Transforming World Trade and Investment Law for Sustainable Development

Transforming World Trade and Investment Law for Sustainable Development

ERNST-ULRICH PETERSMANN

OXFORD
UNIVERSITY PRESS

OXFORD
UNIVERSITY PRESS

Great Clarendon Street, Oxford, OX2 6DP,
United Kingdom

Oxford University Press is a department of the University of Oxford.
It furthers the University's objective of excellence in research, scholarship,
and education by publishing worldwide. Oxford is a registered trade mark of
Oxford University Press in the UK and in certain other countries

First Edition published in 2022

Impression: 1

Published in the United States of America by Oxford University Press
198 Madison Avenue, New York, NY 10016, United States of America

British Library Cataloguing in Publication Data

Data available

Library of Congress Control Number: 2021946726

ISBN 978–0–19–285802–3

DOI: 10.1093/oso/9780192858023.001.0001

Printed and bound in Great Britain by
Clays Ltd, Elcograf S.p.A.

Preface

Can the 2030 United Nations (UN) Sustainable Development Agenda for *Transforming our World* be realized without transforming UN law, the law of the World Trade Organization (WTO) and international investment law? The UN climate mitigation negotiations continue for now more than thirty years without having resulted in effective reductions of greenhouse gas emissions. And the geopolitical rivalries and regulatory competition between neo-liberal, state capitalist, European ordo-liberal, and third world conceptions of multilevel trade and investment regulation have disrupted the WTO legal and dispute settlement system in spite of the UN Agenda's commitments that democracy, good governance and the rule of law are essential for sustainable development and for realizing the human rights of all. In the absence of a functioning WTO dispute settlement system, the introduction of carbon taxes and carbon border adjustment measures (like import tariffs on 'dirty steel' from China) could provoke trade wars and climate mitigation conflicts with reciprocal trade sanctions. Similarly, the decarbonization of economies is bound to provoke investment disputes over compensation claims by coal, gas, and oil companies under the Energy Charter Treaty and other investment protection treaties. As long as citizens leave such regulatory challenges and related, geopolitical rivalries (like the refusal by China and India to phase-out their coal-powered energy by 2050) to the foreign policy discretion of government executives, the intergovernmental power politics dominating UN/WTO governance remain likely to impede realization of the sustainable development goals (SDGs).

How should constitutional democracies respond to the rational ignorance of many citizens vis-à-vis complex global governance problems and to the increasing heterogeneity among UN and WTO member countries, especially if China and India regain their ancient positions as the world's two largest national economies with divergent, nationalist policies? This book explains why UN and WTO law do not—and cannot—effectively protect the SDGs without constitutional reforms protecting human rights and rule of law both inside and among states. The increasing conflicts among Anglo-Saxon neo-liberalism, China's totalitarian state capitalism, Europe's ordo-liberal constitutional approaches to multilevel economic regulation and 'third world approaches' provoke economic disintegration; they increase the need for stronger protection of non-discriminatory regulatory competition, transnational rule of law, and protection of the environment. The book's methodology is interdisciplinary (eg combining legal, economic and political approaches), descriptive and normative (eg exploring justice, fairness, and related values underlying economic law with extensive references to political science and philosophy literature). The answers reflect lessons from my more than forty years of practising world trade law in German, European, UN, the General Agreement on Tariffs and Trade (GATT) and WTO governance institutions and teaching international economic law in universities throughout Europe, the United States, Asia, Latin America, and South Africa.

My main motive for writing this book was to explain the need for strengthening trade, investment and human rights law and adjudication in the current efforts at transforming the world economy. Readers of this book will better understand why UN law—even though it promoted decolonization, human rights revolutions, international economic law revolutions, and development assistance all over the world—has failed to empower citizens effectively by protecting human rights, rule of law, and other SDGs. The current geopolitical, environmental, and public health crises and social inequality reveal systemic legitimacy crises of UN and WTO power politics. Just as polities in the Americas, Africa, Asia, and Europe have evolved from diverse political and legal cultures, so remain the neo-liberal, state capitalist, European ordo-liberal, and third world varieties of regional economic orders driven by diverse, political priorities and principles of justice. As illustrated by the destructive role of German nationalism in the First and Second World Wars and by the assault of US President Trump on UN and WTO institutions, cultivating social market economies, democratic constitutionalism, and reasonable world order treaties protecting sustainable development requires respect for legitimate diversity, constitutional restraints on power politics and institutionalizing public reason. Can this conflict between the obvious need for multilevel governance of global public goods and the popular rejection of multilateral public goods treaties—also in democracies like the United Kingdom, Switzerland, and the United States—be overcome? This book argues that, in order to avoid regular financial, environmental, health, geopolitical crises and social protests by economically less successful groups that feel left behind becoming a permanent feature of 'irresponsible capitalism'—the 'embedded liberalism', non-discrimination-, rule of law-, and human rights principles underlying UN and WTO law must be strengthened, as envisaged in the 2030 UN Sustainable Development Agenda. For example, non-discriminatory human rights standards, environmental protection measures (like carbon taxes), and legal and judicial accountability in international trade and investment regulation (including by multinational corporations in their supply chains) become ever more necessary for maintaining domestic support for open economies, the transnational rule of law, and social justice.

The more UN and WTO reforms are blocked by authoritarian veto practices and political opportunism undermining transnational rule of law, the more sustainable development and democratic civil society struggles for human rights, social justice and protection of the environment risk remaining unsuccessful. If WTO member states should allow American, Chinese, and Russian power politics to destroy the WTO legal and dispute settlement system, the alternative of an authoritarian international law will be incapable of protecting the sustainable development goals. Executive emergency governance without adequate parliamentary, judicial, and constitutional constraints threatens democracy, as illustrated by authoritarian abuses of power in some democracies like the United States under President Trump. The ideological conflicts among American neo-liberalism, China's totalitarian state capitalism, and Europe's economic constitutionalism are likely to promote more regionalization of the international economic order. Civil society struggles for sustainable development (like 'Fridays for future') are of existential importance for transforming human consciousness and power politics so that a cosmopolitan community law can develop beyond Europe and respond to climate change and global health disasters in more responsible and humane ways. Unless democratic institutions challenge the authoritarian disregard for UN and WTO governance failures, the SDGs and their human rights objectives cannot be realized. The book is dedicated to all those daring to understand (ie following the 'enlightenment' call of Immanuel Kant) and struggling for the universally agreed SDGs, notably to my spouse Myszka and our eight children in gratitude for their patience, love, and search for a more humane world.

Ernst-Ulrich Petersmann
European University Institute (Florence) and
World Trade Organization (Geneva)
November 2021

Table of Contents

List of Abbreviations

AB	Appellate Body
AIIB	Asian Infrastructure Investment Bank
ASEAN	Association of South-East Asian Nations
AUKUS	Australia, United Kingdom, and United States security pact
BIT	bilateral investment treaty
BRI	Belt and Road Initiative
BRICS	Brazil, Russia, India, China, and South Africa
C	Celsius
CBAM	carbon border adjustment mechanism
CCP	Chinese Communist Party
CETA	Comprehensive Economic and Trade Agreement
CJEU	European Court of Justice
CO_2	carbon dioxide
COP	Conference of the Parties
COVAX	COVID-19 Vaccine Global Access Facility
CPTPP	Comprehensive and Progressive Trans-Pacific Partnership
CSPP	Corporate Sector Purchase Programme
DSB	Dispute Settlement Body
DSU	Dispute Settlement Understanding
ECB	European Central Bank
ECHR	European Convention on Human Rights
ECT	Energy Charter Treaty
ECtHR	European Court of Human Rights
EEA	European Economic Area
EEC	European Economic Community
EFTA	European Free Trade Area
EMU	Economic and Monetary Union
ETS	Emissions Trading System
EU	European Union
EUCFR	EU Charter of Fundamental Rights
EUI	European University Institute
FAO	Food and Agriculture Organization
FCC	Federal Constitutional Court
FCTC	Framework Convention on Tobacco Control
FTA	free trade agreement
GAL	global administrative law
GATS	General Agreement on Trade in Services
GATT	General Agreement on Tariffs and Trade
GDPR	General Data Protection Regulation

GHG	greenhouse gas
GI	geographical indication
HRL	human rights law
ICCPR	International Covenant on Civil and Political Rights
ICJ	International Court of Justice
ICESCR	International Covenant on Economic, Social and Cultural Rights
ICSID	International Center for the Settlement of Investment Disputes
IEL	international economic law
IIL	international investment law
ILO	International Labour Organization
IMF	International Monetary Fund
ISA	investor–state arbitration
ISDS	Investor–State Dispute Settlement
ITLOS	International Tribunal for the Law of the Sea
LDC	Less developed country
MPIA	Multi-Party Interim Appeal Arbitration
NAFTA	North American Free Trade Agreement
NATO	North Atlantic Treaty Organization
NDC	nationally determined contribution
OECD	Organisation for Economic Co-operation and Development
PEPP	Pandemic Emergency Purchase Programme
PG	public good
PSPP	Public Sector Asset Purchase Programme
PTA	plurilateral trade agreement
RCEP	Regional Comprehensive Economic Partnership Agreement
S&D	special and differential treatment
SDG	sustainable development goal
SOE	state-owned enterprise
TBT	Technical Barriers to Trade
TEU	Treaty on European Union
TFEU	Treaty on the Functioning of the European Union
TMA	Trade Marks Amendment
TNC	transnational corporations
TPP	tobacco plain packaging
TPPR	tobacco plain-packaging regulations
TRIPS	Agreement on Trade-Related Aspects of Intellectual Property Rights
TTP	Trans-Pacific Partnership
TTIP	Trans-Atlantic Trade and Investment Partnership
TWAIL	third-world approaches to international law
UDHR	Universal Declaration of Human Rights
UN	United Nations
UNCITRAL	UN Commission on International Trade Law
UNCLOS	UN Convention on the Law of the Sea
UNCTAD	United Nations Conference on Trade and Development
UNESCO	UN Educational, Scientific and Cultural Organization

UNFCCC	UN Framework Convention on Climate Change
UNGP	UN Guiding Principles on Business and Human Rights
USITC	US Court of International Trade
USMCA	United States/Mexico/Canada
USTR	US Trade Representative
VCLT	Vienna Convention on the Law of Treaties
WEIRD	Western, educated, industrialized, rich, and democratic
WHO	World Health Organization
WIPO	World Intellectual Property Organization
WTO	World Trade Organization

Introduction: Preventing Trade, Investment, Energy, and Climate Conflicts through Rule of Law?

At the 70th anniversary of the United Nations (UN) in 2015, a UN summit meeting with the heads of government of some 150 UN member states adopted the 2030 Agenda for Sustainable Development entitled *Transforming our World* in order to realize the human rights of all, to end poverty and hunger everywhere, and to implement 17 agreed Sustainable Development Goals (SDGs) over the next 15 years with 'the participation of all countries, all stakeholders, and all people'.[1] The Resolution explicitly recognized (in paragraph 9) that 'democracy, good governance and the rule of law ... are essential for sustainable development'. Universal agreement on this ambitious programme for a Global Partnership for Sustainable Development was rendered possible by the fact that notwithstanding agreement on 17 SDGs and on 169 more specific policy targets, the legally non-binding UN General Assembly Resolution neither prescribes precise rights and obligations nor specifies the legal instruments, their legal ranking, sequencing, and other legal changes necessary for implementing the SDGs. Similarly, the 2015 Paris Agreement on climate change mitigation, ratified by 190 countries (as at 2021), relies on nationally determined contributions (NDCs) and governance by science-based indicators without prescribing the precise content of NDCs and policy instruments (like carbon taxes, phasing out of coal subsidies) which need to be progressively clarified. Since 2015, climate change, the digital communication and information revolution, unforeseen global health pandemics, and the need for providing vaccines to all people all over the world increased the regulatory challenges and the need for more precise legal implementation commitments. For example, recent European Union (EU) proposals for introducing carbon taxes aimed at reducing greenhouse gas (GHG) emissions and for concluding a WHO pandemic treaty on reducing the risk of disease outbreaks (eg by pathogens jumping from animals to humans) and disease spread, like proposals (eg from India and South Africa) temporarily to waive intellectual property protections related to COVID-19 health

[1] *Transforming Our World: The 2030 Agenda for Sustainable Development* (UN 2015); the citations are from the Preamble of the Declaration (UN General Assembly Resolution A/RES/70/1) adopted on 25 September.

Transforming World Trade and Investment Law for Sustainable Development. Ernst-Ulrich Petersmann, Oxford University Press. © Ernst-Ulrich Petersmann 2022. DOI: 10.1093/oso/9780192858023.003.0001

technologies, aim at additional UN agreements and WTO decisions at a time when both UN and WTO governance are confronted by geopolitical conflicts. The 25th Conference of the Parties (COP 25) to the UN Framework Convention on Climate Change (UNFCCC) in November 2019—like the COP 26 at Glasgow in November 2021—acknowledged that the world was not on track to meeting the Paris Agreement's long-term goal of holding the increase in global average temperature to well below 2 °C compared to pre-industrial levels, preferably to about 1.5 °C, by GHG emission reductions, transformations of societies, economies, and social progress through multilevel governance cooperation, including assistance for less-developed countries.[2] In 2020/21, the COVID-19 health pandemic killed more than 5 million people; it made realizing the SDGs more difficult by, *inter alia*, increasing the number of people living in extreme poverty by more than 120 million, confronting many less-developed countries with slow rollouts of vaccination, enhancing foreign debt and economic crises, and further limiting policy space (like resources for decarbonizing economies). On 12 May 2021, the Independent Panel for Pandemic Preparedness & Response published its highly critical findings that a swift, collaborative response to the 2019 COVID-19 outbreak in China could have prevented it becoming a global catastrophe in 2020. The Panel's recommendations include setting up a Global Health Threats Council, granting additional powers to the World Health Organization (WHO) to investigate and publish information about disease outbreaks without national government approval, and new funding for an International Pandemic Financing Facility.[3]

At the Leaders' summit of forty countries organized by US President Biden in April 2021 on climate change mitigation, the United States pledged to cut GHG emissions by at least 50 per cent by the end of 2030 (similar to the earlier EU commitment to reduce emissions by 55 per cent during this decade) and to realize a carbon-neutral power sector by 2035 (eg by using commercial solar and wind power). As the SDGs and the goals of the Paris Agreement cannot be achieved without more precise international regulation, multilateral negotiations on additional environmental protection commitments (like limitations of GHG emissions, fossil fuel subsidies, and fishery subsidies) and leadership by the G20 countries become ever more urgent. For instance, similar to the establishment of the Financial Stability Board by the G20 countries in response to the 2008 financial crisis and to proposals for a G20 Global Health Threats Council for coordination of global health pandemic responses, the climate, biodiversity, and other

[2] On the insufficient commitments and political and legal governance structures for securing climate change mitigation, see MT Gunfaus and H Waisman, Assessing the adequacy of the global response to the Paris Agreement: Toward a full appraisal of climate ambition and action, in *Earth System Governance* (Elsevier 23 March 2021) (online only).

[3] *COVID-19: Make it the Last Pandemic*, The Independent Panel for Pandemic Preparedness and Response, May 2021. The Panel criticizes the International Health Regulations of the WHO and proposes numerous reforms.

environmental crises could justify more targeted G20 institutions coordinating multilevel governance of global public goods (PGs). In April 2021, carbon-intensive European industries (eg producing steel, cement, power generation, chemicals) called for introducing carbon border taxes aimed at compensating their increasing production costs and competitive disadvantages caused by the EU's Emissions Trading System (ETS) and its record prices for carbon dioxide (CO_2) allowances; they warned of carbon leakage if manufacturing should move abroad to areas with less stringent environmental restrictions. Yet political and legal views on how to implement the SDGs in conformity with UN and WTO law differ enormously. For example, American techno-optimism relies more on private development of new green technologies (like carbon capture and storage, use of green hydrogen power, and batteries) than on adopting the EU's systemic climate legislation approach, ETS, carbon taxes, and border carbon adjustment proposals. In preparation of the 26th Conference of the Parties to the UNFCCC at Glasgow in November 2021, UN Secretary-General Guterres called on all UN member states to abolish fossil fuel subsidies, phase out coal power plants, and enforce the 'polluter pays' principle with the aim of decarbonizing economies by 2050 (ie shifting from fossil fuels like coal, oil, and natural gas to zero-carbon energy systems based on solar, wind, hydro, geothermal, biomass, and nuclear power). As more than 80 per cent of the increase in CO_2 emissions up to 2050 are likely to come from less-developed countries (notably China and India), leadership and assistance by developed countries (notably the biggest carbon emitters like Australia, Canada, the EU, Japan, Russia, the United Kingdom, and the United States) for less-developed countries in the coming years will be crucial. Will the necessary adjustments of UN and WTO law to the global climate, health, and governance crises be possible without formal amendments of the UN Charter and of the WTO Agreement, as suggested in this book? Can multilevel judicial protection of transnational rule of law—as a constitutional restraint on executive emergency governance neglecting human rights—be protected in order to promote dynamic, systemic treaty interpretations, non-discriminatory regulatory competition, and compliance with the SDGs, as illustrated by the constitutional and human rights litigation discussed in Chapter 9? Will the needed restrictions of fossil fuel investments and the enormous investments needed for the green revolution and digital revolution of the global economy impair the human rights and poverty reduction objectives of the SDGs and further undermine confidence in investor–state arbitration?

This book explores how protecting the SDGs requires going beyond the social idealism of UN General Assembly Resolutions, political declarations, and intergovernmental power politics by promoting legal and constitutional reforms (like implementing legislation protecting individual rights, rule of law, judicial accountability, and remedies) so that world trade and investment law can contribute to transforming our world through limiting environmental pollution and other abuses of public and private power.[4] Restoring the WTO dispute settlement system will be crucial for avoiding and settling trade and environmental conflicts. By emphasizing the value differences between neo-liberal Anglo-Saxon, totalitarian Chinese, and ordo-liberal European constitutional conceptions of international economic law (IEL), this book contributes to the literature on divergent national and regional approaches to international law.[5] Its main claim is that the human rights and rule-of-law objectives of the UN Development Agenda require rules-based, democratic governance, constitutional safeguards of rule of law, and democratic resistance against authoritarian power politics (eg by China, Russia, and other Eurasian states) advocating an international law among sovereign states without effective protection of human and democratic rights. Contrary to the initial focus of sustainable development on converging economic development and environmental protection,[6] the 2030 UN Development Agenda pursues SDGs also in the field of social inclusion and human and labour rights with a view to eradicating poverty in all its forms.[7] As explained in Chapter 2, the SDGs reflect a universally agreed paradigm shift from the neo-liberal, money-driven Washington consensus to an ordo-liberal, citizen-driven 'Geneva consensus' on an international order based on a more inclusive kind of embedded liberalism.[8] However, the more the human rights dimensions of the SDGs and the cosmopolitan 'Brussels consensus' on the need for embedding economic law into human rights law and democratic and judicial institutions remain neglected, the more are

[4] On authoritarian veto powers blocking UN and WTO reforms (eg China and Russia supporting suppression of human rights by military rulers in UN member states like Belarus and Myanmar), neo-liberal regulatory capture of economic rule-making (eg in Anglo-Saxon countries), and explanations of the need for constitutional rather than only managerial mindsets for transforming international law, see Chapters 2–5. In contrast to the agnosticism of critical legal theories towards values, their focus on deconstructing international law (eg by emphasizing its structural biases without proposing ways for a better reconstruction) and their insufficient proposals for a culture of legal formalism, this book uses constitutional constructivism as legal and political methodology for civilizing world trade and investment law (cf EU Petersmann, 'Constitutional Constructivism' for a Common Law of Humanity? Multilevel Constitutionalism as a 'Gentle Civilizer of Nations' in MPIL Research Paper Series No 2017-24). Just as UN, WTO, and EU law introduced transformative legal and institutional changes, so does realizing the SDGs require new multilevel governance rules, institutions, and legal narratives questioning path-dependent neo-liberalism (eg one-sidedly prioritizing private production and supply of medicines, food, and new technologies based on protecting intellectual property rights) as well as authoritarian state capitalism; cf A Saab, *Narratives of Hunger in International Law: Feeding the World in Times of Climate Change* (CUP 2019).

[5] See, eg, L Mälksoo, *Russian Approaches to International Law* (OUP 2015); A Roberts, *Is International Law International?* (OUP 2017); demonstrating how—rather than constituting a single invisible college—international lawyers in different states often pursue different conceptions of international law.

[6] Cf UN General Assembly, Rio Declaration on Environment and Development (1992) A/CONF.151/26.

[7] Cf the Preamble of the UN 2030 Agenda (n 1), 3rd recital; UN 2030 Agenda paras 2 and 9.

[8] This term was coined for describing the dual GATT 1947 objectives of international trade liberalization and domestic political autonomy (eg to regulate markets and their social adjustment problems, and to stabilize the economy in case of external shocks) by JG Ruggie, International Regimes, Transactions and Change: Embedded Liberalism in the Postwar Economic Order, in *International Organization* 36 (1982), 379–415.

UN and WTO power politics contested by civil societies. The EU and other countries use free trade agreements (FTAs) for transforming voluntary NDCs under the Paris Agreement into legally binding and enforceable obligations for climate change mitigation.[9] Legal reforms of world trade and investment law will be crucial for realizing also many SDGs other than climate change mitigation, like freedom from hunger, access to water, protection of biodiversity, universal healthcare, access to electricity and education for all.[10] Democratic support from citizens and parliaments for such legal reforms (like limitation of fossil fuel subsidies, of subsidies to fishing industries, patent rights impeding universal access to vaccines, carbon emissions) requires responding not only more convincingly to populist opposition against protecting the SDGs. The frequent abuses of executive emergency powers during the COVID-19 health pandemic and geopolitical crises—eg for circumventing parliamentary democracy and limiting freedoms of opinion, of assembly, social movements, and trade not only in authoritarian but also in democratic countries—also illustrate threats to democratic governance (eg in Belarus, China, Myanmar, Russia, and even the United States). Why is it that the 'European Green Deal'—announced by the European Commission in December 2019—has enabled the EU to initiate global leadership for transforming Europe into the first carbon-neutral continent by 2050? Why does the EU remain the only regional economic organization that has fully integrated human and constitutional rights and multilevel democratic and judicial institutions into regional economic and environmental law? As the SDGs seek to realize the human rights of all (Preamble) and explicitly recognize (eg in paragraph 9) the need for democracy, good governance, and the rule of law, can the SDGs be realized in and beyond countries without democratic governance and without effective safeguards of rule of law and human rights as constitutional restraints on abuses of governance powers?

[9] Cf M Bronckers and G Gruni, Retooling the Sustainability Standards in EU Free Trade Agreements, in *Journal of International Economic Law* 24 (2021), 25–51. For detailed analyses of the Paris Agreement provisions see G Van Calster and L Reins (eds), *The Paris Agreement. A Commentary* (Edward Elgar 2021). The EU's Taxonomy Regulation of June 2020 entered into force on 12 July 2020 and requires companies to conduct human rights due diligence for designating any good or service as sustainable.

[10] For empirical evidence on the contribution of trade to the seventeen SDGs and related research, see the UN website for the SDGs: <https://sdgs.un.org/goals>.

1
Overview: Sustainable Development without Democratic Protection of Human Rights and Rule of Law?

This chapter gives an overview of the objectives, complexity, and regulatory challenges of the Sustainable Development Agenda, explains their interconnections, and summarizes the book's policy conclusions. Subsequently, Chapters 2 and 3 explore in detail the governance failures and constitutional failures necessitating reforms of world trade and investment law. Chapters 4 and 5 explain why Europe's constitutional responses to long-standing governance and constitutional failures may *not* be politically feasible in worldwide United Nations (UN) and World Trade Organization (WTO) reforms and regional crisis management outside Europe. Chapters 6–9 use the examples of trade, investment, environmental, human, and constitutional rights litigation for demonstrating why stronger judicial remedies and citizen-driven participatory network governance holding governments accountable—and multilevel judicial cooperation in protecting transnational rule of law—must complement intergovernmental rule-making and administrative protection of the Sustainable Development Goals (SDGs) and related global public goods (PGs). Even if multilevel democratic constitutionalism risks remaining limited to European integration, the regulatory competition among neo-liberal, state capitalist, and ordo-liberal approaches to protection of the SDGs will shape international relations for a long time. The following overview of the regulatory challenges of—and dynamic interrelationships between—the economic, environmental, health, geopolitical, social, legal, and political crises will help readers to understand the *systemic nature* of global governance problems, whose main causes and potential remedies are subsequently explored in detail in Chapters 2–9.

1.1 Democracies under Threat

This book is written from the perspective of multilevel democratic constitutionalism as it has evolved in European constitutional law in order to protect human rights and rule of law across national frontiers (for details see Chapter 5). All UN member states have constituted their polities, law-making, and governance procedures through written or unwritten national constitutions and limited their

Transforming World Trade and Investment Law for Sustainable Development. Ernst-Ulrich Petersmann, Oxford University Press. © Ernst-Ulrich Petersmann 2022. DOI: 10.1093/oso/9780192858023.003.0002

regulatory powers through multilateral treaties and general international law obligations recognizing 'inalienable' human rights. Legal obligations (i) to hold free and regular elections based on (ii) a multi-party system, (iii) protection of human rights (including rights to participate in elections and representative governments), and (iv) rule of law are recognized in numerous constitutions and regional and UN human rights conventions; their treaty provisions on restricting human rights explicitly postulate democratic societies (eg in Articles 14, 21, and 22 of the International Covenant on Civil and Political Rights: ICCPR). Yet, outside the Lisbon Treaty on European Union (TEU), the democracy obligations in regional and worldwide human rights law (HRL) are often not effectively transformed in the domestic legal systems of UN member states.[1] As discussed in Chapters 2 and 3, not only is the number of democracies in the world decreasing; also inside democracies (like Brazil, Hungary, India, Poland, Turkey, the Philippines), democratic guarantees (like non-discrimination, free media, independent courts) are under attack, especially during public emergencies like global health pandemics and environmental disasters.

1.1.1 Executive Emergency Governance as a Threat to Democracy

In the United States, for instance, neo-liberal business influence on economic rule-making (eg preventing effective US legislation on gun, tobacco, and climate change control) and election campaign financing by business have contributed to the Republican Party's denial of climate change, opposition to US leadership through inter-regional, economic integration agreements (eg following President Obama's initiatives for the Trans-Pacific Partnership (TPP) and Transatlantic Trade and Investment Partnership (TTIP)), and to the open challenge—since 2020—of one of the core principles of democracy, peaceful acceptance of the outcome of democratic elections.[2] European Union (EU) law limits EU membership to democratic

[1] Cf Chapter 2, section 2.1 and F Ehm, *Das völkerrechtiche Demokratiegebot* (Mohr Siebeck 2013). On the limitation of the path-dependent principle of effectiveness by principles of democratic legitimacy limiting power-based claims by illegitimate military governments to represent a state, see: M Weller, Myanmar: Testing the Democratic Norm in International Law, *European Journal of international Law: Talk* Blog of 31 March 2021. On the unconvincing criticism of the international law requirement to protect at least some human rights dimensions of democracy see: A Rasulov, 'From the Wells of Disappointment': The Curious Case of the International Law of Democracy and the Politics of International Legal Scholarship, *European Journal of International Law* 32 (2021). The democracy deficits of intergovernmental UN and WTO governance are criticized in Chapters 2–9 of this book.

[2] Cf M Wolf, The struggle for the survival of US democracy, *Financial Times* 11 May 2021 (criticizing the 'unambiguously anti-democratic' turn of the Republican party dominated by D Trump and by his '*Führerprinzip*' penalizing any party members criticizing Trump's 'big lie' that the 2020 congressional election was 'stolen' from the Republicans: 'They are increasingly an anti-democratic cult with a would-be despot as their leader'); similarly Republican congress-woman L Cheney, the third-highest ranking Republican in the House of Representatives, in her statement on 10 May 2021 before the Republican party members decided to remove her from her Republican leadership role: 'I will not sit back and

states and prescribes (eg in Articles 9–12 TEU) principles of constitutional democracy (eg EU citizenship rights), representative democracy (eg parliamentary democracy at national and EU levels of governance), participatory and deliberative democracy for the multilevel governance of the EU. UN and WTO law lack corresponding constitutional guarantees of—and political and judicial remedies for—enforcing human rights to democratic governance. During the Trump presidency (January 2017–January 2021), the lack of moral US leadership accelerated the decline in the number of liberal democracies and the increase in political authoritarianism blocking UN and WTO reforms.

The COVID-19 lockdowns since 2020 also prompted democratic governments to impose far-reaching governmental restrictions of social mobility rights through executive orders, often imposed without adequate parliamentary scrutiny; in many democracies, some of the government restrictions were challenged by citizens and occasionally overturned by judicial remedies. UN member states ruled by authoritarian dictators (eg in Belarus and Myanmar) used the health emergencies as pretexts for suppressing political freedoms.[3] The 2019 Sustainable Development Goals Report identified climate change (eg cutting record-high greenhouse gas emissions so as to prevent displacement of up to 140 million people by 2050) and increasing inequality among and within countries as the two most challenging issues of our time.[4] Intensifying climate, health, migration, and social crises may prompt even more executive emergency governance measures, as illustrated by the collapse of the health infrastructures in India's capital New Delhi in response to India's more than 400,000 daily COVID-19 infections in May 2021. Did this obvious governance failure in New Delhi confirm the prediction by Peter Drahos[5] that the authoritarian Chinese government might be more capable of survival governance and of decarbonizing national economies than democratic countries? This book argues that the current global health, climate change, international migration, and geopolitical crises—like trade wars between China and the United States; Russian annexation of Crimea and President Putin's military threats against other countries; vaccine nationalism disregarding the health needs of poor people in Africa, Asia, and Latin America—reveal Titanic challenges for international law

watch in silence while others lead our party down a path that abandons the rule of law and joins the former President's crusade to undermine our democracy'; 'Liz Cheney launches blistering attack on fellow Republicans over Trump', *Financial Times* 12 May 2021). On fears by top US military officials of a Hitlerian 'Reichstag moment' where Trump would launch a coup in order to prevent Biden from taking over the White House see *Financial Times* of 16 July 2021 ('Donald Trump lashes out at top US military officer: 'I'm not into coups').

[3] Cf N Schenkkan and I Linzer, *Out of Sight, Not Out of Reach. The Global Scale and Scope of Transnational Repression* (Freedom House Washington 2021); documenting politically motivated assassinations, illegal abductions, and deportations abroad of political dissidents by Chinese, Turkish, Rwandan, Saudi Arabian, Russian, and Iranian agents).

[4] *The Sustainable Development Goals Report 2019* (UN 2019), 3, 42, 48.

[5] Cf P Drahos, *Survival Governance: Energy and Climate Change in the Chinese Century* (OUP 2021).

and governance. To extend the metaphor, state ships risk hitting an iceberg, potential rescue teams may not be adequately prepared, and survival governance based on governmental invocations of national security and emergency powers—as invoked by China in order to suppress free information on the COVID-19 disease outbreak in Wuhan in 2019, or by US President Trump in starting his trade wars against China and other countries without requesting authorization from the US Congress—all threaten parliamentary and constitutional democracy.

Since Plato's *Republic* (*ca* 375 BC), the metaphor of the state ship is used in Western republicanism for describing the legal structure that protects society from the dangerous waters surrounding it. The Chinese proverb attributed to the Confucian philosopher Xunzi (298–220 BC) used the same metaphor in a significantly different way: 'The heavens create the people and appoint the ruler. The ruler is like a boat, the people are like the water. The water may support the boat, and it may also capsize it.' In the Western metaphor, society and its rulers are on the boat together; the captain acts as an *agent* of the people who are the democratic principal and constituent power. The Chinese metaphor described the people as keeping the state afloat without being on board the ship and without being capable of reforming or steering it. Such preconceptions of law, the state, and of citizens are bound to influence legal interpretations. For instance, the 1982 Constitution of the People's Republic of China is based on the democratic principle that all power belongs to the people (Article 2). Democratic constitutions derive from this principle the need for protecting human rights and for delegating only limited powers to democratically elected legislative, executive, and judicial government branches so as to protect constitutional, participatory, representative, and deliberative self-government of, by, and for citizens and peoples. China's constitution, however, emphasizes the need for dictatorship by the proletariat (Preamble) and the people's democratic dictatorship led by the working class (Article 1), as postulated by Karl Marx based on his claims to know historic truth about the domination of the human condition by materialism. Authoritarian claims to know truth seem to be related also to the neglect for individual rights in the two philosophical schools of Confucianism and Legalism in China, which

> shared a vision of society in which individual lives were led within hierarchies and social distinctions and proper behavior derived from an individual's status in those hierarchies ... Western thought makes the individual the bearer of rights and bases rights on the fundamental dignity and equality of every human being. There were no such concepts in Chinese thought; in the Confucian view, 'identity constantly changes, varying with the context; duties and, correspondingly, rights/rites are also constantly being redefined as other actors change'.[6]

[6] Cf SB Lubman, *Bird in a Cage: Legal Reform in China after Mao* (Stanford UP 1999), 15–16, 19.

The Confucian view of subordinating individual rights and corresponding duties to collective interests continues to inform many Chinese and Marxist conceptions of individual rights in modern China.[7] It reflects patriarchal and communitarian, socialist traditions that are fundamentally different from the more antagonistic, Western conceptions of human and constitutional rights as constitutional constraints aimed at protecting diverse individuals and peoples as constituent powers and democratic principal vis-à-vis all governance agents by corresponding legal duties of governments with only limited, delegated, and separated, regulatory powers. Article 51 of China's Constitution of 1982[8] illustrates how Chinese conceptions of individual freedoms and rights differ from Kantian interpretations of respect for human dignity in terms of equal freedoms as the first principle of justice asserting moral and constitutional priority over governmental limitations of the diverse civil, political, economic, social, and cultural human and constitutional rights and corresponding governmental duties to protect. Yet, both Chinese and Western lawyers acknowledge that the multilevel nature of modern human rights law (HRL) and constitutional law require respect for legitimate constitutional pluralism, depending on the diverse constitutional contracts, democratic preferences, and ratification of human rights treaties in different jurisdictions. As modern China and other Asian countries adopt ever more legislation and international agreements protecting trading rights, investment rights, intellectual property rights, and other economic, social, constitutional, and human rights, generalizations contrasting rights in the East and in the West may no longer be justifiable. For instance:

- in 2011, China's patent office received more patent applications than any other patent office in the world;
- China also seems to comply with most WTO dispute settlement rulings as well as with international investment law and adjudication.

As will be discussed in Chapter 3, China has chosen a power-oriented approach disregarding some of the systemic legal obligations under WTO law, the UN

[7] Cf J Chan, *Confucian Perfectionism. A Political Philosophy for Modern Times* (Princeton UP 2014), arguing that China should adopt liberal democratic institutions that are shaped by the Confucian conception of the good rather than the liberal conception of equal rights.

[8] Article 51 of the 1982 Constitution sets clear limits upon the free exercise of rights by emphasizing the subordination of the individual to the community: 'in exercising freedoms and rights, citizens of the People's Republic of China may not infringe upon the interest of the state, of society or of the collective or upon the lawful freedom and rights of other citizens'. In the Chinese constitutional order, human rights must conform to state-sponsored policies as determined by the Communist party (as the ultimate elite and authority) in order to maintain the 'social harmony between individual and state interests' (similar to the Confucian emphasis on maintaining harmony inside the family as the existential unity of human relationships). Conflict (as opposed to social harmony) is considered an ethical and ontological evil that needs to be limited through proletarian class struggles and redistribution of benefits rather than through rights-based constitutionalism and adjudication.

Convention on the Law of the Sea (UNCLOS), and under UN HRL. China's political use of history for justifying its territorial and maritime claims over large swathes of the South China Sea echoes long-standing imperial strategies reflecting the ancient Chinese board game *wei qui* (also known in the West by its Japanese name *go*), such as building artificial islands and extending military positions surrounding oil, gas, and other natural resources aimed at occupying territories and excluding other countries without regard to international law (eg the UNCLOS provisions on exclusive economic zones and archipelagos). Inside China, the Constitution of 1982 is not effectively enforced in domestic courts, and human rights are not protected. Most other UN member states have recognized constitutionalism as imposing legally binding, reasonable self-restraint on the bounded rationality and often base instincts of human beings and as the most important political invention for decentralized, citizen-driven protection of PGs. China's Communist party, by contrast, rejects national constitutionalism for protecting citizens against abuses of power. And yet, China uses legal self-commitments to UN, WTO, investment, and regional law for justifying China's market liberalization and regulations of non-market concerns.[9] Even though China seems to have suppressed the COVID-19 health pandemic comparatively effectively, Chinese survival governance—without regard to democratic and republican constitutionalism—offers no model for protecting the SDGs and related PGs inside democracies.

The effectiveness of the Chinese regulatory system (eg for obtaining compliance with patent targets set by the central government) has been explained in terms of an authoritarian 'pressure-driving mechanism',[10] yet China's communist governance methods should not be imposed on free societies. UN HRL and democratic constitutionalism proceed from the Kantian premise that because the limits of cognitive human reason (eg in terms of time, space, causality, subjective human senses) exclude knowledge of absolute truth, constitutional protection of individual autonomy rights (eg to choose one's individual conceptions of a good life and of social justice, individual and democratic freedoms to falsify claims of truth) offer more efficient and more legitimate information, coordination, and sanctioning mechanisms for providing private and public goods demanded by citizens. Republican constitutionalism focuses on participatory rights as incentives for citizens to use their republican virtues and assume responsibility for protecting the collective supply of PGs (*res publica*). This book explains why emergency governance at national, regional, and worldwide levels of governance cannot remain legitimate and

[9] Cf PD Farah and E Cima (eds), *China's Influence on Non-Trade Concerns in International Economic Law* (Routledge 2016). Also, Chinese human rights scholarship transcends Confucian Chinese traditions and Marxist ideologies in response to China's ratification of UN human rights conventions and human rights discourse outside China (eg justifying human rights as protecting human freedoms, basic interests, and capabilities).

[10] Cf X Yang, Pressure Driving Mechanism: A Concise History of the Concept, in *Social Science* 2012, 11; W Cheng and P Drahos, *How China Built the World's Biggest Patent Office: The Pressure Driving Mechanism* (unpublished manuscript 2017).

effective without constitutional restraints. The EU's multilevel constitutionalism entailed trial and error responses to the COVID-19 health pandemic inside many EU member states, which facilitated democratic agreements on additional reforms of EU law.[11] Similarly, as will be discussed in Chapter 9, the EU's democratic institutions exercised leadership in designing the European climate law of June 2021 and the thirteen legislative proposals published on 14 July 2021 for decarbonizing the European economy. Democratic, legislative and judicial 'checks and balances' can increase the effectiveness, legitimacy and accountability of executive emergency governance and promote voluntary compliance by citizens.

1.1.2 Intergovernmental Power Politics as a Threat to Democracy

Constitutional, democratic, parliamentary, and judicial restraints remain underdeveloped in UN and WTO legal practices, as illustrated by power-oriented abuses of veto rights in the UN Security Council and by the illegal disruption of the WTO dispute settlement system since December 2019 (as discussed in Chapter 3). Most UN and WTO diplomats prioritize state-centred intergovernmentalism over multilevel constitutionalism for multilevel governance of public goods,[12] just as economists (like Rodrik's claims concerning a 'globalization paradox')[13] and politicians outside Europe disregard multilevel constitutionalism. There are thousands of economic, political, legal, and environmental micro studies of the 17 SDGs and of the 169 specific policy targets identified in the 2030 UN Sustainable Development Agenda. But there seems to be no macro study of what structural changes in UN law, international economic law (IEL), and domestic legal systems are needed for realizing the citizen-oriented SDGs. This book offers such a macro analysis of the interdependent economic, political, legal, and social dimensions of global governance in the field of world trade and investment law from the competing perspectives of neo-liberal, state capitalist, and European ordo-liberal, constitutional conceptions of law and governance. This chapter offers a bird's eye view of structural, methodological, legal, economic, and political problems confronting the realization of the SDGs and a summary of the conclusions of this book. Chapters 2–9 delve deeper into governance failures and constitutional failures of

[11] Cf B de Witte, The European Union's COVID-19 Recovery Plan: The Legal Engineering of an Economic Policy Shift, *Common Market Law Review* 58 (2021), 635–82.

[12] Cf EU Petersmann, *International Economic Law in the 21st Century* (Hart 2012); EU Petersmann, *Multilevel Constitutionalism for Multilevel Governance of Public Goods* (Hart 2017).

[13] Cf D Rodrik, *The Globalization Paradox. Democracy and the Future of the World Economy* (WW Norton & Company 2011) and his unconvincing 'incompatibility proposition' that we cannot have national sovereignty, democratic politics, and global economic integration at once (pp 200–1); the EU's multilevel democratic constitutionalism does protect national sovereignty (eg in terms of democratic capacity to protect national and international PGs), democratic politics, and rules-based global economic integration at once, as discussed in Chapter 5, section 5.5.

multilevel trade and investment regulation and possible remedial responses. They explain in detail the hypothesis of this book: that the governance and constitutional failures described in Chapters 2 and 3 require constitutional responses as identified in Chapters 4 and 5, and why—if such multilevel constitutional responses may not be possible beyond Europe[14]—UN and WTO member states must prioritize, *inter alia*, multilevel judicial protection of transnational rule of law and human rights through promoting trade, investment, environmental, constitutional, and human rights adjudication for holding governments more accountable for implementing the SDGs, as discussed in Chapters 6–9.

The parliamentary ratification of multilateral UN and WTO agreements implies that citizens and their democratic institutions have granted only limited mandates to government executives to implement UN and WTO law for the benefit of citizens. The EU–US summit meeting communiqué of 15 June 2021 mentions, *inter alia*, the need for coordinating trade policies 'to help fight climate change, protect the environment, promote workers' rights, expand resilient . . . supply chains' and protect the world trading system from being undermined by 'non-market economies'.[15] Most SDGs relate to aggregate global PGs (like food security, public health, sustainable energy for all, climate change mitigation, sustainable marine resources and ecosystems, peaceful cooperation, access to justice, human rights) that interact and cannot be protected by national actions alone. Hence, the 2030 UN Agenda emphasizes the need for a global partnership with the participation of all countries, all stakeholders and all people based on 'universal respect for human rights and human dignity, the rule of law, justice, equality and non-discrimination'.[16] Implementation of the communitarian and cosmopolitan SDGs was seriously impeded by the nationalist assault by the US Trump administration on global governance institutions and multilateral treaties, ushering in trade wars and additional governance failures (eg regarding health protection, climate change mitigation, deliberative democracy, parliamentary accountability of President Trump). Trump's denial of climate change—and his executive orders withdrawing the United States from numerous multilateral agreements—illustrated constitutional problems of many SDGs: as long as authoritarian power politics can prevail even in democracies like the United States, the realization of the citizen-oriented SDGs can be upset by unaccountable, opportunistic rulers at any moment. Is it naïve to hope that the UN Sustainable Development Agenda can transform conceptions of international law among sovereign states and intergovernmental UN and WTO power politics

[14] Modern textbooks on *International Economic Law*—especially if written from African, American, or Asian perspectives (like L Choukroune and JJ Nedumpara, *International Economic Law: Text, Cases and Materials* (CUP 2021))—continue to disregard constitutional approaches to multilevel governance of the SDGs and related PGs, just as authoritarian and populist governments in many less-developed and BRICS countries (Brazil, Russia, India, China, South Africa) neglect human rights.

[15] US–EU Summit Statement of 15 June 2021 (https://www.whitehouse.gov/briefing-room/statements-releases/2021/06/15/u-s-eu-summit-statement/).

[16] UN, *Transforming our World* (UN 2015), eg paras 3–9.

by human rights conceptions of multilevel governance of the peoples, by the peoples, and for the peoples protecting the SDGs and related PGs like climate change mitigation and public health? Can the cosmopolitan project of the SDGs succeed in empowering citizens—and localizing protection of the SDGs by stronger rights, responsibilities, and judicial remedies of citizens and other local stakeholders—at a time when global climate, energy, and health crises call for emergency governance and strong states changing the direction, speed, and scale of innovation for green technologies, decarbonization of the world economy, and protection of ecosystems (like biodiversity, fish stocks, clean water, clean air, climate)? Will geopolitical rivalries impede the need for stronger protection of citizens against abuses of power? How should UN and WTO law respond to the geopolitical and regulatory competition among diverse neo-liberal, state capitalist, European ordo-liberal, and third-world conceptions of law and governance and the need for stronger rule of law institutions limiting abuses of public and private power?

During more than seventy years of European integration, European institutions responded to political, economic, legal, environmental, and health crises by innovating and constitutionalizing multilevel governance of European PGs through European regulatory agencies embedded in multilevel democratic, legislative, executive, and judicial institutions, protecting transnational human and constitutional rights of EU citizens which Europeans had never enjoyed before. Nationalist predictions of the collapse of the EU—eg due to its successive monetary, debt, migration, health, and environmental crises—were refuted by new integration initiatives and progressive enlargements of the EU. In the field of climate change mitigation and many other SDGs, Europe's regional multilateralism and experimental governance (eg of the Emissions Trading System (ETS)) demonstrated political and legal leadership for adjusting multilateral treaties, institutions, and regional communities to new regulatory challenges (like transforming Europe into the first carbon-neutral continent by 2050). For example, similar to the SDG of realizing human rights for all through multilevel governance of global PGs, the EU's constitutional constraints on common market regulation, and on foreign policy powers by multilevel guarantees of human and constitutional rights of citizens, democratic governance, rule of law, and judicial accountability revealed 'demoi-cratic taking back control' by EU citizens insisting on multilevel constitutional and citizen rights and on their multilevel, judicial protection beyond national borders.[17] UN and WTO law constitute communities of states rather than—as

[17] Cf K Nicolaïdis, European Demoicracy and Its Crisis, *Journal of Common Market Studies* 51 (2013), 351–69; R Bellamy, *A Republican Europe of States: Cosmopolitanism, Intergovernmentalism and Democracy in the EU* (CUP 2019). The 'no European demos thesis' of these authors is criticized by J Habermas, *The Crisis of the European Union: A Response* (Polity Press 2012); K Nicolaïdis, Citizen and State Equality in a Supranational Political Community: Degressive Proportionality and the Pouvoir Constituant Mixte, *Journal for Common Market Studies* 55 (2017), 171–82. The rights-based character and multilevel, democratic, and judicial control of the EU's common market and foreign policy constitutions are discussed in Chapter 5, section 5.5.

inside the EU—also of citizens and peoples. The emergence of global UN HRL, the citizen-oriented SDGs, and the vast impact of UN/WTO law on citizens all over the world justify the increasing calls from civil societies and democratic parliaments for reforming the power-oriented UN and WTO practices (like arbitrary abuses of veto powers, democracy deficits, disregard for rule of law, human rights, and for judicial remedies). The 2030 Agenda for Sustainable Development not only reaffirms (eg in its Preamble and paragraphs 4 and 9) the universal recognition of human rights based on the acknowledgement that the dignity of the human person is fundamental, and 'democracy, good governance and the rule of law … are essential for sustainable development'; its focus on human rights and 'people-centred transformative goals' (paragraph 2) also requires reviewing UN law and IEL in terms of their contribution to promoting human rights and other SDGs as agreed principles of justice, morality, and ethically responsible sovereignty.[18]

The UK referendum of 2016 and the subsequent UK exit from the EU in 2020 (Brexit) illustrated how nationalist calls for withdrawing from multilateral agreements are supported by populist politics in an increasing number of countries. The civil society protests (eg in Northern Ireland and Scotland) against the reintroduction of welfare-reducing trade barriers were a reminder of how much the European common market had promoted peaceful social, democratic, and political integration throughout Europe. The increasing conflicts between Anglo-Saxon neo-liberalism (including Prime Minister Johnson's declared dream of a 'Singapore on Thames' rather than Global Britain leading the EU), authoritarian state capitalism, European ordo-liberalism, and third-world conceptions of economic regulation prompted President Trump to withdraw the United States from the Doha Round of negotiations in the WTO and unilaterally to disrupt the WTO legal, dispute settlement and appellate review systems. Does nationalist backlash against globalization and IEL render the UN SDGs for transforming our world unrealistic? Can the WTO legal and dispute settlement systems and the more than 3,200 investment treaties remain legal foundations for protecting the SDGs? Or do the geopolitical and environmental transformations of our world, regulatory competition, trade conflicts, and civil society struggles for sustainable development require a more decentralized reconstruction of the international legal and economic order? As UN and WTO power politics adversely affect also distributive and interpersonal justice inside states (eg UN member states governed by authoritarian dictators), does the universal recognition of human rights require redesigning global

[18] On the need for justifying UN and WTO law no longer only in terms of state consent but also in terms of agreed procedural, constitutional, distributive, corrective, and commutative principles of justice, equity, and cosmopolitanism, see Petersmann (2017) (n 12), 38f, 177ff, 334f. On the different kinds of moral, ethical, and pragmatic reasons for justifying result-oriented theories of justice (eg about rights and obligations, conceptions for a good life, choices of efficient policy instruments) and agency-oriented, democratic discourses, see J Habermas, *Justification and Application: Remarks on Discourse Ethics* (Polity Press 1995).

society by empowering cosmopolitan citizens so that they can use their human and cosmopolitan rights more actively in order to hold governments accountable for the ubiquity of governance failures, constitutional failures, and market failures in protecting the SDGs more effectively, as described by the human rights, constitutional, and environmental litigation in Chapter 9? This book explains why realizing the SDGs requires transforming the UN and WTO legal systems and strengthening trade, investment, and human rights adjudication. Without empowerment and participation of civil societies, implementing the SDGs through legislative, administrative, judicial, economic, democratic, and technological reforms in the 193 UN member states risks lacking political drivers, democratic support, vigilant guardians, and self-interested defenders of rule of law and of enlightenment now.[19] And yet, will such rules-based UN and WTO reforms be possible in the 'Chinese century' with an increasingly authoritarian government in Beijing resisting protection of human rights, supporting authoritarian governments outside China (like Iran, North Korea, Myanmar, Russia), and with China's aggressive wolf warrior diplomacy[20] responding to human rights criticism by discriminatory sanctions prompting the European parliament to freeze ratification of the 2020 EU–China Agreement on Investments? As China and India are expected to become once again—as during most of the recorded history—the world's two largest national economies, how will this geopolitical change affect UN, WTO, and other world order treaties and legal practices?

1.1.3 Disruption of the Rules-Based World Trading System as a Threat to Democracy

As human survival and governance powers depend on legal rules allocating economic resources (eg by means of property rights, contract law, state sovereignty), commercial and trade law belong to the oldest fields of legal systems. Yet, a coherent public law system of world trade law emerged only with the 1947 General Agreement on Tariffs and Trade (GATT 1947) and its replacement by the 1994 Agreement establishing the WTO. As discussed in Chapter 3, section 3.1, the embedded liberalism compromise underlying GATT/WTO rules reconciles the need for protecting national sovereignty and legitimate diversity (eg sovereign freedoms to apply non-discriminatory national trade restrictions under Articles III, XX–XXI, XXVIII GATT) with the need for promoting regional and global PGs through legal harmonization, coordination, consultation, and dispute settlement

[19] Cf S Pinker, *Enlightenment Now. The Case for Science, Reason, Humanism and Progress* (Penguin 2018).

[20] Cf T Mitchell, 'China's "wolf warriors" refuse to back down', *Financial Times* 11 April 2021 (wolf warrior was the title of a successful 2015 Chinese action film now used as a nickname for unapologetically aggressive Chinese diplomats).

procedures and negotiations (eg pursuant to GATT Articles XI, XXII, XXIII, XXIV, XXVIII*bis* GATT). In the twenty-first century, world trade and investments remain of existential importance for poverty reduction, human welfare, sustainable development, and political order protecting the global environment. In his acclaimed book on *World Order*, Henry Kissinger compared the diverse regional political orders among states and explained why, due to the 'multifariousness of the human condition and the ingrained human quest for freedom', order 'must be cultivated; it cannot be imposed':

> Any system of world order, to be sustainable, must be accepted as just—not only by leaders, but also by citizens. It must reflect two truths: order without freedom, even if sustained by momentary exaltation, eventually creates its own counterpoise; yet freedom cannot be secured or sustained without a framework of order to keep the peace. Order and freedom ... should ... be understood as interdependent.'

According to Kissinger, regional and world orders base themselves on two components:

> a set of commonly accepted rules that define the limits of permissible action and a balance of power that enforces restraint when rules break down, preventing one political unit from subjugating all others. A consensus on the legitimacy of existing arrangements does not—now or in the past—foreclose competition or confrontation, but it helps ensure that it will occur as adjustments within the existing order rather than as fundamental challenges to it.[21]

Chapters 2–5 compare the diverse regional varieties of neo-liberal, state capitalist, and ordo-liberal economic orders and their impact on the implementation of SDGs in the world trade and investment order. Chapters 6–9 explain why the SDGs, decarbonization, and digitalization of economies require limitation of regulatory competition by multilateral trade and investment adjudication for the peaceful settlement of disputes promoting rules-based adjustments of world trade and investment law to the requirements of sustainable development. The US Biden administration has acknowledged that the assault by the US Trump administration on the UN and on the WTO requires better protection of PGs like a mutually beneficial world trading system, climate change mitigation, access to vaccines and medical supplies for all countries, protection of data privacy and data security in Internet governance, non-discriminatory tax and competition rules restraining abuses of power and tax evasion (eg in electronic commerce and communications),

[21] H Kissinger, *World Order. Reflections on the Character of Nations and the Course of History* (Penguin 2014), 8–9.

and peaceful cooperation with China (eg on climate change mitigation). Yet China's economic, technological, and military power and assertiveness have upset the balance of power and legitimacy of regional order in the Indo-Pacific.[22] Strengthening the multilateral UN and WTO legal and dispute settlement systems—based on strategic alliances among democratic WTO members (like the EU, Anglo-Saxon, and Asian democracies) including more than 2 billion people and more than half the global economy—offers the best incentive for promoting peaceful cooperation protecting the universally agreed SDGs, for cooperation with China as an economic partner, and for deterring power politics by China, Russia, and other strategic rivals and rogue rulers whenever they disregard the need for responsible sovereignty, and for legal and judicial accountability in the defence of legitimate order in multilevel governance of PGs. If such democratic alliances can agree on common rules for non-discriminatory conditions of trade, climate change mitigation, an open and secure Internet safeguarding digital rights, protection of human and labour rights, such democratically agreed rules could provide leadership for a more legitimate twenty-first-century order.[23] However, as long as the EU and the United States fail to resolve many of their long-standing trade disputes (eg over agricultural regulations, US 'buy American legislation', illegal US import restrictions on steel and aluminium, services taxes, WTO appellate review), will they be able to adequately respond to the regulatory challenges of climate change, global health pandemics, and China's state capitalism? Chapters 2 and 3 explain why the geopolitical rivalries, the protectionist interest group pressures inside the United States, the Republican party's opposition to many trade-related issues (like climate change mitigation), and the expiry in 2021 of the US trade negotiating authority granted by Congress, all risk impeding the much needed trade, environmental, and

[22] Cf KM Campbell and R Doshi, How America Can Shore Up Asian Order. A Strategy for Restoring Balance and Legitimacy, *Foreign Affairs* 12 January (2021): 'China alone accounts for half the region's GDP and *military* spending, a gap that has only grown since the COVID-19 pandemic. And like any rising state, China seeks to reshape its surroundings and secure deference to its interests. The way Beijing has pursued these goals—South China Sea island building, East China Sea incursions, conflict with India, threats to invade Taiwan, and internal repression in Hong Kong and Xinjiang—undermines important precepts of the established regional system. This behavior, combined with China's preference for economic coercion, most recently directed against Australia, means that many of the order's organizing principles are at risk.'

[23] For explanations of why democratic states are more likely to agree on liberal international rules protecting human dignity, human rights, rule of law, and third-party adjudication, see AM Slaughter, *A New World Order* (Princeton UP 2004). Recent examples include the EU agreements with Japan in 2019—and with India in 2021—on jointly promoting infrastructure projects in less-developed African and Asian countries on more transparent and more favourable terms than China's Belt and Road projects. The insistence on 'buy America' preferences by the United States illustrates, however, the political limits of rules-based cooperation among democracies and the 'regulatory capture' of economic rule-making inside the United States. See also M Wolf, 'China is wrong to think the US faces inevitable decline' *Financial Times* 28 Aril 2021, explaining why US dominance of the most valuable, productive, and innovative companies and universities renders it likely that the United States 'has a good chance of staying the most influential country far into the future' provided it remains democratic, free, and open. The share of democracies in world production, trade, and innovation remains much larger than that of authoritarian countries.

legal reforms, possibly further undermining the WTO legal and dispute settlement system and its constitutional functions for rules-based, multilateral trade and environmental governance and judicial accountability.

The necessary shift away from fossil fuels (coal, gas, and oil) to renewable green energy (eg based on wind, solar, biomass, hydropower, ocean energy, and geothermal power), new green technologies, and decarbonization of the world economy, is bound to transform the world trading system as dramatically as in earlier industrial revolutions. The inevitable changes—increasingly prescribed in national and international legal commitments—take place in different legal and political contexts characterized by global governance crises (like geopolitical rivalries, health pandemics, climate change, migration, and refugee crises), frequent recourse to executive emergency powers (eg for restricting movements of persons) and decreasing dependence on fossil fuels. Since 2017, the return by the United States to nationalist mercantilism and the UK's exit from the EU reveal a retreat from Anglo-Saxon leadership of multilateralism: both President Trump and Prime Minister Johnson prioritized withdrawing from multilateral agreements and erecting new trade barriers. The UK and US calls for 'taking back control' strengthened neither parliamentary democracy nor popular sovereignty, even if the latter is defined in terms of *national legal autonomy* (which is a delusion in a globally integrated world) rather than as *democratic capacity* to provide citizens with more and better PGs.[24] Both the US and UK governments often used executive powers for withdrawing from multilateral treaties,[25] for introducing new trade taxes, and for bypassing parliaments in the adoption of important policy decisions (like starting a US trade war with China by imposing Section 301 tariffs, and another trade war with NATO allies by imposing Section 232 tariffs on steel and aluminium, without asking for specific parliamentary approval). What comes after 'America First', Brexit, the US disruption of the WTO dispute settlement system, and 'the nightmarish end to Donald Trump's presidency',[26] when false claims of election rigging

[24] Brexit confirmed the legal sovereignty of EU member states to withdraw their consent to EU law, albeit at the high social cost of reducing economic welfare and capacity to protect European aggregate public goods like rule of law, the common market, EU freedoms, and constitutional rights of citizens beyond states. President Trump's 'America First' ideology ignored global PGs like climate change mitigation. On the political undermining of parliamentary democracy and judicial independence in both the United Kingdom and the United States, see R Shrimsley, 'America's warning for British democracy' *Financial Times* 13 January 2021.

[25] Examples include US withdrawal from the Trans-Pacific Partnership and from the draft Transatlantic Trade and Investment Partnership Agreement, and initial invocation by the UK government in 2017 of medieval royal prerogatives and 'Henry VIII powers' for implementing the Brexit withdrawal from the EU; cf J Sumption, *Law in a Time of Crisis* (Profile Books 2021).

[26] E Luce, 'The nightmarish end to Donald Trump's presidency' *Financial Times* 7 January 2021. The democratic Senate leader Charles Schumer called for the immediate removal of Donald Trump from office, saying that the outgoing president was directly responsible for the riots in the Capitol: 'What happened at the US Capitol yesterday was an insurrection against the United States, incited by the president ... This president should not hold office one day longer.' See also '"A coup d'état attempted by Trump": America's failed insurrection' *Financial Times* 9 January 2020.

and stolen victory provoked Trump supporters to storm the Capitol building on 6 January 2021 in order to prevent Congress from certifying the electoral result? Richard Haas, the president of the US Council on Foreign Relations, tweeted that day: 'No one in the world is likely to see, respect, fear, or depend on us in the same way again. If the post-American era has a start date, it is almost certainly today.'[27] The democracy deficits of the US Constitution (eg in terms of racial discrimination, privileging of small states in the US Senate like Wyoming, whose 600,000 inhabitants have the same voting powers in the US Senate as the 40 million citizens of California), and of US political practices (eg dominated by the small 'donor class' of rich Americans, Republican politicians obstructing democratic governance and packing US courts with Republican-leaning judges) have led to money-driven regulatory capture that poses systemic threats to governance of PGs inside and beyond the United States (as illustrated by the high US death toll of COVID-19 victims, the US withdrawal from the World Health Organization (WHO) under the Trump administration, and the risk of a return to Trump politics in 2024).

President Biden has committed himself to rebuilding alliances among democratic countries for reforming economic, health, and climate change governance. Yet, his policy agenda gives priority to reuniting America and repairing democracy, public health, and the economy at home following the socially divisive Trump presidency. Biden's trade policies remain committed to 'Buy American policies' and to false US claims that WTO rules and appellate review are stacked against US interests.[28] Notwithstanding the pragmatic EU–US agreement of June 2021 on de-escalating their trade disputes over aircraft subsidies, US Trade Representative (USTR) Katherine Tai emphasizes enforcement of existing trade rules, whose frequent ambiguity (eg in areas such as subsidies, new digital services taxes, border carbon adjustment taxes proposed by the EU) risks provoking new trade conflicts in the absence of a functioning WTO dispute settlement system. US trade policies (eg on discretionary trade remedies, invocation of security exceptions, extraterritorial economic sanctions) remain unpredictable due to regulatory capture by money-driven Washington politics[29] and the polarization of US politics. In December 2020, the EU Commission and the EU Council suggested more than twenty trade policy initiatives by the EU for joint cooperation with the Biden administration (like the EU and the United States jointly initiating work on health policy issues, digital supply chain security, cybersecurity, carbon border adjustment measures

[27] G Rachman, 'America's disarray is China's opportunity' *Financial Times* 19 January 2020. The Republican party election result deniers used populist 'stab-in-the-back' theories similar to the successful discrediting of German democracy by nationalists after the First World War.

[28] Cf S Charnovitz, How Biden Treats Trade in his first Foreign Policy Speech, *International Economic Law and Policy* Blog of 5 February 2021; M. Wolf, 'The US should spurn the false promise of protectionism' *Financial Times* 15 June 2021.

[29] On the 'regulatory capture' of the more than 500 trade remedies (ie anti-dumping, countervailing duty and safeguard measures) protecting US industries in 2021, see, eg S Lester and S Lincicome, Some New Data on US Anti-Dumping Abuse, *Cato at Liberty Blog* of April 9, 2021.

in the WTO). The lack of specific US responses, however, seemed to confirm that after 'America's political madness'[30] prevented protection of the US constitutional order at the doors of the Capitol, future US leadership for world trade reforms (eg for re-establishing the WTO Appellate Body, renegotiating the Transpacific and Transatlantic free trade agreements (FTAs) denounced by President Trump) lacks democratic support: 'the US is less united at home and less credible abroad than it has been for decades'.[31] As explained in this book, transatlantic leadership for rebuilding a coherent world trading system, reforming international investment law, mitigating climate change, and protecting the rule of law in a legitimate world order risks being impeded by nationalist interest group politics inside the United States.

China's centrality to the world trading system is illustrated by the fact that in 2020, over 130 countries traded in higher volumes with China than with the United States. China became also the EU's largest partner for trade in goods in 2020. Over the past ten years, China's economy has grown faster than that of any other country (eg due to China's more effective handling of the COVID-19 pandemic, China's annual economic growth was around 8 per cent in 2020 compared with less than 4 per cent US economic growth). According to the United Nations Conference on Trade and Development (UNCTAD) statistics, foreign direct investment increased in China by 4 per cent and India by 13 per cent in 2020, in contrast to its fall by 69 per cent in advanced economies. When China acceded to the WTO in December 2001, US President Clinton said that China imported 'one of democracy's most cherished values, economic freedom', and this, he added, 'may lead to very profound change. The genie of freedom will not go back into the bottle'.[32] Yet, according to President Xi Jinping, China 'must never follow the path of Western "constitutionalism", "separation of powers" or "judicial independence"'.[33] Since Xi Jinping became president in 2013, China has become more authoritarian and less liberal. China's communist dictatorship claims to have lifted more than 700 million poor people out of poverty and to have coped with the COVID-19 health pandemic more effectively than democracies; its increasing economic, political, military, and

[30] G Rachman, 'Europe is not immune from America's political madness' *Financial Times* 12 January 2020.

[31] Financial Times Editorial Board, 'Donald Trump's woeful legacy' *Financial Times* 16 January 2021 ('Do not mistake the exit of a rogue President for the end of America's troubles'). The Trump administration's disregard for protection of the environment in order to maximize business profits undermined trust in US economic policies no less than the US handling of the financial crises since 2008 and US tradition of extra-territorial, unilateral economic sanctions.

[32] Quoted from C Prestowitz, *The World Turned Upside Down. America, China and the Struggle for World Leadership* (Yale UP 2020), according to whom 'constructive engagement' by investing in communist China in the hope of promoting greater freedom was a tragic delusion. US corporations became China's must potent lobby in Washington DC using their corporate profits in China for influencing US policies and appease the Chinese government.

[33] Quoted from one of President Xi's major policy speeches in 2018 (cf S Shih, 'In China, many are impressed that, yes, you can sue the US government' *Washington Post* 8 March 2019).

technological power appeals to many poor people and authoritarian governments (eg in Eurasian countries) more than the political and social polarization inside many democracies. China's centralized governance might also find it politically easier to lead the transformation to a green economy.[34]

China's bilateral cooperation with more than 100 countries along the ancient maritime and territorial Silk Road relies on soft law and management approaches that differ fundamentally from the multilateral treaties and institutions characteristic of the post-1945, US-led world trading and financial system. The EU–China investment agreement signed on 30 December 2020, like China's participation in the multi-party interim appeal arbitration procedures in the WTO initiated by the EU, signal the intention of both China and the EU to continue cooperating on reforms of the world trading and investment systems. The conclusion of the Regional Comprehensive Economic Partnership Agreement (RCEP) on 15 November 2020—the world's largest regional trade agreement between ten ASEAN (Association of South-East Asian Nations) countries, Australia, China, South Korea, Japan, and New Zealand—confirms the determination of other Asian countries to continue liberalizing and regulating trade through multilateral agreements with China. India, however, after China, the most populous national economy in the world, decided not to join the RCEP. Upon his inauguration on 20 January 2021, President Biden found the United States outside both the RCEP and the Comprehensive and Progressive Trans-Pacific Partnership (CPTPP) agreement between eleven countries bordering the Pacific Ocean (with China, Korea, and the United Kingdom having expressed interest in joining the CPTPP). The African Continental FTA of 2018, which aims at creating a continental free trade area among fifty-four of the fifty-five member states of the African Union, initiated another new regionalization of world trade. The new nationalism, bilateralism, and regional initiatives illustrate how diverging value premises and geopolitical rivalries among utilitarian Anglo-Saxon neo-liberalism, China's totalitarian state capitalism, Europe's ordo-liberal economic constitutionalism, and third-world economies (like the BRICS (Brazil, Russia, India, China, and South Africa) countries Brazil, India, and South Africa) are transforming the world trading system.[35]

[34] Cf Drahos, *Survival Governance* (n 5) and N Inkster, *The Great Decoupling: China, America and the Struggle for Technological Supremacy* (Hurst 2020).

[35] The notion of the 'third world' includes an enormous variety of less-developed countries with very diverse economic, political and legal systems (eg in Cuba and India); legal scholars proposing 'third-world approaches to international law' (TWAIL) or criticizing international law as empire and 'new colonial order', are 'hardly a homogenous group of like-minded intellectuals' (cf A Bianchi, *International Law Theories. An Inquiry into Different Ways of Thinking* (OUP 2016), at 205ff). This book focuses on neo-liberal, state capitalist, and ordo-liberal varieties of capitalism that can be found also in less-developed countries and contribute to the reality of 'legal pluralism', diversity of legal cultures, and complex interactions between private and public, national, transnational, and international legal and normative orders. The constitutional constructivism advocated in this book (eg for promoting judicial protection of human rights, rule of law, and systemic coherence of fragmented legal sub-systems) emphasizes the need for respecting legitimate diversity and pluralism in order to enhance the legitimacy and effectiveness of world order treaties and of regulatory competition responding to diverse rationalities of social

Will this regulatory competition undermine the WTO, provoke new trade wars, and impede coherent responses to the global health, environmental, economic, and other governance crises? Or should it be welcomed as a discovery process for improving multilevel governance of transnational PGs like better prevention of global health pandemics and of environmental disasters? Will the return of the US Biden administration to active government interventions in the economy (eg by expansive fiscal and monetary policies, subsidies, 'buy American' legislation, social assistance, environmental, and health protection measures) diminish the value differences between Anglo-Saxon neo-liberalism and European ordo-liberalism? How can we reconcile bilateral, regional, and worldwide governance of the SDGs and related transnational PGs with legitimate calls for national sovereignty and diversity?

1.1.4 Transnational Democracy? 'We Have Met the Enemy and He Is Us'

Many social problems (like nationalist xenophobia vis-à-vis foreigners, climate change denial) are aggravated by psychological prejudices.[36] Climate change and sustainable development require citizens and their democratic institutions to think globally, reasonably, and long term, yet domestic politics often forces politicians to think nationally, opportunistically, and short term. Just as some religions proceed from the idea of human sin (eg requiring the expulsion of Adam and Eve from Paradise and justifying God's punishment of Cain for having murdered his brother Abel by condemning Cain to become a restless wanderer on earth), so legal philosophers perceive the unruly nature of human beings (Thomas Hobbes: '*homo homini lupus est*') and their 'unsocial sociability' (Immanuel Kant) as the main justification of law and of the need for social contracts and for institutionalizing public reason (John Rawls). Modern psychology and behavioural economics confirm that legal and constitutional self-restraints on human freedom (tying one's hand to the mast) are reasonable responses to the social fact that human beings risk acting like social animals—in their private as well as public lives—out of a mix of unconscious

systems; following I Kant, Chapter 5 explains multilevel constitutionalism as a necessary constraint on past abuses of state sovereignty, without denying the pluralist structure of post-national law (as emphasized by N Krisch, *Beyond Constitutionalism: The Pluralist Structure of Postnational Law* (OUP 2010)).

[36] The quotation in the sub-title is from W Kelly, *We Have Met the Enemy and He Is Us* (Simon Schuster 1987). See also M Wolf, 'The healing of democracies starts at home' *Financial Times* 22 June 2021 (arguing that the principal threats to Western democracies come not from China but from their own failures to protect widely shared prosperity and democratic values inside their own societies). Authoritarian states like Russia exploit the openness and polarization of democracies to advance the interests of their kleptocratic ruling classes. For an explanation of the view that the US Trump administration was the logical culmination of decades of negative social and political failures inside the United States, see N Bryant, *When America Stopped Being Great: A History of the Present* (Bloomsburg 2021).

instincts, senses, passions, rational self-interests, morality, and reasonableness. Understanding global governance requires combining (i) rules-based legal with (ii) utilitarian economic, (iii) power-oriented political, (iv) ethical communitarian governance approaches, and (v) natural science methodologies in addition to (vi) principled, philosophical theories of justice.[37] Many human beings respond to this enlightenment challenge by rational ignorance, refraining from acquiring knowledge when the supposed cost of educating oneself on an issue exceeds the expected potential benefit that the knowledge would provide. How to respond to this fact that it is rational for most citizens (eg in Swiss public referenda voting against carbon taxes, British referendum on EU membership) to remain ignorant of complex governance challenges even if they affect individual lives?

All human societies use the rule by law for ordering civil, political, economic, social, and cultural cooperation; constitutional limitations of rulers by rule of law depend, however, on struggles for justice, and remain contested in the politics of law. As legal systems exist only in the human mind, their restraints on human freedom and psychology tend to be perceived differently by different individuals depending on their morality and constitutional mindsets (like Jean-Jacques Rousseau's acknowledgement that equal individual freedoms depend on constitutional restraints of freedom). The interactions among local and national societies, economies, polities, and legal systems vary among countries depending on their diverse traditions, preferences, and cultures. International law has power-oriented origins[38] and power-driven histories (eg of colonialism and imperialism). The latter continue being challenged by human rights revolutions, democratic revolutions, and cosmopolitan civil society struggles for justice and sustainable development. Chapter 2, section 2.1, Chapter 4, section 4.2, and Chapter 9, section 9.1 recall why the universal recognition of sovereign equality of states and of inalienable human rights protecting equal freedoms of citizens are ultimately rooted in the human desire for respect of the diversity and dignity of human personalities and cultures. In the globally interdependent world of the twenty-first century threatened by climate change, health pandemics, power politics, and by the rational ignorance of many citizens towards global governance problems, survival governance of transnational PGs entails ever greater regulatory, democratic, and knowledge challenges (eg by climate change deniers) for realizing the SDGs. The lack of

[37] The distinction of four basic forms of human regulatory systems—ie legal (hierarchical), social (self-regulatory), economic (market), and technological (architectural) modalities that engage with the practical and moral senses of the regulated human beings—by L Lessig, *Code: Version 2.0* (Basic Books 2006) remains contested (eg for neglecting genetic, geo- and climate engineering technologies that are closer to natural regulatory systems than to intentional human regulation). On the diversity of legal methodologies in interpreting and designing international law and legal practices, see R Deplano and N Tsagourias (eds), *Research Methods in International Law. A Handbook* (Elgar 2021).

[38] For example, international legal practices recognize a state whenever a government effectively controls a people in a territory and is capable of representing the state vis-à-vis other states. Since ancient times, the legal institutions of sovereignty, property and contract law were used and abused for justifying public and private power politics.

parliamentary and democratic civil society institutions in the UN and WTO legal and political systems renders adjusting UN, WTO, and domestic power politics to the human rights objectives of the SDGs difficult. As discussed in Chapter 5, the global governance crises call for a new twenty-first-century constitutionalism protecting international public goods (like global supply of vaccines protecting public health).

1.2 Competing Regulatory Paradigms

Albert Einstein criticized the methodological madness of using, time and again, outdated methodologies for resolving problems created by the same methodologies. As discussed in Chapter 2, UN and WTO law reflects the insight that the regulatory problems created by power politics cannot be resolved by power politics alone; the need for transforming our world arises from the existential problems of bounded rationality and selfish egoism disregarding equal rights and agreed rules. The regulatory tasks of institutionalizing public reason for protecting PGs demanded by citizens require not only constitutional self-restraint through just rules and institutions of a higher legal rank enhancing democratic capacities to protect PGs. The effectiveness of international rules also depends on their legislative, administrative, and judicial protection and support by civil societies so that governments and individuals comply with reasonable legal constraints and challenge abuses of power.

1.2.1 Governance Failures in UN and WTO Legal Practices

UN law is committed to human rights and provides for democratic self-determination and judicial remedies, but UN and WTO legal practices often remain dominated by power politics imposed by authoritarian rulers prioritizing their own self-interests. For instance, as discussed in Chapter 3, some of the transformations imposed by US President Trump on UN and WTO institutions risk undermining the SDGs (like rule of law and access to justice). Even though in 2021, the Biden administration reversed the failure of the Trump administration to participate in the COVID-19 Vaccine Global Access Facility (COVAX) initiated by the WHO with more than 180 countries as one example of the revitalized Global Partnership necessary for implementing the SDGs,[39] the periodic US elections make the future of US governance unpredictable. Chapter 2 concludes that the member-driven governance dominating UN/WTO legal practices does not—and cannot—effectively

[39] UN *Transforming our World* (UN 2015), at para 39.

protect human rights, rule of law, and global PGs (like public health, climate change mitigation, and sustainable development) as long as power politics is not more effectively constrained. Just as authoritarian power politics (eg in the UN Security Council) prevents effective protection of human rights through UN law, so do regulatory capture of economic regulation (eg in the US and Bretton Woods institutions) and authoritarian blockage of WTO consensus decisions prevent limitation of market failures, governance failures, and constitutional failures in multilevel economic regulation. Transforming our world through global partnerships requires transforming UN and WTO law by the implementation of stronger rights and remedies for civil society struggles in support of the SDGs so that governance failures become more legally accountable and more democratically and constitutionally constrained.

Chapters 2–5 explain why, similar to the rational use of medicine if the human body falls ill, bounded rationality in politics requires stronger, reasonable self-commitments to agreed principles of justice and to their legislative, administrative, judicial, and civil society implementation. All 193 UN member states have adopted national Constitutions, written or unwritten. They recognize inalienable human rights for holding governments accountable. The 2030 UN Sustainable Development Agenda justifies its SDGs also in terms of human rights, basic needs, and other agreed principles of justice. As discussed in this book, however, legislative, administrative, and judicial implementing rules ensuring rule compliance and accountability by governments and citizens are often lacking. Similarly, economic and political markets and competition remain confronted with market, governance, and constitutional failures, preventing undistorted competition inside and beyond states. Can the extra-territorial harm of such governance failures (like climate change, distortion of world markets, disregard for rule of law, Russian threats of the aggressive use of military power) be remedied if international relations are perceived as power struggles among sovereign states and governments, rather than as an instrument for multilevel governance of PGs demanded by citizens? The illegal trade wars initiated by President Trump against China, and the illegal import restrictions on steel and aluminium justified by former USTR Robert Lighthizer on grounds of national security, illustrated how domestic governance failures (like Republican party tribalism undermining parliamentary control of the US executive, regulatory capture of USTR positions by the appointment of long-standing industry lobbyists, as was the case of Lighthizer)[40] risk disrupting the world trading system. As discussed in Chapters 3 and 6, recourse to judicial remedies in the US Court of International Trade and in the WTO turned out to be indispensable for establishing legal accountability and clarifying abuses of trade policy powers and of national security powers. This book explains why analyses of the world trade order

[40] Cf Q Slobodian, 'You live in Robert Lighthizer's world now' *Foreign Policy* 6 August 2018.

must take into account the interdependencies between economic, legal, and political orders. Human rights proceed from methodological individualism and actively promote responsible citizenship and civil society struggles for justice, democratic self-government, and responsible sovereignty. For example, authoritarian rulers should not be allowed to abuse WTO consensus practices for destroying WTO institutions like the Appellate Body (AB) by arbitrarily blocking consensus-based nominations of AB members. Similarly, contrary to the claims by India and South Africa, WTO members should not be allowed to abuse veto powers for blocking plurilateral trade agreements (PTAs) among willing WTO members, elaborating compromises and reforms among like-minded countries (like PTAs on electronic commerce, investment facilitation, and fishery subsidies). As illustrated by the use of agreed appellate arbitration as an interim substitute for the dysfunctional WTO AB, or by the EU initiative for elaborating agreements on carbon taxes and border carbon adjustments aimed at reducing GHG emissions, the needed adjustments to multilevel trade and investment governance must be elaborated and progressively implemented bottom up, based on leadership by the willing world.[41]

Chapters 4 and 5 explain why globalization—having transformed most national into transnational PGs—requires extending democratic constitutionalism and public–private partnerships to multilevel governance protecting PGs beyond state borders. The effectiveness of treaties protecting human rights, public health, and climate change mitigation has proven to depend on forming political coalitions not only among reasonable governments but also among sub-state and supra-national actors like cities, businesses, civil society groups, and international institutions empowered to participate in multilevel governance of PGs. Normative legal orders cannot remain legitimate and effective without institutionalizing public reason at all levels of governance as a reasonable constitutional restraint on the often divisive politics of legal practices. Just as national legal systems become politically effective through support from civil societies, democratic institutions, and courts of justice, so must UN/WTO governance practices treat citizens not only as *objects* of intergovernmental regulation. Human rights require recognizing and empowering citizens as *legal subjects* and democratic principals entitled to participate in governance and to holding all governance agents legally, democratically, and judicially accountable for the lawful exercise of their limited, delegated powers so as to prevent legal systems being undermined by political opportunism and arbitrary power politics. As illustrated in Chapter 9, public–private partnerships for promoting climate change mitigation, inventing vaccines, supplying medical equipment, and for protecting human rights in business activities have proven ever more important for providing PGs. Without 'greening' and 'constitutionalizing'

[41] J Bacchus, *The Willing World: Shaping and Sharing a Sustainable Global Prosperity* (CUP 2018).

the embedded liberalism[42] underlying the UN/WTO legal system, the universally agreed SDGs will be impossible to realize.[43]

1.2.2 Perspectivism and Existentialism in International Economic Law

The human condition is further complicated by the fact that each human being is a genetically unique creature. Individual perceptions, interpretation, and construction of realities (eg world views, narratives)—and the evolution of local societies, polities, economies, and legal systems—are shaped by the diverse perspectives of people growing up, living, and dying in different local contexts and cultures. For example, Thomas Hobbes' conception of people as at base egoist and nasty led him to construe the social contract as a submission to absolute sovereign rulers mandated to secure social peace. His presentation of autocrats as Leviathans, protecting societies from existential threats, continues to be replicated by authoritarian rulers and their repressive regimes (eg dominated by military, bureaucratic, and business elites) all over the world (eg in Asian, African, and post-revolution Arab countries following the Arab Spring in 2010).[44] Rousseau's positive conception of humans as naturally good was used (eg by Swiss and French republicans) for justifying participatory, democratic governance implementing the general will. From the perspective of industrialized countries, protecting patent rights for pharmaceutical products as incentives and compensation for private research and inventions of medicines may appear reasonable, even if it may be viewed as a death sentence from the perspective of poor countries that cannot afford paying monopoly prices for newly developed vaccines offered and sold initially in developed country markets.[45] The examples of climate refugees, patent protection for medicines, or of unnecessary famines (eg in dictatorships like North Korea and in China under Mao) illustrate how economic regulation may involve existential

[42] Cf JF Ruggie, International Regimes, Transactions and Change: Embedded Liberalism in the Postwar Economic Order, *International Organization* 36 (1982), 379–415.

[43] Characteristically, most of the contributions by Anglo-Saxon lawyers to the book edited by A Santos, C Thomas, and D Trubek (eds), *World Trade and Investment Law Reimagined: A Progressive Agenda for an Inclusive Globalization* (Anthem Press 2019) emphasize the need for protecting 'policy space', legal pluralism, regulatory competition (eg by promoting alternative regionalisms), experimentation, and compensation mechanisms for rebalancing the relation between states and international institutions without addressing the multilevel governance challenges of climate change, global health pandemics, rule of law, and multilevel constitutionalism.

[44] Cf AA Aswany, *The Dictatorship Syndrome* (Russel Harris House Publishing 2020), arguing that autocracies abuse docile ordinary persons and tribal societies who neither understand nor want revolutions and live in despair of ever bringing about justice and fear of any attempt to do so; N Feldman, *The Arab Winter: A Tragedy* (Princeton UP 2020), explaining why feudal, repressive regimes—in spite of their resilience—cannot quell the human urge to dignity: after the winter always comes another spring.

[45] Cf P Drahos, *Public Lies and Public Goods: Ten Lessons from When Patents and Pandemics Meet*, European University Institute Law Working Paper 2021-5.

questions that may be answered differently from different perspectives. What kind of limitations of intellectual property rights do human rights of individual access to public health protection require? Are human rights to education and to freedom of opinion compatible with governmental instructions (eg in authoritarian countries like China) to avoid discussing the importance of human and constitutional rights for designing IEL? Authoritarian and democratic governments offer different answers to many existential questions like whether, and how, the human condition of social conflicts (eg due to different conceptions of the good) can be overcome by reasonable political conceptions of justice in non-homogeneous societies where unreasonable people risk preventing social peace and justice by transforming politics into fights against political enemies. Similar to the Heisenberg principle in quantum physics, the mere fact of observing the world from different perspectives risks changing social realities; individual, communitarian, national, international, or cosmopolitan perspectives may call for diverse regulatory understandings and responses.

Anglo-Saxon constitutional recognition of common law freedoms, like EU law's recognition of constitutional and common market freedoms of EU citizens, has no equivalent in authoritarian states like China. From the two philosophical schools of Confucianism and legalism in ancient China to China's Communist Constitution of 1982, individual freedoms remain severely constrained in China by social, political, and legal hierarchies and corresponding social, political, and legal duties of individuals.[46] This book explores how the varieties of post-feudal, capitalist economic orders—like utilitarian economic neo-liberalism, China's totalitarian socialist market economy with Chinese characteristics, and the EU's competitive social market economy (Article 3 TEU) embedded into ordo-liberal constitutionalism—are driven by diverse political and legal cultures. As illustrated by the US–China trade wars since 2018, the regulatory competition and systemic rivalries[47] risk disrupting world order treaties like the WTO Agreement, the UNCLOS and the constitution (*sic*) establishing the WHO. Chapters 4–9 explain why maintaining rule of law (eg through WTO, the International Court of

[46] Cf Lubman (n 6), 15ff. China's Constitution (as amended in 1988, 1993, 1999, and 2004) continues to describe China's political system as a dictatorship of the proletariat (Preamble), notwithstanding China's neglect for human and workers' rights. On the Confucian, legalist, and Taoist influences in Chinese imperial rule, the communist conceptions of law in China (eg as reflected in the 1947, 1954, and 1975 Constitutions), and the evolution of constitutionalist thinking in China since Mao's death in 1976, see S Balme and MW Dowdle (eds), *Building Constitutionalism in China* (Palgrave Macmillan 2009).

[47] On economic and environmental cooperation, systemic competition (eg between diverse competition and subsidy systems) and strategic rivalries (eg regarding China's support of authoritarian rulers and disregard for human rights) between China and the EU, see EU Petersmann, 'Trade and Investment Adjudication Involving "Silk Road Projects": Legal Methodology Challenges' in W Shan, S Zhang, and J Su (eds), *China and International Dispute Resolution in the Context of the 'Belt and Road Initiative'* (CUP 2020), 51–77. The Brussels Communiqué of 14 June 2021 of the NATO Summit meeting of the thirty allied NATO democracies acknowledged (in para 55) that 'China's stated ambitions and assertive behaviour present systemic challenges to the rules-based international order and to areas relevant to Alliance security'.

Justice (ICJ), and UNCLOS adjudication)—and using institutional economics for justifying economic regulation—remain important tools for reducing systemic conflicts and realizing the 2030 SDGs. And yet people will tie their hands to the mast of democratic constitutionalism only if they understand the systemic dangers of governance failures (like rent-seeking interest-group politics, authoritarian abuses of power). As all individuals and peoples remain diverse, so too will their social contracts and democratic decision-making remain diverse. Enabling readers to understand the complexity of the global governance challenges of the SDGs will be facilitated by the following overview of the main systemic problems of regional and global trade and investment orders—as subsequently explored in detail in Chapters 2–9—as parts of the broader UN system and world order necessary for protecting the SDGs.

1.2.3 From the Washington Consensus to the Geneva and Brussels Consensus?

The post-1945 Bretton Woods system was dominated by the neo-liberal Washington consensus under the hegemonic leadership of the United States, the International Monetary Fund (IMF), and the World Bank Group at Washington, DC. The drafting of the GATT in 1947 was dominated by the US and British delegations representing the then largest market economies. The legal evolution of the GATT 1947 through eight rounds of multilateral trade negotiations was driven by its four largest trading and contracting parties called the Quad, the market-oriented policies of Canada, the EU, Japan, and the United States. In the WTO, the membership of state capitalist countries—and the increasing conflicts among Anglo-Saxon neo-liberalism, authoritarian state capitalism, EU WTO members committed to ordo-liberal economic constitutionalism, and less-developed countries insisting on special and differential treatment even if they are part of the G20 group (like India and South Africa)—have given rise to proposals for additional WTO rules prescribing market-conforming policies and limiting abusive self-selection of less-developed country status. How should WTO members respond to the increasing trade wars resulting from regulatory competition among WTO members practising different varieties of capitalist economic orders such as neo-liberal utilitarianism, China's totalitarian state capitalism, and European ordo-liberalism aimed at promoting equal freedoms, fair competition, and social justice through economic constitutionalism?[48]

Chapters 2–5 discuss the evolution from the neo-liberal Washington consensus to the ordo-liberal, regional Brussels consensus and worldwide UN/WTO

[48] On the history of ordo-liberalism see Chapter 4.

Geneva consensus, and their systemic competition with the totalitarian Beijing consensus imposed by China's Communist party monopoly. Chapter 2 describes the UN Sustainable Development Agenda as an application of the Geneva consensus for protecting human rights and other SDGs. Even if the competing neo-liberal, state capitalist, ordo-liberal, and third-world conceptions of embedded liberalism may be applied in conformity with the interface provisions in Articles III, XVII–XXI, XXIV, and XXV GATT (and equivalent provisions in other parts of the WTO Agreement) coordinating diverse, regulatory instruments, the ordo-liberal SDGs require far-reaching reforms of economic law and institutions. The UN's 2030 Agenda for Sustainable Development strengthens the Geneva consensus by offering guidelines for coherent responses to the global economic, health, environmental, governance, and rule of law crises. Can the constitutional foundations of the world trading system (like compulsory jurisdiction for third-party adjudication of trade disputes) be reinforced so as to prevent authoritarian and populist rulers and rent-seeking lobbyists from destroying, once again, the world trade system, as happened following the US Smoot–Hawley Tariff Act of 1930 and the trade wars by US President Trump ushering in the destruction of the WTO AB system in December 2019? Do WTO rules impede effective climate change regulation, for instance, in view of the failure of the 2015 Paris Climate Agreement to provide agreed disciplines for carbon taxes, border carbon adjustments, and green subsidies aimed at reducing GHG emissions?

GATT 1947 began with flimsy legal foundations due to its lack of parliamentary ratification and its only provisional application as an intergovernmental agreement subject to grandfather clauses exempting existing, mandatory legislation. Yet it evolved into the WTO legal system and the most successful, worldwide trading system prescribing compulsory jurisdictions for the settlement of international and domestic trade disputes, enabling all 164 WTO members to enhance their economic welfare, reform their trade law systems, and lift billions of people out of poverty. Chapter 2 recalls why international peace and justice—as represented by the two statues of the Greek goddesses *Eirene* (peace) and *Dike* (standing for justice, order and judgment) at the main entrance to the WTO's Centre William Rappard at Lake Geneva (as pictured on the cover page of this book)—call for maintaining the WTO as a universal trading, legal, and dispute settlement system open for countries with diverse economic systems as long as WTO members comply with their transparency, non-discrimination, rule of law, and other legal requirements under WTO law, including peaceful dispute settlement and impartial third-party adjudication. The embedded liberalism underlying GATT and the WTO deliberately avoided ordo-liberal constitutionalism (ie linking common markets to respect for human rights and constitutional freedoms). Hence, WTO rules (eg China's Accession Protocol) exclude hegemonic claims that WTO membership is conditional on following Western conceptions of market economies. Similar to the four floors of the Centre William Rappard, the WTO can realize its economic, political, and legal objectives best by respecting regulatory competition among the private and public, national, regional, and worldwide storeys of the WTO legal system as long as WTO rules are being followed. If the WTO consensus practices prevent regulatory progress on the level of global WTO governance, or WTO members fail to comply with WTO law as described in Chapter 3, regional, plurilateral, and bilateral agreements and institutions on the lower floors of the world trading house offer more appropriate ways for initiating bottom-up legal reforms among like-minded countries. This subsidiarity principle also reflects the recognition by all UN member states of popular self-determination and of inalienable human rights empowering citizens as democratic principals to choose diverse forms of self-governance. Yet, even though the world economy is driven by producers, workers, traders, investors, and consumers, and UN HRL recognizes citizens as subjects of inalienable human rights and democratic principals of governance agents with limited, delegated powers, UN and WTO practices condone member-driven power politics. Chapter 2 explains why the post-1945 human rights revolution and IEL revolution have failed to prevent the trade wars and geopolitical rivalries described in Chapter 3. The member-driven governance dominating UN/WTO legal practices does not—and cannot—effectively protect human rights, rule of law, and global PGs (like public health, climate change mitigation, and sustainable development) as long as power politics is not more effectively constrained.[49]

1.2.4 Institutional Economics and Democratic Constitutionalism Confirm the 'Geneva Consensus' and 'Brussels Consensus'

Chapters 2 and 3 explain why UN and WTO law do not effectively constrain the politics of international law and related governance failures; they are not enough for establishing a global community law effectively protecting human rights and PGs demanded by citizens. Chapters 4 and 5 argue that institutional economics, democratic and republican constitutionalism offer the most convincing economic, legal, and democratic justifications of liberal, rules-based multilateral trading systems. If geopolitical rivalries lead to the destruction of the multilateral WTO and European trading systems, WTO and EU law—and their underlying economic constitutionalism limiting abuses of power through rules-based market integration and institutions protecting rule of law—would need to be re-invented. The Geneva consensus and the Brussels consensus have succeeded in institutionalizing

[49] Most textbooks on IEL justify economic regulation by neo-liberal concepts of 'Kaldor–Hicks efficiencies' without regard to human rights, 'development as freedom' (A Sen) and the social inequalities inside so many UN member states; on the lack of citizen-oriented theories of justice in IEL, and my use of Kantian, Rawlsian, and cosmopolitan theories of constitutional justice and human rights for justifying IEL, see Petersmann 2012 (n 12), Chapters I–III.

public reason in multilateral treaty institutions far beyond the Washington consensus, notwithstanding hegemonic Chinese, Russian, and US power politics. Unfortunately, many UN and WTO diplomats, WTO economists, and WTO legal scholars are no longer familiar with the legal civilization and republican cultures necessary for maintaining democratic and civil society support for what former WTO Director-General Pascal Lamy described as the Geneva consensus. Chapters 2, 4, and 5 recount these European foundations of economic, legal, and democratic civilization and the differences between utilitarian, Anglo-Saxon (neo) liberalism, and ordo-liberal economic constitutionalism. They explain why—even if the domestic policy functions and constitutional functions of GATT/WTO law for assisting governments in promoting domestic welfare and reforming trade regulation in order to resist protectionist interest group politics are no longer understood in many WTO member countries—the WTO legal and dispute settlement systems remain of crucial importance for assisting neo-liberal, state capitalist, ordo-liberal, and less-developed WTO members in coordinating their regulatory competition, settling disputes peacefully (if need be through WTO third-party adjudication), and cooperating in their use of trade policy instruments for mitigating climate change and responding to global health pandemics. This book's proposals for greening and constitutionalizing the WTO system call for making GATT/WTO rules *consistent* with environmental policies and human rights, which are determined *outside the WTO* in the framework of the competent national, regional, and UN institutions—without repeating past policy mistakes of using welfare-reducing, third-best trade policy instruments as substitutes for first-best or second-best environmental, development, and human rights instruments. Arguably, both trade and competition policies can contribute to protecting the SDGs and to mitigating climate change (eg by spurring innovation necessary for reducing GHG emissions); neither trade protectionism nor anticompetitive agreements offer efficient tools for protecting human rights and sustainable development. Yet, trade and competition policies need to be adapted to the SDGs (eg by means of carbon border adjustment tariffs, broadening the consumer welfare test of competition policies focusing on in-market negative effects and efficiencies by taking into account also certain out-of-market effects).

1.3 Sustainable Development Requires Protecting Rule of Law and Human Rights

Similar to the recognition of human rights, democracy, and rule of law as the foundational trinity of democratic constitutionalism, the 2030 Development Agenda defines most SDGs in terms of human rights objectives: 'The 17 Sustainable Development Goals and 169 targets . . . seek to realize the human rights of all and to achieve gender equality and the empowerment of all women and girls'; the Agenda is committed to 'democracy, good governance', 'the rule of law at the national and international levels', and ensuring 'equal access to justice for all'.[50] Chapters 6–9 discuss trade, investment, human rights, constitutional, and climate change litigation as instruments for holding governments—and increasingly also private corporations—accountable for protecting PGs like sustainable development and climate change mitigation. As recalled by *Justitia*, the blindfolded Roman goddess of law and justice (armed with a sword, symbolizing power and will, and with a balance, symbolizing reason and justice for peaceful settlement of disputes), power-oriented trade governance without legal and judicial remedies lacks legitimacy and efficient ordering. Statues of justice in court houses all over the world recall this historical insight of legal civilization that rule of law must contain the constant tensions between human reason (eg aimed at maintaining the coherence and impartiality of law, limiting its political instrumentalization) and political will (eg aimed at utility maximization for the benefit of powerful rulers). The human rights approach of the UN 2030 Sustainable Development Agenda implies that neither a utilitarian Washington consensus nor an authoritarian Beijing consensus offer sufficient leadership for protecting rule of law and sustainable development in global governance, health, and environmental crises.

1.3.1 From State-Centred to Cosmopolitan Principles of Justice?

Chapters 5–9 explain how constitutional limitations of foreign policy discretion by constitutional and human rights and judicial remedies can depoliticize conflicts among states by protecting the common interests of their citizens. They also examine the question of how UN and WTO member states should respond to nationalist withdrawals from multilateral PGs agreements (as illustrated by Brexit, President Trump's nationalist mercantilism and his withdrawal of the United States from the Paris Agreement on climate change mitigation) and the US assault on the WTO AB and the WHO. The environmental, health, and economic crises provoked by climate change and the global COVID-19 pandemic since 2020 led to emergency restrictions of fundamental rights in most countries. The geopolitical rivalries led to additional invocations of national security laws for justifying unilateral restrictions among states (eg Internet communications, 5G technologies developed by Chinese companies) as well as inside states (eg suppression of human rights in China, Russia, and other authoritarian countries). Some populist emergency responses have undermined the rule of law, for instance illegal US import

[50] Cf UN *Transforming Our World* (2015), at Preamble and paras 8, 9, and 'goal 16'. On the UN resolutions on rule of law see Chapter 4, section 4.1 and Chapter 6, section 6.1 and H Krieger and G Nolte (eds), *The International Rule of Law—Rise or Decline?—Approaching Current Foundational Challenges* (OUP 2019).

restrictions on steel and aluminium and US blocking of WTO institutions and procedures for protecting the rule of law as prescribed in the WTO Dispute Settlement Understanding (DSU).

Due to the inter-governmental, Westphalian traditions of international law and to the colonial and post-war context of 1945, the UN Charter focuses mainly on state-centred principles of international law among sovereign states (like sovereign equality, prohibition of the use of force, peaceful settlement of disputes, non-intervention, cooperation). Even though the UN recognizes and protects inalienable and indivisible human rights, its practices condone power politics (eg by the veto powers in the UN Security Council) and neglect the lack of democratic governance and of effective protection of human rights inside many UN member states. My 2012 textbook, *International Economic Law in the 21st Century*, used Kantian, Rawlsian, and cosmopolitan theories of justice for criticizing the prevailing, utilitarian, and power-oriented approaches to IEL. Like any other legal system confronted with constant tensions between the *law in the books* (providing for a normative legal order based on legal positivism, principles of justice and public reason) and the *law in action* (based on political, social, and strategic decision-making processes for law-making, administration, adjudication, and rule compliance), IEL cannot remain effective and legitimate without being embedded into some kind of democratic constitutionalism, limiting the politics of international legal practices and protecting human rights and remedies against abuses of power. My 2017 monograph, *Multilevel Constitutionalism for Multilevel Governance of Public Goods*, confirmed—normatively and empirically—the claim of theories of justice that the basic structures of legal systems, including international law, will be recognized as legitimate by citizens only to the extent they are justifiable in terms of the procedural, constitutional, distributive, corrective, commutative principles of justice and equity, which have become recognized in national constitutions and HRL all over the world, as explicitly recalled also in the customary rules of treaty interpretation.[51] From 1995 until the destruction of the WTO AB in December 2019, the dynamic evolution of the WTO legal and dispute settlement system was supported by a rules-based trade policy culture prevailing in most WTO members and in their WTO Dispute Settlement Body (DSB). Chapters 6–9 explain why—without restoring and strengthening the WTO legal and dispute settlement systems—the UN/WTO systems cannot protect transnational rule of law in responding to the regulatory challenges of climate change, global health pandemics, and geopolitical rivalries among WTO members with neo-liberal, state capitalist, ordo-liberal, or third-world economies. Also, the post-war trade policy objectives of promoting 'world peace through world trade' and the UN's 2030 Agenda for

[51] Cf EU Petersmann, 'International Trade Law, Human Rights and the Customary International Law Rules on Treaty Interpretation' in S Joseph, D Kinley, and J Waincymer (eds), *The WTO and Human Rights* (CUP 2009), 69–90.

Sustainable Development cannot be realized without rules-based multilateralism and national and international courts of justice protecting justice and equity principles universally recognized in democratic constitutions and human rights agreements as 'foundations of freedom, justice and peace in the world'.[52] WTO law refers to some principles of justice, for example in its regulation of violation complaints (based on corrective justice principles), non-violation complaints (based on commutative justice principles), and situation complaints (based on equity principles), and their protection by judicial remedies and independent WTO adjudication constrained by the customary law rules of treaty interpretation (referring to principles of justice and human rights and fundamental freedoms for all, as codified in the Preamble and Article 31 of the Vienna Convention on the Law of Treaties (VCLT)). WTO law, however, also departs from otherwise agreed principles of justice like state responsibility for reparation of injury. Chapters 6–9 explain the need for restoring and strengthening rule of law in international trade, investment, and environmental relations as a precondition for sustainable development and climate change mitigation. Rule of law requires resisting claims (eg by the USTR) to disregard the customary rules of treaty interpretation in order to enforce US lobbying interests (eg in benefitting from discriminatory anti-dumping duties) with even fewer legal constraints.

1.3.2 The Geo-political Rivalries Reinforce the Need for Rule of Law

Can the ancient ideal of rule of law be achieved in a globally interdependent world dominated by geopolitical rivalries, as described in Chapter 2? Chapters 4 and 5 explain why the challenges to UN/WTO law—like neglect of human rights and for climate change mitigation, insufficient notification of and cooperation in health pandemics, circumvention of WTO disciplines by state trading practices—increase the need for rules-based dispute settlement procedures. The frequent violations of human rights in so many UN member states reveal that UN law remains a power-driven legal system without effective legal and judicial remedies against many illegal practices of UN member governments. Hence, some environmental experts argue that the Anthropocene, —the recent global context of humans having become a geophysical force provoking climate change, massive biodiversity losses, and other geological changes that risk running out of human control—necessitates global constitutional approaches limiting obvious governance failures (like disregard for 'planetary boundaries') so as to prevent the human destruction of our environmental system.[53] European law illustrates why the normative pull of

[52] The quotation is from the Preamble of the 1948 Universal Declaration of Human Rights.

[53] Cf LJ Kotzé, *Global Environmental Constitutionalism in the Anthropocene* (Hart 2016). While the transition to a net-zero carbon emissions economy by 2050 appears technologically possible, it requires

human rights depends on their normative push: their effective legal implementation through (i) constitutional law, (ii) legislation, (iii) administration, (iv) adjudication, (v) democratic support and public reason, (vi) international treaties, (vii) international institutions, and (viii) the secondary law of international institutions. Their effectiveness often depends on whether citizens can invoke and enforce precise and unconditional international rules inside states and thereby constrain power politics (eg by judicial remedies of citizens in national and European courts), as illustrated by the investment, human rights, constitutional, and environmental litigation discussed in Chapters 7–9. Moreover, the fact that almost half of the individual complaints under the European Convention on Human Rights (ECHR) come from Russia and other Eastern European countries and—even if supported by the European Court of Human Rights (ECtHR)—often do not lead to effective remedies, confirms that international law rules risk remaining ineffective if they are not implemented in domestic laws and supported by independent institutions inside states. Such multilevel legal and democratic implementation of HRL does not exist in many authoritarian UN member states (like China) invoking UN principles (like sovereign equality of states, non-intervention into domestic affairs) as shields against external criticism of their domestic suppression of human rights and minority rights (eg of Uighur and Tibetan minorities, people in Hong Kong). This book argues that even if constitutionalizing the UN system may remain a political utopia, democratic alliances of countries should continue their normative push for constitutional reforms, for example following the example of the successful introduction of worldwide compulsory settlement of disputes through the 1994 WTO Agreement and its provisions on multilevel third-party adjudication.

Asian statesmen warn that the dawn of a new world order, with China and India as the most populous economies, requires Western countries to accept that they can no longer impose their liberal ideologies and wage imperial wars (eg in Iraq after 9/11) on the world.[54] Western advocates for enlightenment now[55] respond that future world peace and sustainable development depend on globalizing the Western inventions of enlightenment, public reason, democratic constitutionalism, and multilateral, rules-based institutions for protecting PGs (including rule

far-reaching changes also in agricultural, food, environmental, political, and social policies; cf Energy Transition Commission, *Making Mission Possible: Delivering a Net-Zero Economy* (Energy Transition Commission September 2020). In contrast to the preceding Holocene epoch, which was characterized by relative stability in ecological conditions, the Anthropocene risks disrupting the earth system, its 'planetary boundaries', and international legal regulation of socio-ecological issues. Do the interactions between human rule of law and rule of nature (eg through natural catastrophes) require not only duties of care but also more inclusive decision-making procedures, as proposed by advocates for constitutionalizing the Anthropocene? Should legal duties to protect human rights have priority over legal duties to protect non-human parts of nature, especially in legal systems (like UN law) which fail to protect human rights effectively?

[54] See K Mahbubani, *Has the West Lost It? A Provocation* (Penguin 2018).

[55] Cf Pinker 2018 (n 19).

of law). In addition, the Thucydides trap of political rivalries ushering into war cannot be avoided without constitutional restraints on foreign policy powers.[56] Can a repetition of the recent trade wars (discussed in Chapter 3) be prevented by transforming the ideological conflicts and geopolitical rivalries among American neo-liberalism, communist state capitalism, and European ordo-liberalism into mutually agreed IEL reforms? How are today's *rivalries among states* related to their *rivalries inside states*, such as totalitarian power monopolies inside communist states suppressing human rights, or Republican party tribalism and deniers of election results inside the US Congress undermining democratic control of executive powers in the United States under President Trump? Can the regulatory capture and social inequalities caused by neo-liberal interest group politics inside the United States be reversed?[57] Why have past democratic struggles for compensating bounded rationality of citizens through ordo-liberal, constitutional self-restraints, and multilevel constitutionalism been successful in post-1945 European integration? Can the EU's multilevel constitutionalism succeed in containing abuses of power inside the EU (eg in illiberal EU member states like Hungary and Poland) and within the EU's near neighbourhood? Does European constitutionalism offer lessons for reforming the UN legal system and the protection of the SDGs?

This book argues that the geopolitical rivalries preventing the UN Security Council from effectively protecting a global security order—and increasingly also undermining the UN human rights system and the WTO legal and dispute settlement system—are related to the value conflicts driving the systemic competition among utilitarian Anglo-Saxon neo-liberalism, authoritarian state capitalism, and ordo-liberal constitutionalism in UN and WTO member states. Outside Europe, many people are unfamiliar with the history of ordo-liberalism and of its impact on European integration. Chapters 2–5 explain the major varieties of capitalist economic systems,[58] as well as their increasing systemic conflicts as evidenced by, *inter alia*:

[56] Cf G Allison, *Destined for War: Can America and China Escape Thucydides' Trap?* (Harcourt 2017). The Greek historian Thucydides described the risks of war when a rising power (like Athens in Ancient Greece, China today) threatens to displace the ruling power (ushering in the Peloponnesian wars between Athens and Sparta devastating ancient Greece). The First and Second World Wars reflected democratic failures and 'Thucydidean' wars in the twentieth century.

[57] On paranoid minds in US domestic struggles (eg against slavery, racist right-wing extremism, Republican tribalism) see R Hofstadter, *The Paranoid Style in American Politics* (Vintage 2008). K Pistor, 'Saving US Democracy from Corporate America' *Project Syndicate* 12 January 2021, notes that '(o)ver the past four years, the Trump administration has delivered on pretty much everything that corporate America could have wanted. It cut corporate taxes, rolled back many of the regulations that were instituted to protect the financial system from another crisis, and gutted environmental-protection policies, even as the disastrous effects of climate change have become more obvious.' Due to the appointment of more than 200 Republican judges during the Trump presidency, the US Supreme Court remains unlikely to change its jurisprudence that spending by corporations or wealthy individuals to influence politics is no different from the free speech exercised by natural persons. On the pro-worker rhetoric and pro-billionaire and white nationalism practices of the Republican party, see E Luce, 'Trump's grip on Republicans is still growing' *Financial Times* 5 April 2021.

[58] The term 'neo-liberalism' was coined at the international 'Lippmann colloquium' in Paris in 1938 as a response to liberalism's crisis caused by Marxism, communism, fascism, and Keynesian economics.

- the US trade war initiated in 2018 against China;
- US President Trump's illegal destruction of the WTO AB in December 2019;
- the WTO-inconsistent Economic and Trade Agreement signed by China and the United States on 15 January 2020; and
- by China's illegal trade retaliation (eg since 2018 against the USA, in 2020 against Australia).

Law and legal cultures are of existential importance for extended peaceful cooperation (*ubi societas, ibi jus*). Today, they are embedded in globally interconnected economic, political, social, environmental, national, and international systems of enormous complexity; the interactions and rationalities driving societies, economies, polities, and legal systems remain deeply contested. Normative *legal orders* reflecting the public reason and rationality of their legal subjects and rulers dynamically interact with institutionally framed *legal practices* (eg of law-makers, governments, judges, legal scholars, citizens, companies) shaped by political cultures, politics, self-interests, and the will (power) of legal actors. Together, the *legal orders* and the *legal practices* constitute *legal systems* developing in response to dialectic interactions between law (reason, rationality) and practices (will, psychology).[59] The creation of the UN in 1945 showed that if world powers face a common, existential threat like genocide and nuclear war, dramatic legal and institutional changes are possible. But neither the universal rules and institutions of the UN system nor the regulatory competition among sovereign states have prevented the current economic and environmental crises, health pandemics, trade wars, increasing nationalism and populist tribalism prioritizing separate identities (eg America First, Brexit, the power monopoly of China's communist party vis-à-vis

It was only in the late 1970s that British Prime Minister Thatcher and US President Reagan began using this term in the narrower sense of market fundamentalism (eg prioritizing liberalization, deregulation, privatization, and financialization of economic activities as recommended by Chicago School economists relying on markets as decentralized, largely self-regulatory cybernetic information, coordination, and sanctioning mechanisms driven by the economic rationality and decentralized knowledge of the *homo economicus*). The Trump administration's protectionist policies are described in this book as a hegemonic version of nationalist mercantilism, yet they are viewed as a logical consequence of the regulatory capture by neo-liberal US interest group politics (eg as illustrated by the appointment of long-term business lobbyists as USTR and US ambassador to the WTO, President Trump's deregulation and tax cuts demanded by business) and discussed under the neo-liberal category of economic orders in this study. The new Biden administration in the United States is expected to return to multilateral liberalization and regulation of trade, including recommitment of the United States to some of the multilateral agreements unilaterally denounced by President Trump; its supply-side social and industrial policies provide for massive government interventions into the US economy. The US–China rivalries and global health and climate change crises further contribute to a return to active industrial policies also in the United States. It remains to be seen to what extent neo-liberal traditions (eg of corporations being solely responsible for maximizing shareholder value in terms of profits; corporate tax systems allowing tax avoidance through profit shifting to tax havens; corporations as rule-makers by financing the elections of US congressmen and influencing their work; toleration of anti-competitive practices of dominant US tech and services corporations) will continue to prevail in the United States.

[59] For an explanation of this conception of law and legal systems, see Chapter 2, section 2.1.

local autonomy in Hong Kong and Taiwan). Agreement on the UN Sustainable Development Agenda was possible because, as a Declaration by the UN General Assembly, its guidance is not legally binding but only recommended. As the centre of gravity of international politics and of the world economy is moving to Asia, how will the systemic rivalries between American neo-liberalism, European ordo-liberalism, China's totalitarian state capitalism, and Asian values affect international economic order and international law? Will they render impossible the strengthening of the WTO legal and dispute settlement system so as to fortify resistance against future, similar attacks (eg by Chinese or Russian power politics)? Will US democracy hinder President Biden's attempts at offering leadership for reforming multilateral treaty systems for providing global PGs like public health protection, climate change mitigation, and transnational rule of law? Which governments and national legislatures will accept transformation of the SDGs into legally binding commitments? What are the lessons from the global health pandemic for reforming capitalist economies and their social welfare systems in order to cope with the long COVID health problems of 10–20 per cent of COVID-19 victims and the enhanced insecurity of working from home in digital economies?

1.3.3 Judicial Administration of Justice Must Protect Rule of Law as Constitutional Restraint on Regulatory Competition

Another historical lesson from the post-1945 Cold War between Western democracies and the Soviet Union, which resulted in the political disintegration of the USSR in 1991, was that structural changes in multilevel governance and international relations may be brought about peacefully by coalitions of the willing (like the North Atlantic Treaty Organization (NATO) countries) promoting regulatory competition. Yet, in contrast to the implosion of the Soviet Union's economy, China's socialist market economy has transformed China into the largest trading country with what will soon be the world's largest national economy. The rivalries between American neo-liberalism, China's state capitalism, and Europe's economic constitutionalism remain deeply rooted in diverse cultures and value conflicts that are likely to continue for a long time. Will utilitarian neo-liberalism and power-oriented state capitalism continue to disrupt the WTO dispute settlement and legal system and politicize WTO legal practices, leading to progressive disintegration? How will regionalism, plurilateralism, bilateralism, and other forms of decentralized regulatory competition transform UN and WTO world order treaties? Can the inconsistencies between the realities of legal pluralism and of the politics of international legal practices with the human rights objectives of the SDGs be overcome? How should reasonable citizens and democracies respond to the unprecedented structural changes caused by climate change, global health pandemics, and by authoritarian neglect for human rights, the rule of law, and other global PGs?

Can unilateral commitments, for example by the EU, Japan, and the United States to make their economies carbon neutral by 2050, China's commitment to a carbon-neutral economy by 2060, and India's commitment to a carbon-neutral economy by 2070 be realized without provoking conflicts with third countries if carbon taxes and related border-carbon adjustments measures (CBAMs) are unilaterally introduced vis-à-vis third countries aimed at limiting GHG emissions and carbon leakage abroad (as discussed in Chapter 9)?

Chapters 4–9 explain why—even if the post-1945 Anglo-Saxon neo-liberal economic orders, totalitarian state capitalism, and Europe's ordo-liberal economic constitutionalism remain governed by different principles (values)—institutional economics, multilevel protection of rule of law, judicial remedies, and systemic treaty interpretation methods enable continuing what was successfully begun with the UN and GATT/WTO legal systems to design: rank, and limit policy instruments by law (eg for SDGs like climate change mitigation, public health protection, economic welfare, Internet regulation) in more precise, efficient, and socially just ways, responding better to the environmental, technological, and other regulatory challenges of the twenty-first century. Chapters 6–9 explore how rule of law and legal implementation of the SDGs (eg by carbon taxes and CBAMs aimed at GHG emission reductions) can be promoted in the world trading, investment, and environmental systems. Learning from scientific insights and allowing institutional economics to depoliticize some of the needed UN/WTO reforms is possible only if UN member states heed what President Biden mentioned in his inaugural address on 20 January 2021: 'We must reject a culture in which facts themselves are manipulated and even manufactured'. As explained in Chapters 3 and 6, discussions of WTO legal and dispute settlement reforms have become so badly distorted by false claims (notably those made by the Trump administration) that agreed reforms of WTO trade remedy rules and of independent appellate review may no longer be possible. The money-driven regulatory capture inside the United States also raises doubts on whether a democratic alliance of WTO members will find it easier to agree on the needed legal dispute settlement reforms.

In mutually beneficial trade relations, reciprocal legal and judicial remedies not only reduce transaction costs by building trust, mutual understanding, and public reason limiting harmful unilateral restrictions. Maintaining a rules-based, global order is also a precondition for protecting global PGs and avoiding trade wars (eg in response to perceived Chinese violations of multilateral agreements on human rights, trade, intellectual property, health, and maritime law). The more UN and WTO negotiations fail to reach worldwide agreement on rules-based responses to the economic, environmental, health, and geopolitical challenges, the more necessary will unilateral and plurilateral initiatives become (eg for introducing non-discriminatory carbon taxes, a carbon emission trading systems, and carbon border adjustments), provided they remain subject to judicial remedies protecting their legal consistency with the existing UN and WTO agreements and enabling independent, impartial judicial clarifications of how legal conflicts (eg among trade, investment, environmental rules and human rights) should be resolved. Elder statesmen (like Henry Kissinger) and independent observers increasingly warn that aggressive Chinese policies inside China (eg against Tibetan and Uighur minorities, Hong Kong, and Taiwan) and beyond China (eg territorial and military expansion in the South China Sea, military border conflicts with India in the Himalaya, security risks of China's telecommunications, industrial, and military policies) risk provoking a second Cold War between the West and another communist dictatorship which, this time, is unlikely to collapse under the contradictions of its totalitarian ideology. The geographical, economic, environmental, and political contexts of this geopolitical rivalry in the twenty-first century differ from those during the twentieth century. For example, continued cooperation with China in providing global PGs (like protection of the environment) will remain necessary, and most third countries wish to continue economic cooperation with both China and the United States rather than participating in a hegemonic US containment strategy against China. Yet, the geopolitical rivalries risk disintegrating, once again, the global trading, monetary, legal, and communications systems with adverse effects on citizens all over the world. In addition, UN and environmental experts warn of insufficient limitations of GHG emissions and destruction of biodiversity provoking climate change and droughts, reducing food security, and forcing hundreds of millions of climate refugees to relocate from areas likely to be submerged by rising sea levels. The Trump administration's destruction of the WTO AB system and its withdrawal of the United States from numerous multilateral treaties (like the 2015 Paris Agreement on climate change mitigation, the WHO) were supported neither by the EU nor by the BRICS countries. Yet, if UN and WTO treaty systems should disintegrate into regional blocks, IEL and multilevel governance of PGs risk disintegrating as well. Chapter 5 explains why executive powers to withdraw from multilateral treaties should be subject to parliamentary approval, especially if treaty implementation was regulated by domestic legislation that protects individual rights (eg to health and environmental protection, property rights, and judicial remedies). Chapter 6 explains why executive powers to invoke national security exceptions must remain subject to limited good faith review by independent courts of justice. The environmental and health crises also illustrate the need for democratic and judicial balancing of foreign investor rights with the public interests of the host state, as discussed in Chapter 7. Similarly, an important lessons from the COVID-19 health pandemic is that executive powers to restrict fundamental rights require stronger parliamentary control and judicial remedies, including more transparent balancing of the civil, political, economic, social, and cultural rights of citizens affected by lockdowns imposed by executive orders. Chapter 8 uses the judicial comity and constitutional proportionality principles elaborated in multilevel judicial cooperation among national and European courts for clarifying legal balancing principles protecting transnational rule of law in multilevel governance of PGs and in the national and European constitutional, human rights, and environmental litigation discussed in Chapter 9.

1.3.4 International Economic Law at a Crossroads: Constitutional Justice?

Many politicians and economists neglect the constitutional role of law for social, economic, political, legal, and cultural ordering of societies and for limiting abuses of public and private power. Chapter 2, section 2.1 and Chapter 4, section 4.2 explain why the interactions and interdependencies among societies, economies, polities, and legal systems require interdisciplinary approaches to economic regulation. All WTO members use private commercial law and public international law conceptions of IEL. However, their multilevel economic regulation, their support for global administrative law (as advocated by US legal scholars) or for constitutional conceptions of IEL (as practised by national and European courts inside the EU) vary enormously. Consensus on WTO reforms and prevention or settlement of long-standing trade conflicts (eg over agricultural and aircraft subsidies, trade remedies, electronic commerce, intellectual property rights) are impeded by the historical evolution and politicization of five competing conceptions of IEL since the Second World War, which often entail competing legal interpretations and conflicting legal practices (as discussed in Chapter 3). The more civil societies contest neo-liberal and state capitalist abuses of power (eg neglecting financial, environmental, health, social, and human rights crises), the more citizens and courts of justice in democratic countries are challenging related legal practices. The citizen-driven environmental litigation discussed in Chapter 9 focuses on adverse environmental and health impacts of fossil fuel production and consumption that had been neglected for decades.[60]

The 1948 Universal Declaration of Human Rights (UDHR) succeeded in codifying universal agreement on inalienable and indivisible human rights. Yet, as recalled in Chapter 2, section 2.3, the diversity of moral, political, and legal conceptions of human rights impedes their effective, legislative, and judicial protection in many UN member states, thereby weakening democratic support also for IEL. As UN practises prioritize sovereign equality of states, UN member states remain free to decide whether they will ratify and domestically implement UN human rights conventions. Unlike the EU Charter of Fundamental Rights (EUCFR), most UN human rights conventions do not protect market freedoms

[60] See also 'WHO chief: the G20 must invest in a healthier, greener post-pandemic world' *Financial Times* 7 July 2021 ('Fossil-fuelled air pollution causes about 13 premature deaths a minute or 7m every year. It is the silent pandemic, the consequence of decades of inaction despite stark warnings from scientists'). Coal emissions are responsible for as many deaths every day as the Chernobyl nuclear accident has been in total.

(like freedom of profession), private property, and other legal foundations of what the Lisbon Treaty calls a competitive social market economy (Article 3 TEU), nor do they effectively protect constitutional principles of justice like judicial remedies, democratic constitutionalism, and proportionality balancing of competing civil, political, economic, social, and cultural rights. The 1944 Bretton Woods Agreements and GATT 1947 were designed and progressively developed without references to human rights based on a neo-liberal Washington consensus.[61] Since the 1950s, the ECHR and the European economic integration agreements contributed to a progressively emerging ordo-liberal Brussels consensus embedding FTAs into democratic constitutionalism committed to limitation of market failures, governance failures, and constitutional failures which had devastated Europe through both World Wars and resulting in social, economic, and political crises also during the interwar period. Some of the UN treaty constitutions (*sic*), like those establishing the International Labour Organization (ILO), the WHO, the Food and Agriculture Organization (FAO), and the UN Educational, Scientific and Cultural Organization (UNESCO), and the UN General Assembly resolutions establishing the UN High Commissioners for Human Rights and for Refugees justified their respective legal mandates by explicit references to labour rights, health rights, rights to food, public health protection, and other human rights. This rights-based approach to UN law and the worldwide legal and compulsory dispute settlement systems of trade and investment law extended multilevel judicial remedies for protecting transnational rule of law to public and private economic agents. These rights-based reforms were described by former WTO Director-General Lamy as the Geneva consensus on promoting human rights, rule of law, and other PGs for the benefit of humankind.[62] Chapter 2 explores this rules-based Geneva multilateralism, which underlies also the UN's 2030 Sustainable Development Agenda linking social and environmental protection to human rights. Chapter 3 discusses its increasing disregard by authoritarian power politics disrupting the governance of SDGs and related PGs (like the WTO AB, the WHO, climate change mitigation, human rights). The increasing violations of both procedural and substantive WTO rules render the future evolution of IEL uncertain. Similarly, as illustrated by the 1997 Kyoto Protocol which the USA signed but never ratified, UN commitments for realizing the SDGs and mitigating climate change must become legally more effective in order to change the world's current path toward 2.7C of global warming by the end of this century.

[61] On the very limited role of human rights in the practices of the Bretton Woods institutions see D van den Meerssche, *The World Bank's Lawyers: An Inquiry into the Life of Law as Institutional Practice*, EUI doctoral thesis defended on 27 September 2019 (available in the EUI library and on Cadmus: https://cadmus.eui.eu/handle/ 1814/64344. On the neo-liberal traditions of the Bretton Woods institutions, and the only recent conversion of the IMF and the World Bank in support of active fiscal, health, environmental, and massive deficit spending policies in response to the global health and climate crises, see M Sandbu, 'A New Washington consensus is born' *Financial Times* 12 April 2021.

[62] Cf P Lamy, *The Geneva Consensus. Making Trade Work for All* (CUP 2013).

1.3.5 The Neoliberal US Assault on the WTO Legal System Remains Arbitrary

Chapter 3, section 3.1 outlines the newly emerging multipolar geo-economic security order resulting from the increasing politicization of trade and investment policies. The more some areas of trade regulation (like trade remedies, subsidies, Internet services, intellectual property rights, appellate review, national security exceptions) became dominated by business-driven, neo-liberal interest-group politics, or were circumvented by non-transparent practices of state capitalism and state-owned enterprises, the less successful have the regulatory functions of WTO law become. From the entry into force of the WTO Agreement in 1995 up to 2019, the now more than 420 WTO panel, appellate, and arbitration findings—similar to the more than 1,100 publicly known investor–state arbitration (ISA) cases and related national court decisions (eg enforcing ISA awards) extant by the end of 2020—protected higher degrees of transnational rule of law in *worldwide* trade and investment relations than in any previous period (Chapter 3, section 3.2). Since 2017, the hegemonic US assault on the WTO legal and dispute settlement system has disrupted WTO appellate review by blocking the nomination of WTO AB judges. Since December 2019, this has rendered the AB incapable of accepting new appeals, thereby reintroducing power politics into the WTO dispute settlement system and enabling the now regular blocking also of the adoption of WTO panel reports by appealing them into the void of a dysfunctional AB. Similar to the criticism of neo-liberal investor biases in ISA (eg regarding the investment protection standards, conflicts of interests of commercial arbitrators, excessive arbitration costs), the US assault on the AB and on its jurisprudence revealed political biases in support of money-driven US interest group politics (Chapter 3, section 3.2–3.4). The trade wars and illegal, discriminatory trade sanctions unilaterally introduced by the Trump administration—and China's no less illegal trade retaliation—exempted large parts of the bilateral trade between the world's two largest trading nations from the effective reach of WTO law.

China's opening to the world since the late 1970s, ushering in its accession to the WTO and other multilateral agreements, was followed, since 2013, by China's Belt and Road Initiative (BRI) networks of bilateral trade and investment cooperation with more than 100 countries along the ancient territorial and maritime Silk Roads. This enabled China to become a rule-maker, prioritizing its own strategic policy objectives (like access to foreign raw materials, communication networks, and export markets helping Beijing to dominate Eurasia). China's authoritarian state capitalism, financial assistance, and bilateral policies favour managed bilateralism, administrative soft law regulation, and commercial law practices. This Chinese domination of bilateral foreign policy networks differs fundamentally from the rules-based, multilateral treaties, institutions, and liberal constitutionalism which characterized the post-1945 US-led neo-liberal economic order (Chapter 3, section

3.5–3.6). How should democracies respond to the fact that China is bound to remain the world's biggest trading nation with what will soon be the largest national economy, based on totalitarian state capitalism and increasing geopolitical power politics? Can recourse to the WTO dispute settlement system (eg by Australia in December 2020) offer sufficient legal remedies against China's use of discriminatory trade sanctions against countries (like Australia) daring to criticize China's disregard for human rights and insufficient cooperation in the COVID-19 health pandemic? Can President Biden deliver on his promise to rebuild political alliances among democratic countries for protecting liberal internationalism, mitigating climate change, and for collective responses to the regulatory challenges of state capitalism? Can the US-led, neo-liberal Bretton Woods system, the China-centred bilateral BRI networks, Europe's ordo-liberal constitutionalism, and the increasing number of mega-regional FTAs in Africa, Asia, and Latin America co-exist peacefully if non-compliance with the Paris Climate Agreement should lead to increasing trade conflicts (eg in case of rejection of the EU-Mercosur FTA by the European parliament because of Brazil's burning of tropical forests), unilateral introduction of carbon taxes, and border carbon adjustments by the EU?

1.3.6 Lessons from Institutional Economics for Reforming Trade and Investment Law

Chapter 4 uses institutional and constitutional economics to explore why and how reforms of international trade, investment, and environmental law and institutions are increasingly hampered by conflicting neo-liberal, state capitalist, and ordo-liberal conceptions of multilevel trade regulation. For example, utilitarian Anglo-Saxon neo-liberalism (eg promoting tax cuts and self-regulatory market forces privileging the *homo economicus*), constitutional European ordo-liberalism (eg protecting common market freedoms through multilevel constitutional rights and judicial remedies of EU citizens), and authoritarian state capitalism (eg protecting totalitarian power monopolies of the communist party in China) pursue different legal and institutional designs of trade, investment, and Internet agreements, as illustrated by the Brexit agreement (eg its avoidance of supra-national institutions and European courts) and by China's refusal in its EU–China investment agreement of December 2020 to accept investment adjudication and human rights commitments.[63] Drawing from ordo-liberal traditions, institutional economics

[63] The intention of China and the EU to continue their negotiations on investment protection standards and procedures, and the recent support by the IMF and World Bank of activist fiscal, economic, health, and environmental policies in response to the global health pandemic and climate change, illustrate that academic terms like 'neo-liberalism', 'state-capitalism', and 'ordo-liberalism' refer to policy trends that elude precise legal definitions and continue to evolve. Even in the United States, government spending, budget deficits, central bank interventions, welfare payments, regulation, and corporate bailouts have increased over the past decades. The neo-liberal focus on business efficiency in

departs from narrow assumptions of neo-classical paradigms by acknowledging the communitarian and cosmopolitan dimensions of individuals, their civil, political, economic, social, and cultural rights, and the multilevel interactions between democratic, executive, and judicial governance institutions confronted with bounded rationality of economic actors (eg neglecting human rights and transnational rule of law). Constitutional economics examines how to improve the incentives of constitutional rights, procedures, and institutions for enhancing economic welfare, for example by using common market freedoms of citizens for the decentralized enforcement of Europe's common market and competition rules. Globalization and its transformation of national into transnational PGs require extending constitutional and institutional economics to multilevel governance of transnational PGs in order to enhance the wealth of nations not only through co-operation and division of labour among private economic actors but also among law-makers and governments, such as multilevel parliamentary and judicial institutions, regulatory networks, and multilevel democratic and judicial rights in EU governance (Chapter 4, sections 4.1–4.3).

There are good reasons for adjusting some of the existing principles of WTO law to the changing context of the world economy, such as the WTO practice of self-declaration of the privileged legal status of less-developed country (eg benefitting from special and differential treatment (SDT) based on more than 100 SDT provisions in WTO law). The WTO objective of sustainable development calls for more specific, legal differentiations in order to mitigate climate change and prioritize poverty reduction. The more the initial hopes fade that WTO law could serve as a legal framework for a global market economy, the more it becomes necessary to regulate the interface problems of regional, plurilateral, and bilateral agreements among like-minded countries with mutually inconsistent neo-liberal, state capitalist, or ordo-liberal values and regulatory conceptions. Arguably, maintaining the basic principles of the worldwide legal and dispute settlement system of the WTO[64]—and interpreting the WTO's embedded liberalism (eg Article III GATT) and regional and national exception clauses broadly in order to reconcile diverse national, regional, and plurilateral institutions of economic integration and of embedded liberalism—remain in the interest of all WTO member states (Chapter 4, sections 4.4–4.8).

terms of consumer prices (eg as advocated by RH Bork, *The Antitrust Paradox* (Bork Publishing 1978/2021)) is challenged by focusing also on the welfare of workers, farmers, house owners, and citizens adversely affected by media concentration, rising health and housing costs, and environmental harm; cf R Foroohar, 'Biden and the post-neoliberal era' *Financial Times* 21 July 2021.

[64] Like non-discriminatory treatment, liberalization of discriminatory tariffs and non-tariff trade barriers, transparent policy-making, impartial third-party adjudication protecting rule of law, WTO exceptions protecting sovereign rights to promote non-economic PGs.

1.3.7 Need for Promoting Regional and Plurilateral Economic Constitutionalism

Chapter 5 describes the emergence of human rights and democratic constitutionalism as reasonable responses to the bounded rationality of human beings, the frequent abuses of power, and to past constitutional failures, for instance in the US and French human rights revolutions of the eighteenth century, in the social revolutions following the First World War, and the economic crises during the 1920s (Chapter 5, sections 5.1–5.3). European ordo-liberalism emphasizes not only the need for legally constructing undistorted market competition by means of limiting market failures, governance failures, and constitutional failures. The multilevel economic constitutionalism constituting the EU's common market, monetary union, and common area of freedom, security, and justice also reflects psychological insights (eg based on behavioural economics). Rational utility maximization by the *homo economicus* and political abuses of power by the *homo politicus* need to be constitutionally restrained by institutional checks and balances, constitutional rights and remedies of citizens, and democratic institutionalization of public reason (eg through multilevel parliamentary and judicial governance institutions and accountability mechanisms constraining parochial nationalism). In a globalizing world where domestic and foreign policy powers interact ever more closely, constitutionalism must be extended also to discretionary foreign policy powers (eg to tax and restrict domestic citizens and redistribute domestic income through discretionary trade policies). From such ordo-liberal perspectives, the rise of authoritarianism, neo-liberal interest group politics (eg in the United States), and communist power monopolies in state capitalist economies are linked to inadequate constitutional protection of civil, political, economic, social, and cultural rights and remedies of citizens; such constitutional failures facilitate abuses of public and private power (Chapter 5, sections 5.4 and 5.5). The multilevel protection of civil, political, economic, social, and cultural rights in European law remains unlikely to be acceptable for China's government and for money-driven, nationalist Washington politics. The conflicting neo-liberal, state capitalist, and ordo-liberal conceptions of economic regulation are bound to remain reflected in diverse regional, plurilateral, and bilateral agreements (like President Trump's bilateral trade deals, China's bilateral BRI networks, Russian and Anglo-Saxon rejection of European ordo-liberal economic constitutionalism).

The power monopoly of China's Communist party is rejected by democratic countries as inconsistent with their liberal values. The US refusal to ratify regional and many UN human rights conventions, many ILO conventions, and the WHO Framework Convention on Tobacco Control illustrate the value differences underlying neo-liberalism (eg prioritizing constitutional nationalism, negative civil, political, and economic liberties, market competition as a largely self-regulatory natural phenomenon) on the one side, and ordo-liberal EU constitutionalism (eg prioritizing multilevel constitutionalism and multilevel civil, political, economic, social, and cultural rights as integral parts of social market economies) on the other. The jurisprudence of the European Court of Justice (CJEU) on the inconsistency with EU constitutional law of EU–US agreements on data transfer confirm these systemic differences.[65] Can the EU's functionally limited, multilevel human rights constitution, common market constitution, monetary constitution, and foreign policy constitution (as briefly described in Chapter 5, section 5.6) continue protecting democratic peace throughout Europe? Are systemic regulatory and value differences (eg on data privacy and human rights as positive rights) bound to promote more decentralized, economic orders with different regional, plurilateral, and bilateral agreements among like-minded countries (Chapter 5, section 5.7)? Are there lessons from Europe's successful, multilevel, sectoral constitutionalization of transnational cooperation (eg in the common market) for improving multilevel protection of global PGs and of constitutional, parliamentary, participatory, and deliberative forms of democratic self-governance? How to respond to the many unresolved constitutional problems and regulatory challenges of the EU's monetary constitution and common foreign and security policy, for instance in EU relations with state capitalist countries and the EU–China agreement on investments (CAI) agreed in principle in December 2020?[66]

1.3.8 Rule of Law Requires Protecting Human Rights in International Economic Law

All UN member states have committed themselves to respect for human rights, the rule of law, and related principles of justice. The UN has defined the rule of law at national and international levels as 'a principle of governance in which all persons, institutions and entities, including the State itself, are accountable to laws that are publicly promulgated, equally enforced and independently adjudicated, and which are consistent with internationally recognized human rights'.[67] At the worldwide

[65] Cf A Chander, Is Data Localization a Solution for *Schrems II*? *Journal of International Economic Law* 23 (2020), 771–84. China's insistence on cyberspace sovereignty and localization of data inside China is also a contentious issue in relations between China and the United States.

[66] The conclusion of the EU-CAI seems to have achieved the EU's negotiating objectives of market access, fair competition, and sustainable development; the ongoing investment protection negotiations shall be concluded within two years after the signature of the agreement. In April 2021, the European parliament suspended its deliberations on the CAI due to Chinese sanctions targeting EU officials. It remains uncertain whether China will ratify the fundamental ILO conventions on forced labour, how obligations for state-owned enterprises and for transparency of industrial subsidies can be enforced effectively, and how China will respond to the challenge of phasing out coal-powered energy without compromising its economic growth objectives.

[67] Cf Report of the Secretary-General, Delivering Justice: programme of action to strengthen the rule-of-law at the national and international levels, A/66/49 of 16 March 2012, para 2. This definition of rule of law remains contested, for instance by international and constitutional conceptions of law focusing on whether the agreed rules of law are supported by consistent legal practices not only of governments but also of citizens and other non-governmental actors (cf Chapter 5, section 5.1).

level of governance, it is only since the 1990s that the compulsory WTO dispute settlement system—and the worldwide web of now more than 3,200 bilateral and multilateral investment agreements—have provided for multilevel, judicial remedies aimed at protecting the rule of law at national and international levels. Chapters 6–9 explain why, even in times of global economic, environmental, political, and legal changes driven by conflicting neo-liberal, state capitalist and ordo-liberal ideologies, multilevel judicial remedies aimed at protecting transnational rule of law and legal predictability in conformity with universally recognized human rights remain in the reasonable self-interests of all UN member states. Chapter 6 discusses legitimacy problems of WTO adjudication resulting, *inter alia*, from the limited jurisdiction of WTO dispute settlement bodies. Notwithstanding the only rare invocation of human rights and the reticent use of systemic treaty interpretation methods by WTO governments, GATT/WTO jurisprudence has protected the values underlying HRL (Chapter 6, section 6.1). Chapter 6, section 6.2 uses the example of the Panel and AB findings upholding Australia's tobacco plain packaging regulations for demonstrating that, even if WTO complainants, defendants, and WTO dispute settlement bodies avoid references to the human rights obligations of WTO members, there is no empirical evidence so far that the more than 500 GATT/WTO panel, appellate, and arbitration findings have violated the human rights obligations of GATT/WTO member states. To the contrary, many GATT/WTO dispute settlement findings have balanced the private and public interests and values justifying HRL, for instance by systemic interpretation of WTO rules consistent with multilateral treaties concluded outside the WTO (like the WHO Framework Convention on Tobacco Control). The increasing recourse by rulers to unilateral invocations of national security and public morals for justifying politically motivated trade sanctions has, so far, been successfully contained by WTO panel reports limiting the allegedly self-judging nature of such political sanctions by insistence on the good faith, necessity, proportionality, and other rule of law principles in WTO law and general international law (Chapter 6, section 6.3). Democratic constitutionalism and related theories of justice explain why discretionary power politics in multilevel governance of PGs—including also the sustainable development goals of a rules-based, mutually beneficial multilateral trading system and of transnational rule of law—require multilevel constitutional restraints such as those underlying the WTO dispute settlement system (Chapter 6, section 6.4).

Chapter 7 examines the legitimacy of ISA. Does the transformation of international investment law through more than 3,000 bilateral investment treaties (BITs) and more than 1,100 publicly known, related ISA awards offer lessons for how a more decentralized world trading system could be recreated if the multilateral WTO trading, legal, and dispute settlement systems should become increasingly ineffective as a result of conflicts among neo-liberal, state capitalist, and ordo-liberal policies of WTO members? Like international trade law, the historical evolution of ISA since the 1960s reflects conflicting neo-liberal, state capitalist, and ordo-liberal conceptions of ISA (Chapter 7, section 7.1). Case studies on invocation of human rights in ISA demonstrate that even if human rights were invoked as investor claims, as defences of the host state, by third-party interveners or by arbitrators *ex officio*, the impact of human rights law on ISA awards has tended to remain marginal, for example due to the more precise and higher investment protection standards in BITs (Chapter 7, section 7.2). Arguably, the investor biases reflected in ISA procedures and BITs (eg offering foreign investors higher protection standards than domestic investors) require stronger protection of public interest legislation in investment law and arbitration procedures. Yet, it remains doubtful whether the US Biden administration and China will give up their past resistance against ordo-liberal EU proposals for transforming the multilateral arbitration procedures elaborated by the International Center for the Settlement of Investment Disputes (ICSID) and by the UN Commission on International Trade Law (UNCITRAL) into new forms of public law adjudication by multilateral investment courts (Chapter 7, section 7.3). In contrast to the ordo-liberal preference for permanent, independent multilateral courts of justice (like the EU and European Free Trade Area (EFTA) courts, the ECtHR), neo-liberal and state capitalist interest group politics prefer *ad hoc* arbitration subject to bilateral agreements, as illustrated by the panel procedures provided for in the EU–China 2020 draft investment agreement for the settlement of disputes over labour rights.

1.3.9 Defending Rule of Law through Multilevel Remedies and Judicial Comity

Chapter 8 explores why claims of judicial overreach have become more frequent in national, European, and worldwide trade, investment, and other adjudication systems. It proceeds from the premise that as climate change mitigation and collective responses to global health pandemics require protecting transnational rule of law and the universally agreed SDGs, impartial third-party adjudication becomes ever more important for preventing systemic conflicts among neo-liberal, state capitalist, and ordo-liberal conceptions of international law and legal order. Impartial third-party adjudication of disputes is the most ancient form of constitutional justice; it preceded the historical emergence of democratic constitutionalism (eg in ancient Athens) and republican constitutionalism (eg in ancient Italian city republics). National 'constitutionalism 1.0' explained the need for democratic constitutionalism and for BITs exporting constitutional principles of justice for protecting investors in less-developed, foreign jurisdictions without liberal constitutionalism. The CJEU's *Achmea* judgment has drawn the consequences of the EU's 'multilevel constitutionalism 3.0' by finding that ISA inside the EU in relations among EU member states has become inconsistent with the multilevel constitutional and judicial guarantees of EU law (Chapter 8, section 8.1).

The multilevel guarantees of national and international judicial remedies in multilateral treaties—like the WTO Agreement and the European Economic Area (EEA) Agreement—could have evolved into a new kind of treaty constitutionalism 2.0 if national and international courts had cooperated in protecting rule of law for the benefit of citizens through mutually consistent interpretations (Chapter 8, section 8.2), for example based on the obligation of each member 'to ensure the conformity of its laws, regulations and administrative procedures with its obligations as provided in the annexed Agreements' (Article XVI:4 WTO Agreement) and to provide judicial remedies also at national levels of governance (eg pursuant to Article X GATT). The EU's supranational constitutionalism 3.0—notably the EU common market constitution embedded into the European human rights constitution with multilevel guarantees of human rights, constitutional rights, proportionality of governmental restrictions, and judicial remedies, as described in Chapter 5—was invoked by the CJEU not only for confirming the legal obligations of the twenty-seven EU member states to replace ISA in intra-EU relations among EU member states by the multilevel judicial remedies and institutional guarantees of EU law. EU constitutional law requires public law restraints on ISA also in the external relations of the EU, as provided for in the EU FTAs with Canada, Mexico, Singapore, and Vietnam. While EU law has limited judicial overreach in ISA, the German Constitutional Court judgment of 5 May 2020 has declared monetary policy decisions of the European Central Bank—and their legal confirmation by the CJEU—to be *ultra vires* acts violating the proportionality requirements of EU constitutional law (Article 5 TEU). Chapter 8, section 8.3 explains why multilevel judicial protection of rule of law inside the EU—and the EU's constitutional principles of limited delegation of power, proportionality, subsidiarity, and judicial comity—have evolved not only into the most effective, international legal and dispute settlement system for protecting constitutional rights of citizens in economic integration. The constitutional principles also offer lessons for multilevel judicial comity and avoidance of judicial overreach outside the EU in multilevel judicial cooperation in commercial, trade, investment, human rights law, and other fields of international cooperation. The jurisprudence of European courts illustrates how judicial overreach must be avoided based on commonly shared principles of interpretation and of constitutional restraints on abuses of power, for example by more precise legal requirements of limited delegation of powers, respect for democratic constitutional pluralism and subsidiarity principles, judicial protection of rule of law, and judicial proportionality review. Arguably, multilevel governance of transnational PGs (like climate change mitigation) depends on multilevel judicial remedies protecting transnational rule of law (eg in the unilateral application of carbon taxes and border carbon adjustments). The constitutional principles constituting and limiting multilevel judicial governance and protection of rule of law need to be clarified so as to define and exclude judicial overreach and protect rule of law in the ongoing transformation of IEL aimed at better protection of sustainable development.

1.4 Need for Empowering Civil Societies and Democratic Leadership

Chapter 9 concludes the book by criticizing utilitarian and power-oriented justifications of IEL—in most legal, economic and political science textbooks focusing on economic efficiency and respect for sovereign equality of states—for neglecting human rights, democratic constitutionalism and development as freedom (Amartya Sen). Chapter 9, section 9.1 explains why authoritarian power politics runs counter to the SDGs of protecting human rights, democracy, and rule of law. Chapter 9, section 9.2 describes the need for greening the embedded liberalism by rendering WTO law consistent with climate change mitigation and the SDGs. Chapter 9, section 9.3 discusses the increasing environmental and human rights litigation in European courts holding governments—and increasingly also multinational corporations like the Anglo-Dutch Shell Company—accountable for climate change mitigation. Chapter 9, section 9.4 explains why cosmopolitan human rights constitutionalism and judicial enforcement of corporate social responsibilities beyond Europe—with multilevel judicial remedies of citizens and other private and public actors—risk remaining opposed by authoritarian and neo-liberal interest group politics, as illustrated by the false US allegations of judicial overreach in the AB jurisprudence and the power-driven US destruction of the WTO AB. The SDGs require stronger network governance including all public and private stakeholders (Chapter 9, section 9.5). In view of the conflicting neo-liberal, state-capitalist and ordo-liberal conceptions of IEL, negotiations on additional trade, investment, and environmental disciplines are more likely to succeed at bilateral and regional levels among like-minded countries rather than at global levels of governance. Increasing regulatory competition among mega-regional economic integration agreements (eg with competing Chinese, EU, and US regulations of digital trade) may promote functionally limited agreements (eg on particular topics like e-commerce, government procurement, and infrastructure cooperation among BRI countries). Adverse effects from regulatory competition must remain actionable through judicial remedies as restraints on power politics. Yet, even if reforms can be agreed at international levels of governance, how are such agreements to be protected from being blocked in domestic politics (eg where US approval of international agreements requires a two-thirds majority in the US Senate or majority support in both Houses of the US Congress), or being subsequently denounced by authoritarian governments? Closer cooperation among governments, parliaments, and civil societies in negotiating and implementing agreements for the protection of PGs can prevent some of the governance failures of the currently disconnected UN/WTO governance of PGs. The four years of the Trump administration have taught the world that the rational ignorance and bounded rationality of many citizens vis-à-vis multilevel governance of transnational PGs in distant UN/WTO institutions can easily undermine democratic support for international law, which risks being captured by selfish politicians, business interests, and political extremists. The fact that the USA remain the largest emitter of CO_2 emissions per head and many republican members of the US Congress continue denying climate change, raises doubts as to the capacity of US governments and US citizens to be leaders for implementing the SDGs.

1.4.1 Democratic Leadership for Multilevel Governance of Sustainable Development?

The United Kingdom, China, India, and the United States prioritize national constitutionalism and international law among sovereign states over the EU's multilevel constitutionalism. The realities of UN/WTO power politics and of geopolitical rivalries refute hopes for developing a transnational twenty-first-century constitutionalism beyond Europe. Neo-liberal Anglo-Saxon, totalitarian state capitalist, and third-world countries resort to executive emergency governance (eg in response to climate change, health pandemics, the digital revolution and related economic crises). The frequent abuses of emergency powers, regulatory competition, and international conflicts require supplementing constitutional and parliamentary by stronger participatory and deliberative democracy supporting transnational rule of law. The EU's multilevel constitutionalism is not only more consistent with the rules-based 2030 UN Sustainable Development Agenda than nationalist constitutionalism. The EU's foreign policy commitments (eg in Articles 3 and 21 TEU) entail also EU duties for leadership in multilevel governance of the seventeen agreed SDGs, as illustrated by the EU leadership for climate change mitigation measures (like emissions trading systems, carbon taxes, transforming Europe into the first carbon-neutral continent by 2050) and for supplying COVID-19 vaccines to more than ninety countries in 2021 at a time when the United Kingdom and the United States still prioritized vaccine nationalism. Yet, the G7 summit meeting in June 2021 and the G20 meeting in July 2021 were convincingly criticized as missed opportunities for democratic leadership in the global health pandemic (eg by supplying vaccines for all countries) and climate change crisis (eg by acknowledging the need for more financial assistance and carbon taxes).[68]

[68] Cf M Wolf, 'G7 and G20 opportunities missed' *Financial Times* 17 June 2021 and 14 July 2021.

Authoritarian countries (like China and Russia) and many national democracies (eg in Commonwealth countries and the United States) deny the need for multilevel constitutional reforms. Their nationalism renders them less capable than the multilateral EU to lead rules-based universal reforms for multilevel governance of the SDGs. EU leadership for the SDGs requires maintaining strategic autonomy and global cooperation without taking sides in geopolitical power rivalries unless there are rules-based justifications (like human rights and other SDGs). As explained in Chapter 5, Europe's twenty-first-century constitutionalism aims at limiting market failures (like abuses of corporate power, social injustices), governance failures (like inadequate fiscal and debt policies, insufficient proportionality balancing), and constitutional failures (eg in protecting human rights and rule of law) by linking external policy reforms (eg for realizing climate change mitigation and other SDGs) to internal EU reforms (like decarbonizing the economy, strengthening health infrastructures, and human rights remedies). Continued democratic support by EU citizens requires better information, public reason, more participatory democracy, and judicial remedies. The increasing nationalism and political authoritarianism outside Europe render it unlikely that decarbonization of the world economy by 2050 and the SDG of realizing the human rights of all can be actually achieved. Elaborating coherent strategies for transforming world trade and investment law and promoting democratic and judicial accountability of governments for protecting sustainable development must become political and academic priorities.

1.4.2 From Governance Failures and Constitutional Failures to Constitutional Reforms?

The following chapters understand governance failures and constitutional failures in terms of failures of governments and citizens (as democratic principals of governance agents) to protect, legally and institutionally, the human rights and rule of law objectives of domestic and UN HRL, the UN Sustainable Development Agenda, and the agreed seventeen SDGs like ending poverty in all its forms everywhere, ensuring healthy lives, taking urgent action to combat climate change, and providing access to justice for all. UN HRL and the SDGs confirm the interpretation of UN/WTO rules as protecting embedded liberalism, including also democratic constitutionalism and non-discriminatory regulatory competition among UN and WTO member countries. HRL, UN, and WTO law provide also for legal constraints limiting abuses of emergency governance (eg based on invocation of national security exceptions like GATT Article XXI). Yet, as the constitutional and human rights obligations of UN and WTO member countries differ considerably, regulatory competition between liberal and state capitalist, democratic, and non-democratic UN/WTO member states risks provoking competitive distortions and regulatory challenges (eg over unilateral trade remedies, competition disciplines, protection of fundamental rights, economic sanctions in response to human rights violations).

Each of the following chapters can be read independently from the other chapters but the eight chapters tell a coherent narrative: UN law, WTO law, Anglo-Saxon neo-liberalism and authoritarian state-capitalism regulate market failures, governance failures, and constitutional failures comparatively less effectively than European integration law (Chapters 2–5). Strengthening transnational rule of law in world trade and investment law (as proposed in Chapters 6–8) and promoting constitutional, human rights, and environmental remedies empowering civil societies to hold governments to account for realizing the SDGs (as discussed in Chapter 9) should be recognized as political priorities. Citizens—in their never ending struggles for justice—must assume cosmopolitan responsibility for implementing the Sustainable Development Agenda.

Each chapter begins with a brief overview of its various sections enabling the reader to understand the *systemic nature* of the global governance failures that prevent effective protection of human rights and of other common interests of citizens as defined in the SDGs.

2
Governance Failures: UN Law and WTO Law Fail to Protect Sustainable Development

Since ancient times, the human desire for more, better and a larger variety of goods and services has given rise to trade, division of labour, and regulation of markets.[1] This human desire for increasing individual welfare through trade interacts—as illustrated by centuries of feudalism and colonial and imperial conquests—with the human hunger to possess land and natural resources: 'if goods can't cross borders, soldiers will'.[2] The International Chamber of Commerce was created in 1919 by business leaders who described themselves as 'merchants of peace' pursuing 'world peace through world trade'.[3] The technological transformations of the international economy (eg based on steam power, electricity, automation, digitalization)—and legal limitations of 'market failures' (eg through competition, social and environmental rules) and governance failures (eg through tax reforms, protection of PGs and related human rights)—progressively transformed international economic law (IEL). The first globalization during the nineteenth century, like the second globalization since the 1970s, of production, supply chains, trade, and communications confirmed how different economic actors often prioritize different values and perspectives of IEL, such as:

- *private autonomy* advocated by private traders, producers, and investors, as illustrated by the pursuit of utility- and profit-maximization strategies of commercial companies and rent-seeking industries;

[1] Cf P Coggan, *More: The 10,000 Year Rise of the World Economy* (Profile Books 2020).

[2] The quotation reflects the trade and investment agreements and colonial policies since ancient time (eg the practice of the republic of Venice to protect its foreign trading posts by military force, if necessary). On the interrelationship between struggles over land and human conflicts, see S Winchester, *How the Hunger for Ownership Shaped the Modern World* (W Collins 2020).

[3] Cf F Lehmann and JP Lehmann (eds), *Peace and Prosperity through World Trade. Achieving the 2019 Vision* (CUP 2010). On 8 July 2021, the UN High-Level Political Forum on Sustainable Development 2021 hosted an event on 'Trade for Peace: Addressing Fragility Through Economic Integration and Shared Prosperity: The case of WTO membership for Liberia and Afghanistan'. Moderated by WTO Deputy Director-General Xiangchen Zhang, the event celebrated the five-year anniversary of Liberia and Afghanistan joining the WTO and reflected on how integration into the multilateral trading system provides an opportunity to consolidate peacebuilding efforts; cf *WTO News* of 13 July 2021.

Transforming World Trade and Investment Law for Sustainable Development. Ernst-Ulrich Petersmann, Oxford University Press. © Ernst-Ulrich Petersmann 2022. DOI: 10.1093/oso/9780192858023.003.0003

- *public autonomy* ('sovereignty') advocated by governments representing states;
- *economic efficiency* and consumer welfare emphasized by consumers;
- *democratic input legitimacy* emphasized by citizens and their democratic institutions;
- *republican output legitimacy* emphasized by counter-majoritarian, republican institutions (like central banks, competition, health, environmental, and other regulatory agencies); or
- *transnational rule of law* and *equal individual rights* protected by courts of justice.

This fact of legal pluralism underlying IEL reflects the reality of political disagreements on whether law and governance need to be justified vis-à-vis citizens by prioritizing private autonomy (eg human rights), public autonomy (eg democratic governance, representative and deliberative democracy), or authoritarian protection (eg by 'Leviathans') of law and order. For instance, the UN Charter prioritizes sovereign equality of member states and veto powers of the five victorious powers in the Second World War; UN human rights law (HRL) prioritizes individual and popular self-determination, and the Sustainable Development Goals (SDGs) aim at reconciling protection of private and public autonomy of individuals and peoples and sovereign equality of states. International legal practices are driven by diverse conceptions of law and governance as discussed in section 2.1. This chapter argues that both (inter)governmental power politics and rent-seeking practices of private economic actors have led to governance failures preventing effective protection of the SDGs through UN and Word Trade Organization (WTO) legal practices.

The competing 'legal perspectives' have contributed to five competing conceptions of IEL, as discussed below in section 2.2. These (i) private law and (ii) international public law, (iii) multilevel economic, (iv) global administrative law, and (v) multilevel constitutional law conceptions of IEL reflect diverse regulatory approaches, policy options, and value choices. Utilitarian neo-liberalism, authoritarian state capitalism, and rights-based, ordo-liberal constitutionalism prioritize diverse values like individual utility maximization by the 'economic man', power monopolies of communist parties, or equal rights of citizens and democratic constitutionalism. The value differences often entail diverse economic policies prioritizing different conceptions of IEL (eg regarding protection of individual rights and judicial remedies). The economic and legal conceptions interact closely with political and strategic policies and conceptions of social justice. For example, the First World War took most people in Europe by surprise because the close economic cooperation among European countries was believed to render war between economic partners unreasonable. Will the commercial and technological decoupling, distrust, and great power rivalries between China and the United States increase the risk of military conflicts? As a nuclear conflict would threaten the livelihood of all humanity, what contribution could Europe and other democracies (like India and Japan) make to avoiding another cold war or military conflict? Does the return to nationalism enhance the lack of accountability and impunity of authoritarian leaders for breaching multilateral agreements and neglecting 'shared responsibilities' for protecting human rights and other public goods (PGs)? Should democratic countries insist that China's disregard for human rights (eg of minorities in Tibet and Xinjian), for China's 'one state, two systems' commitments (eg vis-à-vis Hong Kong and Taiwan), for multilateral treaties, transparency, and dispute settlement obligations (eg in the South China Sea, in the World Health Organization (WHO)) justify strategic decoupling of economic cooperation? Should democracies define regulatory conditions for trading with the enemy, for instance by setting limits for private investments in China, by screening Chinese investments in democracies, or by reducing oil and gas imports from Russia?

Sections 2.1 and 2.2 briefly explain why law, legal practices, and legal systems, including IEL, are inevitably shaped by politics and civil society struggles for human rights and democratic governance. Over the past few years, the backlash against globalization and democratic governance has aggravated the failures to realize the SDGs. Section 2.3 recalls how the post-1945 human rights revolution—as illustrated by the 1948 Universal Declaration of Human Rights (UDHR(= (UDHR), dozens of UN and regional human rights conventions, and hundreds of other UN human rights instruments—has not prevented authoritarian governments and insufficient legislative, administrative, and judicial protection of human rights in many UN member states. UN HRL does not prescribe specific economic policies; hence, as confirmed by the case studies in Chapters 6 and 7, human rights are rarely invoked in WTO adjudication and investor–state arbitration (ISA) for constraining abuses of power in trade and investment regulation. Section 2.4 explains how the utilitarian 'neo-liberal Washington consensus' underlying the 1944 Bretton Woods Agreements and the General Agreement on Tariffs and Trade (GATT) 1947 differs from the multilevel European ordo-liberal constitutionalism aimed at limiting market failures, governance failures, and constitutional failures in multilevel governance of transnational PGs. Section 2.5 describes the more cosmopolitan 'Geneva consensus' (Pascal Lamy) and the 'ordo-liberal Brussels consensus' constraining economic regulation by multilevel human rights agreements embedded into European law (eg based on the European Convention on Human Rights (ECHR), the EU Charter of Fundamental Rights (EUCFR) and their multilevel, legal, and judicial protection in European Union (EU) and European Free Trade Area (EFTA) states). Section 2.6 interprets the SDGs as a concretization of this Geneva consensus; they offer governments and civil societies arguments for more 'systemic interpretation' of UN HRL, economic, social, and environmental law in mutually consistent and supportive ways. Yet, like the Washington consensus, the Geneva consensus and the SDGs on promoting human rights, trade, and other international PGs lack sufficient legal and judicial remedies, as illustrated by President Trump's mercantilist assault on the WTO legal and dispute settlement system, his neo-liberal disregard for environmental protection and other PGs inside the United States, as well as by authoritarian power politics in China, Russia and other states.

2.1 Law, Politics, and Democratic Struggles for the SDGs

All states use law for the ordering of civil, political, economic, social and cultural cooperation among citizens. Depending on their histories, geographical contexts, cultures, and democratic preferences, the interactions among societies, their polities, economies, and legal systems differ from country to country. In the twenty-first century, 'positive law' tends to be defined and identified by (i) 'primary rules of conduct'; (ii) 'secondary rules of recognition, change and adjudication'; and by (iii) the ever larger number of principles and policy objectives (like the SDGs) recognized in legislation and in the 'secondary law' adopted by administrative, regulatory or judicial institutions.[4] Path-dependent legal positivism continues being challenged by human rights revolutions and democratic revolutions resulting in ever more social challenges of power-oriented rules of international law and of social injustices (eg regarding the unequal distribution of power, money, and social welfare in and among states). Normative *legal orders* reflecting the 'public reason' and rationality of their legal subjects and governments evolve through politicized *legal practices* and 'dynamic interpretations' of indeterminate rules and principles, for instance if citizens, governments, or courts of justice invoke—as in the case of the SDGs—human rights and agreed principles of justice for justifying 'new interpretations' or implementing rules in order to respond to regulatory challenges (like climate change mitigation), as illustrated by the trade and investment litigation discussed in Chapters 6–8 and the climate change and human rights litigation discussed in Chapter 9.[5] Positive legal orders constantly interact with institutionally framed *legal practices* (eg of law-makers, governments, judges, legal scholars, citizens, companies) shaped by political cultures, politics, self-interests, and the will (power) of legal actors. Together, the *legal orders* and the *legal practices* constitute *legal systems* developing in response to dialectic interactions between law (reason, rationality) and practices (will, political choices, psychology).[6]

[4] For details, see EU Petersmann, *Multilevel Constitutionalism for Multilevel Governance of Public Goods* (Hart 2017), 59ff.

[5] On the need for 'critical legal positivism' acknowledging the 'dual nature' of modern legal systems as including also 'principles of justice', see R Alexy, *The Argument from Injustice: Reply to Legal Positivism* (Clarendon Press 2002); K Tuori, *Ratio and Voluntas: The Tension between Reason and Will in Law* (Routledge 2016); J Raz, *Between Authority and Interpretation: On the Theory of Law and Practical Reason* (OUP 2009).

[6] For an explanation of this conception of law and legal systems, the constant tensions between reason and will (power), and the interactions between the surface level of positive law and the sub-surface level of legal and political cultures and social psychologies (or pathologies) influencing

The dialectic and often adversarial evolution of legal systems does not justify academic claims 'that law is incapable of providing convincing justifications to the solution of normative problems'.[7] True, due to the frequent indeterminacy of legal rules, their legal meaning depends on the decision-making institutions and their particular context. Adversarial argumentation between claimants and defendants advancing mutually inconsistent, legal interpretations (eg based on competing understandings of the text, the context, object, and purpose of treaty provisions, principles, and policy objectives) is an often inevitable consequence of the indeterminacy of international law rules and the politics of legal practices (eg advancing strategic interpretations privileging particular interests). Yet, as recalled in Chapter 5, theories of justice explain how the politics of international law can be transformed into public reason, for instance by means of constitutionally limited democracies institutionalizing representative, deliberative, and participatory democratic governance and third-party adjudication of disputes by independent and impartial courts of justice. Legal constitutionalism allocates authoritative decision-making powers to legislative, administrative, judicial, and non-majoritarian, regulatory institutions or to the private autonomy of citizens and non-governmental organizations (NGOs). It provides procedures for clarifying rules by intersubjective agreements on rules, principles of justice (like human rights) and public reason (like intergovernmental agreements), thereby justifying agreed interpretations and progressive clarifications of the law. HRL, constitutional, participatory, and deliberative democracy require protecting both formal and substantive justice beyond mere legal formalism: the democratic monopoly of the use of public force entails a democratic responsibility of jurisdiction (ie to state what the law is) and justification. The systemic treaty interpretation requirements of international law (eg in Article 31.3,c of the Vienna Convention on the Law of Treaties (VCLT)), the normative and judicial tasks of interpreting treaties 'in conformity with the

law-making, application, and adjudication of legal rules and principles, see also K Tuori, *Critical Legal Positivism* (Routledge 2016).

[7] This claim by M Koskenniemi (*From Apology to Utopia. The Structure of International Legal Argument* (CUP 2005), at 69) is refuted by the rules-based decisions of democratic, administrative, and judicial, national, and international institutions settling disputes over the interpretation and application of rules of conduct through legally binding legislation, administrative decisions and court judgments. Koskenniemi's 'critical legal theory' neglects inter-subjective 'constitutional agreements' on human rights, democratic constitutionalism, and the customary rules prescribing treaty interpretation 'in conformity with the principles of justice', including 'human rights and fundamental freedoms for all' (eg as recalled in the Preamble and Article 31 VCLT), which justify interpreting UN law in the twenty-first century as a cosmopolitan project for protecting the SDGs through a responsible global community of states, peoples and citizens. As discussed in Chapter 6–9 on trade, investment, environmental, and human rights adjudication, impartial and independent judicial interpretation can also be perceived as part of 'legalized politics' protecting identifiable public and private interests (eg as called for in the SDGs) through diverse legal procedures with often diverse legal outcomes. Even if legal decisions involve factual, value, and policy choices, law is a precondition for transparent allocation of inclusive and accountable decision-making powers and procedures.

principles of justice of international law', including 'human rights and fundamental freedoms for all' (as universally recognized in the Preamble of the VCLT), and the universal recognition of human rights require interpreting international law no longer as constituting only a power-oriented 'international community of states' (Article 53 VCLT), where rulers can collaborate in violating human rights of citizens and peoples (eg by perceiving interpretation of international law as argumentative and opportunistic games). The universal recognition of human rights and the citizen-oriented SDGs also justify democratic contestation and 'cosmopolitan interpretations' of treaty provisions in agreements among states like the WTO Agreement, whose Preamble acknowledges 'sustainable development' as a treaty objective and whose WTO provisions provide for international and domestic, legal, and judicial remedies. As long as human rights and the sovereign equality of states are protected, such interpretations will often remain contested:

Was the 1999 bombing of Serbia (causing around 500 civil casualties) by the North Atlantic Treaty Organization (NATO) 'both formally illegal and morally necessary'?[8] Or could the formal violation of the prohibition of force (Article 2.4 UN Charter) be legally justified by obligations to protect human rights and self-determination in Kosovo and prevent another genocide by Serb military forces through forcible 'humanitarian countermeasures'? Can the power-oriented UN Charter rules (eg Articles 51ff) prevent NATO countries from transforming European HRL into a regional security order permitting humanitarian intervention as a 'duty to protect'?

Can human rights to life justify judicial clarifications prescribing precise governmental duties to limit GHG emissions, as it was done in the 2019 *Urgenda* judgment discussed in Chapter 9 and in the 2021 judgment of Germany's Constitutional Court discussed in Chapter 8, section 8.4? What kind of emergency measures are justifiable (eg vis-à-vis climate refugees) by the global climate emergency, which the European Parliament formally declared in 2019? The very diverse emergency responses to the COVID-19 health pandemic illustrate that justice is always contextual (ie depending on the factual circumstances and decision-makers). But this fact of 'reasonable disagreements' does not justify renouncing 'struggles for justice' and for 'enlightenment' aimed at reducing the social injustices in the distribution

[8] Cf M Koskenniemi, The Lady Doth Protest Too Much: Kosovo and the Turn to Ethics in International Law, in m Koskenniemi, *The Politics of International Law* (Hart 2011), 112–30, at 115. Koskenniemi examines 'eight steps through which international lawyers are transformed into moralists by the logic of the argument from humanitarian intervention' (ie textual interpretation *stricto sensu*; value-based interpretation *lato sensu*; instrumental interpretation of 'object and purpose'; utilitarian balancing; human rights as 'trumps'; legislative discourse; law as a procedure for inclusive argumentation; turn to ethics, wisdom and responsibility). Yet, Koskenniemi's 'argumentative carousel', where answers are 'born out of legal nothingness', neglects HRL, constitutional law (eg proportionality balancing), judicial administration of justice, and theories of justice incorporated into positive law through inter-subjective agreements aimed at 'institutionalizing public reason'; arguably, such practical disregard for justice is inconsistent with the customary rules of treaty interpretation and the 'dual nature' of modern 'positive legal systems'.

of power and wealth, and promoting humanism, deliberative democracies, 'public reason', and scientific progress in the hope of realizing the Kantian ideal of 'democratic peace through law'.[9]

Authoritarian governments (eg in China, Russia, and other Eurasian countries) resist struggles for justice and for global community law protecting inalienable individual and democratic rights. Yet, peoples and citizens continue challenging state-centred conceptions of 'international law among states' by democratic conceptions of international law prioritizing rights of individuals and peoples, as recognized in the SDG 'to realize the human rights of all' (Preamble). As long as UN and WTO law remain dominated by state-centred power politics, the actual realization of citizen-centred SDGs—like SDGs 1–8[10]—depends on 'struggles for justice' by civil societies, democratic institutions, governments, and courts of justice.[11] Protest movements continue to take place in all regions of the world illustrating widespread popular demand for the SDGs. Yet, the decrease in the number and quality of liberal democracies since 2005—and the increase in the number of authoritarian governments—contributed to declining freedom, increasing assaults on democracy and on pluralism (notably in the two largest democracies India and United States), climate change, health pandemics, and impoverishment of societies in 2020.[12] According to a recent UN report,

> (t)he 15-year global effort to improve the lives of people everywhere through the achievement of the 17 Sustainable Development Goals (SDGs) by 2030 was already off track by the end of 2019. And now, in only a short period of time, the COVID-19 pandemic has unleashed an unprecedented crisis, causing further

[9] As critique is essential for emancipation, including criticism of 'elite power' based on alleged 'expert knowledge', Chapters 2 and 3 explain why neo-liberal nationalism and totalitarian state capitalism are power-oriented crusades neglecting human rights and abuses of power. Yet, in contrast to Koskenniemi's efforts at deconstructing international law without offering positive responses to the injustices of UN/WTO power politics, Chapters 4–9 elaborate proposals for protecting the SDGs more effectively.

[10] Cf *Transforming our World* (eg 'Goal 1: End poverty in all its forms everywhere. Goal 2: End hunger, achieve food security and improved nutrition' ... 'Goal 3: Ensure healthy lives and promote well-being for all at all ages. Goal 4: Ensure inclusive and equitable quality education and promote lifelong learning opportunities for all. Goal 5: Achieve gender equality and empower all women and girls. Goal 6: Ensure availability and sustainable management of water and sanitation for all. Goal 7: Equal access to affordable, reliable, sustainable and modern energy for all. Goal 8: Promote sustained, inclusive and sustainable growth, full and productive employment and decent work for all').

[11] On defining justice in terms of 'justification' by agreed procedural, constitutional, distributive, corrective and commutative principles of justice and equity, as they underlie many GATT/WTO provisions like GATT Article XXIII.1 on 'violation complaints', 'non-violation complaints', and 'situation complaints', see Petersmann (n 4), 38f, 177ff, 334f. More generally, R Forst, *The Right to Justification. Elements of a Constructivist Theory of Justice* (Columbia UP 2012).

[12] On democratic 'backsliding' even in Europe and the United States where democracies were long thought most securely established, see *Freedom in the World 2020: A Leaderless Struggle for Democracy*, the annual country-by-country assessment of political rights and civil liberties published by Freedom House in March 2020; *Democracy under Siege. Freedom in the World 2021* (Freedom House 2021).

disruption to SDG progress, with the world's poorest and most vulnerable affected the most.[13]

2.2 Strategic Choices: Competing Conceptions of 'International Economic Law'

International trade and investment agreements have been concluded since ancient times, for instance among city republics bordering the Mediterranean Sea. The mutually beneficial nature of division of labour through liberal trade remains one of the few areas on which most economists continue to agree, notwithstanding their disagreements on whether and how individual 'losers' in trade and competition deserve compensation, assistance, or trade protection. Today, all UN and WTO member states share the view that the *laissez faire* liberalism of the eighteenth and nineteenth centuries must be replaced by some kind of 'embedded liberalism' protecting the rights and duties of states to enhance social and economic welfare and human rights of their citizens.[14] Yet, liberal and state capitalist approaches to regulating the economy reflect a large variety of diverse forms of capitalism due to different social, political, economic, legal, and institutional infrastructures and traditions of countries influencing their comparative advantages.[15] For instance, sociologists like Max Weber (explaining European and North American economic welfare by protestant ethics and asceticism) and Joseph Henrich argue that cultural evolution (like Christian marriage laws promoting Europe's transformation from tribal societies to autonomous individualism) explain better (eg than Darwinian natural selection theories) why some societies—in their competition with other societies—prospered more due to their greater 'collective intelligence' (referring to norms, habits, and ideas).[16] Since the Second World War, the local, national, and

[13] Cf *Sustainable Development Goals Report 2020* and related UN Press release of 7 July 2020.

[14] For detailed discussions of 'embedded liberalism', neo-liberalism, ordo-liberalism, and authoritarian state capitalism as competing post-war paradigms of economic policies, see Chapter 3–5.

[15] On different conceptions of domestic economic law systems see PF Kjaer (ed), *The Law of Political Economy: Transformation in the Function of Law* (CUP 2020). Both Marxist and neo-liberal views identifying societies with the economy (eg profit and welfare maximization and 'creative destruction' driving economic and social processes), or emphasizing the shaping of societies by private economic interests (eg of the capitalist *homo economicus*, rent-seeking interest groups), neglect the ordo-liberal emphasis on protecting human and constitutional rights and remedies against abuses of both public and private power. Today's diversity of economic law conceptions is linked to the diverse conceptions of societies (eg individual vs communitarian conceptions of society as being more than its constituent individuals) and of the interactions among societal sub-sectors (like the economy, the polity, law, working classes, social welfare institutions, religious traditions, education, information, and communication systems). Ordo-liberalism emphasizes that the economy, the polity, and society must be governed by constitutional rules, democratic legislation, civil self-determination, and non-majoritarian institutions (like courts of justice, independent competition authorities, central banks) protecting non-discriminatory conditions of competition, the rule of law, and social welfare among free and equal citizens.

[16] Cf J Henrich, *The Weirdest People in the World: How the West Became Psychologically Peculiar and Particularly Prosperous* (A Lane 2020; WEIRD stands for Western, educated, industrialized, rich, and democratic people, and is explained by Henrich in terms of, *inter alia*, Christian prohibitions of

international regulation of economic transactions, trade, and investments has progressively given rise to five competing conceptions of IEL.[17] Neo-liberal, state capitalist, and ordo-liberal conceptions of IEL differ in their views on how the private and public, national and international conceptions of IEL should be implemented and how they need to be adjusted to the regulatory challenges of the twenty-first century.

2.2.1 IEL as Private Commercial Law and International Private Law

Most transnational trade, financial, and investment transactions are based on private contracts, property rights, national private law, and the law of conflicts. From the Roman *jus gentium* governing trade with foreigners, the medieval *lex mercatoria* serving as transnational commercial law in many parts of Europe, up to the common law freedoms in Anglo-Saxon countries and modern codifications of private and commercial law, international private law continues to evolve through national court decisions and commercial arbitral awards supervised and enforced in national jurisdictions. Some textbooks describe IEL from this bottom-up perspective of private contract law regulating international trade transactions, financial services, investments, and the global division of labour across hundreds of national and international legal systems and thousands of non-governmental regulations by transnational corporations. They emphasize

- the reality of competition, rivalry, and decentralized legal coordination in transnational society;
- the 'private ordering ideal' and inevitable limits of 'top-down global governance';
- lessons from private international law for coordinating and resolving conflicts among jurisdictions and among transnational governance mechanisms; and
- the advantages of using private international law concepts for resolving conflicts among multiple systems of governmental and private ordering.

marrying relatives, which forced people to overcome tribalism and promote autonomous research and voluntary associations based on shared interests). Theories of justice (eg of J Rawls) and constitutional theories use the idea of 'public reason' to explain why democratic constitutionalism succeeded in limiting abuses of public and private power—and promoting economic and social welfare—more successfully than authoritarian societies; cf Petersmann (n 4), 34, 109ff.

[17] For a detailed discussion of the five competing conceptions of IEL and related theories of justice, see EU Petersmann, *International Economic Law in the 21st Century* (Hart 2012), Chapters I–III.

Yet does the confrontation of private and public international law with common regulatory problems—such as the need for overcoming parochial legacies of discrimination (eg against foreigners)—justify the conceptualization of IEL as the law of conflicts? Arguably, the recognition by all UN member states of 'inalienable' human rights and of corresponding PGs requires justifying IEL also in terms of constitutional rights of citizens, rather than only in terms of private law principles, economic utilitarianism, and 'state sovereignty'.[18] Conflicts law principles of private law for determining whether foreign jurisdictions, conflicting government regulations, and transnational governance mechanisms deserve recognition are no substitute for the necessary review of the constitutional legitimacy and coherence of IEL. They cannot replace legal and judicial balancing of diverse constitutional principles in applying and interpreting IEL in conformity with principles of justice and the human rights obligations of governments, as prescribed by the customary rules of treaty interpretation (as codified in the Preamble and Article 31–33 VCLT) as well as by constitutional law systems. Private law doctrines offer no coherent answers for the constitutional and collective action problems of multilevel governance of transnational PGs, nor for the social injustices of the existing distribution of power and wealth in the world.

2.2.2 IEL as Public International Law of States Regulating the Economy

The state-centred 'Westphalian conception' of international law and 'political realism' emerged from the power struggles against the Church, the Holy Roman Empire, and colonialism in support of a new system of states with 'sovereign equality' (Article 2 UN Charter). It continues to dominate UN law and IEL textbooks in spite of the increasingly comprehensive human rights obligations acknowledged by all UN member states in hundreds of UN and regional human rights instruments. Government executives often have self-interests in prioritizing 'state immunity' and 'diplomatic immunity' in order to avoid accountability; they claim broad foreign policy powers to conclude intergovernmental agreements regulating international movements of goods, services, persons, capital, and related payments among states. The 1944 Bretton Woods Agreements establishing the IMF and the World Bank, the 1945 UN Charter, GATT 1947, UN institutions (like the United Nations Conference on Trade and Development (UNCTAD)) and UN specialized agencies regulating international services (like the Universal Postal

[18] On the mutation of 'sovereignty' as describing an 'unlimited, undivided and unaccountable locus of authority' (eg during the European wars of religion in the sixteenth and seventeenth centuries, in communist countries) to its modern conception as being constitutionally limited, divided, and accountable to citizens with 'inalienable' human and democratic rights to self-government, see D Herzog, *Sovereignty RIP* (Yale UP 2020).

Union, the International Telecommunications Union, the International Civil Aviation Organization, the International Maritime Organization) were all negotiated by diplomats representing states, under the leadership of the most powerful industrialized countries.

State sovereignty, the 'weighting' of voting in the Bretton Woods institutions according to the financial contributions by states, and the consensus practices in UN, GATT and WTO decision-making processes entail power-oriented, intergovernmental bargaining (eg on reciprocal tariff liberalization in GATT and the WTO) prioritizing rights among states over duties vis-à-vis citizens within states. Intergovernmental rule-making often identifies 'state interests' with those of powerful, domestic interest groups (eg agricultural and industry lobbies demanding subsidies and 'safeguard measures'). The diverse legal structures of UN specialized agencies (eg exclusive membership of states, 'tripartite representation' of workers, employers, and governments only in the International; Labour Organization (ILO)) and of the WTO (eg WTO membership of some sub-state customs territories like Hong Kong, Macao, and Taiwan) are more due to power politics (eg the strong political influence of trade unions after the First World War when the ILO was created) than to principles of justice. The neo-liberal bias of the Bretton Woods Agreements—eg their lack of effective protection of non-economic PGs due to the economic doctrine of separation of policy instruments—is often criticized for its lack of democratic legitimacy. 'Black box conceptions' of states and 'chess-board conceptions' of 'international law among states' leave domestic rule implementation to the discretion of governments. Such focus on reciprocal rights, obligations, and bargaining among states is not only challenged by civil societies. It also explains why most worldwide economic agreements often fail to protect human rights and other global PGs inside many countries, as long as the constitutional priority of human rights and judicial remedies inside constitutional democracies has no equivalent in most areas of international relations among UN member states.

2.2.3 IEL as 'Multilevel Economic Regulation' Informed by 'Law and Economics'

All UN member states participate in transnational economic cooperation in order to advance their economic welfare through division of labour. Conceptions of IEL as multilevel economic regulation are informed by economic theories of 'separation of policy instruments' (eg of trade and monetary restrictions as prescribed in Article XV GATT) and of economically efficient 'optimal policy instruments' (eg prioritizing *non-discriminatory* internal taxes, product and production regulations over trade-distorting subsidies and border discrimination).

The Chicago School of law and economics and the Virginia School of public choice and constitutional economics, like the German Freiburg School of ordo-liberalism and Cologne School of social market economy, focused on interactions of legal rules and economic principles in the regulation of *national economies*. The economists and lawyers cooperating in the Geneva School of multilevel ordo-liberalism[19] and in the construction of European economic integration law were more attentive to questions of *international economic order* as a condition for empowering welfare states and limiting abuses of public and private powers through multilevel, legal, institutional, and judicial guarantees of non-discriminatory market competition. The 1944 Bretton Woods Agreements and GATT 1947 were strongly influenced by US neo-liberalism (eg advocating reciprocal liberalization of monetary, financial, and trade restrictions, deregulation, privatization, and 'financialization' of economies) so as to promote the information, coordination, and sanctioning functions of market competition and private ordering ideals. The ordo-liberal constitutionalism underlying European economic integration perceives common markets as legal constructs requiring systematic limitations of market failures (eg by means of competition law, banking law, investment law, labour law, environmental law), of governance failures (like welfare-reducing protectionism), and constitutional failures (eg to protect human rights and restrain abuses of power). Anglo-Saxon law and economics and authoritarian state capitalism offer no coherent legal and political theories for protecting the 'input legitimacy' and 'output legitimacy' of multilevel governance of transnational PGs, for example by protecting rights of citizens in global cooperation beyond state borders and limiting the collective action problems in multilevel governance of PGs.

2.2.4 IEL as Global Administrative Law (GAL)?

In order to enhance transparency, rule of law, and legal accountability in multilevel governance of PGs, an increasing number of lawyers interpret the law of international organizations as administrative law of regulatory agencies.[20] GAL

[19] For a discussion of the 'Geneva school of law and economics' and its comparison with other schools of 'law and economics', see EU Petersmann, 'International Economic Theory and International Economic Law—On the Tasks of a Legal Theory of International Economic Order' in RSJ Macdonald and DM Johnston (eds), *The Structure and Process of International Law* (Nijhoff 1983), 227–61; Q Slobodian, *Globalists: The End of Empire and the Birth of Neoliberalism* (Harvard UP 2018), 7ff, 183ff, 208ff, 260ff. See also my critical review of this book, which overlooks the categorical differences between utilitarian, Anglo-Saxon neo-liberalism and rights-based, European ordo-liberalism: 21 *Journal of International Economic Law* (2018), 915.

[20] Cf R Stewart and R Sanchez Badin, 'The WTO and Global Administrative Law' in C Joerges and EU Petersmann (eds), *Constitutionalism, Multilevel Trade Governance and International Economic Law* (Hart 2011), chapter 16 ('Much global regulatory governance – especially in fields such as trade and investment, financial and economic regulation – can now be understood as administration, by which we include all forms of law-making other than treaties or other international agreements on the one

approaches seek to ensure that 'global regulatory decision-makers are accountable and responsive to all of those who are affected by their decisions'. For instance, 'the challenges faced by the WTO can be addressed by greater application of GAL decision-making mechanisms of transparency, participation, reason-giving, review and accountability to the WTO's administrative bodies including its councils and committees and the Trade Policy Review Body'. GAL principles and procedures should be strengthened in three dimensions:

1. The efficacy and legitimacy of the *internal WTO governance structures* and decision-making procedures could be improved by strengthening transparency, participation, reason giving, and the law-making role of the WTO's regulatory, administrative, and adjudicatory bodies. For instance, just as WTO Director-General Pascal Lamy's initiative for convening regular parliamentary meetings inside the WTO enhanced transparency and 'deliberative democracy' in WTO decision-making processes, the transparency and legitimacy of WTO third-party adjudication could be enhanced by opening panel and appellate hearings to the public.
2. In the *vertical interrelationships between the WTO and its regulation of members' domestic administrations*, the incorporation of GAL principles and procedures into domestic administrative rules and procedures could strengthen the rule of law, transparency of trade regulation, uniform and impartial administration, due process of law, and judicial review.
3. In the increasingly close *'horizontal linkages' among different global regulatory institutions*, the WTO should recognize regulatory standards issued by other global regulatory bodies only if generated through transparent procedures and regulatory due process, affording rights of participation and based on public reason supported by the decisional record and reflecting fair consideration of all affected interests. Interpreting and applying the Washington consensus underlying the law of the Bretton Woods institutions and GATT/WTO law in conformity with the Geneva consensus, which underlies UN HRL and the law of rights-based UN specialized agencies (like the ILO and WHO), could promote common GAL principles, and strengthen and legitimize multilevel governance of overlapping PGs.

The focus of GAL norms on the procedural elements of administrative law has 'served not only to secure implementation of the substantive norms of liberalized trade but also to promote broader goals including open administration, even-handed treatment of foreign citizens, and the rule of law'. The standards seek 'to provide safeguards against abuse of power, counter-factional capture, and temper

hand and episodic dispute settlement on the other'). The following quotations in the text are from these authors.

the tunnel vision of specialized regulatory bodies'; they pragmatically respond to the accountability gaps in the administrative practices of international institutions and the recognition that the ultimate aim of many of these regimes is to regulate the conduct of private actors rather than states. Yet, GAL proponents acknowledge that, due to the absence of democratic legislation and democratic accountability at the global level, administrative procedures alone may be relatively ineffective in overcoming disparities in power and the biases of specialized mission-orientated organizations.

2.2.5 Multilevel Constitutional Conceptions of IEL

The more territorially based national sovereignty is transformed by functionally limited, multilevel governance of transnational aggregate PGs, the stronger becomes the need for reconceiving sovereignty in terms of duties of governments to protect human rights and transnational aggregate PGs demanded by citizens. Both territorially limited *national governments* and functionally limited *transnational governance* must be reconstituted, limited, regulated, and justified more coherently in terms of the inalienable human rights and constitutional rights of citizens and of their democratic self-governance. The multilevel constitutional approaches underlying European economic law emphasize that the legitimacy and effectiveness of IEL—as an instrument for promoting consumer welfare and human rights of citizens—depend on its consistency with HRL and other constitutional obligations of governments. Such approaches are practiced by the European Court of Justice (CJEU), the EFTA Court, and the European Court of Human Rights in cooperation with national courts, parliaments, and governments throughout Europe. They interpret and develop an increasing number of trade, investment, competition, common market rules, labour law, and HRL as 'cosmopolitan law' empowering private actors.[21] Transnational rule of law is protected for the benefit of citizens (eg EU citizens, investors, migrant workers and their families), with due respect for the legitimate diversity of constitutional democracies.[22] The legal primacy of constitutional rules over post-constitutional rule-making prompts many states to grant international treaties only an *infra*-constitutional legal rank in domestic legal systems, and to exclude direct applicability of many IEL law rules in domestic courts. As international law's claim (as codified in Article 27 VCLT) to legal primacy over domestic law must remain subject to constitutional restraints, constitutional democracy may require higher levels of *national* protection of human rights than the

[21] Cf A Stone Sweet and C Ryan, Kant, Cosmopolitanism and Systems of Constitutional Justice in Europe and Beyond *Global Constitutionalism* 9 (2020), 562–80.

[22] See Petersmann (n 17) chapter III; A Stone Sweet, A Cosmopolitan Legal Order: Constitutional Pluralism and Rights Adjudication in Europe, *Global Constitutionalism* 1 (2012), 1, 53.

minimum standards prescribed in UN HRL. Whenever *international guarantees* of freedom, non-discrimination, and rule of law go beyond those of *national legal systems* (as in many areas of IEL), countries increasingly use IEL for complementing incomplete, national Constitutions by limiting government failures through international agreements. EU constitutional, common market, and competition laws, for instance, empower citizens and NGOs to invoke and enforce common market freedoms and other fundamental rights of European law in national courts vis-à-vis welfare-reducing, national border discrimination against foreign goods and services. The EUCFR protects legal and judicial remedies of citizens against abuses of multilevel economic regulation within and beyond state borders. Worldwide agreements—like the UN Charter and the agreements establishing the fifteen UN specialized agencies—tend to focus on reciprocal rights and obligations among states with only few constitutional dimensions like the UN Security Council powers to adopt legally binding decisions, treaty provisions on international legal responsibilities and judicial remedies, and UN human rights conventions.

2.2.6 How to Respond to the Reality of Legal Pluralism in IEL?

The conceptions of IEL diverge for many reasons. For instance, different private and public, constitutional and administrative law, and economic and political conceptions of legal regulation are influenced by diverse understandings of whether

- societies are a singular whole which is larger than its parts or, rather, a mere collection of parts (eg as claimed by some neo-liberal politicians, for whom society only consists of individuals, and 'cosmopolitans come from nowhere');
- how the hierarchical and spontaneous, civil, political, economic, cultural, legal, and other social dimensions interact;[23] and
- whether national and international HRL can be interpreted as effective constitutional restraints on the delegation of governance powers by citizens and governments.

The regulatory functions of 'constitutionalization' of EU common market law, and of the monetary crises responses in the Eurozone, continue to dynamically change, for instance focusing now less on 'integration through law' than on 'integration through governance' and 'integration beyond law'.[24] Attempts at instrumentalizing IEL (eg by judicialization and 'constitutionalization' of national, regional, or worldwide IEL aimed at making particular legal perspectives the dominant legal order) challenge the impartiality and legal methodologies of adjudication, as illustrated

[23] For more detailed discussion of these questions see the Introduction by Kjaer (n 15) to his book.
[24] For detailed discussion of these questions see Parts I and III of the book edited by Kjaer (n 15).

by the US assault on the WTO legal and dispute settlement system discussed in Chapter 3. The role of law in the global political economy remains contested, for instance by challenging the conception of IEL as an ordering device aimed at introducing stability into the global political and economic systems while promoting peace, justice, and prosperity, as illustrated in Chapter 4 by the widespread civil society criticism of abuses of IEL provoking injustices, inequality, environmental exploitation, and climate change. Hence, the question arises—as discussed in Chapter 4 —whether proposals from 'institutional economics' and 'constitutional economics' for reforming economic, labour, and environmental regulation (eg by prioritizing markets as the most efficient form of resource allocation, limiting market failures, protecting rights of individuals against abuses of both public and private power) can justify and depoliticize IEL reforms responding to the economic, political, technological, and societal transformations of the global economy in the twenty-first century. Arguably, multilevel constitutional law and GAL conceptions of IEL remedy some of the regulatory deficits of international private law and international public law conceptions of IEL in respect of multilevel governance of transnational PGs, which are not spontaneously provided in private markets and are frequently neglected by authoritarian governments prioritizing power politics and national interests. Yet, beyond the regional scope of HRL and economic integration law in Europe, constitutional law conceptions of IEL are resisted by neo-liberal and authoritarian power politics. How should reasonable citizens and democracies respond to this reality of legal pluralism and widespread, multilevel power politics? As discussed in section 2.3, UN legal practices offer no coherent answers.

2.3 From UN Human Rights Law to Global Community Law?

Democratic constitutions emerged since the eighteenth century long before the emergence of international HRL. Just as national constitutions (eg in the United States and Germany) tend to be construed by national courts as *not* prescribing specific varieties of market economies, so do UN human rights conventions refrain from prescribing specific economic orders. What is the legal relationship between national constitutions and international HRL, for example in federal states that protected common market freedoms and judicial remedies long before they accepted international human rights conventions? Why do the 1966 UN human rights conventions on civil and political rights (ICCPR) and economic, social and cultural rights (ICESCR) not include legal guarantees of market freedoms (like freedom of contract, freedom of profession, freedom of trade), private property, and other legal guarantees (like monetary stability) for mutually beneficial division of labour, private trade, and competition? Why do EU law and its EUCFR include constitutional guarantees of civil, political, economic, and social rights, multilevel judicial remedies, and explicit guarantees of a 'competitive social market economy' (Article 3 of the Treaty on European Union (TEU)) with common market freedoms (like free movements of goods, services, persons, capital and related payments, freedom of profession), protection of private property and social rights across national borders, which the more than 450 million EU citizens never enjoyed before the creation of the European Community?

2.3.1 Principles of Justice and Multilevel Democratic Constitutionalism

Since ancient times, theories of justice are being invoked by rulers (eg for justifying their powers by alleged 'mandates from heaven') and by citizens (eg for justifying their 'common law freedoms') for justifying law and governance vis-à-vis citizens. In his *Theory of Justice* (1971), the US philosopher John Rawls described constitutionalism as a 'four-stage sequence' as reflected in the history of the US Constitution: reasonable citizens, after having agreed (i) on their constitutional 'principles of justice' (eg in the 1776 US Declaration of Independence and Virginia Bill of Rights), (ii) elaborate national constitutions (eg the US Federal Constitution of 1787) providing for basic rights and legislative, executive, and judicial institutions; (iii) democratic legislation must progressively implement and protect the constitutional principles of justice for the benefit of citizens; and (iv) the agreed constitutional and legislative rules need to be applied and enforced by administrations and courts of justice in particular cases so as to protect equal rights and promote rule of law and rule-compliance by citizens.[25] Globalization transforms ever more *national* into *transnational PGs* (like human rights, rule of law, sustainable development) requiring multilevel governance and multilevel constitutional restraints on abuses of public and private powers beyond the national 'four-stage sequence' described by Rawls. Hence, the legitimate demand by citizens for regional and global PGs requires transforming the national four-stage sequence of democratic constitutionalism into a multilevel 'six-stage sequence' taking into account the need for (v) international law and (vi) multilevel governance institutions for protecting ever more PGs in a globalizing and dynamically changing world.[26] These new forms of multilevel governance of transnational, often interdependent and 'overlapping, aggregate PGs' (like a mutually beneficial world trading system, rule of law, human rights, climate change mitigation, and other SDGs) should take into account two additional 'constitutional insights' from Rawls' theory of justice:

[25] Cf J Rawls, *A Theory of Justice* (Revised edn, Harvard UP 1999), at 171ff.

[26] This need for a multilevel, transnational 'six-stage constitutionalization process' was explained in Petersmann (n 4), at 112f, 126ff, 174ff.

- *Multilevel constitutional perspectivism*: The 'four-stage sequence is a device for applying the principles of justice and for constraining legal systems from different perspectives of justice. This scheme is part of the theory of justice as fairness and not an account of how constitutional conventions and legislatures actually proceed. It sets out a series of points of view from which the different problems of justice are to be settled, each point of view inheriting the constraints adopted at the preceding stage.'[27] Hence, as illustrated by the German Constitutional Court judgment of 28 April 2021 annulling parts of the German Climate Protection Act (as discussed in Chapter 9, section 9.4), the legal design of democratic legislation protecting SDGs should take into account—and remain constitutionally and institutionally restrained—by 'multilevel constitutionalism' (as reflected in EU and UN law) respecting the constitutional principles and institutional restraints democratically agreed upon at the six different levels of multilevel governance from six legitimately diverse, but complementary 'constitutional perspectives'. Only together can they secure legitimate governmental protection of transnational PGs demanded by citizens. For example, even though a 'party may not invoke the provisions of its internal law as justification for its failure to perform a treaty' (Article 27 VCLT), international treaties must be interpreted 'in conformity with the principles of justice' as embodied in international law, including also 'respect for, and observance of, human rights and fundamental freedoms for all' (as recalled in the Preamble and Article 31 VCLT). Hence, national and international guarantees of human and constitutional rights, non-discrimination, rule of law, judicial remedies, and protection of SDGs should be construed in mutually consistent ways. This is also acknowledged in the legal obligation of each WTO member to 'ensure the conformity of its laws, regulations and administrative procedures with its obligations in the annexed Agreements' (Article XVI:4 WTO Agreement). Even if the 'embedded liberalism' underlying GATT/WTO law (eg Articles III, XVIII–XXI, XXIV GATT) protects national political autonomy of member states, the GATT/WTO policy objectives (like reciprocal trade liberalization, 'sustainable development'), rules (like guarantees of non-discriminatory market access, rule of law), and compulsory jurisdiction for peaceful dispute settlement and third-party adjudication protect transnational PGs that should be

[27] Rawls (n 25), at 176. Arguably, individual and social perspectivism creates regulatory problems similar to the 'Heisenberg principle' in quantum physics: the mere fact of observation from different perspectives risks changing realities; individual, communitarian, national, international, or cosmopolitan social perspectives may justify diverse regulatory understandings and responses, whose overall consistency and social impact are shaped by principles of justice. As Heraclitus of Ephesus claimed, 'everything flows and nothing stays'.

construed consistently with corresponding domestic rights and obligations of governments.[28]

- *Multilevel constitutional pluralism*: Moreover, as emphasized by Rawls in his later book, *Political Liberalism*, the legitimacy challenges arising from the permanent fact of diverse religious, philosophical, moral, and political doctrines endorsed by citizens entail that the democratic exercise of power must remain consistent with the constitutional principles and institutionalize an 'overlapping consensus' supporting 'public reason' by free, equal, reasonable, and rational citizens in spite of their diverse moral beliefs.[29] For example, in contrast to the social contract theories proposed by Thomas Hobbes (eg interpreting social contracts as submission to the absolute powers of a monarch protecting social peace) and by Jean-Jacques Rousseau (eg interpreting social contracts as submitting free and equal citizens to the 'general will' of democratic legislators), the US founding fathers were inspired by John Locke's conception of social contracts among citizens delegating only limited governance powers restrained by human and constitutional rights retained by the citizens, as specified in the US Bill of Rights added to the US Constitution in 1791. Hence, multilevel constitutionalism for limiting abuses of power and for protecting human rights in multilevel governance of PGs must respect legitimate constitutional pluralism, such as reflected in Anglo-Saxon neo-liberal democracies and European ordo-liberal constitutionalism. Yet, is WTO law also consistent with totalitarian conceptions of embedded liberalism as advocated by China? Does the judicial mandate in the DSU for interpreting WTO rules and settling WTO disputes entail that WTO dispute settlement bodies may interpret the WTO sustainable development objectives in conformity with the SDGs universally adopted by UN member states and with their references to some of the human rights obligations of UN member states?

Invocation of human rights played an important role in the justification of democratic revolutions since the eighteenth century (eg in the United States, France, and in post-colonial struggles for justice). Yet, what is the role of HRL in democratic struggles for multilevel constitutionalism constituting, limiting, regulating, and justifying multilevel governance of PGs beyond states? The need for respecting constitutional pluralism is reflected not only by the fact that national constitutions often prioritize diverse principles of justice; for instance, while the US founding fathers emphasized 'life, liberty and the pursuit of happiness' in their 1776 US Declaration of Independence, the republican French Constitutions referred

[28] On multilevel constitutionalism as a normative imperative for constitutional democracies in a globally integrating world see Petersmann (n 4) and, more specifically for IEL, Petersmann (n 17), chapters II and III.

[29] J Rawls, *Political Liberalism* (Harvard UP 1993).

to 'liberty, equality, fraternity' and 'solidarity of the peoples' as 'the motto of the Republic' (eg as recalled in Articles 1 and 2 of France's 1958 Constitution), placing comparatively more emphasis on economic and social rights in addition to civil and political rights. Moreover, both the 1791 and 1793 French Constitutions remained short-lived, for instance due to the termination of the French Republic by Napoleon's military rule since 1799. As further discussed in Chapter 5, all national constitutions—including the US Constitution's neglect for protecting, for example, slaves, indigenous people, and gender equality—tend to be incomplete. Influenced by the eighteenth-century human rights declarations, the end of the Second World War brought about a new wave of recognition and legal protection of inalienable and indivisible human rights notwithstanding disagreements about justifications of such rights (eg by conceptions of divine law, natural law, or humanist law, diverse democratic preferences, social and political traditions, experiences of constitutional failures as in China's, Russia's, and Germany's post-First World War republics).

2.3.2 UN HRL Does Not Effectively Protect Sustainable Development

The UN Charter was adopted in the name of 'We the Peoples of the United Nations' so as, *inter alia*, 'to reaffirm faith in fundamental human rights, in the dignity and worth of the human person, in the equal rights of men and women and of nations large and small, and to establish conditions under which justice and respect for the obligations arising from treaties and from other sources of international law can be maintained' (Preamble). Yet, UN membership is limited to states; Article 2 defines the UN 'principles' by focusing on 'sovereign equality of all its Members' and other state-centred principles (like prohibition of the use or threat of force, peaceful settlement of disputes, international cooperation, non-intervention into domestic jurisdictions). The 1945 UN Charter included seven references to human rights. The UDHR, approved in the 3rd UN General Assembly by forty-eight UN member states without opposition (albeit subject to eight abstentions), listed civil and political liberties, democratic participatory rights, economic, social, and cultural rights with due respect for the diversity of views on how to justify the universal recognition that

> [a]ll human beings are born free and equal in dignity and rights. They are endowed with reason and conscience and should act towards one another in a spirit of brotherhood (Article 1 UDHR).

For example, the 'inherent dignity' and 'equal and inalienable rights of all members of the human family' proclaimed as 'the foundation of freedom, justice and peace in the world' (Preamble) continue being construed in different ways as

- metaphysical (ie empirically not observable) '*inherent moral birth rights*' and 'justice claims' (eg to have rights) of every human person derived from 'moral intuitionism', human conscience, other common humanity values (like responsibility, moral powers for conceptions of a good life and social justice), and universally shared responses to what the Preamble describes as 'disregard and contempt for human rights' (eg during the preceding World Wars, Nazi dictatorship, and the Holocaust) that resulted 'in barbarous acts which have outraged the conscience of mankind';[30]
- deriving from '*reasonable free good will*' respecting human dignity (eg in the Kantian sense of a 'categorial imperative') and acknowledging the moral need for human rights, 'cosmopolitan international law' and an international federation of liberal republics protecting equal freedoms and 'democratic peace';
- moral rules deriving from the '*golden rule*', reciprocity requirements and agreed prohibitions of discrimination (eg in Article 2 UDHR protecting human rights 'without distinction of any kind, such as race, colour, sex, language, religion, political or other opinion, national or social origin, property, birth or other status');
- moral '*natural rights*' deriving from respect for human dignity in the sense of 'free' and 'full development of his personality' (Articles 22, 26, 29 UDHR) based on the species-wide, human capabilities (such as life, health, reason, conscience, etc) and basic human needs;
- *legal (rather than only moral) human rights* universally recognized by all 193 UN member states in, *inter alia*, the UN Charter, UN and regional human rights agreements, national constitutions, and other legal acts implementing the moral human rights recognized in the UDHR; or as
- *political, participatory human rights* recognized in UN member states, notably by democratic institutions in constitutionally restrained 'deliberative democracies' acknowledging the 'co-originality' (Jürgen Habermas) of individual and democratic autonomy.[31]

The drafters of the UDHR were driven by a shared vision of 'cosmopolitan justice' perceiving all human beings as members of the same family of mankind, rather

[30] On metaphysical inherence, epistemic awareness, moral intuitionism, and universal acknowledgment of moral human rights solely by virtue of being born human, see J Morsink, *Inherent Human Rights. Philosophical Roots of the Universal Declaration* (University of Pennsylvania Press 2009).

[31] For a discussion of diverse human rights conceptions and philosophies, see P Tiedemann, *Philosophical Foundations of Human Rights* (Springer 2020); Morsink (n 30); S Gosepath and G Lohmann (eds), *Philosophie der Menschenrechte* (Suhrkamp 1998); A Follesdal, JK Schaffer, and G Ulfstein (eds), *The Legitimacy of International Human Rights Regimes: Legal, Political and Philosophical Perspectives* (2014).

than by national state interests and negotiations based on reciprocity. UN HRL promoted *universal recognition* of moral, political, and legal human rights and related struggles for justice (like decolonization, racial and gender equality). It was less successful in institutionalizing multilevel, *legislative and judicial protection* of human rights and of democratic governance inside many UN member states—notably in Africa and Asia, if compared with the more effective regional human rights conventions and human rights protection in American and European democracies. The disagreements underlying UN HRL (eg among China, the EU, Islamic countries, the United States) not only continue to prevent 'constitutionalization' of UN law and powers (eg of the UN Security Council and UN specialized agencies); human rights are also 'not enough'[32] for justifying the basic structures of social and legal systems, for example because HRL protects legal 'status equality' of human beings without guaranteeing the rules, democratic institutions, resources, goods, and services necessary for satisfying popular demand and essential needs of citizens, which depend on constitutional, economic, social, and other legal rules and institutions (like economic markets supplying consumers with needed private goods, democratic 'political markets', and governments providing PGs).

2.3.3 From the UN Community of States to Global Community Law?

The disagreements underlying the moral and political consensus among UN diplomats on the UDHR entail inadequate constitutional, legislative, and judicial implementation and protection of HRL in many UN member states. UN HRL leaves it to the discretion of each UN member state whether it ratifies UN human rights conventions and which ones, and whether it joins UN specialized agencies for providing global PGs. For example, the United States ratified the ICCPR but not the ICESCR; China ratified the ICESCR but not the ICCPR; EU member states ratified most UN human rights conventions and implemented them within national and EU legal systems through additional, national, and European human rights guarantees and multilevel judicial remedies as prescribed, for example, in the ECHR and in the EUCFR. From the citizen- and people-oriented perspectives of Rawls' *Theory of Justice*, UN HRL can be construed as a 'constitutional foundation' for the democratic task of 'humanizing' and 'constitutionalizing' multilevel governance of PGs for the benefit of citizens. Yet, it is not enough for establishing a mutually beneficial division of labour based on global community law protecting global PGs for the benefit of all humankind. It remains up to the peoples and governments inside UN member states to decide to what extent they wish to incorporate UN

[32] Cf S Moyn, *Not Enough. Human Rights in an Unequal World* (Harvard UP 2018).

and WTO law into their domestic legal systems and economic orders and, thereby, overcome the existing 'disconnect' between UN/WTO treaties empowering states and national legal systems empowering citizens. While hegemonic governments (eg in China, Russia, and the United States) tend to deny rights of citizens to invoke UN and WTO agreements in domestic courts, EU law incorporates international agreements of the EU into the Community legal system with a legal rank higher than the national legal systems of EU member states, albeit subject to legal restraints on individuals to invoke such external agreements in EU courts.[33] As long as power politics and the state-centred principles of UN law prevail over people- and citizen-centred human rights in UN legal practices, UN law remains a power-oriented 'international community of states' (Article 53 VCLT) without constituting 'global community law' empowering humanity. This 'state-driven governance' is illustrated also by the fact that—as discussed in section 2.4—economic cooperation across national borders remains mainly regulated in GATT/WTO law outside the formal UN system and without references to UN HRL.

2.4 The Neo-Liberal Washington Consensus Versus the Ordo-Liberal Brussels Consensus

Human rights were not mentioned in the 1944 Bretton Woods Agreements establishing the International Monetary Fund (IMF) and the World Bank, in GATT 1947, the WTO Agreement, and in most international investment agreements. The economic theory of separation of policy instruments and the utilitarian, neo-liberal market fundamentalism favoured by the Washington consensus prompted states to keep GATT and the WTO deliberately outside the UN legal system. During and beyond the post-1945 Cold War, HRL remained neglected in most worldwide economic organizations. The 1966 ICCPR and ICESCR were ratified by more than 150 UN member states, yet these conventions neither protect private property rights nor citizen-driven market-economies. IMF, World Bank, and GATT/WTO law and practices prioritize macro-economic goals, usually without referring to human rights. Due to the separation of the intergovernmental Bretton Woods and WTO institutions from HRL, worldwide IEL fails to promote the political and legal synergies, which characterize the rights-based, ordo-liberal economic constitutionalism in the EU and in some of the EU's external free trade agreements (FTAs) (eg providing for human rights clauses, judicial protection of rule of law, and fundamental rights). Some of the 2015 UN Millennium Goals and 2030 UN SDGs refer to human rights (eg to food and health protection); yet, proposals for stronger integration of human rights into the law of worldwide

[33] For details, see, M Cremona, A Thies, and R Wessels (eds), *The European Union and International Dispute Settlement* (Hart 2017).

organizations continue being resisted by many governments and also by some human rights advocates prioritizing UN human rights bodies (eg over WTO institutions).[34] The customary law requirement of 'systemic treaty interpretation' of IEL treaties in conformity with modern HRL is not always respected in WTO and investment adjudication.[35] The US refusal to ratify the 1966 ICESCR, China's refusal to ratify the 1966 ICCPR, and the EUCFR reflect conflicting human right conceptions among the major economic powers, which influence their neo-liberal, state capitalist, and ordo-liberal rivalries and diverse IEL conceptions. Theories of justice explain why the basic structures of legal systems must be justified inclusively bottom-up by constitutional contracts among citizens and democratic legislation; top-down interpretations and justifications of WTO rules by WTO and UN bodies (eg including representatives from countries, whose national legal systems do not effectively protect human rights) may be accepted by governments, but risk lacking democratic support and legitimacy from the point of view of adversely affected citizens.

For instance, when the post-1945 embedded liberalism was transformed by Prime Minister Thatcher and President Reagan into neo-liberal prioritization of liberalization, privatization, deregulation, and 'financialization' of transnational markets, Thatcher famously claimed that 'there is no such thing as society'. Such reductionist assumptions of methodological individualism (eg that the sum of individual actions constitutes society) are rejected in UN HRL, the SDGs, in the EU's social market economies, and also in the ECHR, as illustrated by their recognition of legal rights, corporate social responsibilities, and judicial remedies for NGOs. The 1957 European Economic Community (EEC) Treaty incorporated the GATT obligations of the six EEC member states for establishing a customs union; it embedded the EEC common market rules into economic and democratic constitutionalism, as advocated by the Freiburg School of ordo-liberalism, the Cologne

[34] On the 'Alston and Petersmann debate' in 2002, see EU Petersmann, Time for a United Nations 'Global Compact' for Integrating Human Rights into the Law of Worldwide Organizations: Lessons from European Integration, *European Journal of International Law* 13 (2002), 621–50; EU Petersmann, Taking Human Dignity, Poverty and Empowerment of Individuals More Seriously: Rejoinder to Alston, *European Journal of International Law* 13 (2002), 845–51. Most theories of justice, constitutional lawyers, and governments reject claims (eg by some UN human rights specialists like P Alston) that international economic organizations and their member states should implement policies as recommended by politicized UN human rights bodies rather than as approved by parliaments and governments democratically accountable to citizens and legally constrained by democratically approved constitutions justifying the basic structures of legal and governance systems; cf T Cottier, J Pauwelyn, and E Bürgi (eds), *Human Rights and International Trade* (OUP 2005); FA Abbott, C Breining, and T Cottier (eds), *International Trade and Human Rights* (Michigan UP 2006); both books include contributions of mine refuting Alston's criticism that governments, parliaments, and economic courts are less qualified than UN human rights bodies for clarifying the human rights dimensions of IEL. On the 'subsidiarity' of international human rights conventions vis-à-vis domestic, more comprehensive, or more specific human and constitutional rights guarantees, and the 'margin of appreciation doctrine' regarding domestic protection of human rights, see PG Carozza, Subsidiarity as a Structural Principle of International Human Rights Law *American Journal of International Law* 38 (2003), 41ff.

[35] Cf Chapters 6 and 7.

School of social market economy, and as practised in German constitutional and economic law (eg providing for competition, labour, and social policies, monetary stability, freedom of payments, multilevel democratic and judicial protection of civil, political, economic, and social rights).[36] Some leading advocates of these 'law and economics' schools (like Alfred Müller-Armack and Walter Hallstein, who became the first President of the EEC Commission) represented Germany in the EEC Treaty negotiations; also the first EEC Commissioner for competition policy (ie Hans von der Groeben) and some of his influential legal advisors (like Professor EJ Mestmäcker) contributed to designing and interpreting EEC common market and competition rules and policies not only as instruments for promoting economic efficiency and non-discriminatory market competition but also as constitutional safeguards protecting equal common market freedoms and transnational rule of law (eg as justified by Kantian legal theories derived from respect for human dignity and cosmopolitan, equal liberties). Such constitutional approaches influenced not only the progressive 'constitutionalization' of EEC common market law through the jurisprudence of the CJEU and successive treaty amendments. It also furthered acceptance of the ECHR as a condition for EU membership. The EU commitments to a 'competitive social market economy', as specified in the Lisbon Treaty on European Union (eg Article 3 TEU), and the EUCFR confirmed the EU's 'micro-economic common market constitution'.[37] Since the 1992 Maastricht Treaty, this micro-economic constitutionalism was progressively supplemented by the EU's 'area of freedom, security and justice without internal frontiers' and by the EU's 'macro-economic monetary constitution'.[38] The Lisbon Treaty also provides for a 'foreign policy constitution' limiting the EUs common foreign, commercial, and security policies by the EU's constitutional principles of 'democracy, the rule of law, the universality and indivisibility of human rights and fundamental freedoms, respect for human dignity, the principles of equality and solidarity, and respect for

[36] The Freiburg school (initiated in the 1930s by, *inter alia*, law professor F Böhm and economics professor W Eucken) responded to the 'constitutional problems' of economic markets (eg as described in the books by FA Hayek like *The Road to Serfdom* (University of Chicago Press 1944)) in order to legally constitute and protect market competition against authoritarian government restrictions and distortions. The Cologne school (initiated by Professor A Müller-Armack) explained the need for a 'social market economy' (as transformed into government policies by German chancellor Professor L Erhard) in response to the social and political problems resulting from the lack of 'social embeddedness' of economic markets (eg as criticized by K Polanyi, *The Great Transformation: The Political and Economic Origins of our Time* (2nd edn, Beacon Press 1944/2001)). For discussion and criticism see Chapter IV and J Hien and C Joerges, (eds), *Ordoliberalism, Law and the Rule of Economics* (Hart 2020).

[37] For example, based on multilevel common market freedoms, competition, environmental, and social rules, multilevel competition institutions, and 'regulatory competition' constrained by multilevel judicial protection of civil, political, economic and social rights; cf Chapter 5, section 5.5.

[38] For example, based on EU legal disciplines for monetary, fiscal, debt, and economic policies supervised by multilevel, independent central banks and intergovernmental economic cooperation; for details see Chapter 5, section 5.5 and HCH Hofmann, K Pantazatou, and G Zaccaroni (eds), *The Transformation of the European Economic Constitution* (Edward Elgar 2019); C Kaupa, *The Pluralist Character of the European Economic Constitution* (Hart 2016).

the principles of the United Nations Charter and international law' (cf Articles 3, 21 TEU).[39]

2.5 The Geneva Consensus on Rules-based Multilateralism: An Ordo-Liberal Constraint on Power Politics?

The rights-based, ordo-liberal Brussels consensus and constitutional economics underlying the EU's common market law shaped also the EU's *external* policy initiatives for designing FTAs with third countries and for negotiating international trade, competition, investment rules and the compulsory WTO dispute settlement system. Similarly, the legal culture of EU institutions and the jurisprudence of the CJEU influenced the EU negotiation positions in the WTO's Doha Round negotiations since 2001 and the jurisprudence of GATT/WTO dispute settlement bodies.[40] For instance, at the 1996 WTO Singapore Ministerial Conference, the EU proposals for negotiating trade-related competition and investment rules led to the establishment of two WTO Working Groups on 'trade and competition' and 'trade and investments'. European ordo-liberal reform initiatives were particularly visible when former EU Trade Commissioner Pascal Lamy (1999–2004) became WTO Director-General (2005–2013) and initiated regular parliamentary meetings inside the WTO in cooperation with the Inter-Parliamentary Union, as well as joint reports of the WTO with other international organizations at Geneva like the ILO, the WHO, and the World Intellectual Property Organization (WIPO). In his 2013 monograph, *The Geneva Consensus—Making Trade Work for All*, Lamy promoted the Geneva consensus as an alternative to the neo-liberal Washington consensus by emphasizing the need for, *inter alia*,

- stronger policy coherence through better coordination among the legally separate, international monetary, financial, trade, investment, environmental, and human rights institutions and policies in order to enhance their potential synergies in protecting interdependent PGs (like economic welfare, sustainable development, and human rights); and
- strengthening the democratic legitimacy of the world trading system by stronger involvement of national parliaments, civil societies, and NGOs protecting human rights, social justice and the SDGs.[41]

[39] Cf EU Petersmann, The EU's Cosmopolitan Foreign Policy Constitution and its Disregard in Transatlantic Free Trade Agreements, *European Foreign Affairs Review* 21 (2016), 449–69.

[40] Cf T Soave, European Legal Culture and WTO Dispute Settlement: Thirty Years of Socio-Legal Transplants from Brussels to Geneva, *The Law and Practice of International Courts and Tribunals* 19 (2020), 107–33 and chapter 6.

[41] Cf P Lamy, *The Geneva Consensus. Making Trade Work for All* (CUP 2013), eg 148ff: 'human rights and trade rules, including WTO rules, are based on the same values – individual freedom and

Similarly, the jurisprudence of GATT/WTO panels and of the WTO AB was influenced by the jurisprudence of European courts regarding the customs union and common market rules of the EU. For example, the GATT/WTO jurisprudence on the 'necessity' principle and on 'proportionality balancing' in GATT Article XX—as developed notably in the 1989 GATT panel report on *US—Section 337* (with former CJEU judge Pierre Pescatore serving as one of the three panel members) and in the 2001 WTO AB report on *Korea—Various Measures on Beef* (with the former Director-General of Legal Affairs in the EU Commission Claus-Dieter Ehlermann serving as one of the three members of the Appellate Body (AB) Division)—followed the judicial clarifications of similar necessity and proportionality principles in German and EU law and jurisprudence distinguishing the following fours elements:

1. ensuring that the actor (eg the state) is constitutionally legitimated to take the action (the legitimacy test);
2. ensuring that the means adopted by the actor are rationally and carefully designed to achieve the stated policy objective (the suitability test);
3. ensuring that the measure does not curtail other rights any more than is necessary to achieve the stated objective by, if possible, searching for less restrictive means (the necessity test); and
4. ensuring that the effects of the contested act are balanced against the infringement of the right in light of the objectives sought to be attained by the contested act (the proportionality balancing test in the strict sense).[42]

This proportionality balancing of rights and obligations of states under HRL and IEL based on legal standards developed by domestic courts for the reconciliation of competing constitutional rights of individuals and constitutional duties (eg to protect PGs like public health)—rather than based on the more restrictive 'necessity standards' under customary international law as codified by the International Law Commission—has been interpreted as an example of 'judicial constitutionalization' of HRL and IEL.[43] Yet, as illustrated by the 'AB crisis' discussed in Chapter 3,

responsibility, non-discrimination, rule of law and welfare through peaceful co-operation among individuals'; 'Human rights and trade are mutually supportive'; 'It is through the extension and deepening of such fundamental rights that the benefits of trade must finally be measured'; 'One could almost claim that trade is human rights in practice!'

[42] Cf A Stone Sweet and J Mathews, Proportionality Balancing and Global Constitutionalism, *Columbia Journal of Transnational Law*, 47 (2008), 72, 76–7. See also M Andenas and S Zleptnig, Proportionality: WTO Law in Comparative Perspective, *Texas International Law Journal*, 42 (2007), 371–427; A Stone Sweet and J Mathews, *Proportionality Balancing and Constitutional Governance: A Comparative and Global Approach* (OUP 2019).

[43] Stone Sweet and Mathews (n 42), at 75: 'Strikingly, proportionality has also migrated to the three treaty-based regimes that have serious claims to be considered "constitutional" in some meaningful sense: the European Union, the European Convention on Human Rights, and the World Trade Organization.'

'judicial constitutionalization' in WTO law is much more limited than in European law among states with similar constitutional traditions. For instance, the 2015 UN Resolution on the 2030 Agenda for Sustainable Development seeks to implement the seventeen SDGs (like overcoming poverty, hunger, and global warming, protecting health, education, gender equality, access to water, sanitation, and clean energy, urbanization, the environment, human rights, and social justice) by 'localizing the SDGs' through empowerment of local institutions, actors, and civil society support. It recognizes 'that the United Nations Framework Convention on Climate Change is the primary international, intergovernmental forum for negotiating the global response to climate change' (paragraph 31). As the SDGs aim at reconciling climate change measures with other sustainable development objectives (like poverty reduction, sustainable agriculture, sustainable use of marine resources, terrestrial ecosystems) and with trade rules, do they offer relevant context for interpreting WTO rules and for evaluating the WTO-consistency of 'nationally determined contributions' under the Paris Agreement?

It is this human rights-based approach—as recognized in the 'constitutions' (*sic*) establishing the ILO and WHO (eg in their definitions of their respective treaty objectives in terms of basic human rights like labour rights and health rights), in UN HRL, and in the appeals by the UN High Commissioner for Human Rights and Pascal Lamy for interpreting modern IEL in conformity with the human rights obligations of states—which distinguishes the ordo-liberal Brussels and Geneva consensus from the utilitarian, macro-economic Washington consensus and the totalitarian Beijing consensus neglecting human rights and 'development as freedom' (Amartya Sen) aimed at protecting human dignity, the rule of law, human capacities, and 'decent work'.[44] As discussed in Chapter 5, EU constitutional law—including the EU's sectoral common market and monetary constitutions—protect constitutional rights and judicial remedies embedding and constraining the dynamic, legislative, and administrative development of EU economic law. Alison Bradford, in her book on 'the Brussels effect', describes how—in spite of the many EU crises (like sluggish growth, political turmoil following a decade of austerity politics, Brexit)—EU economic regulations influence and elevate business standards worldwide in areas such as data privacy, consumer health and safety,

[44] On judicial protection of 'common market freedoms' in the thirty member states of the European Economic Area (EEA), and on European common market law and HRL as cosmopolitan legal and judicial systems prioritizing individual rights over multilevel governance powers, see Petersmann (n 17), at 189ff, 204ff, 237ff; C Barnard, *The Substantive Law of the EU: The Four Freedoms* (OUP 2019); C Baudenbacher, *The Fundamental Principles of EEA Law* (2018); Stone Sweet (n 22). On the neo-liberal Washington and the authoritarian Beijing consensus see Chapter 4; as China's 'economic miracle' since 1978 took place in a unique domestic and global context, the 'Beijing consensus' does not seem to offer a replicable model for other countries (cf W Chen (ed), *The Beijing Consensus? How China has changed Western Ideas of Law and Economic Development* (CUP 2017)). For example, Singapore combines a different kind of authoritarian state capitalism with government-linked corporations. China rejects legalistic, rights-based, and court-centred constitutionalism and prioritizes social stability and political control by the communist party monopoly.

environmental protection, antitrust, and online hate speech.[45] As explained in sections 2.2 and 2.3, comprehensive conceptions of IEL (ie as comprising private and public, national and international constitutional, administrative and multilevel economic regulation and related legal and judicial practices) respond better to the demands of constitutional and democratic theories of justice for constituting, limiting, regulating, and justifying IEL and multilevel governance of PGs from the diverse perspectives of procedural, constitutional, distributive, corrective, commutative principles of justice and equity. The narrower conceptions of IEL (eg as the public international law regulating the global economy) are more prone to power politics neglecting human rights, democratic governance, and rule of law.[46] Power-oriented legal practices pursuing the rational self-interests of actors risk neglecting principles of justice and public reason underlying positive law as a normative legal order. In order to contain power politics, all legal systems—including IEL—must aim at institutionalizing public reason and accountability mechanisms limiting incoherent interactions between *normative law* and power-/interest-based *legal practices*, which together constitute *legal systems.*

The neo-liberal US assault on the WTO legal and dispute settlement system (as discussed in Chapter 3) undermines not only the multilateral 'constitutional constructivism' underlying, for example, the separation of legislative, executive, and judicial WTO institutions, their mutual 'checks and balances', and the compulsory WTO jurisdiction for AB review. It also impedes WTO reforms responding to the regulatory challenges of China's state capitalism, climate change, and global health pandemics. Economic disintegration (eg due to the US–China trade wars, related dismantling of global value chains) and regulatory competition among North American, European, and Asian trading regimes risk disrupting the rules-based, global trading community, WTO law, and UN law. Does the rising number of authoritarian governments render the democratic, cosmopolitan reconstitution of the global society—as envisaged by UN HRL and the SDGs aimed at promoting multilevel governance of global PGs—a utopia? The increasing number of WTO disputes over nationalist invocations (eg by the United States, Russia, Saudi Arabia) of security exceptions (eg in Article XXI GATT) as justifications of discriminatory trade sanctions illustrates how reasonable, deductive legal interpretations (eg in WTO panel and AB jurisprudence) risk being refuted by power-oriented, inductive claims that states did not consent to such deductive, judicial rule-clarifications. Yet, as discussed in Chapters 3 and 8, the power-oriented US claims of 'judicial overreach' in AB jurisprudence—and academic claims

[45] Cf A Bradford, *The Brussels Effect: How the European Union Rules the World* (2020). The General Data Protection Regulation (GDPR) of the EU, which entered into force in May 2018, aims at reconciling the free flow of data among controllers and processors for the sake of economic development and innovation with protection of related fundamental rights of the data subjects, such as rights to privacy and personal data protection of individuals and other fundamental rights and freedoms (such as integrity, non-discrimination, or consumer protection in the context of data processing).

[46] On embedding theories of IEL and multilevel governance of PGs into Kantian, Rawlsian, and cosmopolitan theories of justice see Petersmann (nn 4 and 17).

'that law is incapable of providing convincing justifications to the solution of normative problems'[47]—are inconsistent with the customary rules of treaty interpretation. The 'systemic treaty interpretation' requirements of international law (eg in Article 31.3,c VCLT), the normative and judicial tasks of interpreting treaties 'in conformity with the principles of justice of international law', including also 'human rights and fundamental freedoms for all' (as recalled and universally recognized in the Preamble of the VCLT), and the universal recognition of human rights require interpreting international law no longer as constituting only a power-oriented 'international community of states' (Article 53 VCLT), where human rights of citizens and peoples are not effectively protected. Even if many governments resist struggles for justice and for global community law protecting 'inalienable' individual, social, and democratic rights, peoples and citizens are likely to continue to challenge state-centred conceptions of international law among states by calling for more inclusive conceptions of international law of states, peoples, and humanity. Mere conflicts of law methodologies prioritizing inter-regional coordination and 'inter-legality' of China-, Europe-, and US-centric regional, legal, and political systems are 'not enough' to protect global PGs like climate change mitigation, which requires limiting harmful greenhouse gas (GHG) emissions and other environmental pollution by governmental and non-governmental actors throughout the globe.

2.6 The 2030 UN Sustainable Development Agenda as a Concretization of the Geneva Consensus

In September 2015, 170 heads of governments adopted the UN 2030 Agenda for Sustainable Development specifying 17 SDGs and 169 policy targets as an integrated framework for guiding national and global development actions up to 2030. In contrast to the Millennium Development Goals adopted by the UN in 2000, the 2030 Agenda is grounded more in HRL. Almost all the seventeen SDGs relate to human rights values like ending poverty in all its forms everywhere (SDG 1), ending hunger and achieving food security (SDG 2), ensuring healthy lives (SDG 3) and inclusive, equitable quality education (SDG 4), achieving gender equality (SDG 5), availability of water and sanitation for all (SDG 6), access to affordable and sustainable energy for all (SDG 7), promoting economic growth and decent work for all (SDG 8), sustainable industrialization (SDG 9), reducing inequality within and among countries (SDG 10), and promoting sustainable development (SDGs 11–17), including combatting climate change (SDG 13) and promoting peaceful societies with access to justice and accountable, inclusive institutions for all (SDG 16) (see Table 2.1 below). The SDGs 'seek to realize the human rights of all' and 'balance the three dimensions of sustainable

[47] Cf Koskenniemi (n 7), at 69 and Chapter 2, section 2.1.

Table 2.1 The Seventeen Sustainable Development Goals (from *Transforming our World: The 2030 Agenda for Sustainable Development*, United Nations A/RES/70/1, 2015)

Sustainable Development Goals
Goal 1. End poverty in all its forms everywhere
Goal 2. End hunger, achieve food security and improved nutrition and promote sustainable agriculture
Goal 3. Ensure healthy lives and promote well-being for all at all ages
Goal 4. Ensure inclusive and equitable quality education and promote lifelong learning opportunities for all
Goal 5. Achieve gender equality and empower all women and girls
Goal 6. Ensure availability and sustainable management of water and sanitation for all
Goal 7. Ensure access to affordable, reliable, sustainable and modern energy for all
Goal 8. Promote sustained, inclusive and sustainable economic growth, full and productive employment and decent work for all
Goal 9. Build resilient infrastructure, promote inclusive and sustainable industrialization and foster innovation
Goal 10. Reduce inequality within and among countries
Goal 11. Make cities and human settlements inclusive, safe, resilient and sustainable
Goal 12. Ensure sustainable consumption and production patterns
Goal 13. Take urgent action to combat climate change and its impacts*
Goal 14. Conserve and sustainably use the oceans, seas and marine resources for sustainable development
Goal 15. Protect, restore and promote sustainable use of terrestrial ecosystems, sustainably manage forests, combat desertification, and halt and reverse land degradation and halt biodiversity loss
Goal 16. Promote peaceful and inclusive societies for sustainable development, provide access to justice for all and build effective, accountable and inclusive institutions at all levels
Goal 17. Strengthen the means of implementation and revitalize the global partnership for sustainable development

* Acknowledging that the United Nations Framework Convention on Climate Change is the primary international, intergovernmental forum for negotiating the global response to climate change.

development: the economic, social and environmental'.[48] The Agenda describes itself as being

> guided by the purposes and principles of the Charter of the United Nations, including full respect for international law. It is grounded in the Universal Declaration of Human Rights, in international human rights treaties, the Millennium Declaration and the 2005 World Summit Outcome.[49]

Arguably, the universal endorsement of the 2030 Agenda is relevant legal context also for interpreting and implementing the WTO sustainable development commitments. It concretizes what Chapter 2, section 2.5 described as the Geneva consensus embedding UN/WTO law and politics into the UN human and labour rights systems; these include also the UN Guiding Principles for Business and Human Rights as endorsed by the UN Human Rights Council on 16 June 2011. The latter confirm

- *state duties* to protect against human rights abuses by third parties, including business, through appropriate policies, regulation, and adjudication;
- *corporate responsibilities* to respect human rights, which means to avoid infringing on the rights of others and to address adverse impacts with which a business is involved; and the need for
- *access to effective remedies for rights-holders* when abuse has occurred, through both judicial and non-judicial grievance mechanisms.[50]

As explained in Chapter 4, the UN SDGs and its 169 agreed policy targets may offer more coherent benchmarks for evaluating economic and environmental measures than neo-liberal conceptions of 'Kaldor–Hicks efficiencies', for instance if the WTO 'sustainable development' objectives, related WTO exceptions (eg for national health and environmental protection measures) and UNFCCC standards are interpreted in conformity with the universally accepted SDGs for evaluating whether national climate change mitigation measures, 'green subsidies', regulatory restrictions of GHG emissions, and other nationally determined contributions under the 2015 Paris Agreement are consistent with the proportionality balancing

[48] Cf n 10 and O de Schutter, *Trade in the Service of Sustainable Development. Linking Trade to Labour Rights and Environmental Standards* (Hart 2017).

[49] UN Resolution A/RES/70/1 (n 10), para 10. On interpreting 'sustainable development' commitments in conformity with HRL in the sense of A Sen's 'development as freedom' protecting basic needs and human capacities for individual and social self-development see Petersmann (n 17), at 190, 340, 374ff.

[50] Cf *Guiding Principles on Business and Human Rights. Implementing the UN 'Respect, Protect and Remedy' Framework* (UN 2011). The 'human rights due diligence' principles based on these Guiding Principles are increasingly applied also to corporate responsibilities regarding climate change and supply chain responsibilities as recognized in recent German legislation and EU Directives (as discussed in Chapter 9).

of competing policy objectives required under Article XX GATT and other world trade rules. The SDGs (like SDG 16 on protecting rule of law) also support the arguments in Chapter 6–9 for strengthening multilevel judicial protection of transnational rule of law in international trade, investment, and environmental policies. Chapters 5 and 7–9 use the examples of economic, investment, and human rights litigation by NGOs for illustrating how governmental commitments to implement the SDGs can offer national courts, European courts, and human rights courts legal context for supporting civil society claims that governments have legal obligations to meet their commitments to reduce GHG emissions and protect SDGs for the benefit of their citizens. Yet, the UN's 2030 Agenda for sustainable development remains a legally non-binding UN Resolution that—so far—lacks adequate implementing legislation, administration and judicial remedies inside many UN member states for effectively protecting human rights and realizing the ambitious SDGs, as illustrated in Chapter 3. The political idealism underlying the 2030 Agenda remains confronted with the political realities of UN and WTO power politics, governance failures, and constitutional failures leading to disregard for human rights in many UN member states, as discussed in Chapter 3.

3

Constitutional Failures: Neo-Liberal and State Capitalist Trade Wars Undermine Sustainable Development

Modern trade theory assumes that the mutual efficiency and productivity gains from specialization and division of labour depend on the scope of markets. The ubiquity of governmental restrictions of international movements of goods, services, persons, capital, and related payments—and the insufficient governmental regulation of market failures—point to widespread governance failures in economic relations in addition to the neglect for human and democratic rights discussed in Chapters 1 and 2. Textbooks on international economic law (IEL) written from third-world perspectives often focus on past constitutional failures of economic regulation (eg during centuries of colonial exploitation, the slave and opium trades),[1] which are rarely discussed in IEL textbooks written by lawyers from Europe and the United States, who focus rather on liberalization of welfare-reducing trade protectionism and regulation of market failures (eg by competition, environmental, and social rules, legal and judicial remedies). This chapter describes the emergence of a geo-economic security order (section 3.1) resulting from the trade wars and disruption of multilateral treaty systems by US President Trump since 2018, based on executive powers without effective parliamentary and judicial control (sections 3.2–3.4), provoking retaliatory treaty violations by adversely affected third countries like China (section 3.5). The arbitrary abuse of executive powers for destroying the World Trade Organization's (WTO) dispute settlement system revealed constitutional failures in protecting transnational rule of law and other UN Sustainable Development Goals (SDGs). China's state-led industrial policies and intergovernmental Belt and Road system of bilateral trade, financial, investment, and infrastructure agreements (section 3.6) are based on different paradigms of economic integration, prompting an increasing number of economists and politicians to ask how far the US and Chinese economies need to be decoupled and whether trade wars can promote foreign policy goals (section 3.7). Yet, responding successfully to the global regulatory challenges of climate change, health pandemics, and the SDGs requires more cooperation and connection rather

[1] Cf L Choukroune and JJ Nedumpara, *International Economic Law: Text, Cases and Materials* (CUP 2021), at 3f.

Transforming World Trade and Investment Law for Sustainable Development. Ernst-Ulrich Petersmann, Oxford University Press. © Ernst-Ulrich Petersmann 2022. DOI: 10.1093/oso/9780192858023.003.0004

than a short-sighted retreat to nationalism. China's economic statecraft, public policy (like its initial cover up of the COVID-19 outbreak in Wuhan in 2019), and authoritarian Internet manipulations lack democratic legitimacy in view of their failures to protect human rights, the rule of law, transparent governance, and non-discriminatory competition.

The negotiations leading to the 1944 Bretton Woods agreements and General Agreement on Tariffs and Trade (GATT) 1947 were dominated by the United States (US), the United Kingdom (UK), their Anglo-Saxon economic liberalism, and utilitarian trade policies. US hegemony and British colonialism contributed to the legal design of GATT as a club of like-minded market economies prioritizing market-based trade policies (eg based on tariffs rather than non-tariff barriers), principles of non-discriminatory treatment (eg in Articles I, III GATT) and reciprocal, intergovernmental negotiations.[2] The embedded liberalism underlying GATT 1947 protected the regulatory autonomy of GATT contracting parties for non-discriminatory, internal regulations (eg taxes, product and production regulation, social laws consistent with GATT Article III), border tariffs subject to reciprocally agreed tariff bindings (Articles II, XXVIII, XXVIII*bis*), border restrictions adopted for non-economic policy purposes (like public morals, health protection, and national security as provided for in Articles XX–XXI)), certain subsidies (Articles III:8, XVI), state-trading enterprises (Article XVII), free trade agreements (FTAs), customs unions, and certain colonial preferences (cf Article I.2 GATT). Since the late 1970s, the shift to Anglo-Saxon neo-liberalism led to increasing regulatory challenges from ordo-liberal EU member countries, less-developed third-world economies, and the newly emerging alliance of Brazil, Russia, India, China, and South Africa (the BRICS countries). The United States played not only a leading role in establishing the embedded liberalism underlying GATT 1947 and in the turn to neo-liberalism since about the Tokyo Round Agreements of 1979. The hegemonic power politics of the US Trump administration also initiated the changing relationship between trade and security policies since 2017, ushering in a new geo-economic order driven by geopolitical rivalries in a multipolar world, where China, Russia, Iran, and also the EU (eg because of the Nord Stream 2 gas pipeline with Russia) are targeted by US economic sanctions in order to contain perceived military and security threats.[3] The WTO crisis was caused not only by WTO governance failures like insufficient supervision of WTO appellate jurisprudence by the Dispute Settlement Body (DSB). The geopolitical rivalries, President Trump's disregard for multilateral agreements, and his neo-liberal

[2] GATT's intergovernmentalism was due, *inter alia*, to the parliamentary non-ratification of GATT 1947, its only provisional application based on a Protocol subject to grandfather clauses exempting mandatory legislation, and the US rejection of the 1948 Havana Charter for an International Trade Organization.

[3] Cf A Roberts, H Choer Moraes, and V Ferguson, Toward a Geoeconomic Order, *Journal of International Economic Law* 22 (2019), 655ff.

interest group politics (as illustrated by tax reductions, economic deregulation, and regulatory capture of the Trump administration by short-term business interests) also revealed constitutional failures undermining the SDGs and international rule of law. The new geo-economic logic and increasing industrial policy interventions in order to advance social, health, digital, supply, and military security, climate change mitigation, and other strategic objectives also drive the EU's quest for strategic autonomy, US President Biden's policies to strengthen the resilience of the American supply chains as well as China's measures aimed at fostering indigenous innovation and self-reliance. This chapter argues that trade wars and incoherent responses to global health pandemics confirm past lessons since the Second World War. The UN, Bretton Woods, and WTO governance systems cannot effectively protect the SDGs if autocratic and populist rulers disregard human rights and democratic constitutionalism. Peace, prosperity, public health, and sustainable development, like human rights, are indivisible. Yet, unlike the post-1945 trust in US leadership, Brexit and President Trump have destroyed public faith in the superiority of British and US power politics.

3.1 A New Geo-Economic Security Order?

Political scientists tend to explain Britain's leadership of a liberal trading system during the second half of the nineteenth century—and the post-1945 US leadership of the multilateral GATT/WTO trading system—by the economic and political self-interests of the hegemonic nation state. Having the largest and most efficient economy, the hegemon has the most to gain from trade liberalization, access to foreign markets, and rule-making. The economic disintegration between the two World Wars was due, *inter alia*, to a lack of hegemonic leadership for creating a multilateral trade, financial, and monetary system.[4] China's accession to the WTO in December 2001 has enabled China to become the world's largest exporting country as of 2010 and one of the world's top destinations for and the largest source of foreign direct investment. Even though China remained a rule-taker inside the WTO, it continues to develop its technological and military power to a point that the declining US relative power is widely perceived as a major cause of the US shifting its attitude to unilateral disregard for WTO rules, increasing US protectionism, and provoking President Trump's trade war restricting imports and investments from China (cf section 3.2). WTO dispute settlement rulings against US justifications of discriminatory antidumping duties, countervailing duties, safeguard measures, and other restrictions on imports of China contributed to

[4] R Keohane, *After Hegemony: Cooperation and Discord in the World Political Economy* (Princeton UP 1984); R Gilpin, *Global Political Economy: Understanding the International Economic Order* (Princeton UP 2001).

increasing US challenges of the WTO legal and dispute settlement system (sections 3.3 and 3.4). As a newly emerging trading, economic, and military power and hegemonic rival of the United States, China continues to support the multilateral WTO legal and dispute settlement system; while its compliance with most WTO rules continues to serve China's economic and strategic interests, it is increasingly becoming a rule-maker in bilateral and regional trade and economic agreements, as discussed in sections 3.5 and 3.6. The increasing cooperation between China and Russia in rejecting human rights challenges and humanitarian interventions by democratic WTO members raises the prospect of a new Cold War between democratic and authoritarian countries that reject democratic constitutionalism.

One of the first disputes under GATT Article XXIII concerned Czechoslovakia's complaint in 1948 that US restriction on exports to that country violated Articles XI:1 and XIII GATT, and they could not be justified as national security measures under Article XXI because the embargoed goods were of no military significance. The controversy was part of the larger Cold War hostility between the two countries. The US counter-argument (ie that the embargoed coalmining equipment could have military significance; for instance, if used for uranium mining) led to a majoritarian ruling of the GATT contracting parties that no violation had been established.[5] Yet, even though the post-1945 Cold War led to systemic export restrictions (eg by countries belonging to the North Atlantic Treaty Organization (NATO)) for military, nuclear, and dual-use goods, the strategic export restrictions were coordinated outside the GATT (eg in the context of the Paris-based Coordinating Committee for East-West Trade). The security exceptions in GATT Article XXI were rarely invoked in GATT Council meetings and gave rise to only a very few GATT disputes. GATT contracting parties exercised self-restraint regarding justifications of trade restrictions on grounds of national security.[6]

The admission of China (2001) and Russia (2012) to the WTO reflected this neo-liberal strategy of world peace through world trade. Increasing the gains from trade and division of labour—and limiting discriminatory protectionism by WTO rules protecting non-discriminatory market competition—were thought to raise the costs of conflict between states and to promote peaceful, mutually beneficial (win-win) cooperation. Judicial third-party adjudication for the settlement of trade and investment disputes and transnational rule of law were intended to depoliticize and stabilize economic and political cooperation. From the entry into force of the WTO Agreement in 1995 up to 2020, the more than 420 WTO panel, appellate, and arbitration findings—similar to the, by now, more than 1,100

[5] The ruling is printed in GATT Basic Instruments and Selected Documents 2 (1952) 28.

[6] Examples included Sweden, when it invoked Article XXI GATT as justification for protecting its shoe industry, and Nicaragua, when it challenged a US trade embargo targeting the Marxist Sandinista military regime; on the rarity of Article XXI invocations, see C VanGrasstek, *Trade and American Leadership. The Paradoxes of Power and Wealth from Alexander Hamilton to Donald Trump* (Harvard UP 2019), at 195ff.

publicly known investor–state arbitration (ISA) cases and related national court decisions (eg enforcing ISA awards), protected higher degrees of transnational rule of law in worldwide trade and investment relations than in any previous period. Yet, hopes that China's accession to the WTO in 2001 would lead to a global market economy with non-discriminatory market access and equal, competitive opportunities in China were progressively disappointed. As discussed in sections 3.3 and 3.4, the more some areas of trade regulation (like trade remedies, subsidies, Internet services, intellectual property rights, appellate review) became dominated by business-driven, neo-liberal interest-group politics, the stronger became the challenges to the post-war domination of international monetary, trade, and investment regulation by European and North American countries. The US Trump administration's perception of international trade as a power-oriented zero-sum game (eg criticizing China's bilateral trade surpluses as relative US losses and stealing US jobs)—and President Trump's disdain for rules-based third-party adjudication of disputes—led to progressive US assaults on the WTO legal and dispute settlement system, as discussed in sections 3.2–3.4, including invocation of national security exceptions for justifying protectionist import restrictions on steel and aluminium (rather than using safeguard or other trade remedies, whose abusive uses had already been limited by WTO dispute settlement rulings against the United States).[7]

The bestselling book by Peter Frankopan, *The Silk Roads. A New History of the World*, begins with the childhood recollection of the author that the

> accepted and lazy history of civilization ... is one where Ancient Greece begat Rome, Rome begat Christian Europe, Christian Europe begat the Renaissance, the Renaissance the Enlightenment, the Enlightenment political democracy and the industrial revolution. Industry crossed with democracy in turn yielded the United States, embodying the rights to life, liberty and the pursuit of happiness.[8]

Frankopan documents how this biased, Western vision of history based on a 'mantra of the political, cultural and moral triumph of the West' ignores many older civilizations (notably in Asia) and the dark side of European civilization (such as imperial opium wars in Asia, colonialism, genocide in Europe). After more than four centuries of colonial domination of many African, Asian, and Latin-American economies by Europeans, China's economy is expected to become larger than that of the United States by 2030. By 2060, even India's economy could surpass that of the United States. The rapid integration of China and India into the world economy

[7] On the need for stronger congressional control over executive abuses of Section 232 tariffs, see S Lincicome and I Manak, *Protectionism or National Security? The Use and Abuse of Section 232*, CATO Institute, Policy Analysis No 912, 9 March 2021.

[8] P Frankopan, *The Silk Roads. A New History of the World* (Bloomsbury 2015), at xiii.

has not only lifted the living standards of more than 2 billion people; it also complicated decision-making in the WTO and continues to shift the global balance of power towards the East.[9] The different domestic and trade policy approaches adopted by China and India (as the world's most populous democracy based on the rule of law) also entailed rivalries (like border conflicts in the Himalaya, non-participation of India in the Regional Comprehensive Economic Partnership Agreement (RCEP), and in China's Belt and Road Initiative (BRI) agreements). Notwithstanding their membership in the G20, both countries present themselves as less-developed WTO members leading the 'struggle for economic development in developing countries'.[10] Yet, like the failure of China's and India's leadership in establishing a New International Economic Order in the 1970s, their cooperation in the Doha Round negotiations for reforming the WTO trading system based on special and differential treatment (S&D) and self-selection of less-developed country status fails to convince most developed WTO member countries.

As discussed below, China's opaque practices of state capitalism, state-owned enterprises (SOEs), totalitarian control of the Internet and of foreign investments in China (eg insisting on joint ventures and technology transfers) further weakened the regulatory functions of WTO law. Together with China's huge annual trade surpluses, increasing military power, and hegemonic rivalries (eg in the South China Sea), they contributed to President Trump's initiation of a trade war against China and the increasing US criticism of WTO third-party adjudication. Economic interdependencies, global supply chains, use of Chinese technologies, and multilateral legal constraints on US power politics (including also on extraterritorial use of US economic sanctions against European NATO allies like Germany because of the EU–Russian Nord Stream 2 gas pipeline) were increasingly viewed by the US Trump administration as strategic vulnerabilities. Since 2017, the US assault on the WTO legal and dispute settlement system has disrupted WTO appellate review by reintroducing power politics. Similar to the criticism of neo-liberal investor biases in ISA practices, the support by some former WTO Appellate Board (AB) judges from the United States for neo-liberal, US trade remedies and trade policies raised questions about protectionist biases in WTO practices (section 3.4). This chapter briefly describes the rise and fall of the WTO legal and dispute settlement system from 1995 to 2020. Chapters 4–6 explain why justice (eg in the sense of impartial

[9] Cf the case studies on China's and India's attitudes towards the existing international trade, investment, and dispute settlement rules in M Sornarajah and J Wang (eds), *China, India and the International Economic Order* (CUP 2010). Due to its rule of law culture, India participated more actively in the Doha Round negotiations and in the WTO dispute settlement system than China's élite-oriented, communist decision-making culture (eg often preferring diplomatic dispute settlements avoiding adversarial judicial adjudication). While both countries began liberalizing their socialist command economies around 1980, China was comparatively more successful in promoting its economic growth and social welfare by liberalizing and developing its economy, yet without respect for rule of law and democratic governance as in India.

[10] Sornarajah and Wang (n 9), at xvi.

justification of law by agreed, procedural, and substantive principles of justice), democratic constitutionalism, and rule of law require protecting impartial WTO third-party adjudication as a precondition for rules-based, multilevel governance protecting global public goods (PGs) like sustainable development, climate change mitigation, poverty reduction, and public health for the benefit of citizens and their human rights, yet with due respect for legitimately diverse constitutional pluralism. Even were it possible under the US Biden administration to return to the rule of law in international trade relations, the new security risks of artificial intelligence, information, and communication technologies, and the new US security strategy of economic security as national security,[11] are likely to entail protectionist changes in the newly emerging, multipolar geo-economic security order.

3.2 President Trump's Return to Nationalist Mercantilism and Regulatory Capture

As announced during his election campaign in 2016, the Trump administration withdrew from the Transpacific Partnership (TPP) Agreement in 2017, discontinued the negotiations with the EU on a Transatlantic Trade and Investment Partnership (TTIP), and requested that Canada and Mexico renegotiate the North American Free Trade Agreement (NAFTA).[12] In March 2018, US President Trump invoked Section 232 of the US Trade Act for imposing—as of 1 June 2018—additional tariffs of 25 per cent on imports of steel and 10 per cent on imports of aluminium from WTO members that had not agreed to limit their exports of these products to the United States. The US Secretary of Commerce also started an investigation into auto imports, based on the same Section 232, to determine whether importation of automobiles and automobile parts was threatening US national security. In July 2018, Trump invoked Section 301 of the US Trade Act for imposing tariffs on $34 billion of imports from China in order to counter Chinese 'acts, policies and practices ... related to technology transfer, intellectual property and innovation' that the US Trade Representative (USTR) had deemed, following a nine-month investigation, to be 'unreasonable or discriminatory and burdensome or restrictive to US commerce'.[13] As China responded with retaliatory tariffs imposed on imports from the United States, in early September 2018, Trump imposed 10 per cent duties on about $200 billion worth of Chinese imports and threatened to increase the tariff rate to 25 per cent as of 2019 if no bilateral trade deal were

[11] Cf National Security Strategy of the United States, White House December 2017, at 17.

[12] On the return to mercantilism and nationalist protectionism in US trade policies under President Trump see VanGrasstek (n 6), at 427ff.

[13] For details see VanGrasstek (n 6) and EU Petersmann, The 2018 Trade Wars as a Threat to the World Trading System and to Constitutional Democracies, *Trade, Law and Development* X (2018), 179–225.

reached with China. The latter retaliated again by imposing additional tariffs of 5 per cent and 10 per cent on imports of goods from the United States worth $60 billion. In response, President Trump imposed additional import duties on imports from China worth up to $350 billion. In August 2018, Trump also imposed discriminatory trade restrictions against Turkey in response to Turkey's detainment of an American evangelical pastor on terrorism charges. Both the discriminatory US sanctions and the Chinese retaliatory trade restrictions violated WTO obligations (eg under Articles I and II GATT, 23 Dispute Settlement Understanding (DSU)).

In response to the US import tariffs on aluminium and steel, many affected WTO members—like Canada, China, the EU, India, Mexico, Norway, Russia, and Turkey—invoked WTO dispute settlement procedures on the ground that, *inter alia*, the discriminatory US import restrictions were inconsistent with WTO law (eg Articles I and II GATT) and could not be legally justified on national security grounds (Article XXI GATT) or as safeguard measures (Article XIX GATT). These WTO members also adopted retaliatory suspensions of market access commitments vis-à-vis the United States, which some of these WTO members justified by invoking Article 8 of the WTO Agreement on Safeguards based on the argument that US import tariffs on aluminium and steel had been introduced for economic rather than national security reasons. China criticized the discriminatory US import tariffs imposed under Section 301 as a trade war violating WTO law but it did not justify its retaliatory tariffs by invoking specific WTO rules. China and the United States invoked the WTO dispute settlement procedures for challenging the consistency of their reciprocal trade sanctions with WTO rules. The breakdown of the WTO AB system in December 2019 enabled the United States to prevent the adoption of adverse WTO panel findings by appealing 'into the void' of a dysfunctional AB.[14]

President Trump's protectionist use of unilateral import restrictions and politically motivated trade sanctions as instruments for imposing bilateral deals aimed at reducing US trade deficits were influenced by rent-seeking, domestic interest group pressures (eg from US steel industries) offering political support in exchange for protection rents (like WTO-inconsistent transfers of income from US anti-dumping and countervailing duties on imports of steel to the protected US industries). The neo-liberal interest group politics and regulatory capture of discretionary US trade policy powers[15]—without requesting Congressional approval for

[14] This is due to Article 16:4 of the DSU, according to which the report of the panel shall not be considered for adoption by the DSB until after completion of the appeal. On details of the US–China trade wars, see P Blustein, *Schism. China, America and the Fracturing of the Global Trading System* (Center for International Governance Innovation 2019).

[15] *Neo-liberalism* refers not only to Chicago School economics as practised by Prime Minister Thatcher, US President Reagan, and many other governments since the late 1970s, ie strong preferences for liberalizing market access barriers, deregulation, privatization, and financialization of the economy so as to empower self-regulatory markets (and the *homo economicus*) as spontaneous information, coordination, and sanctioning mechanisms. The 1979 Tokyo Round Agreements on anti-dumping and

most of these import restrictions imposed by the US executive—reflected long US traditions of public–private partnerships (eg in the legal design of import restrictions), rent-seeking business lobbying influencing economic rule-making (eg discriminatory import protection for cotton, textiles, steel, and car manufacturers), appointment of long-standing US lobbyists to the political positions of USTR (eg Robert Lighthizer) and US WTO representative (Ambassador Shea), tax evasion by multinational corporations (eg through profit-shifting to tax havens), increasing US politicization of judicial appointments and judicial remedies inside and outside the United States,[16] and social inequality inside the United States justified by a money-driven focus on individual utility maximization.[17] Business-driven US safeguard measures, anti-dumping and countervailing duty practices—and their legal contestation in WTO dispute settlement jurisprudence—were among the main motives for the US assault on the WTO legal and dispute settlement system.[18]

Following the UK's 2016 referendum on leaving the EU and the election of US President Trump, the UK and US governments increasingly relied on executive powers for erecting trade barriers and withdrawing from multilateral agreements (eg terminating EU membership, abandoning the EU–US draft agreement on a TTIP). President Trump unilaterally declared the WTO Doha Round negotiations

countervailing duty measures also contributed to the worldwide introduction of US-style trade remedy rules and lobbying practices financed by import-competing industries in order to benefit from protection rents (eg domestic price increases made possible by safeguards, anti-dumping, and countervailing duties restricting imports) at the expense of general consumer welfare. The regulatory capture was illustrated, *inter alia*, by the fact that both USTR Lighthizer and US WTO Ambassador Shea had previously worked as lobbyists for US industries; they defended the maintenance of US trade remedy measures (such as transferring revenue from anti-dumping and countervailing duties to the protected US industries) that had been found to be inconsistent with WTO law by WTO dispute settlement bodies. On the interest group influence on US trade policies, which became institutionalized in US trade policy decision-making by the creation of the advisory committee system that favoured regulatory capture of ever more trade regulation (eg on cotton, textiles, steel, aluminium, trade remedies, labour, intellectual property, environmental, and national security issues). See SN Lester, 'Waiting for Cordell Hull' in M Kolsky Lewis, H Nakagawa, RJ Neuwirth, CB Picker, and PT Stoll (eds), *A Post-WTO International Legal Order. Utopian, Dystopian and other Scenarios* (Springer 2020), 57–70.

[16] Cf A Cohen *Supreme Inequality: The Supreme Court's Fifty-Year Battle for a More Unjust America* (Penguin Press 2019). On the arbitrary politicization of the WTO AB jurisprudence—as reflected in the USTR *Report on the Appellate Body of the WTO* (Washington February 2020)—see sections 3.3 and 3.4.

[17] On the perverse, social effects (like rising mortality of middle-aged, white Americans without college education) of the money-driven US political and health system, and racial discrimination, see A Case and A Deaton, *Deaths of Despair and the Future of Capitalism* (Princeton UP 2020). On the need for socially more inclusive definitions of economic policy goals (eg in terms of promoting human capacities, decent work conditions and satisfying basic needs of everybody), see G Sperling, *Economic Dignity* (Penguin 2020). On why citizens convincingly demand more inclusive social contracts offering better protection against health, environmental, economic, and social emergencies, see M Shafik, *What Do We Owe Each Other? Social Contracts for the 21st Century* (The Bodley Head 2021).

[18] Former US Congressman and WTO AB chairman J Bacchus interpreted US President Trump's blocking of the WTO AB system and US violations of the (according to Trump) 'terrible WTO rules' as an American assault on the rule of law in world trade; cf J Bacchus, *Might Unmakes Right: The American Assault on the Rule of Law in World Trade*, CIGI Papers No 173, May 2018 https://www.cigionline.org/sites/default/files/documents/Paper%20no.173.pdf).

closed. US government positions in the commerce and economic field increasingly reflected US business interests (eg in disrupting Organisation for Economic Co-operation and Development (OECD) negotiations on a global tax framework for technology and Internet companies, unilaterally sanctioning Russia's gas pipeline for supplying gas to EU countries, threatening illegal tariffs on automobile imports from Europe). Even though US technology companies (like Apple, Facebook, Google, and other tech giants) enjoy dominant market positions and avoid taxes in many countries, US antitrust laws and tax avoidance rules were not effectively enforced.

The US Court of International Trade, in a judgment of 14 July 2020, began annulling some of the discriminatory trade sanctions imposed by executive orders of President Trump on the basis of alleged security interests (Section 232).[19] As trade restrictions are about redistributing domestic income from consumers to import-competing producers, economists explain the trade wars and discriminatory bilateral trade deals of President Trump in terms of welfare-reducing, domestic governance failures, notably due to conflicts 'between the very rich and everyone else'[20] and political deals offering economic rents to domestic producers in exchange for their political support. John Bolton's book on his experiences inside the Trump administration described US President Trump as 'erratic and impulsive', 'stunningly uninformed', 'irrational', and 'a danger for the republic'. US policies were also influenced by President Trump's political and business self-interests and by his granting of *ad hoc* exceptions for domestic firms from the US import restrictions on steel and aluminium.[21] Similarly, the abuse of Presidential powers of pardon to the benefit of Trump's former advisors, family members (eg Mr Trump's son-in-law's criminally convicted father, Charles Kushner), and dozens of other people convicted of crimes (many of whom had a personal relationship to President Trump) was criticized by Harvard law professors Jack Goldsmith and Laurence Tribe as possibly illegal efforts 'to place Presidents and their cronies above the

[19] US Court of International Trade (USITC), Slip Op 20-98, *Transpacific Steel LLP v US et al.*, Court No 19-00009, judgment of 14 July 2020; cf S Charnovitz and G Hufbauer, Landmark court decision limits presidential trade restrictions, at https://voxeu.org/content/landmark-court-decision-limits-presidential-trade-restrictions. According to the *Financial Times* of 5 October 2020, there are now more than 3,500 lawsuits by US companies pending in the USICT, which challenge US tariffs on imports from China imposed by executive orders of President Trump. In April 2021, the same USITC annulled additional national security tariffs on steel and aluminium products of President Trump.

[20] Cf M Wolf, 'What trade wars tell us', *Financial Times* 18 June 2020: 'Trade war is often presented as a war between countries. It is not: it is a conflict mainly between bankers and owners of financial assets on the one side and ordinary households on the other—between the very rich and everyone else ... the overall balance in goods and services is explained by savings, investment and capital flows, not by bilateral trade balances, as Donald Trump imagines' (summarizing the conclusions of M Klein and M Pettis, *Trade Wars Are Class Wars* (Yale UP 2020), arguing that the recent financial, debt, and trade policy crises in leading economies can only be understood as pathologies of domestic politics, where wealthy people do not spend what they earn and their savings glut leads to underconsumption resulting in trade and financial imbalances).

[21] Cf A Williams, 'Bolton says Trump poses a danger for the republic', *Financial Times* 22 June 2020; J Bolton, *The Room Where It Happened: A White House Memoire* (Simon & Schuster 2020).

law'.[22] President Trump's hegemonic nationalism ('America First'), his embrace of authoritarian dictators, and his withdrawal of the United States from more than a dozen of multilateral UN agreements entailed US disruption of worldwide and regional organizations (like the WTO, World Health Organization (WHO), NAFTA, NATO). US leadership for multilevel governance of global PGs (like limiting climate change, protecting public health) and for democratic reforms was replaced by power politics and populist recriminations inside the United States and some BRICS countries governed by authoritarian rulers (like China and Russia).

3.3 The US Destruction of the WTO Appellate Body

Article III of the WTO Agreement distinguishes three functions of the WTO as a forum for (i) further negotiations among its members concerning their multilateral trade negotiations; (ii) the settlement of disputes pursuant to the WTO DSU; and (iii) the facilitation and monitoring of the implementation of WTO rules and deliberations on trade policies. Since the beginning of the Doha Round negotiations in 2001, the 164 WTO members reached agreement on very few new trade agreements (like the 2013 Trade Facilitation Agreement). The increasing number of WTO dispute settlement proceedings prompted the US Trump administration to criticize the imbalance between the unsuccessful negotiation function and the very active dispute settlement system of the WTO, where WTO dispute settlement bodies progressively clarified the contested meaning of WTO rules through (quasi) judicial procedures and successfully challenged violations of WTO legal disciplines. In view of President Trump's preference for bilateral deals and his disdain for what he called the 'terrible' WTO agreements, the US began challenging judicial functions of WTO dispute settlement bodies, their systemic interpretation methodologies based on the customary rules of treaty interpretation, the WTO dispute settlement system as an ordo-liberal guardian of non-discriminatory conditions of competition (eg as reflected in the GATT/WTO jurisprudence interpreting GATT/WTO rules as protecting non-discriminatory conditions of competition), and the WTO Agreement's separation of legislative, executive, and judicial powers as a restraint on neo-liberal interest-group politics (as reflected in the WTO jurisprudence limiting discriminatory abuses of WTO trade remedy disciplines). The differences between the neo-liberal power politics and interest group politics of the US Trump administration and European ordo-liberalism became also evident in:

[22] Cf L Tribe, 'Donald Trump's pardons must not obstruct justice. Abuses of constitutional clemency power should be investigated and prosecuted', *Financial Times* 26 December 2020 (with further references to the *Financial Times* 24 December 2020).

- the illegal US blocking of WTO AB vacancies since 2017, resulting in the incapacity of the AB, since 11 December 2019, to accept new appeals;
- the 2020 US Report on the AB, which perceives WTO law as an instrument of US power politics and disregards the (quasi)judicial mandates of WTO dispute settlement bodies and their (quasi)judicial methodologies;[23] and in
- the non-participation of the United States in the EU initiative for the Multi-Party Interim Appeal Arbitration (MPIA) Arrangement under Article 25 DSU, which became effective on 30 April 2020 for appellate review among twenty-three WTO members until the WTO AB can resume its lawful functions, as prescribed by parliaments when they approved the WTO Agreement.[24]

According to Article 17.2 DSU, AB vacancies shall be filled as they arise. Since 2017, the United States has blocked all appointments to the WTO AB ushering in the incapacitation of the AB since 11 December 2019, when only one single AB member remained in office. Due to US threats of blocking approval of the WTO budget, WTO members also accepted a drastic reduction of the WTO AB budget and the dissolution of the AB's legal staff (whose director was transferred to another WTO Secretariat division). The legal justifications by the Trump administration of its blocking of WTO AB nominations insist on US interpretations of WTO rules and US criticism of AB findings without any evidence that legal interpretations by the AB violated the customary rules of treaty interpretation or the (quasi)judicial AB mandate for impartial, independent, and prompt third-party adjudication through quasi-automatic adoption of WTO panel and AB reports by the DSB.[25] The 2020 USTR Report—notwithstanding its valid criticism of some WTO rules and dispute settlement practices (eg that the AB no longer consulted with the parties when deciding to disregard the ninety-day deadline in Article 17.5 DSU)—suffers from legal biases and incorrect claims such as:

[23] See USTR, *Report on the Appellate Body of the WTO*, Washington, DC, February 2020, (https://ustr.gov/about-us/policy-offices/press-office/press-releases/2020/february/ustr-issues-report-wto-appellate-body).

[24] The text to the MPIA was notified to the WTO in WTO document JOB/DSB/1/Add.12 of 30 April 2020 and was subsequently accepted also by other WTO members. G Sacerdoti, The Authority of 'Precedent' in International Adjudication: The Contentious Case of the WTO Appellate Body's Practice, *The Law and Practice of International Courts and Tribunals* 19 (2020), 497–514), quotes USTR Lighthizer as having stated in the US Congress that he would not regret the disappearance of the AB.

[25] For a detailed refutation of the false USTR claims concerning (i) the continued service of AB members after the expiration of their term (ie the US disregard for Rule 15 in the AB Working Procedures); (ii) the ninety-day deadline for circulating AB reports (ie the US disregard for inherent judicial powers for due process of law if WTO members make compliance with deadlines objectively impossible); (iii) AB review of facts; and (iv) of municipal law to the extent that such panel findings include legal qualifications; and the false US claims concerning (v) alleged advisory opinions in and (vi) precedential effects of AB reports, see J Lehne, *Crisis at the WTO: Is the Blocking of Appointments to the WTO Appellate Body by the United States Legally Justified?* (Grossmann 2019).

- US denial of (quasi)judicial functions of WTO third-party adjudication, even though numerous WTO publications, WTO dispute settlement reports, and statements by WTO panellists, AB members, and WTO arbitrators over more than twenty years acknowledged the (quasi)judicial mandates of WTO dispute settlement bodies (ie WTO panels, the AB, and the quasi-automatic adoption of their reports by the DSB);
- US disregard for judicial AB arguments in the performance of the DSU's mandate 'to clarify the existing provisions of those agreements in accordance with customary rules of interpretation of public international law' (Article 3 DSU), for instance whenever the AB found compliance with the time limit of ninety days (Article 17.5 DSU)—which was imposed by US negotiators in 1993 notwithstanding the widespread criticism that no other court seems to be limited by such an unreasonably short time limit—impossible to reconcile with the other AB tasks (eg due to illegal US blocking of the filling of AB vacancies, large numbers of pending AB proceedings, inadequate administrative WTO resources for translation and other support services);
- contradictory USTR claims that AB legal findings against the US violated the DSU prohibition to 'add or diminish the rights and obligations in the covered agreements' (Article 3.2 DSU)—even if the AB had justified these legal findings on the basis of the customary rules of treaty interpretation and its (quasi)judicial mandate—notwithstanding the USTR's regular support of AB reports accepting creative WTO interpretations advocated by the USTR as a legal complainant;
- US description of US 'zeroing practices' as a 'common-sense method of calculating the extent of dumping'[26] even if their protectionist biases had been consistently condemned by the AB and DSB as violations of the WTO obligations of fair price comparisons (which are hardly mentioned in the USTR report);
- one-sided focus on WTO texts as interpreted by US negotiators without regard to the customary law and DSU requirements to clarify the meaning of the often indeterminate WTO provisions with due regard also to WTO legal texts revealing the context, object, and purpose of WTO provisions and the explicitly recognized systemic character of what the WTO Agreement calls 'this multilateral trading system' (Preamble) and its dispute settlement system (Article 3 DSU);
- denigration of AB members as 'three unelected and unaccountable persons'[27] whose 'overreaching violates the basic principles of the United States Government' (USTR Report, Introduction), notwithstanding the election of every AB member through consensus decisions of WTO member

[26] USTR Report (n 23), at 2.
[27] USTR Report (n 23), at 8, 13.

governments (including the United States), their (quasi)judicial mandate, and the approval of WTO agreements (including the DSU) by the US government and US Congress;
- insulting claims that the AB Secretariat had weakened the WTO dispute settlement system by not respecting WTO rights and obligations.[28]

The USTR Report acknowledges that its purpose 'is not to propose solutions'.[29] The USTR Report repeats what the US ambassador had stated in DSB meetings since 2017: 'WTO Members must come to terms with the failings of the Appellate Body set forth in this Report if we are to achieve lasting and effective reform of the WTO dispute settlement system'.[30] Yet, nothing suggests that if WTO members should accept the false US claims of the AB's 'persistent overreaching … contrary to the Appellate Body's limited mandate', and 'the Appellate Body's failure to follow the agreed rules', the US would be willing to comply with its DSU obligation of filling AB vacancies as they arise and return to the WTO third-party adjudication, appellate review, and customary rules of treaty interpretation (including judicial interpretations in the prompt settlement of WTO disputes) as prescribed in the DSU. Past WTO members' appeasement of false USTR claims (eg in Ambassador Walker's informal mediation proposal for overcoming the WTO dispute settlement crises) never changed the USTR's refusal to return to WTO third-party adjudication as prescribed in the DSU. So far, the USTR has failed in its efforts at destroying the social and legal legitimacy of AB jurisprudence, even if the previously celebrated 'crown jewel' of the WTO dispute settlement system has been stolen by the USTR without any intention of giving it back. Paradoxically, compared with other WTO members, the USTR seems to have been the most successful litigator in past WTO dispute settlement practices. Yet, it remains isolated in its efforts at delegitimizing the AB; up to 2020, most AB findings continued being supported and implemented by the WTO membership.

The Economic and Trade Agreement signed by China and the United States on 15 January 2020 provides for discriminatory Chinese commitments to buy US products, discriminatory US import tariffs and trade restrictions (eg targeting Chinese technology companies) without third-party adjudication. This bilateral opt out by the two largest trading nations from their WTO legal and dispute settlement obligations seems to be the policy option preferred by those USTR officials who pursue additional bilateral US trade deals.[31] In June 2020, the USTR publicly considered the US withdrawal from the WTO Agreement on Government Procurement—and unbinding US tariff and market access commitments in the

[28] USTR Report (n 23), at 120.
[29] USTR Report (n 23), at 121.
[30] USTR Report, Introduction.
[31] Cf 'Superpower showdown—trading blows in a new cold war', *Financial Times* 4 July 2020 (citing USTR Lighthizer as publicly stating: 'The only fucking arbitrator I trust is me').

WTO—in order to use power asymmetries for rebalancing US trade deficits through bilateral reciprocity negotiations, as advocated by Trump's trade policy advisor Peter Navarro.[32] The US–China trade deal provides for dispute settlement through unilateral USTR determinations; this unilateralism illustrates the hegemonic trade mercantilism which USTR Lighthizer would like to impose on the rest of the world. The ever more frequent disregard by the Trump administration of WTO rules (eg GATT Articles I, II, and III) and dispute settlement procedures, the unwillingness of other WTO members to protect the WTO appellate review system by majority decisions on the filling of AB vacancies (as, arguably, prescribed by Article IX:1 WTO Agreement),[33] and the dissolution of the AB Secretariat inside the WTO in spring 2020 (following US threats to block adoption of the WTO budget) illustrate a progressive *de facto* breakdown of rule of law in the WTO trading system.

The MPIA agreement presented by the EU on behalf of its 27 EU member states and 21 other WTO members in the DSB meeting on 29 June 2020 provides for arbitration procedures under Article 25 DSU as a temporary substitute for appeals pending the incapacity of the AB, which no longer has the minimum of 3 members necessary to review appeals due to the continued US blocking of Mexico's regular requests—on behalf of 121 WTO members—to initiate the nominations of the six vacant AB positions. Longer-term appeasement of the US destruction of the WTO legal and dispute settlement systems would have systemic repercussions far beyond the WTO. Without a multilateral WTO dispute settlement system, not only the UN goals for sustainable development, climate change mitigation, and future WTO negotiations but also the US efforts at inducing market-oriented reforms in China's totalitarian state capitalism are bound to fail. Citizens all over the world will suffer from neglect of the ordo-liberal task of limiting governance failures and constitutional failures in multilateral governance of transnational PGs.

[32] On the disagreement of most economists with Trump's trade theory (eg rejecting multilateralism and bilateral trade deficits) as advocated by his main trade policy advisor P Navarro, see eg A Lowrey, 'The "Madman" behind Trump's trade theory', *The Atlantic* December 2018 (https://www.theatlantic.com/magazine/archive/2018/12/peter-navarro-trump-trade/573913/); M Wolf, 'Dealing with America's trade follies', *Financial Times* 20 April 2017. In November 2020, the US trade deficit in goods and services rose 8 per cent to $68.1 billion, its highest since 2006 (the US trade deficit in goods hit $85.5 billion, its highest on record). China's trade surplus hit its highest ever monthly level in December 2020, as the country's exports continued to boom during the COVID-19 health pandemic.

[33] On the legal duties under Article IX:1 WTO Agreement to overcome illegal abuses of veto powers in the DSB by recourse to administrative majority voting on the filling of AB vacancies see Chapter 6 and EU Petersmann, 'Between "Member-Driven Governance" and "Judicialization": Constitutional and Judicial Dilemmas in the World Trading System' in C-f Lo, J Nakagawa, and Tsai-fang Chen (eds), *The Appellate Body of the WTO and its Reform* (Springer 2020), 15–42, at 33ff.

3.4 US Politicization of the AB Jurisprudence

The unprecedented and unconvincing attacks against the WTO AB in the 2020 USTR Report and in a speech by the former WTO AB member Tom Graham on 5 March 2020,[34] the UK's rejection of any control by the European Court of Justice (CJEU) or another court over the EU–UK Brexit Trade Agreement, and the limitation of investment adjudication in the United States/Mexico/Canada (USMCA) FTA are reminders of the frequent politicization of judges (eg their political appointments) in many Anglo-Saxon jurisdictions. Court houses in all 164 WTO members are decorated by statues symbolizing justice by the blindfolded figure of *Justitia* holding a scale and a sword. The two statues representing Justice and Peace, which flank the main entrance to the WTO's headquarter at Lake Geneva, recall what WTO publications, the International Chamber of Commerce, and also many US lawyers have long emphasized: rules-based multilateral trading systems play a crucial role in promoting peace. In his book *Supreme Injustice: Slavery in the Nation's Highest Court*, US history professor Paul Finkelman recalls how the 'slavery jurisprudence' of the three most important, pre-Civil War US Supreme Court justices (John Marshall, Roger Taney, and Joseph Story) contributed to the US Civil War responding to a systemic hostility in US law to human rights and social justice.[35] US law professor Richard H Fallon, in *Law and Legitimacy in the Supreme Court*,[36] concurs with other US constitutional lawyers that the politicization of the US Supreme Court judges and judgments calls into question the legitimacy and reputation of the Court. Recent critics of the US Supreme Court, like Adam Cohen, in *Supreme Inequality: The Supreme Court's Fifty-Year Battle for a More Unjust America*, point to social injustices, which the Court's jurisprudence continues to cause by often protecting powerful rather than vulnerable interests.[37] Just as the US government blocked the nomination of NAFTA panel members in order to avoid third-party adjudication of most of its trade disputes with Canada and Mexico, the US blocking of the nomination of WTO AB members reflected the preferences of the US Trump administration for political rather than judicial settlement of WTO disputes in view of the WTO jurisprudence challenging, *inter alia*, US trade remedy measures and US trade sanctions against other countries. The politicization of US criticism of the AB jurisprudence is also illustrated by the contradictory speeches given by former WTO AB member Tom Graham.

[34] Text published in *International Economic Law and Policy* Blog (Washington, DC) of 9 March 2020.
[35] P Finkelman, *Supreme Injustice: Slavery in the Nation's Highest Court* (Harvard UP 2018), at 76ff.
[36] RH Fallon, *Law and Legitimacy in the Supreme Court* (Harvard UP 2018), 155ff.
[37] Cohen (n 16), 309ff.

3.4.1 Contradictory Pronouncements by AB Member Tom Graham

Graham is one of Washington's best-known trade remedy lawyers. He served on the AB from 2011 until 10 December 2019. On 6 February 2013, he gave a public speech, 'It Sure Looks Different from the Inside: Deciding International Disputes at the WTO', at Hofstra University Law School in the United States,[38] in which he emphasized, *inter alia*:

- AB members, 'although they don't call us that, are in effect judges, on what is in effect the highest appeals court for the rules of global trade ... applying a legal craft'; 'it is as craftsmen—not statesmen—that we work together to get it right'; 'we are the final arbiters of what the rules of international trade mean';
- the AB staff 'serves the Appellate Body as a whole—that is, Members don't have their own law clerks—which contributes to the sense of group commitment and collegiality, that is part of our tradition'; 'the sense of responsibility and dedication to the institution of my fellow Members have been enormously impressive, as has been the extraordinary ability and dedication of our truly great multinational staff';
- 'No decision of the Appellate Body has ever been overturned by the WTO Dispute Settlement Body—the committee of the whole WTO membership that oversees us'; 'losing governments have complied with all but a very small handful of our decisions in 110 cases over the past 18-year history of the Appellate Body. In terms of the percentage of disputes resolved successfully, and the record of compliance, this is perhaps the most successful international dispute settlement system in the history of the world.'
- 'As a practical matter, we have the final word not only in deciding cases but also in creating a body of jurisprudence for this global trade institution that is still new in the sense of the usual timeframe for creating international law.'

In his speech 'The Rise (and Demise?) of the WTO Appellate Body' on 5 March 2020,[39] back in Washington DC after the end of his term as an AB member, Graham contradicted his legal findings in his 2013 speech, for instance by:

- criticizing 'an orthodoxy of viewpoint about the role of the Appellate Body as a self-anointed international court, with much broader authority to

[38] See the text at: https://pdfs.semanticscholar.org/f76f/889303add145bdcaad7d7aa4dc13bc45f5a3.pdf.

[39] Cf H Gao, It Sure Looks Different from the Inside, and Now the Outside Too (or 'Graham on Graham'), *International Economic Law and Policy* Blog (Washington, DC) of 11 March 2020. The text of Graham's 2020 speech was published in *International Economic Law and Policy* Blog (Washington, DC) of 9 March 2020.

over-reach the rules and create judge-made law than I thought was permitted by the WTO agreements, or intended by the negotiators who created them'; as a result, 'the Appellate Body acting like a court ... was not accountable to anyone'; 'the negotiating history strongly indicates that (the AB) was intended not as an international court, but as a check on occasional egregious mistakes by panels';

- proposing to '[p]rohibit anyone other than the team—deciders, and staff working directly on a case—from discussing the case' ('no private lobbying of individual deciders by staff leadership not part of the team on the case');
- 'Belief in a single, correct interpretation, and seeking it through expanded analyses, encouraged gap filling and overreach. It made the Appellate Body strain to look for that "one correct" interpretation instead of asking whether the panel made a serious error, whether the challenged measure was prohibited by the rules as written';
- stretching 'the words of agreed text, and to stretch decisions beyond merely resolving a particular dispute so as to create a body of jurisprudence, or to head off future disputes, (was) beyond the Appellate Body's mandate'; 'an undue adherence to precedent ... bake[s] in mistakes'.

According to Graham, his criticism of 2020 reflects his seven years of practical experiences as an AB member. He said: 'increasingly as I saw things from the inside, I mostly agreed with what has been ... the overall view of the United States as to the Appellate Body's proper role as negotiated by governments and written into the WTO Dispute Settlement Understanding. And I mostly agreed with the US critique of the Appellate Body's departure from that proper role.'[40] Yet, neither the USTR's denial of (quasi)judicial WTO dispute settlement functions nor the USTR's claims of the AB exceeding its powers by violating the DSU prohibitions of 'add[ing] to or diminish[ing] the rights and obligations provided in the covered agreements' (Articles 3.2 and 19.2 DSU) are convincing:

- Even though 'hidden in plain sight', WTO law prescribes impartial, independent, and compulsory third-party adjudication of WTO disputes. Notwithstanding the deliberate avoidance, at the insistence of USTR negotiators in 1993, of references to 'judges', 'courts', and 'adjudication' in the DSU treaty provisions, the (quasi)judicial dispute settlement mandate is emphasized in the DSU (again, 'hidden in plain sight'), in WTO working procedures for WTO panellists, AB members, and arbitrators, in numerous WTO dispute settlement reports, annual AB reports, official WTO publications, hundreds of books, and thousands of articles published by WTO lawyers over the past

[40] See 4–5 of this 2020 speech (n 39).

twenty-five years. For years, even the official WTO badge given to AB members by the WTO Secretariat used the title 'judge' (until this administrative practice was terminated by a WTO Deputy Director-General from the United States).

- All practising WTO adjudicators (panellists, AB members, arbitrators) and WTO litigators representing WTO member governments (except some USTR lawyers and their trade remedy clientele) have consistently acknowledged the (quasi)judicial duties of independent, impartial, prompt settlement of WTO disputes through, *inter alia*, clarifications of 'the existing provisions of those agreements in accordance with customary rules of interpretation of public international law' (Article 3 DSU). In his 2013 speech, Graham convincingly described these tasks of AB members as 'judges applying a legal craft—not statesmen'.[41] As all AB reports have been (quasi)automatically adopted by negative consensus decisions of the DSB, their legal interpretations and clarifications of WTO rights and obligations—including interpretation as: (i) a process of cognition (eg of the common intentions of the law-maker as declared in the legal texts, whose words may have different meanings); (ii) an act of volition and choice by the interpreter constrained by the customary rules of treaty interpretation; and (iii) as an 'authoritative rendering of the meaning of the applicable rules of law' for the settlement of the specific dispute[42]—have been exclusively determined by the AB, even if the legally binding nature of the dispute settlement rulings derives from the adoption of panel and AB reports by the DSB.
- As explained by the AB in its long-standing jurisprudence, the WTO legal interpretations clarifying WTO provisions in conformity with the customary rules of treaty interpretation—as prescribed in Article 3 DSU—cannot simultaneously violate the DSU prohibitions (inserted into the draft DSU in 1993 at the request of US negotiators) of 'add[ing] to or diminish[ing] the rights and obligations provided in the covered agreements' (Articles 3.2 and 19.2 DSU).[43] Having served myself as secretary to the Uruguay Round Negotiating Group 13 that elaborated the DSU, I recall that this same legal reservation was expressed during the drafting of Articles 3 and 19 DSU when these DSU provisions were inserted into the draft text upon the insistence of the USTR even though—as pointed out by other negotiators—no similar provisions exist

[41] See https://pdfs.semanticscholar.org/f76f/889303add145bdcaad7d7aa4dc13bc45f5a3.pdf, p 11.

[42] On these three dimensions of legal interpretation, see G Abi-Saab, '"Introduction" in A Meta-Question' in G Abi-Saab, K Keith, G Marceau, and C Marquet (eds), *Evolutionary Interpretation and International Law* (Hart 2019), 7–12.

[43] Cf AB Report, WT/DS110/AB/R, *Chile-Alcoholic Beverages* (2000), para 79. For an explanation of the interpretative approaches of the AB, see P Van den Bossche and W Zdouc, *The Law and Policy of the World Trade Organization. Text, Cases and Materials* (4th edn, CUP 2017), 190ff.

in the founding texts for other international courts and dispute settlement bodies.

3.4.2 Tensions between the Washington Consensus and the Geneva Consensus

Graham's justification, as a trade remedy lawyer back in Washington, DC, of his support for the lack of respect for the AB by the Trump administration[44] remains difficult to reconcile with his support—as an AB judge—for his previous judicial tasks. As an AB judge in Geneva, Graham was legally required and institutionally pressured to construe the WTO agreements impartially and independently 'in accordance with customary rules of interpretation of public international law' (Article 3.2 DSU). The conclusion of Graham's 2020 speech in Washington, DC after the end of his judicial tenure—'[t]he Appellate Body is gone and it is not returning'[45]—flatters the illegal power politics by the USTR and offers incentives for Washington's trade remedy lobbyists to continue WTO-inconsistent trade remedy practices (eg of transferring revenue from illegal US dumping and countervailing duties to the protected US industries), but it fails to convince the more than 120 WTO members requesting, at each DSB meeting, to proceed to the filling of AB vacancies. The contradictory reasoning of Graham offers a taste of how contradictory WTO dispute settlement practices risk becoming without appellate review of panel reports pursuant to Article 17 DSU. Graham suggests in his 2020 speech that the AB should limit itself to reviewing whether the panel made a serious error without creating a body of jurisprudence or to head off future disputes. Such a limitation of AB review would not only be inconsistent with the text of the DSU as interpreted by the AB and all WTO members for twenty-five years. It would also undermine the central DSU objective of 'providing security and predictability to the multilateral trading system' in the 'prompt settlement' of WTO disputes through quasi-judicial clarifications of 'the existing provisions of those agreements in accordance with customary rules of interpretation of public international law' (Article 3.2 DSU).

US government pressures on US AB members to act patriotically in support of US legal positions, and US opposition to reappointments of former AB members from the United States (like Merit Janow and Jennifer Hillman) after they concurred with AB findings against the United States, reflect long-standing US traditions—also of the US Trump administration, as illustrated by its hasty appointment of another conservative US Supreme Court judge just a few days before

[44] See his short reply on the *International Economic Law and Policy* Blog (Washington, DC) of 11 March 2020: https://ielp.worldtradelaw.net/2020/03/it-sure-looks-different-from-the-inside-and-now-the-outside-too-or-graham-on-graham.html?.

[45] See n 39, at p 6.

the 3 November 2020 US presidential elections—of politicizing the appointment of judges and the exercise of judicial powers. The WTO AB crisis, and the US refusal of accepting the compulsory jurisdiction of any other international court (like the International Court of Justice, the International Tribunal for the Law of the Sea, the International Criminal Court, the Inter-American Court of Human Rights), reflect this politicization of independent, impartial third-party adjudication by American interest group politics. The Washington DC speech of former AB member Graham seems to confirm two important policy lessons:

- the rights-based Geneva consensus, as described by former WTO Director-General Pascal Lamy[46] and embodied in the AB jurisprudence, protects a higher degree of institutionalized public reason than the money-driven Washington consensus; and
- the three psychological principles of thinking automatically (eg fast and spontaneous rather than deliberative and reasonable slow thinking), thinking socially (eg adjusting to social contexts of corruption) and thinking with context- and culture-specific, mental models (like rent-seeking in under-regulated financial and trade-remedy industries), as described by 2017 Nobel Prize-winning economist Richard Taler,[47] shape the political discourse and neo-liberal cost–benefit calculations of Washington's trade remedy lawyers like USTR Lighthizer and former AB member Graham. The financial and political influence of US corporate interests on US elections and economic rule-making is increasingly acknowledged as a threat to US democracy.[48]

Fortunately, among the twenty-seven AB members since 1995, Graham remained the only one who seemed to be proud of pleading for the destruction of what he himself praised in 2013 as the most successful international dispute settlement system in the history of the world. History confirms that legal civilizations evolve dialectically; they never remain guaranteed, unless citizens defend PG and public reason and resist power politics. The DSU and its AB system can certainly be improved, even if the DSU reform negotiations in special DSB sessions since 1998 have so far eluded any agreements. Neither the 164 WTO members nor their citizens have reasonable self-interest in destroying the uniquely successful AB system of the WTO. The reform proposals by Graham (eg for disregarding the customary methods of treaty interpretation and the principle of collegiality practised in AB

[46] Cf P Lamy, *The Geneva Consensus. Making Trade Work for All* (CUP 2013).

[47] On these three principles, see *World Development Report 2015:* Mind, Society and Behavior (World Bank 2015) (discussing rational choice, behavioural economics, public choice, and deliberative democracy theories explaining how individuals, institutions, and societies often adopt unreasonable decisions, laws, and social practices).

[48] See SN Lester (n 15) and A Schiffrin (ed), *Media Capture. How Money, Digital Platforms and Governments Control the News* (Columbia UP 2021).

deliberations) would further undermine the WTO dispute settlement system; in any judicial system, interpretative methods—within the constraints prescribed by the applicable law—remain a matter for each individual judge to decide, as long as each judge adopts a legally consistent method in good faith and remains open to modifying her interpretive method in response to the judicial arguments of her colleagues.[49]

3.5 China's Totalitarian State Capitalism and Illegal US–China Trade Wars

China's accession to the WTO in 2001, like Russia's accession in 2012, was influenced by the expectation that its WTO commitments for trade liberalization and market-conforming trade policy instruments would offer non-discriminatory trade opportunities to all other WTO members. This importance of market-oriented conditions to the world trading system was repeated, *inter alia*, in a joint statement from Brazil, Japan, and the United States in the WTO General Council in October 2020, which:

- recalled that the WTO was established to promote Member economies participation in a world trading system 'based on open, market-oriented policies and the commitments set out in the Uruguay Round Agreements and Decisions';[50]
- expressed 'serious concerns with non-market-oriented policies and practices that have resulted in damage to the world trading system and lead to severe overcapacity, create unfair competitive conditions, hinder the development and use of innovative technologies, and undermine the proper functioning of international trade'; and
- affirmed that WTO members' enterprises should operate under market-oriented conditions and note the following elements indicate and are important so that market-oriented conditions exist for market participants:
  1. decisions of enterprises on prices, costs, inputs, purchases, and sales are freely determined and made in response to market signals;
  2. decisions of enterprises on investments are freely determined and made in response to market signals;
  3. prices of capital, labor, technology, and other factors are market-determined;
  4. capital allocation decisions of or affecting enterprises are freely determined and made in response to market signals;

[49] This is also acknowledged by Fallon (n 36), at 131.
[50] Marrakesh Declaration of 15 April 1994, fifth preambular paragraph.

5. enterprises are subject to internationally recognized accounting standards, including independent accounting;
6. enterprises are subject to market-oriented and effective corporation law, bankruptcy law, competition law, and private property law, and may enforce their rights through impartial legal processes, such as an independent judicial system;
7. enterprises are able to freely access relevant information on which to base their business decisions; and
8. there is no significant government interference in enterprise business decisions described above.[51]

According to the US WTO ambassador Dennis Shea, the core problem at the WTO is not a lack of trust but a lack of like-mindedness. We simply disagree on some fundamental issues. These divides make progress here at the WTO exceedingly difficult and threaten the institution itself ... unfortunately, some WTO members apparently do not believe that market orientation is part of the WTO's DNA. In their view, the WTO is agnostic between market and non-market economies—both belong here on an equal footing. This is not just a philosophical difference; it also has a practical impact ... today, we see an economic system in China in which state-owned and -influenced 'national champions' are lavishly funded by state-owned banks, charged with meeting state-determined industrial policy goals, assisted in this effort by state-sanctioned intellectual property theft and cyber espionage, and supported by a panoply of policies that discriminate against foreign competition. Add to this mix the absence of an independent judiciary where business disputes can be decided fairly, highly restrictive information controls, increasing Party involvement in state-owned and private enterprises alike, and an overall lack of transparency, and the playing field becomes even more unlevel ... such a state-led, non-market economic system is incompatible with the WTO and its norms. To believe the WTO can manage this system's trade-disruptive impact under current rules and through the dispute settlement process is fantasy.[52]

China is committed to what it calls a socialist market economy, which differs from the economies of other countries in at least three important respects:

[51] WTO document WT/GC/W/803/Rev.1 of 2 October 2020.

[52] Statement by US Ambassador DC Shea of 14 December 2020 in a WTO meeting of Heads of Delegations, https://geneva.usmission.gov/2020/12/14/us-statement-by-ambassador-dennis-shea-at-the-wto-heads-of-delegation-meeting/.

- as the most populous country in the world (18 per cent of the world population), the gigantic size of China's domestic market entails enormous market power, which the government uses, for example, for conditioning access to China's market on transfer of technology and formation of joint ventures with Chinese companies;
- the totalitarian power monopoly of China's Communist Party (CCP) extends not only to thousands of SOEs but also to formally private companies controlled by internal CCP committees, (in)formal state interventions, totalitarian digital control technologies, administrative privileges (eg subsidies, tax and legal exemptions), and restrictions of fundamental rights (like freedom of information and expression, labour rights) without independent judicial remedies, transparency, and democratic control;[53]
- state planning and subsidies have enabled Chinese producers to export structural surpluses (eg for steel, cement, aluminium, solar panels) at very low prices, distorting world markets and disrupting production and competition in other countries. Yet, the openness of China's economy and active industrial policies have also promoted a rapid industrialization, technological developments, and the lifting of more people out of poverty than in any other country over the past four decades.

The fact that China has become the largest trader in goods and second largest trader in services, and China's persistent trade surpluses with Europe and the United States, were increasingly perceived as a systemic WTO problem by the US Trump administration. Similar to Prime Minister Johnson's programme aimed at economic deregulation (like rejection of EU competition, single market and free movement rules) for establishing what he called a 'Singapore on Thames', President Trump rejected the draft TTIP agreement and preferred managing foreign trade deficits through bilateral deals (eg with China, Korea, and other countries aimed at exploiting US power emulating the trade management by authoritarian countries). In contrast to Anglo-Saxon neo-liberalism (prioritizing individual liberty and market-driven utilitarianism) and European ordo-liberalism (prioritizing protection of human dignity through constitutional rights and a social market economy), China's state capitalism prioritizes totalitarian control of the state, the polity, and

[53] Cf M Wu, The 'China, Inc.' Challenge to Global Trade Governance, *Harvard International Law Journal* 57 (2016), 261ff. On the enormous impact of WTO law on changing China's economy and legal systems, see Y Tan, How the WTO Changed China, *Foreign Affairs* March/April 2021. On China's use of anti-trust law as an instrument not only of economic and administrative regulation, but also of strategic rivalries, see AH Zhang, *Chinese Antitrust Exceptionalism* (OUP 2020). On the ambiguities and contested meanings of China's 1982 Constitution and its 2004 amendments (eg providing for the first time for constitutional recognition of human rights and private property), see Q Zhang, *The Constitution of China: A Contextual Analysis* (Hart Publishing 2012). On the totalitarian history of the CCP (like the famine during Mao's 'Great Leap Forward' campaign 1958–1962 and Mao's 'Cultural Revolution' 1966–1976 causing the deaths of millions of Chinese people), see Y Jisheng, *The World Turned Upside Down: A History of the Chinese Cultural Revolution* (Macmillan 2020).

economy by the CCP and nationalist 'Xi Jinping thinking'.[54] China presents its communist state capitalism as a socialist market economy with Chinese characteristics based on SOEs, an increasing number of private-owned enterprises, and totalitarian control of the Chinese economy by the CCP and its state apparatus. In contrast to China's territorial expansion in the South China Sea in open disregard of China's legal obligations under the UNCLOS as interpreted by the Permanent Court of Arbitration in July 2016,[55] China remains an active supporter of the WTO legal and dispute settlement system. Its selective adaptation to WTO rules is complemented by innovative networks of bilateral trade, investment, and financial agreements and regulations with the more than 100 countries participating in China's Belt and Road Initiative (BRI) financing Chinese investments and building infrastructures (like railways, maritime- and air-ports, electricity networks, and communications systems) connecting China's economy with those of the BRI countries.[56] As the world's largest trading nation and, by 2030, the world's largest economy, China is mistrusted by the United States as a technological, geopolitical, and also military rival using state subsidies, SOEs, government procurement practices, regulatory, administrative, and financial privileges for distorting markets and pursuing totalitarian, political goals without respect for most UN human rights conventions and International Labour Organization (ILO) conventions. China's foreign policies under President Xi are becoming ever more assertive using external power politics (eg for appropriating more than 80 per cent of the South China Sea, China's contested borders with India) and internal disregard for minority rights (eg of Tibetan and Uighur people) and for China's 'one state, two systems' agreements protecting autonomy in Macau, Hong Kong, and Taiwan.

[54] 'We must never follow the path of Western "constitutionalism", "separation of powers" or "judicial independence"', President Xi warned in one of his major policy speeches in 2018. Yet, he also stated that '(i)n the struggle against foreign powers, we must take up legal weapons, occupy the high ground of the rule-of-law' (quoted from S Shih, 'In China, many are impressed that, yes, you can sue the US government', *Washington Post* 8 March 2019). In 2012 and 2014, Xi Jinping had still acknowledged: 'Rule of the nation by law means, first and foremost, ruling the nation in accord with the constitution'; on subsequent assaults on constitutionalist thinking inside the CCP, see H Patapan, Towards a Cosmopolitan Constitutionalism: On Universalism and Particularism in Chinese Constitutionalism, *The Chinese Journal of Comparative Law* (2015), 78–96.

[55] See China's rejection of the arbitration award of 12 July 2016 under UNCLOS Annex VII concerning the Chinese claims to control more than 80 per cent of the South China Sea without regard to UNCLOS obligations: Permanent Court of Arbitration Case No 2013-19 in the matter of the South China Sea Arbitration (*The Republic of the Philippines v The Peoples Republic of China*). The award is published on the PCA website at http://www.pcacases.com/web/view/7. For critical analysis of the award, see J Wang, 'China and International Dispute Settlement: Implications of the South-China Sea Arbitration' in W Shan, S Zhang, and J Su (eds), *China and International Dispute Resolution in the Context of the 'Belt and Road Initiative'* (CUP 2020), 280–316. The geopolitical dimensions of this dispute over whether China can unilaterally control one-third of world maritime trade passing through these disputed waters were made evident in May 2021 when Belarus forced a Ryanair jet plane flying over the territory of Belarus to land at Minsk airport in order to imprison a political journalist flying on the plane.

[56] Cf H Wang, A New Chinese Economic Order? *Journal of International Economic Law* 23 (2020), 563–82.

The regulatory challenges of SOEs result not from their *existence*, but from the financial and regulatory advantages granted to SOEs (eg monopolies and exclusive rights), the advantages (such as capital and inputs) transferred from SOEs (eg state banks, raw material producers) to other economic actors, related competitive distortions affecting competitors and consumers, and the use of SOEs for political or military objectives (such as technological domination and Internet control). The existing WTO legal disciplines (eg in Articles XVII GATT, VIII GATS, China's Protocol of WTO Accession, WTO subsidy and trade remedy rules) are insufficient for controlling discriminatory, often non-transparent trade and financial distortions caused by SOEs or by non-transparent government privileges. There is broad agreement on the need for additional WTO trade, competition, subsidy, dumping, safeguard, and investment rules for limiting abuses by SOEs, which also exist in many other WTO member states.[57] In the absence of such WTO reforms, many WTO members unilaterally adjust their trade remedy laws (eg by focusing on cost distortions and particular market situations in applying anti-dumping and countervailing duty regulations).[58] Leaving related clarifications of WTO rules to WTO dispute settlement practices is widely perceived as insufficient and risky.[59]

The United States, under President Trump, considered the WTO incapable of responding adequately to China's alleged violations and circumvention of WTO rules. President Trump's bilateral US–China negotiations and trade wars have thus far not limited China's state influence on public and private enterprises (eg China's active industrial policies), Chinese non-compliance with certain WTO rules, China's military expansion (eg in the South China Sea), military threats (eg vis-à-vis Taiwan), and related strategic challenges to US hegemony. Unlike the multilateral disciplines for SOEs in Chapter 17 of the TPP Agreement, the bilateral US–China trade negotiations prioritize short-term managed trade deals (eg on China's purchase of US soya beans). The geopolitical and technological rivalries and policy divergences risk decoupling certain sectors of economic integration (eg digital trade using dual use technologies of strategic importance), diverting global supply chains (eg from China to other Asian countries like Vietnam), and emulation by other authoritarian rulers of China's bilateralism, state interventions, and

[57] Cf Y Wu, *Reforming WTO Rules on State-Owned Enterprises* (Springer 2019).

[58] For comparative analyses of how WTO members use their trade remedy laws for responding to non-market situations in China, see JJ Nedumpara and W Zhou (eds), *Non-market Economies in the Global Trading System* (Springer 2018). On recent EU legislation responding to trade distortions by subsidized, foreign SOEs and providing for screening of foreign investments inside the EU and of corporate responsibilities in supply chains, see 'The EU is trailing China's trade distortions all round the world', *Financial Times* 11 May 2021.

[59] This is illustrated by China's challenge of EU anti-dumping calculations based on a competitive distortion standard that was upheld in a WTO panel report, which remained unpublished due to China's withdrawal of its complaint after China's legal arguments had been rejected in the confidential interim panel report; see WT/DS516/14 of 15 June 2020 (notifying the lapse of authority of the WTO panel on China's complaint against EU measures related to price comparison methodologies following China's withdrawal of the complaint after having received the interim panel report).

managed trade. The communist ideologies underlying China's CCP state render it unlikely that its pervasive government control of the economy and polity can be liberalized through WTO negotiations. Yet, there remain many economic and political voices inside China recognizing that Chinese citizens could enormously benefit from additional WTO competition, e-commerce, and rule-of-law disciplines preventing abuses of public and private power inside China. Similarly, China continues using its participation in the WTO dispute settlement system and China's implementation of most WTO dispute settlement findings on illegal trade restrictions inside China for reforming trade laws inside China.

China remains committed to compliance with the WTO dispute settlement system in relations with most third WTO members (eg except in its trade war with the United States, and its authoritarian national policies vis-à-vis Hong Kong, Macao, and Taiwan). Empirical studies suggest that China's formal record of complying with WTO dispute settlement rulings is comparatively good.[60] As for the claim that '17 years, from its entry into the WTO in December 2001 to December 2018, China has timely and satisfactorily implemented the findings and recommendations of WTO tribunals in all but one dispute',[61] China's record of compliance with WTO dispute settlement rulings compares favourably with US dispute settlement practices.[62] Yet, China's good record of complying with adverse WTO dispute settlement rulings does not justify generalizations on China's compliance with WTO rules, which remains problematic in many respects (eg regarding transparency and subsidy disciplines, SOEs, intellectual property obligations, and judicial remedies). The empirical finding that:

> at the core of China's approach has been the use of WTO rulings as an external lever to facilitate domestic economic reforms while at the same time limiting the impacts of the rulings on its policy objectives and regulatory framework designed to pursue such objectives,[63]

[60] Cf W Zhou, *China's Implementation of the Rulings of the World Trade Organization* (Hart 2019). By December 2018, China had been a complainant in twenty WTO disputes, a respondent in forty-three disputes, and a third party in 143 disputes. Zhou's book examines China's implementation measures in the forty-three disputes, where China had been a respondent, also including cases that have not (yet) been adjudicated. The fact that China had never been subject to requests for authorization of retaliation confirms the empirical conclusion of Zhou that China, as a respondent, has fully participated in the dispute settlement and adjudication processes, including ten disputes settled without WTO rulings (analysed in Part II of Zhou's book) and implementation of adverse WTO rulings in twelve WTO dispute settlement findings by the end of 2018 (as demonstrated in Parts III–VII of Zhou's book). The book shows how WTO law and WTO dispute settlement rulings were used for reforming China's own legal system.

[61] Zhou (n 60), 183.

[62] For example, in contrast to China, the United States has faced many WTO requests for authorizing retaliation following WTO findings on US non-compliance with WTO dispute settlement rulings.

[63] Zhou (n 60), 184.

corresponds with similar findings on the impact of adverse WTO dispute settlement rulings on domestic policy-making and legal implementation of WTO law in other states like Canada and the United States.[64] Thus, even if President Xi rejects Western constitutionalism, the separation of powers, and judicial independence as restraints on his CCP state monopoly, he seems to support international rule of law as a legal restraint on China's trade policy powers and as a strategic policy tool for regulatory reforms inside as well as beyond China's borders.[65] Yet, as illustrated by China's illegal retaliatory trade sanctions in response to President Trump's trade war targeting China and Chinese tech companies, the Chinese government does not hesitate to respond to what it perceives as illegal, unilateral aggression by employing equally illegal (eg in terms of GATT Articles I and II, Article 23 DSU) trade retaliation if member-driven WTO governance turns into arbitrary power politics.[66]

3.6 China's Belt and Road Networks: An Alternative Trading System?

As a WTO member since December 2001, China continues supporting the multilateral WTO trading, legal, and dispute settlement system. Its steadily increasing trade surpluses since 2001, successful handling of WTO dispute settlement proceedings, and use of WTO rules for legal and economic reforms of China's domestic economic and legal system explain why most WTO members perceive China as one of the most successful users of the WTO legal system. The signing of the Regional Comprehensive Economic Partnership (RCEP) on 15 November 2020 among the ten ASEAN states, China, Australia, New Zealand, Japan, and South Korea has created the world's most populous FTA. Its comparatively low ambitions for liberalizing tariffs and regulating non-tariff trade barriers are interpreted as reflecting China's increasing role as a rule maker outside the WTO. In 2021, China applied for joining the Comprehensive and Progressive Agreement for Trans-Pacific Partnership (CPTPP), which was negotiated and accepted by eleven transpacific countries after US President Trump withdrew the United States from the TPP Agreement signed in 2016 by twelve transpacific countries. President Xi's new economic doctrine of dual circulation reflects an increased emphasis on developing China's domestic market, the advantages of China's unique market size

[64] JD Krikorian, *International Trade Law and Domestic Policy* (University of British Columbia Press 2012), 81: 'the US government has acted in its own self-interest and thwarted the potential impact of the dispute settlement mechanism either by effectively ignoring its decisions or by implementing them in such a way as to minimise their overall effect'.

[65] Cf Y Tan, How the WTO Changed China. The Mixed Legacy of Economic Engagement, *Foreign Affairs* March/April 2021.

[66] Cf J Ya Qin, WTO Reform: Multilateral Control over Unilateral Retaliation—Lessons from the US–China Trade War, in *Wayne State Law School Legal Studies Research Paper Series* No 2020-73.

(eg for attracting foreign investments), domestic demand, political control, and domestic technological independence; it seems to aim at reducing China's dependence on the global trading system ('producing in China for China') rather than at protectionism.

Even though the TPP and CPTPP were negotiated as models for collective responses to the regulatory challenges of China's state capitalism (eg by providing for high regulatory standards protecting labour, environmental sustainability, intellectual property rights, prohibitions of subsidies, and other limitations on SOEs), the US Biden administration has so far (2021) not decided whether to rejoin the CPTPP in pursuit of its strategy of using alliances among democratic WTO members for inducing China to accept additional, market-oriented regulatory reforms. As the Trade Promotion Authority of the US government for fast-track legislation on trade agreements has run out in July 2021, congressional support for US accession to the CPTPP remains uncertain. A strengthened CPTPP could also be used as institutional framework for pushing back against China's land grabs in the South China Sea and for developing collective counter-strategies containing Chinese power politics threatening democratic countries (like Australia) with economic sanctions if their governments and public media dare criticize Chinese domestic policies.[67] If Indonesia, the Philippines, South Korea, the EU, and other democracies would consider joining the CPTPP, the latter could even operate as a plurilateral strategic substitute for China's opposition against market-oriented reforms of worldwide WTO rules.

The 2013 BRI by President Xi Jinping envisages investing more than $1 trillion for the construction and infrastructures of a Silk Road economic belt (following the ancient Silk Road from China through central Asia and the Middle East to Europe) and for a twenty-first-century maritime Silk Road (linking China to South East Asia, East Africa, and the Mediterranean Sea) so as to promote international policy coordination, infrastructure facilities connectivity, unimpeded trade, financial integration as well as human people-to-people bonds among more than 100 countries bordering these Silk Roads.[68] China's BRI initiative recreates China-centred, bilateral networks of transnational road and maritime infrastructures—supported by financial, technical, and government procurement assistance from

[67] The warning—'if you make China your enemy, China will be yours'—has been attributed to a Chinese government official; cf *Financial Times* editorial board, 'The worrying precedent in China's quarrel with Australia. Democratic countries should coordinate responses to pressures from Beijing', *Financial Times* 27 November 2020 (eg quoting a foreign ministry spokesman in Beijing responding to a joint statement on Hong Kong by the 'Five Eyes' security cooperation group of Australia, Canada, New Zealand, the United Kingdom, and the United States by saying 'No matter if they have Five Eyes or 10 eyes, if they dare to harm China's sovereignty . . . they should be aware of their eyes being poked and blinded').

[68] Details of the Chinese BRI can be found at http://en.ndrc.gov.cn/newsrelease/201503/t20150330_669367.html. Trade over the Silk Road by land and by sea is documented from about 200 BC up to the fall of Constantinople in 1453 BC; it connected the economic centres from the east to the west ends of Asia, Arabia (eg Baghdad, Damascus, Cairo), Venice, and Rome.

Chinese and Asian institutions—following China's ancient perception of itself as the Middle Kingdom. China's incremental development of a decentralized hub-and-spokes model—with China at the centre—for bilateral trade, investment, and financial cooperation is perceived as a potential new model of Chinese economic order dominated by Chinese industrial and development policies and SOEs.[69] China's new initiatives for digital silk roads, green silk roads, and polar silk roads have prompted the EU, India, and the United States to offer less-developed countries more market- and democracy-centred alternative infrastructure assistance. In contrast to the post-1945 Anglo-Saxon international economic order—which was based on liberal constitutionalism, multilateral treaties and institutions, and neo-liberal liberalization and deregulation of market access barriers—the BRI is based on China's authoritarian nationalism, asymmetrical, and informal bilateral arrangements, lack of multilateral agreements and institutions coordinating the web of bilateral BRI arrangements, and Chinese economic sanctions if partner countries dare criticize China's state capitalism and its disregard for human rights and the rule by law.[70] The BRI's bilateralism offers China more economic means for influencing BRI partner countries (eg to accept Chinese industrial standards and internet governance methods) compared with the post-war American and European methods of establishing multilateral organizations to reform the world,[71] including admission of China's WTO accession in the hope that WTO law would induce China to strengthen non-discriminatory market competition, the rule of law, and judicial remedies also inside China.[72]

Europe, like other countries (such as the United States with its high dependence on raw material imports from China for US production of many pharmaceutical products), depends on raw material imports from China in many important sectors (eg 98 per cent of rare earth materials used in the EU for certain products like

[69] Cf Wang (n 56); G Shaffer and H Gao, A New Chinese Economic Order?, *Journal of International Economic Law* 23 (2020), 607–35; L Zucca, 'Two Conceptions of Global Order' in G Martinico and X Wu (eds), *A Legal Analysis of China's Belt and Road Initiative: Towards a New Silk Road?* (Palgrave MacMillan 2020), 21–43.

[70] Cf n 67 and R Guo, Is China's Belt and Road Initiative Moving towards a Silk Road Union? *China and WTO Review* 6 (2020), 49–80. On China's use of trade sanctions, see R McGregor, 'China sends a message with Australian crackdown', *Financial Times* 25 November 2020 (reporting on China's publication of fourteen grievances justifying China's import restrictions targeting Australian products by Australian criticism of China's disregard for human rights of Uighur minorities and in Hong Kong, exclusion of China's 5G Internet technologies, China's illegal military expansion in the South China Sea, Australia's unilateral call for a WHO inquiry into the Chinese origins of the COVID-19 health pandemic, and Australia's opposition to the direct participation of the state government of Victoria in the BRI arrangements, which Canberra has refused to sign so far).

[71] Cf GF Sinclair, *To Reform the World. International Organizations and the Making of Modern States* (OUP 2017).

[72] W Yuhua, *Tying the Autocrat's Hands: The Rise of the Rule of Law in China* (CUP 2015). Discussion of judicial independence from the CCP remains a forbidden subject inside China. Chinese officials argue that separation of powers, democracy, and human rights are not required by China's WTO accession protocol. In the WTO dispute on *China-Publications and Audiovisual Products* (WT/DS363/AB/R of 21 December 2014), the potential violation of China's content review (censorship) of freedom of speech was not even mentioned.

making the magnets that run electric vehicles). As China has exploited its dominant market position in the past (eg by introducing export restrictions, increasing prices, and diverting supplies to Chinese producers), bilateral trade with China outside the multilateral WTO legal rules (eg on non-discrimination, prohibition of export restraints) risks being abused by anti-competitive practices.[73] Most of the bilateral BRI agreements and contractual arrangements for the financing and implementation of China's bilateral infrastructure investments, trade and financial projects in BRI countries use soft law (eg memoranda of understanding, political declarations, dispute settlement through mediation or commercial arbitration) rather than hard treaty law and third-party adjudication of disputes.[74] Yet, the long duration of infrastructure projects may turn out to promote more stable cooperation than fragile FTAs. Also the draft China–EU investment agreement signed on 30 December 2020 focuses on additional, reciprocal market access commitments (eg granting access for EU investors to additional sectors of China's economy, prohibiting forced technology transfers) without providing for independent judicial remedies and unequivocal Chinese commitments to accept the core ILO labour conventions (eg prohibiting forced labour).[75] Yet many of China's existing bilateral investment treaties (BITs) include most-favoured-nation clauses,[76] and China's Supreme People's Court has confirmed the importance of protecting rule of law and judicial remedies in the BRI cooperation with third countries.[77] The establishment of the Chinese–European Arbitration Centre at Hamburg (Germany) and of China–Africa Joint Arbitration Centres at Johannesburg (South Africa) and Shanghai (China) confirms China's preference for settling BRI disputes through commercial arbitration or mediation. The limited number of ISA proceedings initiated so far by foreign companies against China—or by Chinese companies against foreign host states[78]—seems to confirm this Chinese preference for

[73] Cf A Beattie, 'The EU plan to live in a raw materials world. China supplies 98% of the bloc's rare earths, and has exploited that bottleneck in the past', *Financial Times* 26 November 2020: the EU is up 'against Beijing in a game of low costs, lax standards, managed prices and state handouts in a mass production industry with a dominant position in strategic commodity markets at stake. China tends to win those most of the time.'

[74] Cf Martinico and Wu (eds), (n 69).

[75] For a summary of this draft agreement, which still requires ratification (eg by the European parliament), see *Financial Times* 1 January 2021 and 31 December 2020.

[76] Cf J Chaisse and J Kirkwood, Chinese Puzzle: Anatomy of the (Invisible) Belt and Road Investment Treaty, *Journal of International Economic Law* 23 (2020), 245–69.

[77] See the Opinion, issued on 16 June 2015 by China's Supreme People's Court, that 'the rule of law is an important safeguard for China's Belt and Road Initiative, in which the role of the judiciary is indispensable' ('Several Opinions of the Supreme People's Court on the Judiciary's Provision of Judicial Services and Safeguard for the Belt and Road', Fa (2015) 9 Hao, 16 June 2015, quoted by J Wang, *China's Governance Approach to the Belt and Road Initiative: Partnership, Relations, and Law*, in NUS Law Working Paper No 2019/005, available at https://papers.ssrn.com/sol3/papers.cfm?abstract_id=3346427.)

[78] Even though China has signed more than 130 BITs, there seem to have been only two complaints initiated against China under the ICSID rules by 2017, and only five arbitration complaints initiated by Chinese foreign investors against foreign host states; cf Y Hua, *China's Legal Obligations in the Field of Foreign Investment: How Trade Agreements Influence the Formation of Investment Agreements*, EUI doctoral thesis defended on 15 June 2017.

alternative dispute settlement methods that avoid recourse to international or domestic courts (eg also in view of the often inadequate independence and judicial expertise of local courts in some African and Asian countries). Promotion of such alternative dispute resolution may become one of the important legal innovations of China's BRI cooperation. Yet, involvement of third parties (as mediators or conciliators) in dispute settlement proceedings also raises questions of justice and of legal methodology.[79]

The 2015 Agreement establishing the Asian Infrastructure and Investment Bank (AIIB) and the 2001 Shanghai Cooperation Organization—even though initiated by China and having their headquarters at Beijing—have mandates far beyond BRI cooperation. China's preference for using flexible legal instruments for implementing BRI projects, and for avoiding multilateral BRI treaties and institutions, confirms China's economic and political dominance in designing and implementing its BRI strategy.[80]

China's promotion of BRI investments may give rise to

1. trade disputes and WTO dispute settlement proceedings;
2. investment disputes settled through China's more than 130 BITs, International Center for the Settlement of Investment Disputes (ICSID), or UN Commission on International Trade Law (UNCITRAL) arbitration proceedings;
3. financial disputes settled through bilateral negotiations, arbitration courts, and other jurisdictions in China rather than through multilateral treaty institutions like the AIIB;
4. intellectual property disputes settled through Chinese jurisdictions (like China's Patent office and Chinese courts) or through WTO, World Intellectual Property Organization (WIPO), and other multilateral dispute settlement procedures;
5. commercial disputes settled through Chinese courts and commercial arbitration procedures, subject to various limitations of the legal admissibility of ad hoc arbitration inside China; as regards

[79] Cf Shan, Zhang, and Su (eds), (n 55); EU Petersmann, 'Trade and Investment Adjudication Involving Silk Road Projects: Legal Methodology Challenges' in Shan, Zhang, and Su (eds), (n 55), 51–77.

[80] The *Financial Times* of 11 December 2020 reported ('China pulls back from the world: rethinking Xi's "project of the century"') that annual lending by the China Development Bank and the Export-Import Bank of China collapsed from a peak of $75 billion in 2016 to just $4 billion in 2019. Between 2008 and 2019, the two Chinese banks had lent $462 billion, just short of the $467 billion extended by the World Bank. The sharp reduction of lending by the Chinese banks is linked to at least eighteen debt renegotiations by China with over-indebted BRI countries. President Xi's recent speeches favouring domestic self-reliance on Chinese technology policies are widely interpreted as a potential retreat from export-led globalization strategies and acceptance of decoupling of China's economy from foreign supply chains.

6. maritime disputes, China refused participating in the UNCLOS arbitration initiated by the Philippines and rejected the UNCLOS arbitration award of 2016 concerning the South China Sea[81];
7. as regards energy trade and investment disputes, China has not yet ratified the Energy Charter Treaty (ECT) providing for international state–state and investor–state arbitration.[82]

Avoidance of multilateral treaties and lack of a multilateral dispute settlement approach distinguish the BRI from past US leadership for multilateral dispute settlement systems in GATT, ICSID, the WTO, and regional FTAs. Chinese BRI investments inside the eleven EU member states that, so far, have concluded memoranda of understanding on their participation in China's BRI, risk running into legal problems if they neglect the EU legal guarantees of civil, political, economic, social, and cultural rights, EU competition and social laws, and open government procurement procedures. For instance, in legal conflicts about justice at work in the power relationships between Chinese employers and their employees inside EU member states, the multilevel judicial remedies protected by EU law risk being invoked by adversely affected workers inside the EU if their individual rights, privacy, and co-determination are disregarded. Beijing's annual 17+1 meetings with 17 European countries (mostly from eastern, central, and southern Europe) participating in BRI projects reflect China's preferences for informal, pragmatic diplomacy (eg preferring to divide and rule rather than negotiate multilateral rules with the EU). It remains to be seen whether the ongoing negotiations on reforms of ICSID and UNCITRAL arbitration procedures, and the EU proposals for a multilateral investment court system, will strengthen the public law dimensions of investor–state disputes in ways that will also be accepted by China and strengthen judicial remedies in BRI economic cooperation. The jurisprudence of the CJEU and of the ECtHR on protecting worker rights (eg based on EU anti-discrimination law, Articles 8, 11, and 14 ECHR) has reinforced the legal disciplines for foreign investors inside the EU and for the protection of their workers (eg against being treated like commodities or robots), for instance by limiting the terms of labour contracts through mandatory principles of constitutional law and HRL aimed at guaranteeing justice at work for all.[83]

[81] See n 55.

[82] For a discussion of alternative dispute settlement procedures governing BRI projects see EU Petersmann, 'International Settlement of Trade and Investment Disputes over Chinese "Silk Road Projects" inside the EU' in Martinico and Wu (eds), (n 69), 45–68.

[83] Cf H Collins, *Justice at Work*, LSE Law, Society and Economy Working Papers 18/2019.

3.7 Responding to China's Regulatory Challenges

China has become less liberal—and militarily more assertive—under President Xi Jinping than it was in 2001 at the time of its accession to the WTO. The US–China rivalry and the global health, climate change, and digital regulatory challenges also induce many other governments to adopt active industrial policies, state interventions (like governmental carbon emissions trading systems), and develop strategies to counter Chinese influence (eg by new geostrategic G7 and EU infrastructure investment initiatives offering market-based alternatives to China's BRI programme). The increasing conflicts among American neo-liberalism, China's totalitarian state capitalism, and Europe's multilevel, economic constitutionalism are likely to promote more regionalization of the international economic order driven by regulatory competition and civil society struggles for protecting sustainable development. Yet, it is not impossible that Chinese leaders—after having successfully emulated the export-driven industrialization and liberalization of Asian 'tiger' economies (like Singapore, Hong Kong, Japan, South Korea, Taiwan)—might also discover the benefits of political liberalization. China's rules-based economic cooperation with constitutional democracies protecting human rights and transnational rule of law may continue to induce rule of law reforms inside China, such as the labour law reforms envisaged in the China–EU Agreement on Investments of December 2021. Arguably, the more China's CCP becomes meritocratic and realizes its cultural-political objectives of protecting China's political unity against humiliating foreign power politics (as during the time of the Opium War in 1842 up to 1945), the more may the changing geopolitics (eg with China becoming the largest and India the second-largest national economies in the twenty-first century) set incentives for rules-based international cooperation.

China continues participating in UN policies aimed at mitigating climate change and implementing the SDGs (like provision of Chinese vaccines in order to mitigate the COVID-19 health pandemic in less-developed UN member states, Chinese financial and economic assistance for less-developed UN member states). The current EU- and US-led efforts at offering less-developed countries more market- and democracy-oriented, alternative infrastructure assistance are likely to counter the geopolitical significance of China's BRI strategies. Even if China currently remains the largest GHG emitter, the Chinese contribution to climate change mitigation and to decarbonizing the economy will be crucial for realizing many SDGs inside and outside China (eg in many BRI countries).[84] The geopolitical rivalries between China and the United States confront third countries with increasing political pressures to choose between economic cooperation with the United States or China (eg regarding use of 5G Internet technologies) or to seek

[84] Cf P Drahos, *Survival Governance: Energy and Climate Change in the Chinese Century* (OUP 2021).

more strategic autonomy (eg as demonstrated by Japan's leadership for concluding the CPTPP, the entry into force of the EU–Japan Economic Partnership Agreement on 1 February 2019, India's refusal to participate in the RCEP). The EU and the United States share many concerns about Chinese practices (like forced technology transfers, trade subsidies, counterfeiting, anti-competitive business practices, reciprocity of market access, political influence over China's foreign direct investments, human rights abuses inside China); yet, in contrast to the geopolitical US policies (eg promoting strategic alliances with Australia, India, Japan, and other Asian countries aimed at containing Chinese power politics), most European states prioritize their self-interest in continuing economic cooperation with China. For multinational corporations, access to the Chinese market not only offers profit opportunities but even more so incentives for developing new technologies needed for the planned transformation of Chinese cities and urbanization projects. The more globalization and economic integration become affected by geopolitical divisions, authoritarian contestation, climate and technological changes and related conflicts (eg caused by cyber wars, disorderly climate migration, border pollution, disputes over scarce resources like border rivers), the more important international dispute settlement procedures and institutions will become.

The declining US willingness to maintain the WTO legal and dispute settlement system responds to the changing power relationships with China and to other challenges of US hegemony (like US domination of the global financial system, extra-territorial US power politics, and increasing US nationalism). It mirrors the decreasing willingness also of other authoritarian countries (like China and Russia) to limit their power politics by national, regional, and worldwide courts of justice (like the International Tribunal for the Law of the Sea and the International Court of Justice). As a result, global governance is becoming more difficult. Most countries seem to prefer responding to trade distortions caused by competition from China through invocation of WTO rules (eg on trade remedies, WTO exceptions, negotiation of new WTO disciplines, WTO dispute settlement procedures) without being drawn into the China–US trade wars. In view of the difficulties of a WTO-centric strategy for any joint alliance-based approach to tackle the regulatory challenges of China's industrial, technology, Internet, and intellectual policies and non-tariff trade barriers, the US Biden administration seems intent on developing multi-prong bilateral, regional, and multilateral approaches in its US strategy vis-à-vis China.[85] Most of these regulatory challenges were not addressed in the bilateral US–China phase one trade agreement of January 2020. Successful WTO negotiations on these issues may depend on overcoming the differences with US allies (like the EU and Japan) over reforms of WTO appellate procedures, regulation of digital trade, carbon taxes, and border carbon adjustments, and on

[85] Cf M Wu, *Managing the China Trade Challenge: Confronting the Limits of the WTO* (unpublished working paper 2021).

actively using other multilateral fora (like the G20, OECD, the Paris Agreement) for progressive coalition-building. As the global health, environmental, energy, and political crises require new regulatory responses, the continuing regulatory competition between WTO member countries with diverse neo-liberal, state capitalist, ordo-liberal, and third-world regulatory systems may reveal new insights into how best to respond to China's regulatory challenges. For instance, the WHO's independent commission on health and sustainable development—in its interim report of 16 March 2021—recommended (i) creating an international panel on health threats (following the example of the intergovernmental panel on climate change) as an early warning system for scientific assessment of health risks from future emerging infections caused by the interdependence of human, animal, and environmental health (eg micro-organisms jumping from animals to humans); (ii) improving data systems on disadvantaged communities with precarious health conditions; (iii) financing investments in health infrastructures so as to make it more difficult for viruses to spread and mutate; (iv) to create a Global Health Board (following the example of the Financial Stability Board) to address vulnerabilities of public health systems and promote the necessary supervisory policies to overcome them; and (v) promote innovation of vaccines, medicines and technologies for neglected tropical diseases.[86] If the WTO should take decisions, as proposed by WTO Director-General Ngozi Okonjo-Iweala on 9 March 2021, for increasing production and supplies of COVID-19 vaccines in less-developed countries (eg by authorizing compulsory licensing of related patent rights), such trade, health, intellectual property rights, financial, and sustainable development decisions would require close coordination at national, regional, and worldwide governance levels, and among international agencies (like the World Bank, WTO, WHO, WIPO) in order to be effectively implemented. China's plans to create more than fifty new 'green' cities will create incentives for decarbonizing the economy and developing new 'green technologies' in cooperation with foreign firms. If US–China trade wars should further undermine the WTO trading, legal, and dispute settlement systems, the BRI networks connecting more than 3 billion people could become a China-led framework for worldwide economic, environmental, and health cooperation competing with regional FTAs initiated by democratic trading countries and with other regional free trade areas (eg among African countries). The US withdrawal from inter-regional economic integration agreements (like the TPP and TTIP) will further diminish US geopolitical influence. China's cooperation with rogue states (like North Korea and Myanmar under their military rulers, Russia under Putin waging covert military aggression against neighbouring states like Georgia and Ukraine) in rejecting human rights criticism and humanitarian interventions by democratic countries could even lead to political BRI coalitions of (formerly

[86] Cf M Monti, 'An ambitious agenda is needed for the post-Covid "normal"', *Financial Times* 16 March 2021.

communist) authoritarian countries. Similar to the eruption of the First World War by the assassination of Archduke Ferdinand in June 1914 at a time of emerging powers (like Germany, Japan, the United States) challenging the hegemonic British empire, another accident (eg among Chinese and US military forces in the South China Sea) could set off conflict like a spark in a powder keg.[87]

[87] On China's expansive ambitions, see R Doshi, *The Long Game. China's Grand Strategy to Replace American Order* (OUP 2021).

4
Constitutional Economics for Multilevel Economic Regulation

The United Nations (UN) 2030 Sustainable Development Agenda recognizes:

> International trade is an engine for inclusive economic growth and poverty reduction and contributes to the promotion of sustainable development. We will continue to promote a universal, rules-based, open, transparent, predictable, inclusive, non-discriminatory and equitable multilateral trading system under the World Trade Organization, as well as meaningful trade liberalization (paragraph 68).

Yet, neither the UN Sustainable Development Agenda nor World Trade Organization (WTO) law clarify what kind of adjustments to world trade and investment law will be necessary for realizing the citizen-oriented Sustainable Development Goals (SDGs). Nor does the UN Sustainable Development agenda clarify the legal relationships between its references to human rights, democracy, and rule of law, on the one side, and sovereign equality of states and international cooperation in UN and WTO institutions, on the other. The Paris Agreement relies on nationally determined contributions (NDCs) as well as on contributions from other international organizations which—in the absence of a global environmental organization—need to be coordinated in specialized regional and worldwide organizations (like the International Maritime Organization coordinating greenhouse gas (GHG) emissions caused by shipping, the International Civil Aviation Organization coordinating GHG emissions caused by air transport); these contributions lag far behind what is necessary for realizing the SDGs (eg to limit global temperature increases to 1.5 °C or well below 2 °C). The 2030 UN Sustainable Development Agenda (described in Chapter 2, section 2.6 as a concretization of the Geneva Consensus) leaves open how UN member states will implement the SDGs through worldwide, regional, and national legal practices (eg new WTO rules on carbon border tax adjustments as discussed in Chapter 9) and how they will resolve conflicts among competing goals (eg if termination of fossil-based energy enhances local unemployment and poverty, or if the costs of substituting 'green' energy for 'dirty' energy prevent the financing of other social programmes).

Section 4.1 recalls the progressive changes in the embedded liberalism underlying UN and GATT/WTO law. Section 4.2 discusses legal methodology

Transforming World Trade and Investment Law for Sustainable Development. Ernst-Ulrich Petersmann, Oxford University Press. © Ernst-Ulrich Petersmann 2022. DOI: 10.1093/oso/9780192858023.003.0005

challenges of the increasingly science-based foundations of UN and WTO climate change and health protection policies. Sections 4.3 and 4.4 point to incoherencies among the economic, legal, and policy paradigms underlying the clashes between American neo-liberalism and China's state capitalism; as explained by European ordo-liberalism, the utility maximization paradigm of neo-classical economics (focusing on rational choices within rules that are assumed as given) must be complemented by legal contract/exchange paradigms of institutional economics for elaborating and justifying choices among alternative rules and institutions, including also constitutional constraints of a higher legal rank protecting individual and democratic preferences. In contrast to the focus of politics on winners, losers, and distribution of power, the exchange paradigms of law and economics and of constitutional economics—analysing both (i) empirical choices of rules restraining government agents and of their economic effects as well as (ii) their normative justifications (eg by social contract theories, constitutional, and public goods theories)—focus on mutual individual and collective gains enabled by constitutional cooperation improving the laws and institutions of the economic and political order.[1] Sections 4.5 and 4.6 recall that globalization—and its transformation of national into transnational public goods (PGs)—requires extending constitutional and institutional economics to multilevel governance of transnational PGs (like most SDGs) in order to enhance the wealth of nations, not only through cooperation and division of labour among private economic actors but also among law-makers, governments, and courts of justice. Efficient allocation of scarce resources and satisfaction of consumer preferences can be enhanced by both constitutional improvement of the contractarian efficiency of laws and institutions (eg constraining coercive authority, protecting democratic preferences) and post-constitutional economics maximizing the available economic goods, services, and resources. Sections 4.7 and 4.8 explain the conflicts among competing paradigms as reflecting the realities of constitutional pluralism and regulatory competition among authoritarian economic systems (eg in China and Russia) and neo-liberal or ordo-liberal market economies committed to methodological individualism,

[1] For an introduction into constitutional economics as a part of institutional economics, 'law and economics' and 'public choice' analyses, and its analytical distinction between positive and normative analyses of the economic incentives and effects of constitutional rules, principles, and institutions of a higher legal rank, see S Voigt, *Constitutional Economics: A Primer* (CUP 2020). Notwithstanding the diversity of national constitutional systems and the criticism that constitutionalization of international law has evoked in legal scholarship, constitutional principles are increasingly extended to the law of international organizations and invoked in multilevel governance and adjudication—such as human and constitutional rights, constituent power, and national sovereignty, limited delegation of power, proportionality of their exercise, rule of law, separation of legislative, executive, and judicial powers, balance of powers, access to justice and judicial remedies, multilevel judicial cooperation based on principles of judicial comity, executive emergency powers, legal accountability of independent regulatory agencies, multilevel governance through international organizations, principles of subsidiarity, and federalism; cf EU Petersmann, *Multilevel Constitutionalism for Multilevel Governance of Public Goods* (Hart 2017); AF Lang and A Wiener (eds), *Handbook on Global Constitutionalism* (Edward Elgar 2017).

democratic constitutionalism, and rational choices by individuals and peoples. Sections 4.9 and 4.10 emphasize the need for cooperation and coherence among overlapping PG regimes for pursuing the seventeen SDGs; peaceful resolution of disputes (eg over the consistency of legal practices with multilaterally agreed rules) by means of third-party adjudication is economically efficient and reasonable, without prejudice to the sovereign freedom of states to change rules or withdraw from multilateral agreements.

This chapter argues that a better understanding of the value conflicts underlying US neo-liberalism, China's constitutionally unrestrained state capitalism and Europe's ordo-liberal, multilevel constitutionalism can facilitate transforming the world for realizing the SDGs. Respecting the diversity of constitutional traditions—like Anglo-Saxon constitutionalism in island states (like the United Kingdom, Australia, and New Zealand), authoritarian constitutionalism (eg in China and Russia), and multilevel, democratic constitutionalism in continental Europe (eg in EU and European Economic Area (EEA) countries)—is important for designing policy responses to the competing conceptions of economic and trade regulation, regulatory competition, and trade distortions (eg by Chinese subsidy practices and dumping of surplus products like aluminium and steel, US trade remedy practices, non-transparent regulatory discriminations, extraterritorial economic sanctions). Chapters 4–9 explain the systemic importance of independent third-party adjudication as a means of peaceful, rules-based settlement of disputes clarifying legal limits of regulatory competition and protecting transnational rule of law. Conflicts among governmental interests (eg favouring particular lobbying interests over general consumer interests) can be reduced by relying on citizen-oriented SDGs as agreed benchmarks for common general interests. For instance, the EU has linked its common trade policies to its Green Deal[2] by requiring that any future trade agreement with a G20 country be based on a shared ambition to achieve climate neutrality and protection of biodiversity as soon as possible, to be reflected in NDCs and in the sustainable development chapters of EU trade agreements (specifying commitments in areas like human rights, labour rights, the environment, and related dispute settlement procedures). Yet, the EU should avoid hegemonic policies by acting only as a civilian power promoting democratic values (as prescribed in Articles 2 and 3 TEU) and good global governance standards. Realizing the SDGs requires adjusting the embedded liberalism compromise underlying GATT/WTO law (as discussed in section 4.1), notably by making WTO rules consistent with the climate mitigation objectives of the Paris Agreement (as explored in Chapter 9, section 9.2). Arguably, the EU's multilateralism and ordo-liberal constitutionalism render the EU better qualified for rules-based, multilateral leadership aimed at decarbonizing and digitalizing economies in conformity with the citizen-oriented

[2] See *An Open, Sustainable and Assertive Trade Policy*, EU Commission, 18 February 2021 (available on the EU website https://ec.europa.eu/commission/press).

SDGs (eg by protecting environmental and human rights, designing decentralized emission trading systems, carbon border adjustment taxes) than other major GHG emitters like China, India, Japan, Russia, and also Anglo-Saxon democracies. For instance, due to neo-liberal interest group politics and its financial influence on US Congressmen, the US Biden administration lacks political support by a congressional majority for introducing carbon taxes, and for returning to WTO appellate adjudication, as proposed by parliamentary and executive EU institutions, which are subject to stricter, multilevel constitutional restraints (eg in Articles 3, 21 TEU) than foreign policy powers in nation states outside the EU. Constitutional economics explains, *inter alia*, why certain economic rules deserve a higher legal rank, and how the economic welfare effects of international legal disciplines can be enhanced inside domestic legal systems.

4.1 Challenges to GATT's Embedded Liberalism

GATT 1947 (eg its Articles III, XVIII–XXI) was based on embedded liberalism protecting national sovereign rights to regulate the domestic economy, polity, and legal system through non-discriminatory measures.[3] GATT rules legally ranked trade policy instruments according to their economic efficiency: non-discriminatory measures (like taxes, product and production regulations) were left to national sovereignty (Article III); domestic subsidies were allowed unless they created discriminatory trade distortions (Articles III.8, XVI); market-conforming tariffs were progressively liberalized through reciprocal tariff commitments (Articles II, XXVIII); discriminatory non-tariff restrictions were prohibited as a matter of principle (Articles III, XI). And yet GATT's safeguard clauses (Articles VI, XIX) and numerous exceptions (eg Articles XX, XXI, XXIV) permitted import restrictions for (non-)economic reasons, thereby confirming the national sovereignty of GATT members over their pursuit of national policy objectives and non-economic policy instruments. GATT rules had domestic policy functions and constitutional functions in the sense that GATT not only required contracting parties to use transparent, non-discriminatory, and economically welfare-enhancing policy instruments for whatever policy objectives they decided to pursue. They also assisted governments in reforming domestic trade laws so that domestic protectionist pressures from import-competing producers could be resisted better by offering export opportunities and incentives for export industries to support reciprocal trade liberalization politically, which promised more competitive employment opportunities in the export sector as compensation for job losses in import-competing

[3] On embedded liberalism see JG Ruggie, International Regimes, Transactions and Change: Embedded Liberalism in the Postwar Economic Order, *International Organization* 36 (1982), 379–415 and Chapter 9, section 9.2.

industries. From a constitutional perspective (like that adopted by US Secretary of State Cordell Hull and the founding fathers of the EEC Treaty), the self-imposed GATT legal constraints could be seen as responding to the bounded rationality and constitutional failures in national constitutions to limit welfare-reducing abuses of foreign policy powers and protect equal freedoms of citizens (eg as a first principle of justice as explained in Kantian and Rawlsian theories of justice) beyond national borders.[4] From this citizen and economic welfare perspective, the multilevel legal and judicial GATT/WTO safeguards of non-discriminatory trade competition based on transnational rule of law (cf Article XVI:4 WTO Agreement) complemented the cosmopolitan constitutionalism underlying UN and EU human rights law (HRL) by institutionalizing public reason for interpreting domestic law and GATT/WTO rules in mutually consistent ways promoting non-discriminatory conditions of trade and competition.[5]

The utilitarian neo-liberal turn, since the late 1970s, under Prime Minister Thatcher in the United Kingdom and US President Reagan in the United States, its incorporation into some of the 1979 Tokyo Round agreements (eg on anti-dumping duties and subsidies), and its emulation by several other GATT contracting parties rejected such constitutional interpretations. It favoured justifying trade rules in terms of Kaldor–Hicks and Pareto efficiency criteria rather than also constitutional values (like promotion of equal freedoms and rule of law beyond frontiers). This promoted neo-liberal neglect for human rights and for democratic constitutionalism as restraints on legitimate trade policy-making, thereby provoking 'grey area' measures circumventing GATT rules (like voluntary export restraints for cotton, textiles, automobiles) and increasing challenges of GATT/WTO rules by civil societies and national parliaments.[6] In *Globalists: The End of Empire and the Birth of Neoliberalism*, history professor Quinn Slobodian describes the WTO as 'the paradigmatic product of Geneva School neoliberalism' and the 'creation of the WTO (as) a crowning victory of the neoliberal project of

[4] Cf EU Petersmann, *Constitutional Functions and Constitutional Problems of International Economic Law. International and Domestic Foreign Trade Law and Foreign Trade Policy in the United States, the European Community and Switzerland* (Fribourg UP/Westview Boulder Press 1991, reprinted by Routledge 2019), Chapters V–VIII; K Dam, 'Cordell Hull, the Reciprocal Trade Agreements Act and the WTO' in EU Petersmann (ed), *Reforming the World Trading System: Legitimacy, Efficiency and Democratic Governance* (OUP 2005), 83–98.

[5] On such constitutional economics interpretations of GATT rules see also M Hilf and EU Petersmann (eds), *National Constitutions and International Economic Law* (Kluwer 1993).

[6] Cf Petersmann (n 4); A Lang, *World Trade Law After Neoliberalism. Re-imagining the Global Economic Order* (OUP 2011). Note that contrary to Lang's definition of 'neoliberalism as an economic and political ideology over the last three decades of the twentieth century' (p. ix), my publications acknowledge that the term 'neo-liberalism' was coined at the international Lippmann colloquium in Paris in 1938 as a response to liberalism's crisis caused by Marxism, communism, fascism, and Keynsian economics; in contrast to Lang, who describes the period from 1947 to the early 1970s as 'the period of embedded liberalism' (at 16) and the following period up to around 2000 as 'the neoliberal turn' (at 17), some GATT/WTO agreements (like the 1979 GATT 'Enabling Clause', the DSU) and domestic economic law developments (eg in EU competition, monetary, social, and environmental regulation) pursued ordo-liberal regulation rather than deregulation and liberalization of markets.

finding an extra-economic enforcer for the world economy in the twentieth century'.[7] Like many other Anglo-Saxon commentators on neo-liberalism, however, Slobodian overlooks the differences between Anglo-Saxon neo-liberalism and European ordo-liberalism. US neo-liberalism and Chicago School economists prioritize liberalization of market access barriers, deregulation, privatization, and financialization of markets in order to empower utilitarian market actors (*homo economicus*) to pursue their self-interests and enhance the self-regulating forces of market competition as spontaneous information, coordination, and sanctioning mechanisms. The German, European, and Virginia Schools of ordo-liberalism perceive markets as legal constructs of reasonable citizens (rather than as gifts of nature) who cannot maximize their general consumer welfare without legal limitations of market, governance, and constitutional failures.[8] GATT/WTO jurisprudence (eg on interpreting GATT/WTO rules as protecting non-discriminatory conditions of competition) emphasized the systemic, ordo-liberal functions of states and of the GATT/WTO legal and dispute settlement systems as guardians of non-discriminatory conditions of competition. US President Trump's assault on the world trading, health protection, and environmental systems illustrates how constitutional choices—like Congressional delegation of vast trade policy powers to the US President, irresponsible Congressional abdication of control over the trade wars initiated by President Trump, judicial deference vis-à-vis money-driven interest group politics (like corporate financing of election campaigns for the US Congress), and regulatory capture of economic policies at Washington, DC (as illustrated by the appointment of long-standing trade lobbyists to the positions of US Trade Representative (USTR) and US ambassador to the WTO) can quickly disrupt democratic governance and the rules-based international order.[9] Yet, the 1934 US Reciprocal Trade Agreements Act designed by US Secretary of State Cordell Hull also demonstrated how the protectionist interest group politics behind the congressional Smoot–Hawley tariffs of 1930 could be constrained by legislation enabling the Executive branch to negotiate reciprocal trade liberalization agreements subject to fast-track approval by Congress.

The European ordo-liberal schools of thought contrast sharply with the economic paradigm underlying the recent Report on the Appellate Body (AB) of the WTO by the USTR of February 2020,[10] which perceives WTO law as an instrument of US power politics and disregards ordo-liberal constitutional economics justifying the multilateral WTO legal and dispute settlement systems. The legal

[7] Q Slobodian, *Globalists: The End of Empire and the Birth of Neoliberalism* (Harvard UP 2018), at 23–5.

[8] On the differences between Anglo-Saxon, utilitarian neo-liberalism and European, constitutional ordo-liberalism see also J Hien and C Joerges, *Ordoliberalism, Law and the Rule of Economics* (Hart 2020), Chapters 2 and 6.

[9] As discussed in Chapter 3, it was only in a judgment of 14 July 2020 that the US Court of International Trade began annulling some of the executive import restrictions of US President Trump.

[10] For a criticism of this report see Chapter 3, sections 3.3 and 3.4.

justifications by the Trump administration of its illegal blocking of WTO AB nominations insisted on US interpretations of WTO rules—and US criticism of AB findings—without any evidence that legal interpretations by the AB violated the customary rules of treaty interpretation or the (quasi)judicial AB mandate for impartial, independent, and prompt third-party adjudication through quasi-automatic adoption of WTO panel and AB reports by the Dispute Settlement Body (DSB). US trade policies prioritizing reciprocal bargaining (like the WTO-inconsistent China–US deal of January 2020) also ignore the US legal obligations under Article XV:4 WTO Agreement, that is to ensure the conformity of domestic laws, regulations, and administrative procedures with the WTO Agreements. Authoritarian strongmen may benefit from intergovernmental power politics, neo-liberal interest group politics, and from populist (eg anti-elitist and anti-pluralist) nationalism ('America First'). Yet, citizens all over the world will suffer from neglect of the ordo-liberal task of limiting governance and constitutional failures in multilateral governance of transnational PGs. Is ordo-liberal economic constitutionalism— like the WTO appellate review system and jurisprudence—justifiable and politically realistic beyond EU law? Will the worker-centred trade policy announced by the US Biden administration—and its increasing interest in reshaping the relationship between economic globalization and economic inequality in order to respond to the rise of anti-global populism inside the United States and to the illegal migration problems and trade distortions caused by dysfunctional labour markets abroad (eg in many Central and Latin-American countries)—lead to renewed interest in the EU's social market economy traditions?

4.2 The Knowledge Problem of Law and the SDGs: Dare to Understand

Chapter 2, section 2.1 emphasized the dual nature and antagonistic dialectic of modern positive legal systems challenging the internal and external legitimacy of law as a normative order, for instance when citizens and people contest the power-oriented foundations of states, authoritarian rulers, and intergovernmental power politics as being inconsistent with modern HRL and democratic constitutionalism. If power-oriented 'rules of recognition' (eg for determining rules and subjects of international law) used to be social facts up to the start of the Second World War, democratic constitutionalism and the modern rules of treaty interpretation (eg in the Preamble of the Vienna Convention on the Law of Treaties) now acknowledge principles of justice and human rights and fundamental freedoms for all that legally constrain legal recognition of power politics. In the twenty-first century, they also offer an increasing number of legal, democratic, and judicial remedies, including access to justice to regional and international courts of justice. The internal logic of normative legal orders as rules-based frameworks for legal argumentation and decision-making and the external, political challenges of their institutional autonomy (eg of WTO law as interpreted by the AB) raise the question of the interdisciplinary interrelationships between

- *law as an instrument of social regulation* and other social science disciplines (like economics and political science), and
- *law as a legal constraint on economics and politics* if the latter present themselves as strategies for designing legal rules in 'efficient' (eg in terms of cost–benefit analyses) and 'democratic' ways (eg in terms of transparent, participatory, deliberative, and rules-based, democratic discourses).

Lawyers emphasize not only that international law has evolved into a legal system (eg in terms of HLA Hart's criteria) limiting the instrumental usefulness of other social science disciplines and the risks of their manipulation (eg by neo-liberalism as justification of US hegemony, economic power structures, and of extra-territorial US economic sanctions even against allied democracies, as in the case of the Nord Stream 2 sanctions). They also admit that justice requires openness of lawyers to economic, political science, environmental, and other social science proposals for protecting PGs and reforming legal regulation and its underlying politics.[11] If the validity of legal rules is derived from hierarchical normative orders founded on a rule of recognition as a concordant social practice,[12] then the state-centred UN and WTO legal practices reveal path-dependent *status quo* biases privileging power politics; the universal recognition of human rights reinforces the need for understanding legal obligations also in interactional terms as deriving not only from formal criteria (authoritative imposition) but also from the consent of citizens to the morality, justice, and internal legitimacy of norms.[13] Legal obligations lose their legitimacy (eg in terms of providing reasons for actions and rule compliance) if they no longer contribute to realizing legitimate, normative goals such as the SDGs; without such legitimacy, citizens and civil

[11] On Koskenniemi's criticism of the 'hubris of instrumental knowledge' and of 'the anarchy of autonomous functional systems: trade, human rights, environment, security, diplomacy, and so on' (M Koskenniemi, *The Politics of International Law* (Hart 2011), at 324–6), see D Roth-Isigkeit, The Blinkered Discipline? Marti Koskenniemi and Interdisciplinary Approaches to International Law, *International Theory* 9 (2017), 410–35. My 2012 monograph, *International Economic Law in the 21st Century* (Hart 2012), used the New Haven School approach describing law as a process of authoritative jurisprudence and policy decisions oriented toward protection of human dignity (like respect for the intrinsic value, moral autonomy, and fundamental equality of every human being); but it also emphasized the need for respecting legitimate constitutional pluralism and the advantages of Europe's multilevel economic constitutionalism constraining domestic and foreign policy powers by multilevel human rights constitutionalism. The dual nature of modern positive law (ie its incorporation of natural law principles of justice challenging law's internal legitimacy, and the challenges to its external legitimacy through the politics of legal practices) constrains the autonomy of legal systems and of law as a rules-based process of reasoning that structures our social world so as to protect equal freedoms, rule of law, and moral, legal, and constitutional responsibility.

[12] Cf HLA Hart, *The Concept of Law* (3rd edn, OUP 2012), at 110.

[13] J Brunnée and SJ Toope, *Legitimacy and Legality in International Law: An Interactional Account* (CUP 2010), 20–55.

societies have reasons for contesting authoritarian power politics, legal formalism, and legal discourse neglecting the SDGs. The more individual, Kantian morality is being transformed through constitutionalism and democratic discourse into a new democratic public reason challenging authoritarian power politics (eg in the UN Security Council), the more legitimacy can alliances of democratic countries assert for challenging power-oriented interpretations of UN and WTO law (like the illegal US blocking of the WTO AB, India's blocking of Doha Round negotiations) and their path-dependent *status quo* bias by invoking the universally approved SDGs and their underlying social science justifications.

The SDGs aim at transforming the discretionary politics of UN legal practices by empowering everybody through human rights to flourish and develop human capacities in sustainable ways. The legal design of global law for governance of PGs (like regulation of trade, finance, climate change, the Internet, electronic commerce, public health, poverty reduction), and of inalienable human rights as constitutional restraints on power politics, are increasingly influenced also by expert knowledge for dealing with the complexity of regulatory challenges (eg resulting from new technologies for electronic commerce, fighting climate change and health pandemics). Legal interpretation involves not only political choices and a turn to ethics. The universal agreement on 17 SDGs with 169 policy targets also reflects a turn to human reason, as specified by social and natural sciences. Many politicians (like President Trump) and critical legal theorists refuse to engage with economic theories explaining why trade has been instrumental in lifting billions of people out of poverty over the past decades, for instance based on their mercantilist beliefs, self-interests, or populist claims that the correctness of economists' models always depends on a number of assumptions not directly addressed in them.[14] The claim of critical legal theories (eg as represented by Koskenniemi) that 'law is incapable of providing convincing justifications to the solution of normative problems',[15] cannot be derived from descriptions of the politics of indeterminate international law transforming lawyers into moralists, nor from Koskenniemi's critique of liberalism, human rights, and economics:[16]

[14] M Koskenniemi, *International Law and the Far Right: Reflections on Law and Cynicism* (Asser Institute 2020), at 17. According to Koskenniemi, 'the cynicism of the "system" lies in its insufficient scepticism' (at 31). Yet, Koskenniemi's radical scepticism about values and reform proposals—apart from pleading for truthfulness and emancipation—can also be seen as a refusal to clarify public reason and change harmful practices by engaging with the social and natural sciences underlying the SDGs.

[15] Cf M Koskenniemi, *From Apology to Utopia. The Structure of International Legal Argument* (CUP 2005), at 69. Koskenniemi's focus on discretionary political decision-making—and his contempt for liberal theories of justice ('the liberals are my enemies') justifying the need for democratic 'institutionalization of public reason' (J Rawls) and of human rights—resemble the reasoning of C Schmitt for political decision-makers in exceptional situations. For a criticism, see JL Dunoff, From Interdisciplinarity to Counterdisciplinarity: Is there Madness in Marti's Method? *Temple International & Comparative Law Journal* 27 (2013), 309–38.

[16] Cf Chapter 2, section 2.1. Koskenniemi's emphasis on the open-ended nature of international legal discourse and of the purposes and meaning of legal rules, and his endless criticism of false universalism (like human rights and the fight against impunity which he describes as 'hegemonic maneuvers') present themselves as Socratic dialogues, yet without an academic theory of justice, doctrinal,

- The ethical commitment (eg underlying UN HRL, the 17 SDGs and their 169 agreed policy targets) to inclusive reasoning, humanism, and emancipation requires clarifying our understanding of the world through evidence-based science (eg open debates with conjectures and refutations, as explained by Karl Popper) accepting our cosmopolitan responsibilities for transforming our world in order to realize the agreed SDGs. The past technological, economic, and human rights 'revolutions' enabled progressive realization of the US revolutionary ideals of 'life, liberty and pursuit of happiness' and the French revolutionary ideals of '*liberté, égalité et fraternité*', even if the remaining social injustices (like unequal distribution of power and wealth) are reminders of the imperfections of all political and legal struggles.
- Empirical evidence also demonstrates that democratic constitutionalism, deliberative democracy, and institutionalization of public reason (eg in independent regulatory agencies like central banks, competition, public health, and environmental agencies) not only enable but also require going beyond Koskenniemi's semantic and interpretative argumentative games with indeterminate legal rules. While competing legal and social science doctrines are likely to remain controversial, democratic, legislative, administrative, judicial, and other agreed procedures provide for authoritative decision-making powers, including multilevel constitutionalism protecting human rights, multilevel governance, and third-party adjudication of disputes among member states. If 'entropy, evolution and information' can be identified as the 'enlightenment challenges' of our modern human condition,[17] the SDG of a 'global partnership for sustainable development … with the participation of all countries, all stakeholders and all people' deserves support as a humanitarian enlightenment strategy aimed at reducing social injustices, intergovernmental abuses of power, and bad faith governance in authoritarian UN member states. Lawyers have moral responsibilities to criticize the hegemonic purposes of US neo-liberalism and totalitarian state capitalism and the *status quo* bias of intergovernmental power politics, and to resist populist and tribal counter-enlightenment movements that prioritize nationalist

or institutional reform proposals, or practical proposals for improving social justice, in view of his emphasis on the inescapably situated, contextual, and contested nature and politics of legal claims, arguments, and related structural biases favouring certain actors and outcomes. His proposed 'culture of legal formalism' is less about finding correct answers in legal doctrine and professional practices than about protecting adversarial processes of legal argumentation among juridical equals.

[17] Cf S Pinker, *Enlightenment Now. The Case for Science, Reason, Humanism and Progress* (Penguin 2018), at 14ff. Entropy (eg disorder in closed systems) can be transformed into more orderly, open systems through evolution, and better information; 'for all the flaws in human nature, it contains the seeds of its own improvement, as long as it comes up with norms and institutions that channel parochial interests into universal benefits' (at 28).

authoritarianism over cosmopolitan dialogues on universal reason, science, and humanist progress in our search for justice.

4.3 Institutional Economics, Democracy, and International Law

Economic activities, like production, distribution, and consumption of goods and services and related investments, are influenced not only by offer and demand from *private* economic actors like producers, investors, traders, and consumers. They are also strongly influenced by political values (like human rights, public health), legal institutions (like common law liberties, protection of monetary stability by central banks, property rights, contract law, corporate law, rule of law), technological progress (eg enabling past industrial revolutions based on steam power, electricity, information and communication technologies), social institutions (like markets, trust, corruption, religious and cultural traditions like gender equality), political governance institutions and government policies as explored by institutional economics and ordo-liberal analyses of the interactions among law, societies, polities, and economies.[18] Humans create legal institutions (eg as formalized extension of social norms more generally) in order to live and cooperate peacefully, limit risks (such as Hobbesian wars of each against each other), reduce transaction costs (eg due to uncertainty and incomplete information), and promote welfare through agreed rules limiting coordination problems and abuses of public and private power.[19] While the design of legal institutions depends on public and private preferences and traditions, economic analysis offers normative and analytical yardsticks for the design of legal institutions. The focus of institutional economics on legal rules offers a suitable, albeit under-researched framework and interdisciplinary approach to studying international economic law. The

[18] Cf C Ménard and MM Shirley, (eds), *Introduction to a Research Agenda for New Institutional Economics* (Edward Elgar 2018); E Furubotn and R Richter, *Institutions and Economic Theory The Contribution of the New Institutional Economics* (2nd edn, University of Michigan Press 2005); K Viscusi, JM Vernon, and JE Harrington, *Economics of Regulation and Antitrust* (2nd edn, MIT Press 1995). The German and European schools of ordo-liberalism are documented in the more than seventy volumes of the annual *ORDO-Jahrbuch für die Ordnung von Wirtschaft und Gesellschaft*, first published in 1949 by the two founders of the Freiburg School of ordo-liberalism (ie W Eucken and F Böhm) together with FA Hayek. For recent analyses see also Hien and Joerges (n 8). The 'Freiburg I' variant of ordo-liberalism (as elaborated by the economist W Eucken and the lawyer F Böhm) was progressively adapted by 'Freiburg II economists' (like FA Hayek, E Hoppmann, V Vanberg), lawyers (like EJ Mestmäcker), and leading German politicians (from German chancellors L Erhard up to A Merkel) and German EU politicians (like W Hallstein, von der Groeben) supporting ordo-liberal proposals for a social market economy, as later explicitly incorporated into EU law (cf Article 3 TEU). On the need for responsive regulation and the role of procedural justice in promoting voluntary compliance, see P Drahos (ed), *Regulatory Theory. Foundations and Application* (Australian National UP 2017), Chapters 1–3, 7–8.

[19] On the importance of transaction costs in the emergence of firms and other market institutions see: R Coase, The Problem of Social Cost, *The Journal of Law and Economics* 3 (1960), 1–44; OE Williamson, *Markets and Hierarchies. Analysis and Antitrust Implications* (Free Press 1975).

institutional economic benchmark shares with neoclassical economics certain fundamental assumptions (such as methodological and normative individualism); on other accounts, it extends the analysis to other aspects that are typically ignored in neo-classical economics.[20] To the extent that neo-classical economics assumes the existence and market-clearing function of 'perfect' competition and the absence of transactions costs (allowing what is referred to as the Coase theorem), institutional economics instils what lawyers may find more realistic when dealing with interpreting and analysing legal rules: in the real world without perfect market competition and without equal access to human capabilities, economic resources, and opportunities, a move toward free markets may not enhance efficiency.[21] The political economy environment with its heterogeneity of stakeholders and interests matters for the design of legal rules. Given the persistence of transaction costs, legal institutions offer plausible solutions to deal with transaction costs in cost-effective ways. Emphasis should be given to constitutional choices regarding protection of human capabilities, constitutional rights of citizens (like equal access to education, health protection, satisfaction of basic needs), and the principal–agent relationship between citizens and governance agents with limited, delegated powers. From a citizen perspective, both economic markets (eg coordinating supply and demand among producers, workers, traders, investors, and consumers) and political markets (eg among citizens, political voters, and politicians coordinating demand and supply for PGs) can be seen as citizen-driven (democratic) information, coordination, and sanctioning mechanisms in need of legal regulation of market , governance failures, and constitutional failures.

Constitutional economists (focusing on the constitutional rules that constrain the choices and activities of economic and political agents) apply the market assumption of individual pursuit of self-interests to political markets too. Constitutional contracts are interpreted as rules-based, contractarian processes (eg assigning all persons equal values), in contrast to post-constitutional governance that is often more akin to a result-oriented search of truth, for instance when organizations (like firms, political governments) receive limited, delegated powers for realizing specified goals. As political failures may be just as pervasive as market failures, the search for legal protection of individual preferences (eg by means of legal protection of human and fundamental rights) and for legal restraints on abuses of public and private power must explore not only *legislative* but also potential *constitutional rules* and the use of *multilevel governance mechanisms based on international law* and institutional checks and balances. Hence, rather than calculating efficiency only by way of cost–benefit studies, constitutional economists

[20] Furubotn and Richter (n 18), at 482–508.

[21] On the long history of feudal, capitalist, communist, and neo-liberal inequality regimes distorting market competition, the distribution of incomes, and wealth, see T Piketty, *Capital and Ideology* (Belknap Press 2019).

search for inclusive, reasonable agreements among citizens protecting democratic preferences, limiting special interests, and constraining government powers to discriminate (eg in response to rent-seeking pressures). Yet, the social contract ideal of citizens making reasonably informed constitutional choices is often confronted with the reality that economic actors and political regulators have only limited knowledge of the complex interactions among private and public, national, transnational, and international legal, economic, political, and social rules and institutions.[22] Their decisions may be influenced also by 'rational ignorance' and intuitive or irrational motives, as explained by behavioural economics and illustrated by the diversity of social contract theories and assumptions.[23] The paradox of freedom, that is the inherent risks of human freedoms destroying themselves by destructive abuses (eg of public and private power) rather than constructive uses respecting the equal freedoms of all others, has prompted all 193 UN member states to adopt national constitutions (written or unwritten) limiting governance failures in the supply of *national PGs*. The more globalization continues to transform *national* into *transnational PGs*, with increasing spillovers between countries' policies offering the economic rationale for policy coordination, the stronger becomes the need for 'constitutionalizing' *foreign policy powers* and the law of international organizations.[24]

Both neo-classical theory and institutional economics offer valuable analytical tools in addressing international law and economic regulation. For instance, scholarship has put emphasis on the issue of compliance with or disregard for international law rules (like customary law, national jurisdiction, establishment of international organizations) and the extent to which this may be influenced by economic considerations and choices.[25] Likewise, the notion of *institutional competition* normatively inspires the idea of political competition for, within, and between government(s) in order to produce benefits for citizens similar to those generated by economic market competition, for instance by promoting regulatory experimentation and competition. The sovereign equality of states and related

[22] Cf G Brennan and JM Buchanan, *The Reason of Rules. Constitutional Political Economy* (CUP 1985).

[23] On behavioural economics exploring intuitive or irrational economic behaviour, see, eg, A van Aaken and J Kurtz, Beyond Rational Choice: International Trade Law and the Behavioral Political Economy of Protectionism, *Journal of International Economic Law* 22 (2020), 601–28. On the historical evolution and institutional diversity of social contract theories from Plato's *Republic* (conceiving justice as a social contract among rational egoists), T Hobbes (social contracts as rational submission to the absolute political power of a monarch), J Locke (social contracts establishing constitutional governments with limited powers restrained by human rights retained by citizens), JJ Rousseau (social contracts as reconciling equal individual freedoms with the general will exercised by democratic legislators), to J Rawls (constitutional contracts protecting equal freedoms, equal opportunities, and difference principles of egalitarian justice), and their diverse conceptions of human beings (eg as naturally good by Rousseau contrary to Hobbes' conception of '*homo homini lupus est*'), see, eg, D Boucher and P Kelly (eds), *The Social Contract from Hobbes to Rawls* (Routledge 1994).

[24] Cf Petersmann (n 1).

[25] Cf JP Trachtman, *The Economic Structure of International Law* (Harvard UP 2008).

legal freedoms foster regulatory competition among states. However regulatory competition is often abused, for instance by extra-territorial power politics of stronger actors, or if governments (like the US Trump administration) welcome the adoption by the WTO DSB of constructive WTO dispute settlement rulings supporting their legal complaints vis-à-vis other WTO members but reject similar WTO dispute settlement findings against themselves as defendant on the ground that the rulings create new obligations not consented to by their government.[26] Institutional economics explains the need for legal institutions limiting moral hazard inside multilevel governance and federal states,[27] with rules on balanced budgets, governing bailouts of banks, and sovereign defaults (more recently controversially discussed in the Eurozone) as prominent examples.

Democratic constitutions can become effective only through progressive transformation of their constitutional rules into democratic legislation, administration, and adjudication protecting rule of law, equal rights of citizens, and voluntary rule compliance. Similarly, world order treaties—like the UN Charter and the WTO Agreement—can protect global PGs only through additional legislative, administrative, and judicial implementing acts (like political or judicial interpretations clarifying indeterminate treaty provisions) supported by citizens. Unequal distribution of human and economic resources risks aggravating social inequalities to a point that citizens may lose trust (eg in social justice, political élites), circumvent the law (eg through tax avoidance, black markets, illegal transactions), or appoint populist, demagogic rulers advocating narrowly conceived national identities.[28] Normative institutional economics therefore emphasizes the need for social embedding of international economic regulation and for institutionalizing public reason, for instance by HRL promoting humanistic cosmopolitan values, independent monetary authorities protecting monetary stability, independent competition authorities protecting non-discriminatory conditions of competition, impartial third-party adjudication protecting rule of law and equal rights of citizens, and social market economies protecting social rights and social peace.

History confirms this dialectic evolution of law, legal practices, and legal systems as instruments of rules-based social, political, and economic ordering and of result-oriented utility maximization. The often spontaneous emergence and functioning of local markets (eg responding to supply and demand for local goods and services) depended, *inter alia*, on legal guarantees of contract law (*pacta sunt servanda*), private property rights, monetary means of payment or barter, tort and criminal law (eg limiting fraud). In response to abuses of monetary and police powers entailing legal insecurity and market distortions, democratic and republican city states (eg since the ancient Greek and Italian city republics) introduced

[26] See Chapter 3, sections 3.3 and 3.4.
[27] Cf RD Cooter, *The Strategic Constitution* (Princeton UP 2000), 127ff.
[28] Cf A Case and A Deaton, *Deaths of Despair and the Future of Capitalism* (Princeton UP 2019).

republican laws limiting monetary, tax, and fiscal powers of governments. They also regulated monetary, trade, investment, and health policies, related contractual and property rights, and transnational trade and investment agreements (eg among city republics around the Mediterranean Sea, the Hanseatic cities around the North and Baltic seas).[29] The 1944 Bretton Woods Agreements and decolonization initiated progressive worldwide, legal, and institutional reforms of economic regulation aimed at limiting abuses of power (eg in authoritarian and imperial trade regimes) and protecting transnational PGs. The current schism fracturing the global legal, trade, and communication systems through a return to authoritarian nationalism, geopolitical rivalries, and extra-territorial power politics (eg by China, Russia, Saudi Arabia, Turkey, the United States) requires rethinking the design of international economic law (IEL) and of regulatory methodologies.

4.4 Welfare Economics Must Be Complemented by Constitutional Economics

Theories of knowledge (eg by Nobel Prize economist Friedrich A Hayek) justify markets, price mechanisms, and spontaneous emergence of market rules as decentralized information, coordination, and sanctioning mechanisms reflecting decentralized knowledge among individuals which no central government can possess. Classical economists (like Malthus and Ricardo) reduced economic questions to markets and incentives. Welfare economists demonstrate the existence of market failures (like abuses of power, cartel agreements, externalities, information asymmetries, PGs) and of distortions of the efficient functioning of market mechanisms. They may justify governmental trade and competition rules and other market interventions aimed at efficiency gains resulting from governmental limitations of market failures. Public choice economists warn of governance failures and constitutional failures that risk impeding or distorting governmental attempts at correcting market failures. Constitutional economists offer descriptive and normative insights. Descriptively, they assess and compare institutional arrangements of how societies transform individual preferences into collective choices and design institutions to correct market failures and avoid government failures.[30] Descriptive analysis may uncover institutional differences shaped by fundamentally divergent paradigms (eg neglect for racial discrimination, for the human rights of slaves and indigenous people, and for social justice in the US Constitution of 1787). Constitutional reforms (eg in communist economies) may

[29] For institutional economics analyses of the ancient economies of Rome and Greece, see T Terpstra, 'Neo-Institutionalism in Ancient Economic History' in Ménard and Shirley (eds), (n 18), Chapter 26.

[30] S Voigt, 'Constitutional Economics and the Law' in F Parisi (ed), *The Oxford Handbook of Law and Economics: Volume 1: Methodology and Concepts* (OUP 2017), at 206.

be of more existential importance for citizens than the utility maximization paradigm of efficient choices within existing constraints (like the use of black markets). Normatively, constitutional economists address the constitutional question of how people can live together in liberty, peace, and prosperity by using the exchange paradigm for exploring efficient choices of constraints. How should constitutional rights, obligations, and institutions be designed in order to constitute markets, protect democratic preferences, ensure individual freedoms, limit governance failures, and enhance economic welfare and social support through embedding economic law into social justice systems responding to democratic preferences and citizen demand for PGs?[31]

4.4.1 Legal Ranking of Economic Policy Instruments According to Their Efficiency

The economic paradigms inspiring governmental choices of institutions can be categorized along the bipolar relationship between state intervention and market freedom, with country- or region-specific paradigms varying in the degree to which one or the other prevails. For the success of developing legally binding international rules, a careful balancing of state policies and market freedoms in the design of binding law is decisive, both as a matter of political feasibility and economic efficiency. As constitutional pluralism at national levels of governance is likely to remain a permanent fact, international trade law must strike a balance between outlawing policies that cause significant harmful cross-border effects (eg discriminatory quantitative restrictions as prohibited in Articles XI and XIII GATT) on the one hand, and preserving room for states allowing them to pursue policy choices in line with their value system (like use of non-discriminatory tariffs, product regulations, and subsidies) on the other. Economics mirrors this need for balancing along criteria such as market and government failure, with each offering ground for efficiency considerations to allow for optimal intervention (like non-discriminatory carbon taxes aimed at internalizing harmful environmental external effects like carbon emissions contributing to climate change). To that end, GATT and WTO law, regional economic integration law, and domestic implementing laws rank alternative economic policy instruments according to their respective economic efficiency as explained by theories of optimal intervention, while at the same time maintaining scope for national regulation as needed to find support in states to surrender national policies to an international regime. For instance, Article III

[31] Cf V Vanberg, *The Constitution of Markets. Essays in Political Economy* (Routledge 2001); RB McKenzie (ed), *Constitutional Economics. Containing the Economic Powers of Government* (Lexington Books 1984); JM Buchanan, *The Economics and the Ethics of Constitutional Order* (University of Michigan Press 1991). Constitutional economics locates the ultimate sources of value only in individuals and in their constitutionally limited democratic agreements and informed exchange contracts.

GATT allows non-discriminatory domestic economic regulations (like tax, competition, consumer, and environmental protection rules, consumption and research subsidies). Article II GATT allows border tariffs up to the level of reciprocally negotiated tariff bindings. In turn, discriminatory non-tariff trade barriers tend to be prohibited (eg Articles III and XI GATT) unless they can be justified as being necessary for protection of non-economic PGs like public health, public morality (Article XX GATT), and national security (Article XXI GATT). The economic theory of optimal intervention justified GATT's legal ranking of alternative policy instruments in terms of their economic efficiency (eg use of transparent, non-discriminatory tariffs that do not interrupt price and market mechanisms); it promoted mutually welfare-enhancing, legal harmonization, which reduced transaction costs and political conflicts without limiting national sovereignty over non-discriminatory, domestic regulation of the economy and polity.[32]

4.4.2 Constitutional Approaches to Economic Regulation

In contrast to neo-liberal Chicago School recommendations for liberalizing market access barriers, deregulating and privatizing economic activities, and for financialization enhancing the self-regulatory forces of market competition (eg including financial speculation), the ordo-liberal European and Virginia Schools of constitutional economics perceive economic markets as legal constructs in need of systemic regulation of market, governance, and constitutional failures. Their thinking assigns the state the function to formulate and enforce framework policies which set out the general rules applicable to all economic actors without exception to avoid market failures, such as promoting non-discriminatory conditions of competition in the economy as a whole. States should refrain from process policies which distort individual business decisions and market solutions. Rather than steering sectors or individual business decisions on the basis of centralized planning, economic policies ought to be guided by constituent principles (like economic freedoms, property rights, and other fundamental rights of citizens, monetary and price stability protected by independent central banks), regulatory principles (eg for limiting market failures by competition, environmental, and social policies and institutions), and constitutional checks and balances (eg democratic constitutionalism limiting governance failures, protecting the rule of law, and holding governments accountable, judicial remedies of citizens, subsidiarity principles protecting decentralized governance mechanisms). This principled

[32] Cf M Corden, *Trade Policy and Economic Welfare* (OUP 1974). On the economic, legal, and political functions of GATT 1947 see GATT's chief economist J Tumlir, 'GATT Rules and Community Law' in M Hilf, FG Jacobs, and EU Petersmann (eds), *The European Community and GATT* (Kluwer 1986), 1–22.

thinking in terms of rules-based orders reflects the notion of a state seeking to reconcile both respect and promotion of individual liberties associated with the belief in the welfare-enhancing effects of market forces and state powers for value-based interventions to ensure commonly agreed levels of social and environmental results in society. This bipolar paradigm of ordo-liberal constitutional economics influenced the embedding of Germany's social market economy into German and European constitutional law. The EU's micro-economic common market constitution,[33] macro-economic monetary constitution,[34] their progressive evolution and judicial review[35] were influenced by German and European ordo-liberalism.[36] Due to its constitutional embeddedness, the regulatory functions of economic law inside the EU often diverge from those inside neo-liberal and state capitalist countries.[37]

Ordo-liberalism calls for legal safeguards that the *competitive order* (protecting performance competition and price mechanisms) remains embedded in mutually coherent *monetary order* (eg protecting price stability, fiscal discipline), *democratic constitutionalism* (eg holding European network governance accountable through multilevel competition, monetary and other regulatory agencies, and their parliamentary and judicial control), and *social order* (eg protecting labour markets, welfare states, social justice, and judicial remedies). In line with the ordo-liberal paradigm, normative constitutional economics criticizes the neo-liberal focus on utility maximization, rational rent-seeking, assumptions of perfect market competition without transaction costs, and gross domestic products to the extent that satisfaction of the basic needs of all citizens, enhancement of human capacities (Amartya Sen), and their mutually agreed protection through constitutional rights offer better benchmarks for human well-being. The EU Charter of Fundamental Rights (EUCFR) guarantees civil, political, economic, social, and European citizenship rights that protect not only negative freedoms (eg constraining abuses of public and private power). Rights empowering individuals to exercise positive freedoms (eg human rights to education, health protection, freedom of association, decent living and working conditions) through governmental protection of

[33] For example, based on multilevel common market freedoms, competition, environmental, and social rules, multilevel competition institution, and regulatory competition constrained by multilevel judicial protection of civil, political, economic, and social rights.

[34] For example, based on EU legal disciplines for monetary, fiscal, debt, and economic policies supervised by multilevel, independent central banks and intergovernmental economic cooperation.

[35] Cf HCH Hofmann, K Pantazatou, and G Zaccaroni (eds), *The Transformation of the European Economic Constitution* (Edward Elgar 2019); C Kaupa, *The Pluralist Character of the European Economic Constitution* (Hart 2016).

[36] On the EU's sectoral (eg micro-economic, macro-economic, and social) constitutions, see K Tuori, *European Constitutionalism* (CUP 2015), 127ff. On constitutional economics and the controversies over applying ordo-liberalism to the EU's monetary union, see T Biebricher and F Vogelmann (eds), *The Birth of Austerity. German Ordoliberalism and Contemporary Neoliberalism* (Rowman & Littlefield 2017); J Hien and C Joerges (2017).

[37] Cf PF Kjaer (ed), *The Law of Political Economy: Transformation in the Function of Law* (CUP 2020).

individual self-development (eg human dignity) can be seen as constitutional core values of social market economies. The social market economy progressively established in Germany since the 1960s, and the EU law commitments to a competitive social market economy (Article 3 of the Treaty on European Union (TEU)) with ever more guarantees of social rights structured around three priorities—equal opportunities for education, professional training, and access to labour markets; fair working conditions; and access to social protection and healthcare for all—illustrate how ordo-liberal constructivism differs from neo-liberal faith in self-regulatory capacities of markets generating ever larger social inequalities inside neo-liberal economies like the United States.

4.4.3 The Geneva School of Ordo-Liberalism

Constitutional economics justifying multilevel economic constitutionalism (like multilevel legal and judicial protection of EU common market freedoms, European competition law, and fundamental rights) has become an integral part of European integration law as practised in the thirty member states of the EEA. The Geneva School of multilevel ordo-liberalism[38] focused on constitutional justifications of *worldwide economic order* so as to enable welfare states and multilevel legal, institutional, and judicial guarantees of non-discriminatory market competition limiting abuses of public and private powers beyond European integration. Notably, the economists (like GATT's chief economist Jan Tumlir) and lawyers working inside GATT's economic research and legal divisions were more influenced by constitutional economics[39] than by utilitarian Chicago School economists (eg in view of their normative premises underlying the distributive effects of Kaldor–Hicks efficiencies). Some of the constitutional, competition, and social policy principles of ordo-liberalism have influenced the progressive legal construction and political

[38] Cf EU Petersmann, 'International Economic Theory and International Economic Law—On the Tasks of a Legal Theory of International Economic Order' in RSJ Macdonald and DM Johnston (eds), *The Structure and Process of International Law* (Nijhoff 1983) 227–61, and P Lamy, *The Geneva Consensus. Making Trade Work for All* (CUP 2013); H Hauser, P Moser, R Planta, and R Schmid, 'The Contribution of Jan Tumlir to the Development of a Constitutional Theory of International Trade Rules' (in German with English summary) in *Ordo-Jahrbuch für die Ordnung von Wirtschaft und Gesellschaft* 39 (1988), 219–38; Slobodian (n 7), 7ff, 183ff, 208ff, 260ff. My review of Slobodian's book criticizes his failure to recognize the ordo-liberal—rather than neo-liberal—foundations of the Geneva School: cf *Journal of International Economic Law* 19 (2018), 915–21. See also the critical book review by F Roessler in *World Trade Review* 18 (2019), 353–9.

[39] For example, as taught by the ordo-liberal Freiburg School (eg W Eucken, F Böhm, FA Hayek, V Vanberg) and Virginia School (eg J Buchanan) defining economic efficiency not only in terms of Pareto and Kaldor–Hicks efficiency (based on utilitarian premises), but also by (hypothetical) individual and democratic consent to inclusive, reasonable rules reconciling the interests of all affected citizens. Buchanan cooperated with Freiburg School scholars (like Vanberg) and received the 1986 Nobel Prize in Economic Sciences for his development of the contractual and constitutional bases for the theory of economic and political decision-making (eg rejecting any organic conception of the state as superior in wisdom to its citizens).

legitimation of the GATT/WTO legal and dispute settlement systems, for instance in designing multilevel legal restraints of trade policy instruments according to their respective economic efficiency (as illustrated by Articles I–III, XI GATT, VI–IX General Agreement on Trade in Services (GATS)), separating trade and monetary policy instruments (cf Article XV GATT, XI GATS), interpreting GATT/WTO market access commitments as protecting non-discriminatory conditions of competition, protecting and prioritizing sovereign powers to regulate and protect non-economic PGs in non-discriminatory ways (cf Articles XIX–XXI GATT, XIV–XIV*bis* GATS); providing for legal accountability and multilevel judicial remedies limiting rule-violations and other abuses of power (eg in Articles X, XXIII GATT, XXIII GATS); and promoting domestic implementation of WTO rules (cf Article XVI:4 WTO Agreement) and progressive evolution of the incomplete GATT/WTO system through progressive legal, political, and judicial clarifications and development of indeterminate GATT/WTO rules and underlying principles, in close cooperation with trade-related, other international organizations.[40] As reciprocal trade liberalization depends on inclusive policy-making supported by citizens (all politics is local), some GATT lawyers interpreted these domestic policy functions of GATT's embedded liberalism compromise—and the judicial review of the necessity and proportionality of trade restrictions (discussed in Chapter 2, section 2.4)—as constitutional functions of GATT rules for promoting equal freedoms, non-discrimination, rule of law, judicial remedies, and social justice also inside domestic economies and polities for the benefit of citizens.[41]

Policy recommendations from institutional and constitutional economics remain controversial, however, as illustrated by the disagreements on the future design of the European monetary and banking union and related constitutional restraints of the EU (eg for financing EU and national expenses through Euro-bonds). Similarly, the WTO Doha Round negotiations since 2001 have failed to adjust WTO rules to the regulatory challenges of the twenty-first century. The perception that less-developed 'Global South' advocates (like India) had blocked the conclusion of the Doha Round for ideological reasons, and that the ability to self-declare as a less-developed country in order to benefit from the more than 100 WTO provisions on special and differential treatment had been abused, contributed to the US assault on the WTO dispute settlement system ushering in the blocking of the

[40] The GATT/WTO jurisprudence (eg on interpreting GATT/WTO rules as protecting non-discriminatory conditions of competition) reinforces this ordo-liberal function of states and of the GATT/WTO dispute settlement systems as guardians of the competitive order.

[41] Cf the contributions by F Roessler, EU Petersmann, JH Jackson, RE Hudec, J Bourgeois, P Pescatore, T Cottier, M Matsushita, and numerous other American, Asian, and European GATT lawyers to Hilf and Petersmann (eds) (n 5). Some of these GATT lawyers recognized domestic policy functions of GATT rules (eg for improving the transparency and efficiency of domestic trade legislation and administration) rather than constitutional functions (eg in the sense of Cordell Hull's use of reciprocal trade agreements for self-limitation of congressional powers, or for judicial application of certain clear and unconditional GATT prohibitions for protecting non-discriminatory conditions of competition inside states against rent-seeking interest group politics).

WTO AB and its jurisprudence. Similar to the successful EU initiatives for using Article 25 DSU for interim appeal arbitration among WTO members (as briefly discussed in Chapter 3), the additional EU initiatives aimed at replacing investor–state arbitration inside the EU—as well as in the external relations of the EU—by new kinds of multilevel investment adjudication respond to the increasing civil society challenges of investor bias and insufficient guarantees of public interests in international investment arbitration.[42] The systemic rivalries between neo-liberal, state capitalist, and ordo-liberal policies entail increasing challenges of other international jurisdictions too, like the International Tribunal for the Law of the Sea, the International Criminal Court, and the European Court of Human Rights (ECtHR) as independent and impartial institutions for protecting transnational rule of law and, thereby, reducing international transaction costs as well.

4.4.4 Utilitarian vs Rights-Based Approaches to Environmental Law

Environmental regulation in the United States tends to be based on cost–benefit analyses grounded in the Kaldor–Hicks principle of economic efficiency, social net benefit considerations, and pragmatic, neo-liberal neglect for the 'polluter pays' principle rather than on constitutional and environmental rights, principles of corrective justice, and multilevel environmental regulation incorporating environmental treaty obligations into domestic legal systems. For instance, significant levels of environmental pollution are tolerated in the United States based on cost–benefit analyses (eg that the social benefits outweigh the environmental costs), non-enforcement of the 'polluter pays' principle and climate change denial by Republican politicians.[43] Constitutional law in the EU and many European countries, by contrast, protects fundamental rights and corresponding governmental duties and judicial remedies to protection of the environment. For instance, as discussed in Chapter 8, section 8.4.4, the decision by Germany's Constitutional Court of 24 March 2021 upheld some of the constitutional complaints that the state had not implemented sufficient regulations for the immediate reduction of GHGs, especially carbon dioxide (CO_2), which were necessary to keep the rise in the earth's

42 Cf Chapter 7 and ML Marceddu and P Ortolani, What Is Wrong with Investment Arbitration? *European Journal of International Law* 31 (2020), 405–28.

43 Cf ED Elliot and DC Esty, The End Environmental Externalities Manifesto: A Rights-Based Foundation for Environmental Law, *NYU Environmental Law Journal* (2021, forthcoming). The authors criticize the Kaldor–Hicks fallacy underlying US efforts at developing cost-effective ways to reduce obvious pollution and argue for reframing environmental law and policy on an intellectual foundation of environmental rights rather than economic efficiency. Their call for an *end to externalities* is centred on a societal goal of eliminating pollution based on their proposed, legislative recognition of rights to protection of the environment and corresponding obligations of pollution emitters to pay compensation for any residual emissions that remain after technologically feasible pollution controls have been implemented.

temperature from today's average temperatures to 1.5 °C, or at least stop at well below 2 °C. The Court interpreted the constitutional right to protection of life and physical integrity (Article 2.2 Basic Law) of the private, mainly younger complainants as including:

> protection against damage to fundamental rights by environmental pollution, irrespective of by whom and by what circumstances they threaten. The state's duty to protect following from Article 2, Paragraph 2, Clause 1 of the Basic Law also includes the obligation to protect life and health from the dangers of climate change. It can also establish an objective legal obligation to protect with regard to future generations.

The Court followed that from this constitutional right and from Article 20a Basic Law (which obliges the state to protect the climate, including the aim to achieve climate neutrality)—in the event of a conflict—the constitutional obligation of climate protection must be brought into balance with other constitutional principles and requires the democratic legislator to specify carbon reduction commitments in ways that protect future generations, not just today's. As this constitutional requirement for intergenerational climate justice had been neglected in Germany's climate protection legislation, the Court required the legislator to prescribe more balanced carbon reduction commitments also for the period beyond 2030. According to the Court:

> As a climate protection requirement, Art. 20a Basic Law has an international dimension. The national climate protection obligation does not conflict with the fact that the global character of climate and global warming excludes a solution to the problems of climate change by one state alone. The climate protection law requires the state to act internationally for global protection of the climate and obliges to work towards climate protection within the framework of international coordination. The state cannot evade its responsibility by referring to greenhouse gas emissions in other states.[44]

As compatibility with Article 20a of the Basic Law is a prerequisite for the constitutional justification of state interference with fundamental rights, the Court found that the lack of legislative reduction targets for periods from 2031 onwards made

[44] The Decision can be found on the website of the German Constitutional Court (BVerfG, decision of the First Senate of March 24, 2021—1 BvR 2656/18, Rn. 1-270, http://www.bverfg.de/e/rs20210324_1bvr265618.html); the quotations are from the guiding principles summarized at the beginning of the Decision. For a more detailed discussion of this judgment, see Chapter 8, section 4.4. On the advantages of a rights-based approach in German and European economic and environmental regulation (ie empowering rights holders to challenge legally unjustified restrictions through legal and judicial remedies), see EU Petersmann, *International Economic Law in the 21st Century* (Hart 2012), Chapters II–III.

certain parts of the Federal Climate Protection Act of 2019 incompatible with the constitutional rights of the complainants insofar as the adverse impact of climate change and of heavier, future carbon reduction requirements from 2031 onwards—necessary in order to comply with the remaining CO_2 budget corresponding to the temperature threshold of 1.5 °C—risked disproportionately affecting the equal freedoms of younger generations. The Court also refers to Germany's legal obligations under the 2015 Paris Agreement as the declared basis of the Climate Protection Act of 2019, as well as to governmental duties under the European Convention on Human Rights (eg Article 2) and the EU Charter of Fundamental Rights (eg Article 37) to protect individuals from life-threatening environmental dangers; however, these international legal obligations do not modify the constitutional rights and duties under Article 2.2 of the German Basic Law.[45]

4.5 Design of International Economic Law Requires Institutional Economics

The influence of constitutional and institutional economics on the legal design of multilevel trade and investment regulation (as illustrated in section 4.4) is also true for other areas of IEL like monetary, investment, and environmental regulations. Institutional economics explores the organization and institutions related to production, distribution, and consumption of goods and services, including constitutional rules and institutions limiting market failures (eg related to abuses of power, cartel agreements, mergers and acquisitions, externalities, information asymmetries, PGs), governance failures, and constitutional failures through democratic regulation and checks and balances (eg including science-based, regulatory agencies like central banks, competition authorities, and environmental protection agencies). It complements neo-liberal welfare economics (eg focusing on markets and competition as incentives for reducing the scarcity of goods and services through division of labour exploiting comparative advantages) and constitutional economics (eg exploring economic rights of citizens and principles for constituting market competition, monetary stability, and the rule of law reducing transaction costs in free societies). The institutional characteristics of economies and of their legal, political, and social organization vary enormously across space and time. Empirical evidence confirms close interrelationships between legal systems and economic welfare (eg widespread poverty in communist countries like China, Cuba, and the Soviet Union prior to their introduction of market reforms based on private property and commercial laws). Understanding the concrete social and historical factors and cultures shaping the functioning of economies can

[45] For details see paras 137, 147, 204, 209, 210, and 211 of the Court decision (n 44), which is discussed in more detail in Chapter 8, section 4.4.

be enhanced through comparative studies (eg of behavioural production and consumption patterns, informal social belief systems, formal legal and political institutions). Neo-liberal economies (like the United States), ordo-liberal economies (like the European common market), and state capitalist economies (like China) are founded on different values (like Anglo-Saxon utilitarianism prioritizing 'negative' liberties, European rights-based economic constitutionalism prioritizing 'positive' liberties, totalitarian power monopolies in China). They represent dominant models of normativity in the relationship between states, markets, and citizens, without prejudice to other varieties of capitalism.[46]

The institutional economics perspective enables the analysis to differentiate the variable influence of different economic schools on international cooperation and on legal institutions, which they have fostered or undermined. The Bretton Woods agreement and GATT 1947 had been strongly influenced by Anglo-Saxon economic liberalism aimed at liberalizing trade barriers and promoting monetary stability and convertibility of currencies. However, while driven by liberal market paradigms, they were a first step of institutionalization and rules generation with the aim to restrain political and economic power. From an institutional economics perspective, the Bretton Woods environment established an institutional setting that, while maintaining the hegemonic predominance of the US economy (eg due to the use of the US dollar as the global reserve currency and its convertibility into gold), reduced legal uncertainty in international relations and fostered predictability through a web of international treaties. GATT 1947 had been designed as a provisional, intergovernmental agreement that should have been replaced by the 1948 Havana Charter for an International Trade Organization. The design of GATT institutions and of GATT's dispute settlement system progressively evolved through decisions of the GATT Contracting Parties and additional trade agreements resulting from eight GATT Rounds of multilateral trade negotiations. The WTO institutions and multilevel WTO dispute settlement system resulted from the multilateral Uruguay Round negotiations (1986–1994) ushering in the 1994 Agreement establishing the WTO and its DSU. The separation of legislative, executive, and judicial powers of WTO institutions (cf Article III WTO), the multilevel WTO governance structures (cf Article IV), the coordination of WTO activities with those of other worldwide and regional organizations (cf Articles V WTO,

[46] PA Hall and D Soskice, *Varieties of Capitalism: The Institutional Foundations of Comparative Advantage* (OUP 2001). This chapter's focus on neo-liberal, state capitalist, and ordo-liberal paradigms of market regulation does not ignore other varieties of capitalism, which were already noted by M Foucault, *The Birth of Biopolitics: Lectures at the College of France 1978–1979* (Palgrave Macmillan 2010), eg distinguishing the Freiburg School of ordo-liberalism from the Austrian school of neoclassical economics and the Chicago School's 'anarcho-liberalism', and observing at 131: 'the problem of neoliberalism was not how to cut out or contrive a free space of the market within an already given political society, as in the liberalism of Adam Smith and the eighteenth century. The problem of neoliberalism (was) rather how the overall exercise of political power can be modeled on the principles of a market economy.'

XXIV GATT), and the multilevel WTO dispute settlement system providing security and predictability to the multilateral trading system (Article 3 DSU) went beyond the market liberalization logic of economic liberalism by strengthening the ordo-liberal foundations of international cooperation (eg explaining welfare gains from informed consent to rules, rule of law, multilateral treaties, third-party adjudication of trade disputes) rather than only from utilitarian neo-liberalism (eg pursuing maximization of individual utilities and of Pareto and Kaldor–Hicks efficiencies).

With the progressive development from non-enforceable trade arrangements to sanctions-based adjudication, the institutional changes towards closer cooperation were—in line with the seminal work by Douglass North—driven by states pursuing profits from closer cooperation in terms of, *inter alia*, reduced uncertainty and lower transactions costs involved in international relations.[47] However, since the twentieth century when the founding thinkers of institutional economics (like Ronald Coase, North, Elinor Ostrom, Oliver Williamson) received their respective Nobel Prizes in economics, globalization and hegemonic power politics transformed and disrupted worldwide economic regulation. The Brussels School of law and economics (mainly driven by the EU Commissioners for competition policy, common market regulation, and legal services, and their academic advisers like Professor Ernst-Joachim Mestmäcker) and the jurisprudence of European economic courts have influenced the Geneva School of law and economics[48] and the jurisprudence of the WTO AB.[49] The trade wars instigated by the US Trump administration, and Brexit, confirmed, however, that global cooperation is no longer a one-way development trajectory towards a more rules-oriented outlook.[50]

The US Trump administration's assault on the established order, particularly on the WTO legal and dispute settlement systems, was driven by a return to hegemonic, mercantilist power politics and neo-liberal interest group politics, thus allowing a renaissance of political and economic forces, which the trade

[47] Cf DC North and RP Thomas, *The Rise of the Western World: A New Economic History* (CUP 1973); DC North, *Structure and Change in Economic History* (WW Norton 1981).

[48] For a discussion of the Geneva School of law and economics, and its comparison with other schools, see Chapter 2, section 2.5 and Petersmann (n 38) 227–61. The constitutional approach was endorsed also by WTO Director-General and former EU trade commissioner Lamy (n 38), who initiated regular parliamentary meetings inside the WTO and emphasized the synergies among human rights and rules-based trade (eg at 148ff). On the role of parliamentary diplomacy in EU external relations, see K Raubel, M Müftüler-Bac, and J Wouters (eds), *Parliamentary Cooperation and Diplomacy in EU External Relations* (Edward Elgar 2019).

[49] Cf Chapter 2, section 2.5 and T Soave, European Legal Culture and WTO Dispute Settlement: Thirty Years of Socio-Legal Transplants from Brussels to Geneva, *The Law and Practice of International Courts and Tribunals* 19 (2020), 107–33.

[50] Cf M Wolf, 'A deal to end the Brexit delusions', *Financial Times* 27 December 2020, explains why 'Brexit is, in many ways, the English equivalent of Donald Trump's promise to "make America great again". A big difference is that, unlike Mr Trump's time as US president, Brexit is forever. It seems almost certain to damage the country's prosperity and influence permanently'; for detailed criticism of the Brexit Agreement, see R Bhala, Britain's Brexit Deal Debacle, *Manchester Journal of International Economic Law* 18 (2021), 4–49.

systems sought to restrain by rules-based market competition and adjudication. Since December 2019, the illegal US blocking of the filling of AB vacancies enables unilateral blocking of WTO panel reports (eg by appealing into the void of a dysfunctional AB) and thus weakening the legal enforceability of WTO rules: it risks undermining the whole WTO legal and dispute settlement system. Similarly, the rising influence of authoritarian state capitalism threatens to undermine the rules-based trading system through state-induced, anti-competitive practices in guises as different as hidden subsidy practices, forced technology transfers, indirect discrimination, other market distortions, trade sanctions for political reasons, and military threats against WTO members (like India and the Philippines in their border conflicts with China). The geo-political rivalries among Anglo-Saxon neo-liberalism, European social market economies, and authoritarian state capitalism entail new economic risks (eg as illustrated by US justifications of discriminatory import restrictions by invoking national security exceptions), transaction costs, and institutional challenges (eg for limiting market distortions by state-owned enterprises (SOEs)) and security risks (eg resulting from dependence on Chinese SOEs controlling transnational energy, communication, and technology networks).[51] The global health pandemic of 2020 revealed insufficient healthcare institutions and medical supplies in many countries and protectionist, nationalist responses with adverse effects on the public health emergencies in others. The initially uncoordinated responses need to be studied with the analytical tools provided by institutional economics in order to examine what kind of multilateral rule adjustments may assist governments in better protection of the welfare and human rights of their citizens (eg by limiting patents for vaccines and environmental technologies). For instance, the lockdown restrictions of civil, economic, social, and cultural rights of citizens were often imposed by government executives without transparent proportionality examination of whether their enormous macro-economic and social costs (eg adversely affecting the professional activities, income, and social lives of more than 95 per cent of national populations and businesses) could be justified by reducing the infection risks for mainly elderly people and protecting their access to insufficient intensive care units in hospitals.

4.6 Globalization Requires Multilevel Governance of Sustainable Development

Market mechanisms of demand and supply tend to offer spontaneous incentives for decentralized production of private goods and services demanded by people.

[51] Cf C Long, 'The China Experience: An Institutional Approach' in Ménard and Shirley (eds), (n 18), Chapter 15.

In line with standard rational choice theory, optimal market solutions do not occur for the supply of PGs like most SDGs (like mitigation of climate change and biodiversity loss, food and energy security for all). The 'non-excludable' and 'non-exhaustive' characteristics of 'pure PGs', like sunshine or human rights, whose benefits are non-rivalrous in consumption and non-excludable, impede their production and availability in private markets. International legal cooperation governing national defence, clean air, or the absence of armed threat typically allows all citizens to enjoy benefits. At the same time, it gives rise to collective action problems. As for all PGs, the universal regulation of common goods makes intuitive sense because it has the potential to affect every member of global society. The extensive participation necessary for regulating common goods often bears collective action problems such as free-riding, which can diminish the effectiveness of global regimes. PGs theories distinguish different kinds of—and diverse supply strategies for—pure or impure PGs and 'common pool resources'.[52] Globalization transforms *national* into *transnational PGs* (like markets, monetary stability, legal, food and health security, climate change mitigation) requiring multilevel governance institutions limiting the collective action problems of intergovernmental politics. Going beyond the neoclassical externality analysis, institutional economics contributes to PGs analysis by integrating insights of behavioural economics and public choice theories. It explains why intergovernmental supply of PGs requires institutional checks and balances limiting abuses of public and private powers. Just as executive powers inside national jurisdictions have often been abused until democratic and republican constitutionalism progressively succeeded, in many countries, in protecting constitutional rights of citizens and collective supply of *national PGs*, so have the multilevel constitutional checks and balances and judicial protection of constitutional and human rights inside the EU—or the multilevel judicial protection of transnational rule of law among the 164 WTO members—enhanced the

[52] On the economic distinction between private goods, non-excludable and non-exhaustible 'pure PGs', non-exhaustible 'impure PGs', and non-excludable 'common pool resources', their respective collective action problems, and the legal strategies for limiting market failures, governance failures, and constitutional failures (like formation of clubs limiting free-riding among WTO members and among citizens), see Petersmann (n 1), at 190ff. On the distinction between PGs, global commons beyond national jurisdiction (like outer space, the High Seas, Antarctica), fundamental values (like *erga omnes* obligations), and common interests (like democratic self-determination, agreed constitutionalism), see M Iovane, FM Palombino, D Amoroso, and G Zarra, 'The Protection of General Interests in Contemporary International Law. Some Introductory Remarks' in M Iovane, FM Palombino, D Amoroso, and G Zarra (eds), *The Protection of General Interests in Contemporary International Law. A Theoretical and Empirical Enquiry* (OUP 2021), at 3ff. These different concepts originate from different economic, political, and legal disciplines, often overlap, and (as social constructs) are subject to change, as illustrated by the conservation of common pool resources (like fisheries). Hence, also the related governance problems and interactions among national and general interests may be perceived differently by different private and public, national and international actors. Yet, one common feature is that their regulatory challenges go far beyond any one single state and require international cooperation and multilevel governance institutions regulating the transnational dimensions.

efficiency of multilevel governance of *transnational PGs*, for instance by reducing transaction and coordination costs.

Most transnational PGs are aggregate PGs that must be produced collectively through aggregation and integration of local, national, regional, and worldwide building blocks (eg for limiting GHG emissions). Transforming 'pure' into 'impure, PGs (eg by formation of clubs)—like the WTO trading, legal, and dispute settlement systems—can reduce collective action problems (eg by making club membership conditional on cooperation and limitation of free-riding). The particular characteristics of PGs risk leading to actions that may be rational from an individual's perspective (like use of fossil fuels, burning of tropical forests) but harmful from a collective PGs viewpoint (like reduction of GHG emissions so as to promote green, carbon-free economies). International organizations facilitate international cooperation among state actors, for instance by enabling access to information, negotiating agreed rules, supervising and promoting rule compliance. The optimal supply strategies differ depending of the particular characteristics of PGs (like non-proliferation of nuclear weapons) and on the diverse preferences and interests of countries. Hence, the fifteen UN specialized agencies for collective supply of different PGs often use diverse regulatory instruments (like the tripartite structure of labour, employer, and government representatives in the International Labour Organization (ILO), and weighted majority voting in the International Monetary Fund and World Bank).

Multilevel governance of transnational PGs suffers from various gaps diminishing scope and effectiveness of cooperation. *Participation gaps* (eg withdrawal of the United States from the 2015 Paris Agreement on climate change mitigation) occur with increasing numbers of participating states; as the transaction costs on determining a compensation solution (eg for protecting tropical forests as carbon sinks benefitting all countries) increase, achieving Kaldor–Hicks improvements becomes more difficult. The dilemma associated with negotiations among multiple parties is akin to Coasean bargaining, in which parties negotiate towards an equilibrium where cooperation gains are maximized.[53] *Incentive gaps* (eg for less-developed economies dependent on fossil fuels) materialize when some countries do not see any overall improvement from contributing to the PG for their welfare position in terms of the Pareto or Kaldor–Hicks criteria. *Jurisdiction gaps* (eg inadequate international agreements on fossil fuel subsidies, carbon taxes, border carbon adjustments, and emissions trading systems) highlight the existence of significant transactions costs such as *sovereignty costs* (as emphasized by Brexit) occurring whenever states surrender competencies limiting their national prerogatives. *Negotiation costs* increase not only with the number of participating states or the degree of heterogeneity of preferences; they also differ according to the

[53] Cf Coase (n 19).

nature and complexity of the subject matter. *Implementation* and *enforcement costs* depend on the complexity and technicality of the subject matter (like developing, producing, and distributing vaccines limiting health pandemics). *Monitoring costs* increase when compliance with the agreement must be controlled and international organizations are established to administer an agreement and exercise surveillance (eg by the WTO Trade Policy Review Mechanism) over its implementation inside member states.

4.7 Need for Respecting Constitutional, Legal, and Institutional Pluralism

Modern HRL and the sovereign equality of states protect individual and democratic diversity as well as legal diversity among today's 193 UN member states. Almost all states have adopted (written or unwritten) national Constitutions, ratified one or more UN human rights convention(s), and cooperate in the context of hundreds of international organizations for the collective supply of transnational PGs. The hundreds of national legal systems, thousands of international treaty systems, and millions of transnational legal systems (eg governing transnational corporations, their foreign investments, and trade in goods and services) entail legal and institutional pluralism, embedded in diverse national constitutions constituting legal and political governance systems for the collective supply of national PGs. National and transnational governance of aggregate PGs (like monetary, trade, investment, environmental, human rights, and legal systems) interact in complex ways. Regulating the interdependencies between diverse social, political, economic, cultural, and legal systems requires respect for the reality of constitutional pluralism and legal-institutional pluralism constraining human cooperation. From economic perspectives, legal-institutional pluralism promotes institutional competition between jurisdictions, thereby furthering knowledge, enhancing efficiency, restraining power, and promoting experimentation with innovative legal-institutional arrangements.[54] Institutional competition can promote variability and quality, for instance if socially and economically viable institutions (like national central banks, competition authorities, courts of justice) are imitated in intergovernmental cooperation (eg by establishing the European Central Bank (ECB), the CJEU, the European Free Trade Area (EFTA) Court, the ECtHR) with different mandates and *competing* jurisdictions (eg among national and European competition authorities and courts protecting fundamental rights).

Empirical studies of embedded liberalism confirm that the legal design of multilevel institutions in economic integration differs among jurisdictions, for instance

[54] Cf L Gerken, 'Institutional Competition: An Orientative Framework' in L Gerken (ed) *Competition among Institutions* (Palgrave Macmillan 1995).

within and among state capitalist economies (like China and Russia), neo-liberal economies (like the United States), or ordo-liberal economies (like the European common market) and their diverse polities and legal systems. Each of these competing economic systems proceeds from competing value premises, such as the political power monopoly of China's communist party, the US democracy prioritizing civil and political constitutional rights of US citizens and pursuing economic hegemony over foreign countries, and the more comprehensive protection of multilevel civil, political, economic, social, and cultural human and constitutional rights in the multilevel constitutional law of the EU and its twenty-seven EU member states. The initial post-1945 expectation of inducing all GATT member countries to follow the US model of neo-liberal liberalization of market access barriers, deregulation, privatization, and financialization of markets (as spontaneous information, coordination, and sanctioning mechanisms) has proven illusory. As a consequence, GATT/WTO trade rules and investment rules need to be adjusted to the reality of member states with diverse neo-liberal, ordo-liberal, state capitalist, and third-world economic systems and to the resulting geopolitical rivalries (eg between US-dominated Bretton Woods institutions in Washington, DC, and China-dominated Asian institutions like the Asian Infrastructure Investment Bank (AIIB) in Beijing). The competing value premises entail that, for example, China's BRI agreements with more than 100 countries along the ancient territorial and maritime Silk Roads are based on different legal and institutional principles (eg for dispute settlement, government procurement, protection of individual rights) compared with the free trade agreements (FTAs) concluded by the United States or by the EU. Due to the institutional diversity inside and among states, views on how to define market distortions in the global trading system,[55] or how to design international trade and investment adjudication, are increasingly contested.

4.8 Need for Adjusting WTO Rules to Geopolitical Regulatory Competition

President Trump's withdrawal from the 2015 Paris Agreement, his assault on the WTO legal system, the US–China trade wars, China's BRI initiative for bilateral economic cooperation agreements with more than 100 countries along the ancient Silk Road, and China's territorial expansion in the South China Sea challenged the ordo-liberal multilateralism underlying EU law, WTO law, the Paris Agreement on climate change mitigation, and other multilateral agreements from which the US withdrew or which China disregards (like the UN Convention on the Law of the Sea (UNCLOS)). The institutional diversity among the more than 400 regional

[55] Cf A Lang, Heterodox Markets and 'Market Distortions' in The Global Trading System, *Journal of International Economic Law* 22 (2019), 677–719.

economic integration agreements suggests that mankind must learn through 'trial and error' (Karl Popper) and progressive 'institutionalization of public reason' (John Rawls) how to overcome the current geopolitical rivalries among Anglo-Saxon neo-liberalism (as illustrated by Brexit and Britain's rejection of European regulatory harmonization and European courts), Trump's mercantilist disregard for multilateral trade and environmental agreements protecting global PGs (like climate change mitigation), authoritarian state capitalism (eg in China and Russia), European ordo-liberal economic constitutionalism, and third-world ideologies (like India's refusal to accept the July 2008 package presented by WTO Director-General Lamy as a compromise for concluding the Doha Round).

Due to the mutually incoherent value premises of utilitarian neo-liberalism, hegemonic mercantilism, totalitarian state capitalism, and rights-based, multilevel economic constitutionalism, these systemic divergences among WTO members are increasingly disrupting the WTO legal, dispute settlement, and negotiation systems (eg as a result of US invocations of national security exceptions for justifying discriminatory import restrictions on steel and aluminium, US invocation of GATT's 'public morals' exception for justifying trade sanctions against China).[56] In contrast to the end of the post-1945 Cold War between the Soviet Union dictatorship and Western democracies, the current geopolitical rivalries are unlikely to disappear in the near future, particularly in view of the fact that China's successful economic and social transformation since 1978 is transforming China into the world's largest economy and increasingly limiting US military and economic hegemony and political leadership.[57] The systemic rivalries risk further increasing due to the need for mitigating climate change by, *inter alia*, carbon taxes, border carbon adjustments, limitation of fossil fuel subsidies, and GHG emissions trading systems. Moreover, WTO adjudication and investor–state arbitration are challenged not only by neo-liberal and mercantilist WTO member states but also by civil societies in other countries.

If the WTO negotiation and dispute settlement systems should break down, the subsidiarity principle suggests that the WTO provisions on exceptions (eg GATT Articles XX, XXI, GATS Articles XIV and XIV*bis*) and the embedded liberalism compromise underlying WTO law may need more flexible, legal interpretations enabling WTO members to adjust their economic laws and institutions to the changing regulatory challenges (eg by using WTO trade remedy rules for protecting domestic industries against foreign market distortions, use of

[56] For details see Chapter 6, section 6.3. President Trump's introduction of discriminatory tariffs on imports of China worth up to $360 billion was found to be inconsistent with GATT/WTO rules in the panel report in *United States—Tariff Measures on Certain Goods from China* (DS543) of 15 September 2020. The US invocations of the security exception in GATT Article XXI for justifying other trade sanctions are, likewise, likely to be found illegal in the pending WTO dispute settlement proceedings; cf J Bacchus, 'WTO signals national security no longer trump card in trade disputes', *Newsweek* 7 July 2020.

[57] Cf K Mahbubani, *Has the West Lost It? A Provocation* (Penguin 2018).

WTO exception clauses and WTO waivers for making carbon border adjustments WTO-consistent so as to limit GHG emissions and carbon leakage). The more the 'new nationalism' in neo-liberal WTO members (like the United Kingdom and the United States) and in some of the BRICS countries (Brazil, Russia, India, China, South Africa) render the success of WTO reform negotiations unlikely, the stronger become the reasons for decentralized reforms of world trade rules through (inter-)regional, plurilateral, and bilateral agreements among willing and like-minded governments (eg insisting on protection of non-economic *national PGs* like cyber sovereignty inside communist China, cyber security inside democracies, data privacy inside Europe). Constitutional and institutional economics offer transaction cost rationales for moving towards regional or plurilateral approaches, as the costs vary in finding interaction partners, negotiating contract details, monitoring compliance, and enforcing sanctions. Just as reducing complexity is a rationale for non-multilateralism proposed both in the international relations and international law literature, transaction costs in political, technical, or economic regulation can be reduced when moving from multilateral efforts to regional or bilateral agreements.

During the 2020 global health pandemic, many WTO members introduced import and export restrictions on goods and services (like land, air, and maritime transport) in conformity with the medical guidance and advice from the World Health Organization (WHO). Some of these crisis measures are likely to raise strategic long-term questions regarding the previous openness and dependence of countries (eg over 80 per cent of active pharmaceutical ingredients of US medicines coming from abroad) and of industries on foreign supplies (eg by global supply chains, 'just-in-time' deliveries of inputs for manufacturing, access to foreign medicines and food supplies). To the extent that a shift in states' preferences towards more autonomy and autarky in terms of public health, medical supply, and services will ensue from the current crisis, this will have an impact on both globalization and cooperation, with nationalization of production facilities and national stockholding (eg of medical supplies, food reserves) possibly leading to a reduction of economic interdependence.

4.9 Need for Coherence among Sustainable Development Goals

The UN Sustainable Development Agenda emphasizes the need for policy and institutional coherence.[58] The UN pursues its seventeen SDGs in cooperation

[58] Cf *Transforming our World* (2015), paras 17.13ff.

with networks of fifteen UN specialized agencies, the WTO, and additional multilateral treaty regimes (like human rights conventions, the 2015 Paris Agreement on climate change mitigation). In conformity with Nobel Prize economist Jan Tinbergen's theory of 'separation of policy instruments',[59] each of these functionally limited PG treaty regimes focuses on different, complementary policy instruments for protecting a specific global PG. The 2015 UN Resolution on the 2030 Agenda for Sustainable Development coordinates the implementation of the seventeen SDGs (like overcoming poverty, hunger, and global warming; protecting health, education, and gender equality; access to water, sanitation, and clean energy; urbanization; the environment; human rights and social justice). It aims at localizing the SDGs so as to empower local institutions, actors, and civil society to support the SDGs bottom up using local expertise and initiatives. It recognizes 'that the United Nations Framework Convention on Climate Change is the primary international, intergovernmental forum for negotiating the global response to climate change' (2015 UN Resolution on the 2030 Agenda for Sustainable Development, paragraph 31). As trade and climate change regulation are inseparable, the UN also relies on WTO negotiations (eg on promotion of sustainable development through limiting fishery and fossil fuel subsidies) and on comprehensive coordination among national and international actors, including the EU as an international member of both the 1994 WTO Agreement and the 2015 Paris Agreement. This latter Agreement entered into force in November 2016 and was ratified by 190 Parties (2021); 182 countries plus the EU notified their NDCs by 2019. These voluntary contributions to reduce GHGs differ enormously but they remain insufficient for realizing the climate change mitigation objectives of the Paris Agreement. The United States—as the largest economy and second-largest emitter of GHGs—notified its withdrawal from the Agreement under President Trump, and its rejoining of the Paris Agreement under US President Biden in January 2021. During the UN climate conference in Madrid in December 2019 focusing on carbon market systems, other major emitters of GHGs (like China, India, Australia) avoided committing to ambitious limitations of GHGs. The Paris Agreement includes neither trade and competition rules to safeguard a level playing field among competing industries in countries with diverse carbon constraints, nor effective legal disciplines (eg for fossil fuel subsidies, GHG emissions, carbon taxes, border carbon adjustments) and dispute settlement procedures (eg regarding NDCs and their consistency with WTO law).

With climate change mitigation typically suffering from insufficient remedies due to its PG nature, institutional economics highlights how constitutional rights

[59] Cf J Tinbergen, *On the Theory of Economic Policy* (North Holland 1952) (arguing that in order to be effective, a public policy instrument should only aim to secure one goal).

accorded to individuals can help to achieve higher levels of climate protection. This is illustrated by the ruling of the Dutch Supreme Court on 20 December 2019 in *State of the Netherlands v Urgenda*[60] (a Dutch NGO suing the state on behalf of around 900 citizens), which confirmed the 2018 Court of Appeals judgment that Articles 2 (right to life) and 8 of the European Convention on Human Rights (ECHR) (right to private and family life) entail legal duties of the Dutch government to reduce GHG emissions by at least 25 per cent (compared to 1990 levels) by the end of 2020. Similar to recent findings of UN human rights bodies and other national courts acknowledging the human right to live in an environment without pollution endangering human health,[61] the Dutch Supreme Court judgment confirmed—as illustrated also by similar judgments by other courts in Europe—how constitutional rights and democratic and judicial institutions are of crucial importance for protecting PGs.[62]

The legal and economic innovation of the Dutch ruling is to reconcile legal interpretation of HRL with the economic PG character of the environment. Outside the EU, courts often deny direct invocability of international treaty rules by individuals. Individual and judicial efforts at obliging states to take positive action remain confronted with high hurdles posed by the notions of direct effect and direct applicability of international rules inside domestic legal and judicial systems. In order for a provision to gain direct effect, it must be sufficiently clear and precise and enable enforceability by the individual invoking the norm without further implementation through legal acts; courts' reluctance in acknowledging direct effect has been particularly high in relation to international treaties stipulating primarily state obligations (such as WTO law),[63] while international treaties granting individual rights (such as the ECHR) are more likely to be recognized by courts as invocable by individuals and to serve as legality standards of states' measures. With PGs creating positive or negative effects on virtually everyone, it is sound to extend the scope of constitutional rights (such as the right to life in Article 2 ECHR, the right to private and family life in Article 8 ECHR) to protection against encroachments on individual rights resulting from insufficient public efforts to mitigate climate change.

In that vein, the Dutch government's commitment to comply with the judgment sets an important precedent for legal, judicial, and rules-based political

[60] De Staat der Nederlanden (Ministerie van Economische Zaken en Klimaat) tegen Stichting Urgenda, Hoge Raad der Nederlanden, Civiele Kamer, Nummer 19/00135, 20 December 2019.

[61] References to climate change lawsuits can be found at http://climatecasechart.com/. See also J Peel and J Lin, Transnational Climate Litigation: The Contribution of the Global South, *American Journal of International Law* 113 (2019) 679–726.

[62] This jurisprudence is further discussed in Chapter 9 for illustrating the need for moving from state-centred chess-board governance to citizen-centred network governance supporting PGs.

[63] F Martines, Direct Effect of International Agreements of the European Union, *European Journal of International Law* 25 (2014) 129–147.

protection of PGs like climate change mitigation. In order to garner the social and democratic support for implementing the EU's New Green Deal and make the WTO and Paris Agreements mutually coherent, EU leadership for climate mitigation policies must go beyond merely environmental discourse by emphasizing the constitutional and ordo-liberal foundations of EU environmental policies limiting market failures (like environmental pollution) and governance failures (eg to prevent climate change). The EU will elicit sufficient support to overcome internal and external opposition to climate mitigation policies only if limitation of fossil fuels and of GHG emissions, the introduction of carbon taxes and border carbon adjustments, and prevention of carbon leakage (eg by shifting production of cement, steel, and other products using fossil fuel-based energy from the EU to third countries with less stringent restrictions) are not perceived as green protectionism distorting fair competition and creating social injustices. Hence, the border carbon adjustment measures (eg taxes) envisaged in the EU's New Green Deal should be based on multilaterally agreed, non-discriminatory standards rather than being imposed unilaterally at national and EU levels of governance.

4.10 Legitimacy and Efficiency of Economic Adjudication

Institutional economics confirms that legal security and predictability not only reduce economic transaction costs. Just laws and inclusive institutions also promote the social acceptance of economic law and the inclusiveness of market-driven information, coordination, and sanctioning mechanisms. The increasing number of—and interactions among—international PG treaties cannot realize their legal and policy objectives without transnational rule of law and judicial remedies protecting overall coherence between national and international, legal, and political governance systems. As illustrated by President Trump's withdrawal from the 2015 Paris Agreement and his assault on the WTO legal and dispute settlement system, neo-liberal interest group politics and nationalism ('America First') neglect harmful externalities like environmental pollution, climate change, and US violations of multilateral WTO commitments. In a world where multilateralism is increasingly challenged by nationalist power politics, is it realistic to pursue the need for stronger multilateral rules and dispute settlement procedures institutionalizing public reason and holding governments accountable for violations of multilateral treaties protecting transnational PGs?

4.10.1 Legitimacy and Necessity of Judicial Protection of Rule of Law

The UN has defined rule of law at national and international levels as 'a principle of governance in which all persons, institutions and entities, including the State itself, are accountable to laws that are publicly promulgated, equally enforced and independently adjudicated, and which are consistent with internationally recognized human rights'.[64]

The second half of the twentieth century has seen an unprecedented increase in the number of international trade, investment, economic, and other courts at bilateral, regional, and worldwide levels of governance aimed at protecting transnational rule of law. They often interact—for example, in international trade, investment, regional economic integration law, HRL, and international criminal law—with domestic courts aimed at multilevel protection of transnational rule of law for the benefit of citizens. The legitimacy of specialized trade, investment, and intellectual property courts and arbitration tribunals—for example, in the sense of justification of their legal and judicial authority, protection of their independence, and their personal integrity vis-à-vis rent-seeking interests groups—remains contested in democratic and civil societies, just as the politicization of judicial appointments in national courts (eg in the United States) is increasingly contested.[65] Challenges to the legitimacy of courts depend on their diverse judicial mandates, subject matters, specific goals, design choices, applicable law, processes, audiences, institutional contexts, and results.[66] From an institutional economics perspective, legitimacy matters to the extent that it ties public measures back to the claim of normative individualism guiding ordo-liberal 'principled' thinking. While legitimacy may be conceptualized in different guises and draw from different disciplines, it ultimately contributes to stabilizing the relationship between public authority and those governed or affected by public measures. *Source-based legitimacy* and *process-based legitimacy* suggest that the approval of WTO agreements by national parliaments and democratic institutions also conferred legitimacy on the WTO dispute settlement jurisprudence. *Normative legitimacy* derives also from the fact that WTO law promoted and protected non-discriminatory conditions of trade, rule of law, and democratic preferences of citizens. WTO law can claim *result-oriented legitimacy* to the extent that it enhanced rule of law (as defined by national parliaments in their ratification of the WTO and DSU agreements) and economic efficiency satisfying economic and legal demand of citizens benefitting from

[64] Cf Report of the Secretary-General, Delivering Justice: programme of action to strengthen the rule-of-law at the national and international levels, A/66/49 of 16 March 2012, para 2.

[65] Cf RH Fallon, *Law and Legitimacy in the Supreme Court* (Harvard UP 2018); A Cohen, *Supreme Inequality: The Supreme Court's Fifty-Year Battle for a More Unjust America* (Penguin Press 2019).

[66] The legitimacy criteria are explained in N Grosman, H Grant Cohen, A Follesdal, and G Ulfstein (eds), *Legitimacy and International Courts* (CUP 2018).

international trade and the global division of labour. Historical evidence confirms that rights-based, ordo-liberal conceptions of transnational rule of law cannot be realized without legitimate third-party adjudication.

4.10.2 Efficiency Justifications of Judicial Protection of Rule of Law

From an economic perspective, independent and impartial third-party adjudication can limit not only public and private rule violations and related costs in ways promoting constitutionally agreed rights, rule of law, and other PGs for the benefit of all citizens in conformity with their democratically expressed preferences. Adjudication also contributes to reducing transaction costs, in the context of WTO law no less than in the context of national and other international legal systems protecting PGs and rules-based cooperation among citizens. Efficient allocation of governmental authority and jurisdiction for peaceful settlement of disputes is no less important for promoting consumer and citizen welfare than efficient market allocations of private goods and services.[67] In terms of *external legitimacy* (eg beliefs of outside constituencies like EU citizens, traders, producers, investors, and consumers affected by trade and investment adjudication), WTO law protects not only international third-party adjudication among WTO member states and other supra- or sub-national WTO members (like the EU, Hong Kong, Macau, and Taiwan). Numerous WTO provisions also provide for individual access to domestic courts or international commercial arbitration (eg pursuant to Article 4 of the WTO Agreement on Pre-shipment Inspection), which offer less costly judicial remedies for the settlement of transnational trade disputes. Empirical evidence suggests that the 316 dispute settlement proceedings under GATT 1947 and the 1979 Tokyo Round Agreements,[68] and the more than 600 formal dispute settlement proceedings under the WTO Agreement (1996–2020), have considerably enhanced the policy objective of 'providing security and predictability to the multilateral trading system' through compulsory third-party adjudication of disputes over the interpretation and application of WTO rules 'in accordance with customary rules of interpretation of public international law' (Article 3.2 DSU), thereby reducing transaction costs in international trade also for the benefit of traders, investors, and consumers. Judicial protection of rule of law also promotes individual and democratic autonomy by assisting citizens and governments in maximizing long-term benefits and minimizing costs in the pursuit of individual and collective preferences.

[67] Cf Trachtman (n 25).

[68] Cf the list and analyses of cases in *GATT Disputes 1948–1995* (2 vols, WTO 2018).

5

European Economic Constitutionalism: Constitutional Approaches to Sustainable Development?

Chapter 2 explained why, even though they enabled decolonization, human rights revolutions, and international economic law (IEL) revolutions all over the world, the United Nations (UN) Charter and UN human rights law (HRL)—have failed to establish a global community law effectively protecting human rights and public goods (PGs) in all 193 UN member states. Many authoritarian UN member states do not comply with UN HRL and block UN decisions (eg of the UN Security Council) to protect human rights. Chapter 3 demonstrated how the post-1945, US-led world trading system has become disrupted by the US Trump administration and by the rise of China as the world's largest trading country. Can the risks of future, similar attacks by authoritarian, nationalist rulers be mitigated? Chapter 4 explained the turn to constitutional economics in post-1945 multilevel trade and economic regulation as an attempt at institutionalizing public reason and constitutional checks and balances (eg through EU, European Free Trade Area (EFTA), and World Trade Organization (WTO) adjudication) aimed at limiting market, governance, and constitutional failures. This chapter describes Europe's multilevel constitutionalism, which emerged in response to long-standing constitutional failures and ongoing struggles to protect human rights, democracy, and the rule of law in the relations among the now forty-seven member states of the Council of Europe in order to prevent a repetition of past constitutional and governance failures in Europe's long history of feudalism, colonialism, imperialism, wars, and economic crises ushering in dictatorships and the Holocaust (as briefly summarized in sections 5.1–5.4).[1] Whereas the motto of the United States ('*e pluribus unum*')

[1] The term constitutionalism is used here for agreements constituting governance institutions subject to legal restraints and rights of citizens. 'Constitutionalization' refers to legislative and judicial, national, and international clarifications of the constitutional rights of citizens and legal restraints of multilevel governance institutions (eg by national constitutions, judicial remedies, functionally limited treaty constitutions of a higher legal rank). For a case study of constitutional failures in the post-First World War Weimar Republic of Germany, which contributed to the Second World War and which remain representative for the abuses of emergency powers and of anti-liberal politics in many countries, see E Kennedy, *Constitutional Failure. Carl Schmitt in Weimar* (Duke UP 2004). The similarities between Trumpian politics (as described in Chapter 3) and Schmitt's justification, in the 1930s, of charismatic legitimacy of authoritarian leaders using emergency powers and anti-liberal, ethnic identity politics, contesting the legitimacy of their political enemies as existential struggles between friends and

Transforming World Trade and Investment Law for Sustainable Development. Ernst-Ulrich Petersmann, Oxford University Press. © Ernst-Ulrich Petersmann 2022. DOI: 10.1093/oso/9780192858023.003.0006

remains characteristic for unitary states with often hegemonic ambitions (like China and Russia), the motto of post-1945 European integration (*unity in diversity*) draws lessons from Europe's past governance failures by emphasizing universalist enlightenment values (like human rights, democratic constitutionalism, rule of law), respect for the constitutional identities of EU member states, cosmopolitan rights and responsibilities of EU citizens (as codified in the EU Charter of Fundamental Rights (EUCFR)). The commitment to a competitive social market economy (Article 3 TEU) not only prompted the EU to spend comparatively more money on social welfare systems than states outside Europe.[2] The EU's social model (like promoting families, health, and social rights like gender equality, active labour market policies, and professional training, public education, and cultural policies) is also increasingly seen as a source of productivity, competitiveness, and social stability of the European economy (eg responding to the need for social protection in international financial, health, and environmental crises). The periodic amendments of the EU treaties consolidated the progressive constitutionalization of EU law (as described in section 5.5), also including obligations to promote sustainable development and combat climate change both inside the common market as well as in the external EU policies (cf Articles 3.3, 21 of the Treaty on European Union (TEU), and Article 191 of the Treaty on the Functioning of the European Union (TFEU)).

This chapter argues that the emergence of Europe's unique common market law—and the multilevel governance of the thirty member states of the European Economic Area (EEA)—offer lessons also for third countries by using constitutionalism for limiting past market, governance, and constitutional failures. Just as reasonable citizens seek medical advice in order to prevent or cure physical and mental health problems, so has democratic constitutionalism proven to be the most important political invention for containing political problems caused by the bounded rationality of citizens and by the self-interests of political actors in the polity (section 5.1). By changing the psychology and politics of law, democratic constitutionalism assists in providing PGs and limiting harmful political choices in legal practices and political decision-making processes. This is of particular importance for citizen-oriented reforms as envisaged by the SDGs (section 5.2). National and transnational (con)federations offer centuries of regulatory experiences for

foes, rejecting courts as defenders of the Constitution, trusting in illiberal cultures, and undermining democratic constitutionalism by political religions justifying big lies (eg about democratic election results) are obvious.

[2] German chancellor Angela Merkel often remarked that Europe accounts for 7 per cent of the world's population, 25 per cent of its economy, but 50 per cent of its social spending. All post-1945 German chancellors acknowledged Germany's historical responsibility in Europe as a '*Schicksalsgemeinschaft*' (community of fate), which allocates more responsibility on Germany for protecting peaceful integration (notably with its nine neighbouring states and for financing the EU) than on other European states (like the United Kingdom as an island state).

designing integration through law and institutions regulating multilevel governance of PGs (like rule of law, common markets, monetary stability) for the benefit of citizens living in different jurisdictions (section 5.3). The experiences with federalism and transnational confederations—in Europe and beyond—demonstrate the advantages of multilevel constitutional constraints on discretionary foreign policy powers and of related theories of multilevel constitutionalism (section 5.4). In order to be accepted and supported by citizens across states, integration law and its underlying public reason need to be legitimized, embedded in, and democratically institutionalized by social contracts on human rights and other principles of justice, as illustrated by the emergence of rights-based, regional human rights constitutions, common market constitutions, and monetary and foreign policy constitutions in post-1945 European integration law (section 5.5). In worldwide institutions, the disagreements among UN member states on the foundations and scope of civil, political, economic, social, and cultural human rights (as discussed in Chapter 2, section 2.3) permit only pragmatic common law approaches to protecting PGs. Without effective constitutional restraints (like individual rights, democratic accountability, judicial remedies), multilevel market regulations and regulatory competition risk being captured by powerful interest groups (including also authoritarian rulers and their clienteles) favouring regional and bilateral agreements, as increasingly advocated by authoritarian leaders (eg in China) and populist demagogues (eg advocating for Brexit and US withdrawal from multilateral agreements) prioritizing diverse, nationalist, and cultural identities (section 5.6). The declining number of democracies, the rise in authoritarian governments, and the increasing challenges to international adjudication suggest that multilevel democratic constitutionalism may remain limited to Europe.

5.1 Constitutionalism: A Universally Adopted Western Political Invention

All human societies use law as an instrument of social ordering and governance. And in all human societies, abuses of the rule by law have led to struggles for justice aimed at limiting abuses of power through the rule of law.[3] During most of the recorded history of *homo sapiens*, law and governance were justified by 'mandates of heaven' invoked by feudal rulers. When the first humanism since about 500 BC enabled the emergence of *autonomous* rather than *heteronomous* political and legal orders, *democratic constitutionalism* (eg in ancient Athens) and *republican*

[3] On ancient calls for justice and impartial adjudication in the Bible, in the Greek tragedy of Aeschylus' *Oresteia*, in the Athenian democracy and Roman republic, see DD Raphael, *Concepts of Justice* (OUP 2001), 11ff. On humane governance as the moral responsibility of rulers in East Asian Confucian political philosophy, see A Carty and J Nijman (eds), *Morality and Responsibility of Rulers. European and Chinese Origins of a Rule of Law as Justice for World Order* (OUP 2018).

constitutionalism (notably in ancient Rome) were designed and justified (eg by political philosophers like Plato, Aristotle, and Cicero) as being more inclusive, more legitimate, and more effective political strategies for protecting PGs for the benefit of citizens. As the 2030 Agenda for Sustainable Development aims at transforming law and policies for the benefit of citizens and their human rights, the historical lessons from using constitutionalism for transforming power politics into democratic and republican protection of constitutional rights of citizens are of crucial importance for realizing the Sustainable Development Goals (SDGs).

Aristotle, in his *Politics* and *Constitution of Athens*, explained why the rule of law is preferable to that of any individual; even if it is better for the population that certain individuals must govern, they should be regarded as only guardians and ministers of the law.[4] Centuries later, Cicero, in *The Republic* and *The Laws*, emphasized the need for the rule of law in the Roman republic.[5] Democratic constitutionalism focused on improving the *input legitimacy* of law and governance through citizenship rights, democratic elections, participatory democracy (eg in popular assemblies and armies), deliberative democracy, and institutional checks and balances (eg among legislative, executive, and judicial institutions). Republican constitutionalism focused on additional constitutional mandates and restraints aimed at improving the *output legitimacy* of law and governance (eg in terms of protecting non-domination, judicial remedies of Roman citizens, and other PGs like the Roman legal system that became accepted by many other jurisdictions throughout Europe).[6] Even after the ancient city republics around the Mediterranean ceased to exist (eg due to the rise of the Western and Eastern Roman empires), new city republics emerged (eg in Florence, Venice, and the northern European city republics participating in the Hanseatic League protecting peace and trade in the North and Baltic seas). They developed new law and governance institutions (eg maritime law, transnational financial law, arbitration protecting multinational banks and investments abroad) that continue to influence modern legal systems. *Magna Carta* of 1215 and the recognition of *habeas corpus* (as a judicial remedy against unlawful detention) in England during the thirteenth century, the English Bill of Rights of 1689, the democratic US and French Constitutions, Bills and Declarations of Rights of the eighteenth century were other historical milestones on the way to the 1948 Universal Declaration of Human Rights (UDHR) and its recognition of the need for protecting inalienable human rights by rule of law. Chapters 5–9 explain

[4] S Everson (ed), *Aristotle: The Politics and The Constitution of Athens* (CUP 1996), 88 (book III, section 1287).

[5] For details, see BZ Tamanaha, *On the Rule of Law. History, Politics, Theory* (CUP 2004), 11ff.

[6] Notwithstanding disagreements on whether freedom as non-domination, civic virtues, active citizenry, political equality, self-government, rule of law, the community, the common good, or the struggle against domination are the core values of republicanism, modern liberal and republican theories overlap (eg in their separation of powers and of public and private spheres). In national and international law, republicanism is more ancient than liberalism and majoritarian democratic decision-making.

why stronger protection of the rule of law in regional and worldwide economic and human rights agreements is a precondition for realizing most SDGs.

Law (eg as self-commitment to rules of a higher rank) is part of individual and social self-constitution in order to realize personality (eg one's moral powers of choosing a good life and social justice) and order society. Constitutionalism differs from feudalism and related value traditions (eg including Confucianism) by the ideas that (i) all legal public power must be justified vis-à-vis citizens through (ii) limited delegation of governance powers for protecting PGs, and (iii) must remain accountable subject to (iv) agreed higher law as acts of individual and social self-constitution.[7] As a social contract theory on the relationship between the source of the authority of political power (*potestas*, government by the people), the control of its limited delegation and exercise (*auctoritas*, government of the people), and of the duty of governments to protect PGs for the benefit of citizens (*res publica*, government for the people), constitutionalism evolved differently in different societies, for instance depending on the ideas prevailing in particular societies regarding the relationship of their own legal orders with:

- social conceptions of divine or cosmic order (eg justification of legal rules and ultimate sources of public authority by religious beliefs in Islamic states);
- natural law and justice (eg inalienable human rights as higher law limiting legislation); and of
- human nature and the human condition (eg contractual and discourse justifications and construction of constitutional order for representative and deliberative democracy).[8]

5.1.1 Normative Constitutionalism as an Ideal

Societies and their ideas of constitutionalism distinguished between the *legal constitution* (eg as reflected in the positive law of a society), the underlying *constitutional ideals* (eg the constitutional mandates for realizing a better future), and the

[7] The distinction between sovereignty and government appointed by the sovereign people was increasingly discussed since the sixteenth century in view of the impossibility of applying the Athenian model of permanent self-governance through democratic assemblies in city-republics to nation states with vast territories and people. Hobbes's suggestion (in *De Cive*, 1642) that the sovereign—after appointing a government—may be considered as 'sleeping', contributed to the invention of representative parliamentary sovereignty (eg in England) and of constitutional democracy (eg in the United States and France) constituting, limiting, regulating, and justifying limited government powers through democratically agreed, constitutional rules of a higher legal rank and constitutional rights of citizens aimed at 'constitutionalizing' the overall structures of society; cf R Tuck, *The Sleeping Sovereign: The Invention of Modern Democracy* (CUP 2016).

[8] Cf P Allot, *The Health of Nations. Society and Law beyond the State* (CUP 2002) Chapter 12; J Habermas, *Between Facts and Norms. Contributions to a Discourse Theory of Law and Democracy* (MIT Press 1998).

real constitution (eg abuses of power and other constitutional failures in social realities). Today:

- All 193 UN Member States have adopted national constitutions (written or unwritten) constituting, limiting, regulating, and justifying the basic legal order of their respective peoples based on agreed principles of justice, which are progressively clarified and developed through national and international legal instruments (like UN treaty commitments to respect human rights, rule of law, democratic self-governance, and protection of other, transnational PGs for the benefit of citizens).
- This *positive constitutional law* also includes mandates for the progressive realization (eg through additional constitutional, legislative, administrative, judicial, and international rules and institutions) of the *ideal constitution* (eg as reflected in the objectives of national constitutions and specified, *inter alia*, in the 2000 Millennium Goals and 2015 SDGs of UN Member States).
- The social and *constitutional realities*, however, often differ from the constitutional law and ideals set out in the multilevel constitutional commitments adopted by peoples and governments in the name of their citizens. For instance, inside many UN Member States, governments do not effectively protect human and constitutional rights of citizens and corresponding PGs as prescribed in national constitutions, UN law, or regional HRL. In UN and WTO law, power-oriented justifications prioritizing sovereign equality of states coexist with justifications prioritizing public autonomy of peoples (eg as represented by the EU as a WTO member) and private autonomy (eg as protected by individual rights).

5.1.2 Constitutional Politics as Imperfect Realities

Since the 'Glorious Revolution' in England during the seventeenth century and the human rights revolutions in the United States and France during the eighteenth century, constitutionalism has been progressively transformed:

- *Constitutionalism 1.0* (like the democratic US and French Constitutions during the eighteenth century and the German and Swiss Constitutions during the nineteenth century) had focused on emancipation of peoples in nation states, the constitution of government powers, and the creation of common markets.
- A second wave of *treaty constitutionalism 2.0* after the Second World War was based on treaties protecting fundamental rights (like the European Convention on Human Rights (ECHR)) or market freedoms and judicial remedies across national frontiers (like the European Economic Area (EEA

Agreement). The customary law requirement of interpreting treaties in conformity with the principles of justice, including human rights and fundamental freedoms for all (as recalled in the Preamble and Article 31 Vienna Convention on the Law of Treaties), induced national and regional courts of justice (notably in Europe) to cooperate in protecting treaty rights and remedies, which citizens could invoke and enforce against their own governments.

- The European economic integration agreements among the twenty-seven EU member states evolved into supra-national, European democratic constitutionalism protecting constitutional and human rights of EU citizens. This multilevel *cosmopolitan constitutionalism 3.0*[9] aims at protecting and emancipating citizens vis-à-vis abuses of national policy powers through multilevel treaty law and institutions constituting, limiting, regulating, and justifying multilevel governance of transnational PGs (like common markets, transnational rule of law, protection of monetary stability, and of the environment, multilevel legal and judicial protection of cosmopolitan rights).

The repercussions of this multilevel constitutionalism on IEL are illustrated by European constitutional and common market law, EU membership in worldwide organizations like the WTO and Food and Agriculture Organization (FAO), and by European and other international courts protecting the rights not only of states, individuals, and non-governmental organizations (NGOs) but also of EU institutions and EU citizens. Designing and controlling multilevel governance for protecting PGs (eg SDGs like public health and climate change mitigation, development as freedom, satisfaction of basic needs) remains the biggest constitutional challenge of modern legal systems and of survival governance faced with irreversible climate change.

5.2 Democratic Constitutionalism as Reasonable Constraint on Bounded Rationality

Chapter 2, section 2.3 discussed how human rights can be—and have been—justified in different ways as (i) expressions of moral intuitionism; (ii) reasonably self-imposed categorical moral imperatives; (iii) as agreed golden rules and natural rights; (iv) constitutional contracts; or (v) as positive law in national and international legislation. This diversity of moral and legal views reflects the constitutional problem of the indeterminacy of legal rules and of perspectivism of legal interpretations. As explained by Immanuel Kant, rules do not spell out the conditions of their own application; the interpretation and application of any rule

[9] Cf EU Petersmann, *Multilevel Constitutionalism for Multilevel Governance of Public Goods* (Hart 2017); A Somek, *The Cosmopolitan Constitution* (OUP 2014).

require additional judgments about what the rule should mean in a particular case, and whether applying the rule might be better than resorting to an exception. Such judgments may legitimately differ, depending on the particular perspectives and value premises of decision-makers such as their policy objectives and whether they practice constitutionalism as a mindset in order to reconcile their rational self-interest with their moral and legal obligations to respect human dignity and equal freedoms for all. 'Law exists only as identified and interpreted by situated legal actors ... embedded in a particular social and cultural context.'[10] Reasonable people accept third-party adjudication in order to benefit from independent, impartial judgments settling disputes over the interpretation of rules through due process of law, in conformity with agreed principles of justice, applicable rules, and procedures justifying the judgment.

5.2.1 Constitutionalization of the Politics of International Law?

Independent and impartial judges and academics may apply what they perceive as an objective legal approach focusing on the customary law rules of interpretation and deducing, subsuming, and justifying legal interpretations (like external observers) with references to general rules and principles of law. Yet, as illustrated in Chapter 3 by the US criticism of the AB jurisprudence, legal interpretations may focus less on text and context of the rules than on what the interpreters perceive as their object and purpose. International legal practices are often guided by politics rather than by deducing and subsuming meaning from abstract rules and principles of justice; this politicization of international law refers to the reality of choice in legal interpretation and contrasts it with the technical production of the justification of it.[11] Chapter 2, section 2.3 recalled conflicting interpretations of UN HRL, such as human rights to democratic self-determination of peoples and of individual rights to participation in democratic self-governance (eg as universally recognized in Article 21 UDHR). Chapter 3 illustrated diverse legal perspectives, policy choices, and conflicting interpretations of WTO rules in the US criticism of the AB jurisprudence. Chapter 4 explained why, in contrast to the comparatively greater, neo-liberal faith in the perfect rationality of economic actors (*homo economicus*) and of self-regulatory market mechanisms, ordo-liberal economic constitutionalism emphasizes that the rationality of individual and social decisions—in both economic as well as in political markets—is subject to cognitive limitations and biases of the mind, for instance due to the complexity of decision

[10] K Tuori, *European Constitutionalism* (CUP 2015), at 78; Petersmann (n 9), at 81f, 147f; M Koskenniemi, Constitutionalism as Mindset: Reflections on Kantian Themes About International Law and Globalization, *Theoretical Inquiries in Law* 8 (2006), 9–36.

[11] Cf M Koskenniemi, *The Politics of International Law* (Hart 2011), at v.

problems and the limited time and resources available to make informed decisions. Constitutional economics and public choice theories conceive welfare-enhancing economic markets and democratic political markets as legal constructs rather than as largely self-regulatory gifts of nature.[12] The more governance of PGs can be improved by input from natural and social sciences (eg on risk-regulation, health and environmental protection, cost–benefit analyses, and economic ranking of alternative policy instruments), the more democratic law-makers may have convincing reasons for establishing science-based procedures (eg for providing risk and cost–benefit analyses, health and environmental evaluations of legislative proposals) and counter-majoritarian regulatory agencies with specialized expertise, as reflected in the WTO Agreements on Technical Barriers to Trade and on Sanitary and Phyto-Sanitary Measures. As discussed below, the EU treaties also include a foreign policy constitution limiting (eg in Articles 3, 21 TEU) EU foreign policy discretion by respect for human rights, democratic constitutionalism, rule of law, judicial remedies, and other constitutional restraints.

5.2.2 Bounded Rationality Calls for Separation of Powers also in International Law

Democratic constitutionalism began more than 2,400 years ago in the ancient Athenian democracy in Greece. It was only during the English and American revolutions of the seventeenth and eighteenth centuries that lawyers (like John Locke and James Madison) began justifying democratic constitutionalism in terms of the bounded rationality of citizens and their rulers.[13] In economics, the concept of bounded rationality was explored by economic Nobel Prize laureate Herbert A Simon as an alternative to economic modelling of rationality as optimization in the sense of a fully rational process of finding an optimal choice given the information available. Perfectly rational decisions are often not feasible in practice. Most people are only partly rational; they act as boundedly rational agents in other parts of their actions, content with decisions that are satisfactory (rather than economically optimal). Behavioural economists explore these reasoning shortcuts and recommend adjustments to decision-making procedures and institutions in order to respond to human agents' bounded rationality (eg by 'nudges', social networks, and institutions like independent regulatory agencies with specialized, science-based

[12] Cf JM Buchanan, *The Economics and the Ethics of Constitutional Order* (Michigan UP 1991); RD Cooter, *The Strategic Constitution* (Princeton UP 2000).

[13] Cf R Reed, C Curtis, and NP Lovich Jr, Does Democracy Entail an Obligation to Make Rational Decisions? The Muddling Through vs Bounded Rationality Debate Through a Lockean and Madisonian Lens, *Public Integrity* 22(4) (2020) 316–29 (discussing the writings of Locke and Madison advancing the use of reason to manage inevitable conflict in democratic societies and, in so doing, to achieve the public good).

knowledge). Both in private markets and in the public realm, working in groups and institutions (like the firm or governments) may help to reduce bounded rationality, for example by enhancing access to information, computational capacities, and the environments under which decisions are being made. The trade-offs involved (eg between costs, ethical reputation, sustainability and legitimacy of decisions-making) may require different decision-making procedures taking into account multi-valued utility functions (eg of citizens and voters). For instance, by subjecting all government powers and majority decisions to constitutional constraints like individual rights, democratic consent, judicial remedies, and other institutional checks and balances, constitutionalism may increase political transactions costs, privilege the *status quo*, and lead to political gridlock (as, arguably, under the US Constitution privileging small states and the political composition of the US Supreme Court with conservative majorities). Yet, constitutional promotion of 'inclusive, slow and reasonable decision-making' may reduce the influence of special interests and enhance the 'input legitimacy' (eg in terms of better information) and 'output legitimacy (eg in terms of protecting more inclusive 'public interests') of 'deliberative democracy'.[14] The human rights revolutions and democratic revolutions that have occurred since the eighteenth century and since the Second World War prompted people in all states to adopt national constitutions (written or unwritten) constituting, limiting, regulating, and justifying political, judicial, and other non-majoritarian government powers (eg of national central banks). Chapter 4 explained why the legal ranking of economic policy instruments according to their respective efficiency, and promotion of public reason by independent regulatory institutions (like central banks and competition authorities) and courts of justice can reduce transaction costs and enhance efficiency in IEL. Separation of constitutional, legislative, administrative, and executive public and private powers requires protecting overall legal coherence by rule of law, as universally recognized in UN HRL.

The Preamble to the UDHR recalls the human tragedies that 'disregard and contempt for human rights have resulted in barbarous acts which have outraged the conscience of mankind', such as the First and Second World Wars and the Holocaust. The Preamble draws two conclusions from this human condition:

- 'it is essential, if man is not to be compelled to have recourse, as a last resort, to rebellion against tyranny and oppression, that human rights should be protected by the rule of law'; and

[14] Cf N Berggren and N Karlson, Constitutionalism, Division of Power and Transaction Costs, *Public Choice* 117 (2003), 99–124; JM Buchanan and G Tullock, *The Calculus of Consent. Logical Foundations of Constitutional Democracy* (University of Michigan Press 1962).

- 'recognition of the inherent dignity and of the equal and inalienable rights of all members of the human family is the foundation of freedom, justice and peace in the world' (Preamble, UDHR).

The WTO Agreement protects transnational rule of law and is committed to 'sustainable development, seeking both to protect and preserve the environment' as well as 'to raising standards of living, ensuring full employment and a large and steadily growing volume of real income and effective demand' (WTO Preamble). Yet, unlike the 2030 UN SDGs, the WTO Agreement neither refers to human rights nor offers solutions for responding to global emergencies. Proposals for redefining international law as multilevel governance of PGs for the benefit of peoples and citizens and their human rights,[15] and for systemic interpretation re-interpreting IEL in conformity with the human rights obligations and SDGs recognized by all UN and WTO member states,[16] continue to be ignored by most WTO diplomats, for instance by insisting on member-driven WTO governance without any references to human rights. Chapter 3 illustrated why US Trade Representative (USTR) lawyers were often more interested in demonstrating why idealistic-deductive interpretations of WTO rules by the WTO AB could be rejected as lacking consent by adversely affected business interests rather than in promoting public reason through impartial interpretations in conformity with the customary rules of treaty interpretation. Neo-liberal and state capitalist nationalism and power-oriented economic and foreign policies offer no coherent, multilateral models for efficient governance of global PGs. Hence, constitutional struggles for justice (eg for democratic control of US trade policies, protection of China's 'one state two systems' commitments), and for protecting global PGs become more necessary than ever before.

5.2.3 Constitutional Functions of International Economic Law?

As explained in Chapter 4, the GATT and WTO guarantees of equal freedoms, non-discriminatory market competition, transparent policy-making, rule of law, and national sovereignty (eg to protect non-economic PGs) are justified not only on economic efficiency grounds. They also serve constitutional functions for protecting development as freedom by extending domestic constitutional principles to transnational trade relations. For similar reasons, as discussed in section 5.5, European common market law protects common market freedoms and judicial remedies of market citizens as fundamental rights. Arguably, economic globalization has increased the political importance of such constitutional IEL functions for

[15] Cf Petersmann (n 9).
[16] Cf EU Petersmann, *International Economic Law in the 21st Century* (Hart 2012).

supporting producers, workers, traders, investors, consumers, and other citizens in their struggles for protecting the SDGs through reforms of economic and environmental law and adjudication.

If economics is about the arrangements within which individuals and collective actors make efficient choices in response to scarcity, it is important to distinguish *choices within existing constraints* (as studied by ordinary economics) from *choices among alternative legal and institutional constraints* (as studied by constitutional and institutional economics). As explained in Chapter 4, in contrast to the focus of politics on winners, losers, and the distribution of power, the exchange paradigm of constitutional economics focuses on mutual individual and collective gains enabled by constitutional cooperation improving the laws and institutions of the economic-political order. Strategic, economic constitutionalism argues that the design, interpretation, and adaptation of constitutional rules should focus more on their real-world consequences (eg in terms of incentives for citizens, politicians, administrators, judges, enterprises) and for dynamic, multilevel governance of PGs than on the original intentions of constitutional founding fathers in earlier, different historical contexts with different regulatory challenges. For example, if globalization requires the transformation of the four-stage sequence of national constitutionalism into a transnational six-stage process, including international law-making and executive and judicial protection or transnational rule of law, it is important to limit the diverse national constitutional perspectives and principles of justice by transnational, cosmopolitan justice perspectives (such as climate change mitigation).[17] Just as ordo-liberal constitutionalism acknowledges dynamic interactions between moral, political, economic, and legal freedoms and justifies economic competition on economic and non-economic grounds,[18] so can democracy be identified with competitive government dependent on constitutional safeguards of democratic competition (eg promoting 'median democracy' in constitutional democracies, 'political bargain democracy' in neo-liberal democracies, multilevel constitutional democracy inside the EU). Transforming national constitutionalism protecting *national PGs* into multilevel constitutionalism for multilevel governance of *transnational PGs* raises a host of strategic constitutional questions. For instance:

[17] For 'law and economics' approaches to constitutionalism see Cooter (2000); Petersmann (n 9), who explains the need for a multilevel, transnational 'six-stage constitutionalization process' at 112f, 126ff, 174ff.

[18] For example, as information, coordination, and sanctioning mechanism enhancing individual freedom, promoting consumer welfare in terms of consumer surplus, inducing individuals to use their decentralized knowledge and limit abuses of power; cf V Vanberg, 'Consumer Welfare, Social Welfare and Economic Freedom—On the Normative Foundations of Competition Policy' in J Drexl *et alii* (eds), *Competition Policy and the Economic Approach. Foundations and Limitations* (Elgar 2011), 44–71.

- Why are the Bretton Woods Agreements, GATT, and the WTO—and most economic and legal textbooks[19]—neglecting the task of justifying economic law and policies in terms of principles of justice even though voluntary rule compliance depends on the perception of the rules as just? Why are human rights and constitutional principles of justice increasingly invoked in European courts by citizens as legal constraints on modern trade, investment, and environmental regulation, as discussed in Chapters 8 and 9?
- Can European competition law and multilevel networks of regulatory agencies serve as models for reforming international trade, investment, Internet, and environmental law and governance beyond Europe (eg the global competition network reviewing mergers and acquisitions) in order to depoliticize the joint protection of the SDGs?
- The less social, economic, political, and legal interactions can be separated in the determination of economic distortions (eg by currency manipulation and forced labour in China), the more interdisciplinary cooperation is needed for understanding and designing institutions in national and international economic regulation. How can legal disciplines (eg legal budget, fiscal, and debt disciplines in EU law) integrate insights produced in other disciplines (eg about moral hazards in the joint issuance of public debt, currency manipulation) in ways respecting the methodological frontiers of each discipline?
- Can the EU's multilevel common market constitution remain effective without further constitutionalization of the EU's fiscal and monetary constitution and banking union? How can the institutional asymmetry between decentralized fiscal policy and centralized monetary policies in the Eurozone be developed achieving both resilience of the monetary union against crises and avoiding moral hazards undermining EU citizens' trust in EU constitutional law principles (like limited delegation of EU powers, national sovereignty over fiscal and debt policies)? Does the adoption of the EU's 2021–2027 long-term resilience budget and Recovery Fund on 17 December 2020 provide for sufficient constitutional safeguards against the risks of EU financing through Euro bonds?
- Does the political failure of WTO members to hold WTO jurisprudence accountable—for example, by adopting majority decisions on authoritative interpretations of WTO rules (Article IX.2 WTO Agreement), amending WTO rules, negotiating new WTO rights and obligations, or by establishing a DSB Legal Committee for elaborating proposals for reforming WTO

[19] On the neglect of theories of justice in most IEL textbooks see Petersmann (n 16), at 1ff (defining the first principle of justice in terms of Kantian and Rawlsian theories of justice, thereby justifying presumptions of transnational economic freedoms subject to other principles of justice, human rights, and democratic legislation); on human rights approaches to IEL see Chapter 2, section 2.3 and Chapters 6–9. See also O Suttle, *Distributive Justice and World Trade Law. A Political Theory of International Trade Regulation* (CUP 2018).

jurisprudence—undermine the democratic legitimacy of WTO jurisprudence based on quasi-automatic adoption of WTO panel and appellate reports? How can the constitutional problems of the compulsory WTO dispute settlement system (as discussed in Chapters 3 and 6)—such as the insufficient democratic accountability of the WTO AB for its judicial clarifications of WTO rules—be reduced?
- How much will the strengthening of the intra-EU constitutional restraints on economic adjudication of trade and investment disputes and on judicial protection of individual rights influence the ongoing negotiations on reforms of ISA procedures in the external EU relations with third states and foreign investors (as discussed in Chapters 7 and 8)?

Chapter 4 explained how the WTO rules protecting non-discriminatory access to markets, non-discriminatory conditions of competition, use of efficient and transparent trade policy instruments (eg tariffs rather than non-tariff border restrictions), and rules-based dispute settlement procedures enhance the capacity of each WTO member to increase its economic welfare without unduly restricting national sovereignty to protect non-economic PGs. This mutually beneficial, legal limitation on harmful trade protectionism, and the voluntary consent of democratic institutions to the WTO agreements, justify the legal primacy of WTO rules over national laws (eg in terms of legal accountability of WTO members for their compliance with WTO obligations). From the point of view of democratic constitutionalism, the WTO legal guarantees of equal freedoms, non-discriminatory conditions of competition, transparent policy-making, rule of law, and judicial remedies extend domestic principles of justice to international trade. In this limited sense, they serve constitutional functions for complementing the utilitarian maximization paradigms (like Kaldor–Hicks efficiency) by mutually beneficial constitutional contract/exchange paradigms protecting democratic preferences of WTO members and of their market participants in transnational trade.

5.2.4 The Psychology Impeding IEL Reforms

Chapter 4 explained why globalization and its transformation of national into transnational PGs require extending constitutional and institutional economics to multilevel governance of transnational PGs in order to enhance the wealth of nations, not only through cooperation and division of labour among private economic actors but also among law-makers, governments, and courts beyond national frontiers. Efficient allocation of scarce resources and satisfaction of consumer preferences can be enhanced by both constitutional improvement of the contractarian efficiency of laws and institutions (eg constraining governmental market distortions) and post-constitutional economics maximizing the available economic goods, services, and resources. In view of the frequent difficulties of changing national constitutions, most national constitutions and constitutional courts (eg in Germany, the United States) acknowledge legislative and governmental discretion to choose among alternative economic policies subject to constitutional constraints. Such difficulties of amending national Constitutions (eg in the United States) prompted US Secretary of State Cordell Hull to promote trade policy reforms through congressional legislation (like the 1934 Reciprocal Trade Agreements Act) delegating trade policy powers to the Executive subject to additional restraints and Congressional 'fast track approval'.[20]

Chapters 2 and 3 demonstrated how reforms of international trade, investment, and environmental law and institutions are increasingly hampered by the conflicting value principles underlying utilitarian Anglo-Saxon neo-liberalism (eg promoting self-regulatory market forces privileging the *homo economicus*), constitutional European ordo-liberalism (eg protecting common market freedoms and multilevel, constitutional rights and judicial remedies of EU citizens), and authoritarian state capitalism (eg protecting totalitarian power monopolies of the communist party in China). The value conflicts underlying this reality of constitutional pluralism at national levels of governance are unlikely to disappear; they may justify broader reinterpretations of WTO exception clauses and pragmatic adjustments of the WTO dispute settlement system in response to the US assault on the WTO AB, as illustrated by the successful EU initiative for a new Multi-Party Interim Arbitration (MPIA) arrangement enabling mutually agreed appellate arbitration based on Article 25 Dispute Settlement Understanding (DSU) until the WTO AB can resume its lawful functions pursuant to Article 17 DSU.[21] Responding to the Anthropocene—that is, our new global context of humans having become a geophysical force provoking climate change, massive biodiversity losses, and other geological changes that can no longer be prevented through intergovernmental management—increases the need for making international trade, investment, and environmental regulations more coherent, for instance through legal reform-commitments like the EU's 'New Green Deal' for realizing a carbon-neutral, circular, green economy by 2050.

The tensions and geopolitical rivalries between American hegemonic neo-liberalism, European constitutional ordo-liberalism and China's totalitarian state

[20] Psychological studies of how international law works explore other departures from rational choice assumptions of self-interested utility maximization; they can be grouped into the three categories of bounded willpower, bounded self-interest, and bounded rationality of individuals and groups (whose psychology is often different from individual decision-making); cf A van Aaken and T Broude, The Psychology of International Law: An Introduction, *European Journal of International Law* 30 (2020), 1225, at 1227, 1232.

[21] See Chapter 3, section 3.2 and E Baroncini, 'The EU Approach to Overcome the WTO Dispute Settlement Vacuum: Article 25 DSU Interim Appeal Arbitration as a Bridge between Renovation and Innovation' in M Kolsky Lewis, H Nakagawa, RJ Neuwirth, CD Picker, and PT Stoll (eds), *A Post-WTO International Legal Order. Utopian, Dystopian and other Scenarios* (Springer 2020), 115–32.

capitalism render constitutional and institutional economics more contested, for instance due to the lesser constitutional restraints on governmental conferral of privileges and rent-seeking interest groups in neo-liberal and state capitalist economies than in ordo-liberal, constitutionally more restrained democracies. Due to its emphasis on the interdependence of orders, European ordo-liberalism remains an open-ended, economic, legal, and political programme embedded in Europe's multilevel constitutionalism. As European ordo-liberalism and US neo-liberalism face common regulatory challenges (like authoritarian state capitalism, climate change) and share common foundations (like democratic constitutionalism, use of institutional economics and 'constitutional economics' for responding to market and governance failures), US and European legal and economics scholars should join forces in responding to the regulatory challenges of the changing global economy and international order. Also US trade lawyers acknowledge that the current global governance crises, health pandemics, and climate change make constitutional reforms of multilevel governance of PGs ever more urgent.[22] In order to be democratically legitimate and politically supported by citizens, the policies for realizing the SDGs should no longer prioritize 'negative freedoms' (eg from unjustified restrictions) and neo-liberal interest group politics. As reflected in the universally agreed SDGs, they must protect also universally recognized 'positive freedoms' (eg to health, environmental, and other human rights protection) and constitutional, democratic, and environmental reforms. More than forty years ago, Nobel Prize laureate James Buchanan admonished economists not to neglect 'the constitutional-institutional or framework requirements of an economic system'.[23] In view of global governance crises and their existential threats, also politicians must acknowledge that transnational PGs cannot be protected without international law and multilevel governance institutions supported by citizens (rather than only by utility-maximizing economic actors). The conflicts between rational pursuit of *self-interest*, legal promotion of *common interests* (eg through non-discriminatory economic and democratic competition), and reasonable protection of *public interests* and PGs through constitutional law and democratic regulation are at the root of why constitutional economics and reasonable self-restraint are needed for rules-based, efficient responses to the knowledge, incentive, reputation, and legitimacy problems of economies.[24]

[22] See, eg, S Lester, 'Waiting for Cordell Hull' in Kolsky Lewis et al. (eds), (n 21), 57–70.
[23] J Buchanan, *Freedom in Constitutional Contract* (Texas UP 1977), at 5.
[24] Cf V Vanberg, Ordnungspolitik, the Freiburg School and the Reason of Rules, *Freiburger Diskussionspapiere zur Ordnungsökonomik* No 14/2001.

5.2.5 Need for Respecting Constitutional Pluralism

Chapters 2 and 3 described how the current state of IEL faces opposing realities of constitutional pluralism and regulatory competition among authoritarian economic systems (eg in China and Russia) and neo-liberal or ordo-liberal market economies committed to methodological individualism, democratic constitutionalism, and rational choices by individuals and peoples. The remainder of Chapter 5 elaborates on the close links between economic ordo-liberalism and democratic constitutionalism in European integration as illustrated by past European integration through law projects (section 5.3), ushering in increasing constitutionalization of foreign policies (section 5.4) and Europe's functionally limited human rights constitution, common market constitution, incomplete monetary constitution, and foreign policy constitution (section 5.5). The more European integration law differs from regional integration law in Africa, the Americas, and Asia, the stronger becomes the need for basing reforms of IEL on respect for the reality of constitutional pluralism (section 5.6) and for peaceful resolution of conflicts among authoritarian, neo-liberal, and constitutional approaches through reforms of international trade, investment, environmental, economic, and human rights remedies and adjudication (Chapters 6–9).

5.3 Constitutional Failures: Lessons from 'Integration through Law'

Chapter 4 explained why economic law must respond to the reality of market failures, governance failures and constitutional failures as implicitly acknowledged in the SDGs.[25] Are the needed reforms of national and international legal systems feasible in view of the ever greater influence of money in politics—notably in democracies like the United States, where political money (eg financial donations to public media and politicians) by the richest 1 per cent of the US population and US companies are believed to influence politics often more than public opinion?[26] Do the political and legal experiences with integration through law in federal states and regional integration regimes offer lessons for reforming IEL? Why is it that both inside federal states and inside regional economic integration, protectionist resistance against creation of common markets was overcome only on the basis

[25] Cf *Transforming our World* (2015), para 14: 'Billions of our citizens continue to live in poverty and are denied a life of dignity. There are rising inequalities within and among countries. There are enormous disparities of opportunity, wealth and power.'

[26] Cf Institute for New Economic Thinking, 'New INET Research shows once again that it's large firms and the 1%—not the 'median voter'—who drive US policy' (2 November 2020), (https://www.ineteconomics.org/perspectives/blog/affluent-authoritarianism-mcguire-and-delahunts-new-evidence-on-public-opinion-and-policy).

of multilevel legal rules and judicial remedies of a higher legal rank empowering self-interested citizens and other economic actors (like businesses) to invoke and protect their common market freedoms against local protectionism?

5.3.1 Lessons from Federal Integration through Law?

In 1991, Professor Joseph Weiler's influential article on *The Transformation of Europe* described the legal and judicial 'constitutionalization' of European common market law, the political equilibrium and the constitutional tolerance necessary for implementing community policies supported by citizens, parliaments, governments and courts of justice in and among the member states of the European Community.[27] Simultaneously, my book on *Constitutional Functions and Constitutional Problems of International Economic Law* explored the lessons from federal and regional common market projects during the nineteenth and twentieth centuries for the needed reforms of worldwide agreements like the 1944 Bretton Woods Agreements and GATT 1947, whose monetary and customs union rules served as foundations of the 1957 European Economic Community (EEC) Treaty and of its common market project.[28] Methodologically, both Weiler and myself proceeded from comparative studies of common market law in federal states and perceived democratic constitutionalism and common market law as most important building blocks for transnational community law.[29] We argued that the legitimacy of liberal trade and common market rules derived less from enhancing economic efficiency than from protecting agreed principles of justice like equal freedoms, rule of law, non-discriminatory competition, and difference principles enhancing social welfare, respect for human dignity, and cosmopolitan rights. My publications emphasized the constitutional functions of ordo-liberal free trade agreements (FTAs)—like the 1991 FTA establishing the EEA among today thirty EEA member countries—and of the EEC's common commercial policy for transforming GATT 1947 into the more rules-based WTO legal and dispute settlement system resulting from the Uruguay Round of multilateral trade negotiations.[30] In

[27] J Weiler, The Transformation of Europe, *Yale Law Journal* 100 (1991), 2403–283.

[28] EU Petersmann, *Constitutional Functions and Constitutional Problems of International Economic Law. International and Domestic Foreign Trade Law and Foreign Trade Policy in the United States, the European Community and Switzerland* (Fribourg UP/Westview Boulder Press 1991, reprinted by Routledge 2019).

[29] Cf M Seccombe, M Cappelletti, and J Weiler (eds), *Integration through Law: Europe and the American Federal Experience* (3 vols, de Gruyter 1986–1988); M Hilf and EU Petersmann (eds), *National Constitutions and International Economic Law* (Kluwer 1993).

[30] Cf M Hilf, FG Jacobs, and EU Petersmann (eds), *The European Community and GATT* (Kluwer 1986); EU Petersmann, The Transformation of the World Trading System through the 1994 Agreement Establishing the World Trade Organization, *European Journal of International Law* 6 (1995), 161–221; EU Petersmann, Proposals for a New Constitution of the European Union: Building-Blocks for a Constitutional Theory and Constitutional Law of the European Union, *Common Market Law Review* (1995), 1123–75.

spite of Brexit and of selective exits from certain fields of EU law (like the monetary union), the 2009 Lisbon Treaty (eg its EUCFR) and the adoption by the EU Council, in December 2020, of the 2021–2027 EU multiannual budget and economic recovery project (responding to the COVID-19 health pandemic by providing for €1.8 trillion, including €750 billion in common borrowing) justify hopes that the EU's regional community law—embedded in a human rights constitution, micro-economic common market constitution, and macro-economic monetary constitution providing for multilevel, democratic governance of European PGs—will continue protecting the common market, monetary stability, transnational rule of law, and human rights inside the EU and among the EEA member states, notwithstanding global economic and environmental governance crises and health pandemics.[31]

Up to the inauguration of US President Trump in January 2017, the 1994 Agreement establishing the WTO and its AB were celebrated by most WTO members as one of the most transformative, worldwide agreements since the UN Charter, notwithstanding the failures of the Doha Round negotiations to realize most of that Round's objectives. Some likened the transformation of GATT 1947 into a worldwide legal and compulsory dispute settlement system governing the global trading community to a constitutional moment, for instance in view of its inclusion of sub-state actors (like Hong Kong, Macau, and Taiwan) and supra-state actors (like the EU), and the almost universal acceptance of compulsory WTO dispute settlement jurisdiction (including by all permanent members of the UN Security Council). Yet, just as the Bretton Woods Agreements have not prevented repeated financial and sovereign debt crises, so have WTO law and adjudication for a rules-based, non-discriminatory trading system failed to prevent the return to aggressive nationalism (eg by Russia against neighbouring states), extra-territorial expansionism (eg by China in the South China Sea), and illegal trade wars (eg by the United States) disrupting multilateral treaty and dispute settlement systems. Federal market integration (eg in Germany, Switzerland, and the United States during the nineteenth century) succeeded only if protected by federal courts vis-à-vis local protectionism. The US destruction of the WTO AB revealed a constitutional failure of WTO members, similar to other constitutional failures of UN member states briefly discussed in Chapters 2 and 3. The controversies over the failures of the Doha Round negotiations to adjust the world trading system to the regulatory challenges of the twenty-first century (like e-commerce), over the consistency of China's state capitalism with WTO law (as discussed in Chapter 3, sections 3.5 and 3.6), and over alleged judicial overreach in trade, investment, and

[31] On the progressive, legal, and judicial constitutionalization of European economic law since J Weiler's publication in 1991, see MP Maduro and M Wind (eds), *The Transformation of Europe Twenty-Five Years After* (CUP 2017). On the EU's sectoral (eg democratic and economic) constitutionalism, see Tuori (n 10).

European adjudication (as discussed in Chapter 3, section 3.3, and Chapters 6–8) reveal increasing conflicts among Anglo-Saxon neo-liberalism, authoritarian state capitalism, third-world economies, and Europe's multilevel constitutionalism. These geopolitical rivalries undermine multilevel legislative, executive, and judicial protection in worldwide institutions of transnational PGs like human rights, rule of law, sustainable development, and climate change mitigation. The global COVID-19 health pandemic, the World Health Organization's (WHO) lack of adequate leadership in responding to this global health crisis (eg due to China's non-cooperation in clarifying the origins of this health crisis in Wuhan), and the insufficient efforts to realize the climate change mitigation objectives of the 2015 Paris Agreement suggest that global community law for multilevel governance of global PGs may remain a political utopia.

5.3.2 Intergovernmental Power Politics as Constitutional Failure

Many countries have seen that their revolutionary constitutions (like the French Constitutions of 1791 and 1793, the German Weimar Constitution of 1919, China's Constitutions of 1912 and of 1982) failed to effectively protect equal rights of citizens against power politics.[32] Most UN and WTO agreements for protecting transnational aggregate PGs[33]—like sustainable development, international rule of law, climate change mitigation, poverty reduction through a mutually beneficial monetary and trading system, public health, international labour rights, and human rights—have failed to realize their objectives in full and contain domestic governance failures. Some of the founding treaties, such as those of the International Labour Organization (ILO), WHO, FAO, and the United Nations Educational, Scientific and Cultural Organization (UNESCO), were explicitly called constitutions and linked their legislative and executive mandates to specific human rights (like labour rights, health rights, rights to food and education) and corresponding PGs (like public health and education systems, food security, collective bargaining between employers and employees). Yet, due to the intergovernmental domination of UN/WTO governance and the disconnect these institutions had from effective democratic and judicial protection of rights of citizens, UN/WTO governance often remains dominated by authoritarian rulers and special interest groups (eg special producer interests rather than general consumer interests, governmental self-interests in limiting legal, democratic, and judicial accountability vis-à-vis

[32] Cf S Gardbaum, 'Revolutionary Constitutionalism' (2017) 15 *International Journal of Constitutional Law* 173–200.

[33] On the defining characteristics and different kinds of 'pure PGs' (whose use is 'non-rival' and 'non-excludable' like human rights) and 'impure PGs' (like 'club goods' excluding free-riders, common pool resources with rival uses), the related collective action problems, and their limitation through multilevel constitutionalism see Petersmann (n 9), Chapter 2.

citizens). For instance, toxic tobacco products have killed more than 100 million smokers during the twentieth century before WHO members finally adopted the Framework Convention on Tobacco Control in 2003, which has now been ratified by 181 countries. From the point of view of citizens as constituent powers and democratic principals of governments, the power-oriented disconnect of the intergovernmental decision-making processes, and their inadequate democratic control, reveal constitutional failures, ushering in unnecessary poverty and inadequate protection of human rights of billions of adversely affected citizens in UN member states.

There are numerous reasons why the self-constitution of individuals and societies in the twenty-first century requires an extension of constitutionalism beyond state borders to the ever more intense, transnational cooperation in collective supply of PGs. For example:

- The more globalization transforms national into *transnational PGs* which no state can protect unilaterally without international law and multilevel governance institutions, the more necessary become constitutional restraints and democratic control of discretionary foreign policy powers to tax and restrict citizens and redistribute domestic income through foreign policy measures (like import tariffs, export subsidies, discriminatory trade, investment, and Internet restrictions).
- The disconnect between intergovernmental UN/WTO governance and domestic rights of citizens—such as intergovernmental treaty provisions and practices preventing citizens from invoking PGs treaties in domestic jurisdictions—risks undermining constitutional rights of citizens (eg as democratic principals of multilevel governance agents with limited, delegated powers); the primary and secondary law of international PGs treaties often eludes effective democratic control, parliamentary and judicial review, and remedies of citizens.
- Citizen-driven network governance (eg protecting reasonable, common self-interests of citizens though labour rights, human rights, competition, commercial, and common market law and adjudication, global supply chains, climate change governance) has proven to be more effective than intergovernmental UN and WTO 'chess-board' governance treating citizens as mere objects. As legal subjects and democratic principals, citizens must also assume republican responsibilities for promoting transnational PGs like mitigation of climate change.
- The widespread disregard for human rights inside many UN member states creates negative externalities (eg more than 80 million refugees fleeing civil wars and unnecessary poverty) that call for constitutional restraints on abuses of power and for collective assistance limiting governance failures and

constitutional failures (like impunity of rulers violating human rights and committing crimes against humanity).

- As human rights recognize individual and democratic self-development as ultimate values, the universally recognized principle—that '[i]n the exercise of his rights and freedoms, everyone shall be subject only to such limitations as are determined by law solely for the purpose of securing due recognition and respect for the rights and freedoms of others and of meeting the just requirements of morality, public order and the general welfare in a democratic society' (Article 29:2 UDHR)—requires constitutional protection of all human beings against abuses of multilevel governance powers.

5.4 Unrestrained Foreign Policy Discretion as Constitutional Failure

Foreign policy powers include powers to tax and restrict domestic citizens (eg through tariffs, import prohibitions), redistribute their domestic income, and provoke trade or military wars. The practical need for constitutionalizing executive foreign policy powers (eg through legal and institutional limitations of their abuses) have been evident since ancient times, for instance in situations (eg in ancient Greece and Italy) where peace and security inside republican city states depended on mercenary military armies and alliances with powerful foreign rulers. Donato Gianotti wrote his book on the republic of Florence while the war between the French king (Francis I) and the Holy Roman Empire (under Charles V as emperor) was fought mostly in Italy for the dominion of the peninsula. Italian states had to side either with the king or the emperor. The last Florentine republic (1527–1530), in which Gianotti served as secretary to the Council of Ten (*dieci*), had been overthrown by the imperial army and replaced by the imperial recognition of the Medici *signoria* in Florence, which was later transformed into a hereditary lordship based on an agreement between the pope and Florentine aristocrats. Gianotti's book, *Republica Fiorentina*, was designed as a blueprint for a new Florentine republic that could, however, never be realized given Cosimo de Medici's superior, military power.[34] One of the most innovative features of Gianotti's constitutional project for a fourth republic of Florence was the recognition of foreign and security policies as a separate state function subject to constitutional limitations so as to avoid the previous failures of the second and third Florentine republics of 1494 and 1527 (both had been overthrown by the Medici rulers with external support from the Pope).[35] The political lessons from Gianotti's insights remain relevant today, for

[34] On this historical background, the text, and contents of the *Republica Fiorentina*, see D Gianotti, *Republica Fiorentina*, A critical edition and introduction by G Silvano (Droz 1990).

[35] For a detailed analysis of Gianotti's Renaissance republicanism (eg in contrast to modern constitutional contract theories), his concern for limiting arbitrary abuses of legislative, executive, judicial, and

instance in situations like the South China Sea where an authoritarian government (China) exploits its military force for annexing maritime waters at the expense of smaller, neighbouring states. From a constitutional perspective, national constitutions should not leave it to executive discretion whether to withdraw unilaterally from 'world order treaties' that had been ratified by national parliaments for the benefit of their citizens.[36]

5.4.1 Constitutional Foreign Policy Dilemmas

It was Kant who—in *Perpetual Peace*—described the foreign policy dilemma of constitutionalism (ie that freedom and rule of law can prevail inside states only if they prevail also in their external relations and are protected by judicial remedies) in general theoretical terms:

> all men who can at all influence one another must adhere to some kind of civil constitution ... (1) a constitution based on the civil right of individuals within a nation (*jus civitatis*); (2) a constitution based on the international right of states in their relationships with one another (*jus gentium*); (3) a constitution based on cosmopolitan right, in so far as individuals and states, existing in an external relationship of mutual influences, may be regarded as citizens of a universal state of mankind (*jus cosmopoliticum*). This classification, with respect to the idea of a perpetual peace, is not arbitrary, but necessary. For if even one of the parties were able to influence the others physically and yet itself remained in a state of nature, there would be a risk of war, which it is precisely the aim of the above articles to prevent.[37]

foreign policy powers so as to protect man's freedom in society, and Gianotti's proposals for rule of law, see Gianotti (n 34), at 41ff; D Gianotti, *Die Republik Florenz (1534)*, edited by A Riklin and D Höchli (Fink 1997). As the handwritten copies of *Republica Fiortentina* were rediscovered in the eighteenth century and translated into foreign languages only recently, Gianotti's constitutionalism remains little known and under-researched.

[36] President Trump's claim to have independent power to terminate international trade agreements remains contested among US constitutional lawyers in view of the exclusive congressional power under the Commerce Clause and the lack of explicit allocation of authority in the US Constitution to terminate treaties. Some US constitutional lawyers construe US constitutional law as being inconsistent with independent presidential authority to terminate trade agreements; as there is also no statutory authority for the President to terminate trade agreements, they conclude that the President lacks authority—without new authorization from Congress—to terminate existing trade agreements unilaterally; cf JP Trachtman, *Power to Terminate US Trade Agreements: the Presidential Dormant Commerce Clause Versus an Historical Gloss Half Empty*, SSRN Research Paper, 16 October 2017, at 1. By repealing agreements incorporated by Congress into domestic federal law and rendering ineffective entire areas of congressional trade legislation without constitutional or statutory authorization of the President to terminate trade agreements unilaterally, the President would upset the constitutional balance of legislative and executive powers and undermine constitutional democracy in the United States.

[37] I Kant, 'Perpetual Peace. A Philosophical Sketch' in I Kant, *Political Writings* (edited by H Reiss, CUP 1970), at 98f.

Moreover, as explained by Kant, the problem of establishing a perfect civil constitution is subordinate to the problem of a law-governed external relationship with other states and cannot be solved unless the latter is also solved.[38] This constitutional dilemma continues to be widely ignored; it calls for extending democratic constitutionalism beyond national borders (as in EU law) in order to protect human rights, democracy, and the rule of law against executive abuses of foreign policy powers. Defending a liberal international order is not an act of idealism but of reasonable defence of a liberal order at home for the benefit of domestic citizens and their constitutional rights.[39] Similarly, domestic constitutional restraints on foreign policy discretion are a reasonable defence of the domestic constitutional order.

5.4.2 The Unsocial Sociability of Men as Core Constitutional Problem

According to Kant, it is the 'unsocial sociability of men' which drives them to abandon their state of nature and enter a law-governed federation of peoples protecting equal rights and rule of law through law-governed, multilevel constitutionalism enabling mankind to develop all its natural capacities. Kant's confidence in the sociological forces of voluntarily agreed, mutually beneficial trade[40] refers to another dimension of the psychology driving international legal and political actors. Their rational self-interest promote peaceful, welfare-enhancing cooperation, as acknowledged in many empirical and normative studies on the role of trade agreements in preventing military conflicts; as long as goods, services, and investments can cross borders peacefully and the rule of law prevails, soldiers need not cross borders for economic reasons.[41] Economic integration law within federal states and among states in Europe was designed and perceived as an instrument for promoting peaceful cooperation and the rule of law; for instance, the International Chamber of Commerce was created in 1919 with the aim of pursuing world peace through world trade by promoting merchants of peace. Arguably, both GATT 1947 and the WTO have promoted peace and prosperity by integrating the 164 WTO member states and more than 20 accession candidate states into a global division of labour that has helped to lift more than 2 billion people out of poverty. These psychological interactions between ordo-liberal economic, democratic, and

[38] *Idea for a Universal History with a Cosmopolitan Purpose*, in Kant (n 37), at 47.

[39] Cf GJ Ikenberry, *A World Safe for Democracy: Liberal Internationalism and the Crisis of Global Order* (Yale UP 2020).

[40] Kant, 'Perpetual Peace' (n 37), at 114: '[f]or the spirit of commerce sooner or later takes hold of every people, and it cannot exist side by side with war'; 'of all the powers (or means) of the state, financial power can probably be relied on most'.

[41] Cf F Lehmann and JP Lehmann (eds), *Peace and Prosperity through World Trade. Achieving the 2019 Vision* (CUP 2010).

constitutional orders are just another illustration of the psychological dilemmas of bounded rationality necessitating constitutional self-restraints for reducing the human paradox of liberty (eg in the sense of inherent tendencies of liberty rights to self-destruction by abuses of public and private powers) and the paradox of inequality (eg in the sense of social inequalities inside and among countries despite legal status equality guaranteed by human rights).

Democratic, republican, and cosmopolitan constitutionalism do not aim at the utopia of a global super-constitution overruling domestic law in multilevel governance of global PGs. Rather, they argue for functional bottom-up constitutionalization of multilevel governance of transnational PGs through stronger cosmopolitan rights and remedies (eg in constitutional laws, labour laws, human rights law, competition, common market, and environmental legislation) inducing citizens to participate in, and support multilevel governance of transnational PGs (eg by protecting economic and social rights in the global division of labour, rights to participation, privacy, and remedies in global communication systems). The fragmented constitutionalization of multilevel governance is facilitated by the simultaneous internationalization of national constitutional law principles as reflected in the jurisprudence of international courts and the emergence of global administrative law.[42] They promote a convergence of national constitutional law principles by linking the constitutional functions, principles, and constitutional methodologies in multilevel regulation and governance of transnational PGs (eg judicial use of proportionality balancing of competing rights and constitutional principles, multilevel judicial comity, and judicial deference based on principles of subsidiarity and national margins of appreciation in domestic implementation of human rights). The increasing use by national and regional courts in Europe of constitutional methodologies for interpreting the rules of recognition, change, and adjudication of multilevel legal systems (like EU law, EEA law, and European HRL) as principal–agent relationships among citizens and multilevel governance agents remains context-specific; it differs from multilevel judicial cooperation in African, Asian, and other countries.[43]

[42] See Chapter 2, section 2.1 and S Cassese (ed), *Research Handbook on Global Administrative Law* (Edward Elgar 2016); A Peters, 'The Globalisation of State Constitutions' in J Nijman and A Nollkaemper (eds), *New Perspectives on the Divide between National and International Law* (OUP 2007) 251–308.

[43] Cf PJ Yap, *Constitutional Dialogue in Common Law Asia* (OUP 2015), who emphasizes the advantages of dialogic judicial review over alternatives of legislative or judicial supremacy.

5.5 Europe's Ordo-Liberal Economic, Human Rights, and Foreign Policy Constitutionalism

Since the 1950s, the treaties establishing the ECHR, the European Communities, the EFTA, EEA, and other European organizations continue to transform the state-centred international law among European states (as it evolved since the Westphalian peace treaties of 1648) into a citizen-centred European integration law recognizing constitutional rights of citizens, transnational rule of law, multilevel democratic rights, and multilevel parliamentary, governmental, and judicial institutions as common foundations of an emerging European constitutional law.[44] In contrast to power-oriented conceptions of international law among states that risk 're-feudalizing' international relations by prioritizing rights of governments over rights of citizens (eg in many areas of UN and GATT/WTO law),[45] the dynamically evolving European constitutional law reconnects with the ancient idea of European public law including both domestic, transnational, and international public law for multilevel governance of PGs inside and beyond the EU, the EEA, and the forty-seven Member States of the Council of Europe. The more the different domestic and transnational public laws interact both vertically and horizontally, the more the doctrinal separation of the national, transnational, international, and supranational levels of legal regulation neglects the transformative and compensatory functions of multilevel legislative, administrative, and judicial governance for protecting rights of citizens and transnational PGs in the common European zone.[46]

5.5.1 Five Characteristic Features of European Constitutionalism

Europe's multilevel constitutionalism has the following five defining characteristics at least, which distinguish it from other regional law systems in Africa, the Americas and Asia:

1. The multilevel constitution, limitation, regulation, and justification of governance powers (eg in the EU, EEA, EFTA, ECHR, and the Energy Charter

[44] Cf A von Bogdandy and J Bast (eds), *Principles of European Constitutional Law* (2nd edn, Hart 2010).

[45] On the initial unity of human societies, polities, and law (like Roman law and its *jus gentium*) before the doctrinal separation of international law among sovereign states from domestic legal systems and from effective democratic control opened the doors for discretionary abuses of foreign policy powers by what Allot called the '*Hof-mafia*' of diplomats, see Allot (n 8) 289ff ('It was a sad day in the history of humanity when the subtle and complex concept of law was crudely split into two—national law and the law between nations').

[46] Cf A von Bogdandy, *The Idea of European Public Law Today. Introducing the Max Planck Handbooks on Public Law in Europe*, MPIL Research Paper Series (2017).

Treaty (ECT)) are based on respect for constitutional rights, multilevel protection of rule of law and democratic governance, rules-based economic constitutionalism (eg of competition and common market regulations, related fundamental rights and judicial remedies), and protection of constitutional pluralism and diverse constitutional identities of peoples (cf Article 4 TEU).

2. The multilevel regulatory structures (eg of EU, EEA, and EFTA law) have more successfully protected transnational PGs (like transnational common markets, rule of law, non-discriminatory conditions of competition, fundamental rights and social welfare of citizens) than in any previous period of European history—notwithstanding populist contestations (eg prompting Brexit ushering in the unilateral termination of the fundamental rights of British citizens under EU law in 2020 and in the reintroduction of discriminatory trade barriers).
3. Even if European integration law could often not progress in linear ways (eg due to popular opposition against political and defence communities proposed in the 1950s), the economic integration dynamic promoted functional spillovers (eg from the customs union to the progressive creation of a common market and competitive social market economy, monetary union, 'area of freedom, security, and justice'), and multilevel legal and judicial protection of ever more fundamental rights as codified in the EUCFR.
4. The history of European law confirms that intergovernmental power politics can be constitutionalized in diverse ways through multilevel constitutional, parliamentary, participatory, and deliberative democratic principles (cf Articles 9–12 TEU) and multilevel, judicial protection of transnational rule of law accommodating diverse constitutional traditions (eg of common law and civil law countries) inside EU member states as well as in third states insisting on participation in the common market without supra-national constitutional restraints (eg EEA member countries like Norway, EFTA member countries like Switzerland, Muslim countries like Turkey).
5. The economic logic (eg of creating an EU monetary union without common economic policies) and public reason driving European integration (eg its social market economy prescribed in Article 3 TEU) remain contested, as illustrated by the financial crises since 2008/2010, the debt crises in (so far) ten EU member states, the refugee crises and related rule of law crises (as illustrated by widespread disregard for the Schengen rules on free movements of persons, migration, the EU budget and debt disciplines in Article 126 TFEU). Yet, the governance failures have often been used as opportunities for reforms (eg by creating a banking union in response to private and public debt crises inside EU Member States, financing of parts of the EU 2021 budget through joint issuance of Euro bonds). This pragmatic and dialectic evolution of European integration law remains constantly exposed to constitutional challenges (eg from national constitutional courts and European

courts contesting EU regulations, illiberal EU member state governments—such as currently in Hungary and Poland—defying compliance with EU law) that may enable future constitutional reforms (eg of the European monetary union, the reallocation of refugees from Mediterranean 'arrival' countries to other EU member states). Notwithstanding populist dissatisfaction with certain governance failures inside the EU (like monetary crises, financial austerity measures, uncontrolled immigration in 2015, social inequalities, youth unemployment), citizen support for constitutional, parliamentary, participatory, and deliberative democracy remains very high in continental Europe.

5.5.2 Functional Constitutionalism: The Common Market Constitution

National constitutionalism aims at legally constituting a people and its self-government. In contrast to this all-inclusive function, multilevel constitutionalism beyond the state is functionally limited by extending certain constitutional rules, principles, and institutions to limited areas of multilevel governance of transnational PGs. Depending on the policy sectors concerned, economic, political, social, and security policy objectives tend to lead to diverse constitutional approaches. Hence, functionally limited transnational constitutionalism is often sectoral, as illustrated below by the brief discussion of the EU's micro-economic common market constitution, macro-economic monetary policy constitution, and foreign policy constitution. This reflects the relational nature of constitutionalism, that is its dependence on the regulatory object.[47] For instance, the EU's common market constitution is based on common market freedoms for movements of goods, services, persons, capital, and related payments. National and European courts protect these common market freedoms both as individual, directly applicable rights and as objective constitutional principles. The multilevel EU competition law protects non-discriminatory conditions of competition; it is enforced through multilevel, national, and EU competition authorities subject to comprehensive, judicial remedies. The EU's competitive social market economy (Article 3 TEU) is embedded into multilevel constitutional guarantees of civil, political, economic, social, and environmental rights and policies protecting PGs. As illustrated by the EUCFR and by the rights and judicial remedies of 'market citizens' under EU and EEA competition and common market law, the individualization of micro-economic constitutional guarantees and the judicial protection of negative integration (eg by extending free-movement rights of workers to family members) reinforced the legal and political constitutions of EU and EEA member states, for instance by

[47] Cf Tuori (n 10), at 9, 21ff.

transforming the EU's instrumental market freedoms into fundamental rights and EU citizenship rights requiring additional positive integration law.[48]

Whereas national constitutions are often the result of particular constitutional moments (eg following the First and Second World Wars), sectoral, transnational constitutionalization tends to result from evolutionary, multilevel legislative, executive, and judicial governance processes. For instance, the progressive constitutionalization of the 1957 EEC Treaty was initiated by constitutional interpretations of the European Court of Justice (CJEU) (eg on legal primacy, direct effect, and direct applicability) of EEC Treaty provisions, their acceptance by national governments, parliaments, courts, and citizens, and by subsequent EEC legal practices and treaty amendments. Since its *Les Verts* judgment in 1986, the CJEU characterized the founding treaties of the EC/EU as a constitutional charter and has progressively granted constitutional status to the Treaty's general principles, common market freedoms, and other fundamental rights guarantees.[49] The EU's primary and secondary law and related legal practices dynamically evolved into a multilevel common market constitution, notwithstanding the fact that national constitutional courts (eg in Germany) had deliberately refrained from interpreting their respective national constitutions as an 'economic constitution', as advocated by ordo-liberal economists and lawyers.[50]

5.5.3 Evolutionary Human Rights Constitutionalism

The EU's common market constitution was embedded in a multilevel human rights constitution, whose progressive emergence confirmed the evolutionary nature of EU constitutional law limiting EU powers. The 1957 EEC Treaty included no treaty provisions on human rights. Since the *Nold* judgment in 1974, the CJEU recognized and progressively clarified the status of human rights as general principles of EU law deriving from the common constitutional traditions of EU member states and from international human rights obligations accepted by EU member states, notably the ECHR, other human rights treaties, and general international law obligations.[51] In addition, the CJEU progressively clarified its judicial interpretations of EU common market freedoms and fundamental rights based on specific Treaty provisions (eg on prohibition of gender discrimination). The status of human rights as general principles of EU law was explicitly recognized in subsequent EU Treaties (eg Article 6 of the 1992 Maastricht Treaty). With the entry into force of

[48] See A Tryfonidou, *The Impact of Union Citizenship on the EU's Market Freedoms* (Hart 2016).

[49] For detailed references to the jurisprudence, see, eg, Tuori (n 10), 13ff; Weiler (n 30).

[50] Cf C Joerges, 'The Overburdening of Law by Ordoliberalism and the Integration Project' in J Hien and C Joerges (eds), *Ordoliberalism, Law and the Rule of Economics* (Hart 2020), 179ff.

[51] Cf V Kosta and B de Witte, 'Human Rights Norms in the Court of Justice of the European Union' in M Scheinin (ed), *Human Rights Norms in 'Other' International Courts* (CUP 2019), 263–86.

the Lisbon Treaty in December 2009, the incorporation of the EUCFR provided EU law with its own detailed set of civil, political, economic, and social rights. The new Article 6 TEU confirmed not only that '[f]undamental rights as guaranteed by the European Convention for the Protection of Human Rights and Fundamental Freedoms and as they result from the constitutional traditions common to the Member States shall constitute general principles of the Union's law' (paragraph 3). Article 6.2 TEU also prescribed accession of the EU to the ECHR; Article 6.1 TEU specified—together with Article 52 EUCFR—the relationship between ECHR and EUCFR guarantees. Several Lisbon Treaty provisions further confirmed 'respect for human dignity, freedom, democracy, equality, the rule of law and respect for human rights as foundational values' of the EU (Article 2 TEU), which must also guide the EU's external actions and policies (cf Articles 3.5, 21, 207 TEU).[52] Legal systems are defined by dynamic interactions between the normative primary and secondary rules, principles, and legal order and their application and progressive clarification through the legal practices of private and public legal subjects and institutions concerned; the EU human rights *system* continues to evolve dynamically through national and EU legal practices, the jurisprudence of European and national courts, and civil society challenges of EU internal and external practices (like investor–state arbitration, judicial challenges of the EU's and Morocco's neglect for respecting human rights in the western Sahara).

5.5.4 Constructivist Constitutionalism: The EU's Incomplete Monetary Constitution

The entry into force, in December 2009, of the Treaty on the Functioning of the European Union (TFEU) clarified and complemented the EU rules for the Economic and Monetary Union (EMU), including 'provisions specific to Member States whose currency is the Euro' (Articles 136ff). Yet, the global financial crisis of 2008 ushered in increasing disregard by EU member states for the budget and debt disciplines of Article 126 TFEU. The bail out and related credit facility prohibitions in Articles 123–125 TFEU, which reflected Germany's insistence on constitutional commitments to fiscal and monetary stability, did not prevent the EU and its member states to respond positively to requests for—so far—ten sovereign debt programmes disbursing around €500 billion since 2008 in favour of Euro area states (eg Greece, Ireland, Portugal, Cyprus) as well as balance of payments loan assistance under Article 143 TFEU for other EU member states (eg Hungary, Latvia, Romania).[53] The EU responses to the financial crises in some EU member states

[52] For details, see V Kube, *EU Human Rights, International Investment Law and Participation. Operationalizing the EU Foreign Policy Objective to Global Human Rights Protection* (Springer 2019).

[53] Also Greece formally ended its sovereign debt programme and resumed borrowing in private, international capital markets in 2019. This illustrates not only the success of most of these programmes;

led to numerous intergovernmental agreements among EU or Eurozone members providing for additional financial assistance (eg by a new European Stability Mechanism) embedded into additional agreements specifying the fiscal, debt, financial, and economic conditions of these crises measures. The Eurozone crises entailed not only major mutations of the EU's macro-economic constitution, notably resulting from extending 'the primary objective of the European System of Central Banks . . . to maintain price stability' (Article 127.1 TFEU) to safeguarding 'the stability of the euro area as a whole' (Article 136.3 TFEU as amended) by ever more comprehensive Eurozone legislation and European Central Bank (ECB) interventions.[54] The Maastricht Treaty provisions for the EMU and the intergovernmental responses to the Euro crises have brought about increasing convergence of French and German policy responses in the Eurozone crisis, even if the non-conventional policy adopted by the ECB 'has broken with the ordo-liberal approach'[55] and provoked a constitutional conflict with the German Constitutional Court (as discussed in Chapter 8). Can the progressive rule-making and exceptional crisis management in the EU's unique monetary union without common economic and fiscal policies cope with the increasing inconsistencies between the law in the books (eg the TEU provisions limiting fiscal and debt deficits) and the law in practice? Are the principles of liability and conditionality of Eurozone financial assistance ordo-liberal and dangerous (eg by enhancing austerity and price, wage, and competitive adjustments rather than short-term economic growth through reflationary measures in over-indebted Eurozone economies)? Or are they justifiable by institutional economics (eg in view of moral hazards caused by joint liability regimes)? How to avoid intergovernmental authoritarian liberalism in executive emergency responses to unforeseen crisis politics (eg caused by sovereign debt crises or health pandemics)?[56] The initially constructivist nature of the EU's monetary constitution is increasingly challenged by unforeseen developments and by political calls for evolutionary constitutional responses (eg by expansive use of ECB monetary policy powers).

The conflicts between the post-1945 German culture of stability, embedded in the EU's fiscal and debt disciplines, and different cultures in EU member state (eg in Italy) and outside the EU (eg in the United States) become ever more evident.[57]

it also seems to confirm the constitutional problem that in weak political systems where politicians fail to defend the rule of law (eg the budget and debt disciplines of Art 126 TFEU), the public debt is high because the government is willing to pay for the losses of small, well-organized groups rather than to defend the collective interests of taxpayers.

[54] See Tuori (n 10), 191ff.

[55] Cf A Lechevalier, 'Why and How has German Ordoliberalism Become a French Issue?' in Hien and Joerges (eds), (n 50), 14, at 47.

[56] Cf Hien and Joerges (eds), (n 50).

[57] Cf Chapters 3–5 in Hien and Joerges (eds), (n 50). Ordo-liberals criticize US evolution towards a monopoly-friendly and monetarist-oriented framework entailing market and financial deregulation; they criticize US reliance on the speculative truth of deregulated financial markets in view of the financial crises caused by US financial deregulation. Many Italians attribute their country's economic

The ordo-liberal constitutive and regulative principles for constituting a private law society and competitive market economy governed by rules that protect individual rights, share with other economic schools (eg Austrian, Chicago, and Keynesian) the rejection of authoritarian state capitalism and of *laissez-faire* ideas of self-regulating markets as a natural phenomenon. They build on existing constitutional principles (like rule of law, equal freedoms, personal liability, monetary stability), yet differ in their greater emphasis on limiting market failures (like rent-seeking, external effects, social injustices), governance failures (like discretionary protectionism, other governmental market distortions undermining citizen- and consumer sovereignty), and constitutional failures (eg insufficient institutionalization of public reason through science-based regulatory agencies, constitutional neglect for multilevel governance protecting international PGs). In December 2020, the COVID-19 health pandemic and related lockdowns adversely affecting economic activities prompted EU member states and institutions to adopt the largest ever EU long-term budget, together with an EU recovery fund providing for a total of €1.8 trillion to rebuild a post-COVID-19 Europe. A large part of the EU recovery fund will be financed by EU common borrowing in international capital markets, which is expected to boost European monetary integration and the use of the Euro in international financial and capital markets still further. The future evolution of the EU's incomplete monetary constitution remains open.

5.5.5 The EU's Open-Ended Foreign Policy Constitution

The EU's 'cosmopolitan foreign policy constitution' prescribing (eg in Articles 3 and 21 TEU, the EUCFR) protection of human rights, strict observance of international law, and mutual coherence of internal and external market regulations illustrates, likewise, the political limits of EU constitutionalism, for instance if decisions in EU external relations are not taken as openly as possible and as closely as possible to the citizens, contrary to Article 1 TEU, or if EU FTAs preclude citizens from invoking and enforcing FTA obligations in domestic jurisdictions (arguably contrary to the guarantees of fundamental rights and judicial remedies in the EUCFR).[58] The EU's foreign policy constitution continues to evolve pragmatically in response to external challenges and the jurisprudence of the CJEU (eg on the contested consistency with EU law of EU FTAs with Canada, Morocco, and Singapore). Invocation of EU fundamental rights by private EU citizens has

depression and high budget and debt deficits to the EU's ordo-liberal austerity politics and demand a different 'social' Europe modelled on a transfer union rather than on the rules-based Kantian ethics underlying ordo-liberalism.

[58] Cf EU Petersmann, The EU's Cosmopolitan Foreign Policy Constitution and its Disregard in Transatlantic Free Trade Agreements, *European Foreign Affairs Review* 21 (2016), 449–69.

repeatedly prompted EU courts to intervene in EU foreign policies, like the repeated invocation of privacy rights that prompted the CJEU—in judgments of 6 October 2015[59] and of 16 July 2020[60]—to annul EU participation in agreements with the United States on the transfer of private data in view of their inadequate protection inside the United States. FTAs by the EU with third countries are increasingly subjected to conditionality, as in the case of the EU–Mercosur FTA (requiring the parties to comply with certain climate change commitments), EU–Korea FTA (where the EU is pressuring South Korea to strengthen workers' rights), the EU–Cambodia FTA (where the EU has withdrawn trade preferences because of human rights violations inside Cambodia), the EU–Morocco FTA (where the CJEU has insisted on respecting the minority rights of indigenous people in the western Sahara), and EU FTAs with European countries (where the EU insists on level playing-field guarantees of fair competition).

5.6 Regulatory Competition rather than Global Community Law

In contrast to the recognition of national and EU citizenships, multilevel human rights, and of representative, deliberative, and participatory democracy (cf Articles 9–12 TEU) as constitutional foundations of the functionally limited EU community law, UN and WTO law continue to prioritize sovereign equality (Article 2 UN Charter) of member states. The embedded liberalism underlying UN law and WTO law promotes regulatory competition without constituting—as explained in Chapter 2, section 2.3—a global community law effectively protecting human rights. GATT/WTO law includes interface rules acknowledging:

- sovereign rights of WTO member countries to adopt diverse domestic regulations (eg based on Articles III, XIX–XXI GATT);
- state trading enterprises (Article XVII GATT);
- differential treatment for less-developed countries (eg based on Article XVIII GATT and the Enabling Clause);
- FTAs and customs unions (Article XXIV GATT).

Even if GATT/WTO law admits sub- and supranational members (like Hong Kong, Macao, Taiwan, the EU) and provides for compulsory third-party

[59] See CJEU Judgment of 6 October 2015, *Schrems v Data Protection Commissioner*, Case C-362/14, ECLI:EU:C:2015:650.

[60] CJEU Case C-311/18, *Data Protection Commissioner v Facebook Ireland Ltd, M. Schrems (Schrems II)*, ECLI:EU:C:2020:559. For comparative analyses of data protection and fundamental rights in Internet regulation in Europe and the United States, see O Pollicino, *Judicial Protection of Fundamental Rights on the Internet. A Road Towards Digital Constitutionalism?* (Hart 2021).

adjudication—and the UN General Assembly adopts recommendations also on behalf of 'We the Peoples of the United Nations'[61]—implementation of UN and WTO law inside states remains a matter of decentralized, domestic competences. The UN specialized agencies are more akin to regulatory agencies assisting member states in their collective supply of transnational PGs. The constitutional dimensions of European community law—as discussed in section 5.5—remain unique without equivalent constitutional provisions in UN law (with the exception of the UN Security Council) or in regional legal systems outside Europe. Compared with the foreign policies of hegemonic states, the foreign policies of the EU are much more constitutionally constrained by human rights, rule of law, democracy principles, other multilevel constitutional constraints, multilateral agreements, and multilevel institutional checks and balances. The normative ideal underlying the EU's foreign policy constitution—that is, to use the EU's external relations law for progressively transforming international power politics through constitutional restraints protecting rights of citizens—remains confronted with power realities (eg in external relations with authoritarian states like China and Russia) that make the emergence of global community law unlikely.

Constitutionalization of PGs regimes outside Europe differs, as illustrated by non-democratic constitutionalism (eg in China) and by broader parliamentary powers, more limited judicial powers, less comprehensive common law freedoms, and narrower human rights charters in countries practising Commonwealth constitutionalism.[62] Chapter 5, section 5.1 recalled the dialectic tensions between imperfect national constitutions, constitutional ideals and constitutional realities as part of the human condition and of the complex, yet imperfect realities of cosmopolitan constitutionalism. According to Kishore Mahbubani, Singapore's long-time ambassador to the UN, the 'biggest gift the West gave the Rest was the power of reasoning' which 'seeped into Asian minds gradually, through the adoption of Western science and technology and the application of the scientific method to solving social problems'. He said:

> East Asian societies, especially Japan and the 'Four Tigers' (South Korea, Taiwan, Hong Kong and Singapore) were the first to absorb these ideas and practices, such as free market economics and empirical scientific research ... This spread of Western reasoning ... triggered three silent revolutions that explain the extraordinary success of many non-Western societies in recent decades... The first revolution is political. For *millennia*, Asian societies were deeply feudal. The people were accountable to their rulers, not rulers to their people. 'Oriental despotism'

[61] See, eg, the Declaration on the commemoration of the 75th anniversary of the UN, adopted by the UN General Assembly on 21 September 2020 (Resolution 75/A/L.1).

[62] Cf J Komarek and M Avbelji (eds), *Constitutional Pluralism in Europe and Beyond* (Hart 2011); S Gardbaum, *The New Commonwealth Model of Constitutionalism: Theory and Practice* (CUP 2013).

> was a fair description of the political environments in all corners of Asia... The rebellion against all kinds of feudal mind-sets which gained momentum in the second half of the twentieth century was hugely liberating for all Asian societies ... in a big shift from previous 'despotic' assumptions, most Asian leaders now recognized that they are accountable to their people ... The second revolution is psychological: the Rest are going from believing that they were helpless voyagers in a life determined by 'fate' to believing that they can take control of their lives and rationally produce better outcomes ... In the last thirty years, we have carried more people over the threshold of university education than we have in the previous 3,000 years ... The third revolution is in the field of governance ... Fifty years ago, few Asian governments believed that good rational governance could transform their societies. Now most do.[63]

The increasing conflicts between neo-liberal, state capitalist, and ordo-liberal conceptions of IEL, and the emergence of Asia as the new centre of worldwide economic growth and regional economic integration, weaken the influence of European ordo-liberalism as a legal and economic framework emphasizing (i) the ordering functions of law (eg for protecting equal freedoms, non-discriminatory conditions of competition, transnational rule of law, common markets); (ii) the normativity of economic competition (eg as a citizen-driven information, co-ordination, and sanctioning process, performance competition embedded into constitutional and competition laws as necessary legal constraints on the self-constitution and auto-regulation of markets); and (iii) the ethical foundations of ordo-liberalism (eg of constitutional rights empowering and limiting producers, traders, investors, consumers, and democratic citizens) and of ordo-liberal social market economies committed to social justice.

5.6.1 Return to a Cordell Hull Strategy of Global US Leadership?

The 2020 election of Joe Biden as US President makes it unlikely that the WTO trading, legal, and dispute settlement system will completely collapse or become largely irrelevant. Both China and US President Biden recognize the WTO and its commitment to rule of law as worth saving even if it needs substantial reforms. Yet, the diverse neo-liberal, state capitalist, and ordo-liberal conceptions of world trade prioritize different legal, economic, and political values like state-centred power monopolies (prioritized by China's communist party state), business-centred interest group politics (prioritized by money-driven Washington, DC, politics), and citizen-centred, non-discriminatory conditions of competition and social

[63] K Mahbubani, *Has the West Lost It? A Provocation* (Penguin 2018), 11ff.

justice (as emphasized by EU institutions). The global health and environmental crises risk deepening the divides between developed and less-developed countries, as illustrated by the increase in the number of people living in absolute poverty in 2020. The post-1945 multilateral trading system, and US leadership in its creation, were among the most significant accomplishments in legal, economic, and political history. Each of the four dominant WTO actors with diverging trade policy paradigms—China, India, the EU, and the United States—may find it now politically more realistic to continue prioritizing regional, plurilateral, bilateral, or nationalist trade policies, like the US–Mexico–Canada FTA (USMCA) as renegotiated under pressure by the US Trump administration; China's web of bilateral agreements with Belt and Road Initiative (BRI) partner countries and its Regional Comprehensive Economic Partnership (RCEP) Agreement of 15 November 2020 with the ten ASEAN states, Australia, New Zealand, Japan, and South Korea; the global web of FTAs concluded by the EU with third countries in Africa, the Americas, Asia, and Europe; or India's more nationalist third-world ideologies with comparatively much less interest in FTAs (like the RECEP). The post-1945 global US leadership—through the IMF and World Bank Group at Washington and the UN at New York—in a US-centred world appears to be coming to an end, for instance due to resistance inside the United States against WTO appellate review, global carbon taxes (as the most efficient policy instrument for climate change mitigation), and against competitive and other regulatory restraints on private US tech empires dominating communication services. US democracy is less and less perceived as a model for democratic governance in the twenty-first century (eg in view of socially unjust, money-driven internal US politics and US non-participation in numerous UN, ILO, and WHO agreements). The trade policy discourse of the US Trump administration was so heavily based on false claims (eg concerning the AB jurisprudence, use of trade remedies) and on protectionist unilateralism that it will be difficult—both inside the United States and in WTO institutions—to agree on unbiased, reasonable reforms of WTO rules. Since 2020, most WTO panel reports could no longer be adopted (eg because the defendants, like the United States, appealed into the void of a non-functioning AB); with thirty-three WTO panel proceedings and more than a dozen WTO appellate proceedings pending in early 2021, the WTO legal and dispute settlement systems are confronted with an existential crisis.

Since 2001, the Doha Round negotiations have failed to enable consensus-based compromise solutions for many systemic WTO problems (like state capitalist practices, state-owned enterprises (SOEs), forced technology transfers, non-transparent subsidies, industrial policies, the developing/developed country divide, special and differential treatment based on self-selection of less developed country status, independent and impartial third-party adjudication with appellate review, sustainable development). The antagonistic policy divisions inside the United States, past US attacks on the WTO, and the continuation by the

Biden administration of illegal US trading practices all undermine US leadership for WTO reforms. There is also no political agreement on the needed domestic US trade policy reforms—such as legislative reforms of the advisory committee system, which has favoured regulatory capture of ever more trade regulation (eg on cotton, textiles, tobacco, steel, aluminium, trade remedies, labour, intellectual property, environmental, and national security issues). Just as former US Secretary of State Cordell Hull responded to the US Congress' protectionist Smoot–Hawley tariff legislation of 1930 with legislative reforms of US trade policy-making, US democrats look for someone to respond to the US Trump administration's nationalism with a principled case for trade liberalization: 'Trade agreements should no longer be just a collection of interest group favours.'[64] Yet, the populist tribal politics and regulatory capture of US economic rule-making render unlikely such a renewed Cordell Hull vision of peace and prosperity through trade and through domestic legislative reforms limiting domestic interest group politics inside the United States.[65] US trade policies risk not only remaining dominated by interest group politics impeding reasonable reforms of WTO rules (eg on trade remedies, agricultural subsidies, and independent appellate review). China's increasingly assertive industrial, technological, and military policies (eg in the South China Sea, vis-à-vis Taiwan) risk further politicizing the invocations of national and international security exceptions for justifying trade sanctions (eg targeting Chinese SOEs and their dual-use technologies). The global disagreements on 'climate justice'—for instance between the United States emitting 15 tonnes per capita of carbon per year compared with Uganda emitting 0.1 tonnes per capita per year (2018)—are bound to provoke ever more environmental conflicts and trade distortions which, without a functioning WTO dispute settlement system, risk disrupting the world trading system.

[64] SN Lester (n 22), 57ff, at 64f. According to Lester, 'the core principles of the GATT/WTO are good and remain essential: Tariff reductions, non-discrimination and transparency' (p. 65). Bilateral agreements 'should be a small supplemental component to a broadly multilateral system' (p. 66). Intellectual property, labour, and environment issues 'should stay separate from trade agreements and institutions' (p. 66). Liberalization and regulation of services trade and of related public policy exceptions need to be expanded. In order to incentivize less-developed countries to reduce their high tariffs, developed countries should offer liberalization of their protectionist farm subsidies, anti-dumping policies, and abuses of foreign policy powers (like justifying discriminatory import protection on grounds of national security).

[65] Cf KW Dam, 'Cordell Hull, the Reciprocal Trade Agreements Act and the WTO' in Petersmann (ed), *Reforming the World Trading System: Legitimacy, Efficiency and Democratic Governance* (OUP 2005), 83ff (explaining the 'Cordell Hull principles of reciprocity, advance authorization, professional negotiations out of the public eye, and more or less automatic adoption of the results of the negotiations'); Lester (n 22) (explaining the interest group stranglehold on trade remedy issues, subsidy and intellectual property issues in US trade policies as a result of the creation of the advisory committee system in US decision-making procedures on trade policies, which favoured regulatory capture of ever more US trade regulation, as also illustrated by the appointment of long-time industry lobbyists to the positions of WTO ambassador and USTR under President Trump).

5.6.2 Need for Regional, Plurilateral, and Bilateral Bottom-Up Reforms

Similar to the 1919 rejection by the US Senate of US entry into the League of Nations and to the 1949 refusal by the US Congress to ratify the 1948 Havana Charter for an International Trade Organization, the four years of the US Trump administration (2017–2021) undermining multilateral agreements render it uncertain whether there will be sufficient political support inside the United States for US participation in ambitious reforms of the WTO, of the vague 2015 Paris Agreement commitments on climate change mitigation, and of other multilateral agreements for protecting sustainable development. The signing of the RCEP on 15 November 2020 entailed that the United States finds itself now outside three of the world's largest free trade areas: RCEP as the world's most populous FTA; the Comprehensive and Progressive Agreement for Trans-Pacific Partnership (CPTPP 11) among Australia, Brunei, Canada, Chile, Japan, Malaysia, Mexico, New Zealand, Peru, Singapore, and Vietnam; and the EEA Agreement among twenty-seven EU and three EFTA states. Both accession of the United States to the CPTPP and resumption of the EU–US negotiations on the Transatlantic Trade and Investment Partnership (TTIP) Agreement lack political support inside the United States. The CPTPP, and to a lesser degree the RCEP, include specific rules responding to some of the systemic WTO disagreements relating to state capitalist practices using SOEs, politicization of private enterprises, forced technology transfers, non-transparent subsidies, and other politically motivated trade distortions (like discriminatory government procurement) for state-centred industrial policies. Other systemic WTO disagreements relate to neo-liberal interest-group politics like agricultural and industrial subsidies, discriminatory trade remedies, safeguard measures, and US neglect for many other trade-distorting practices (like tax evasion, anti-competitive US domination of certain areas of electronic services trade) benefitting US companies. Sustainable development challenges (like carbon taxes, border carbon adjustments) enjoy greater priority in EU trade policies in response to civil society pressures, which are suppressed in authoritarian countries (like Russia). The systemic WTO disagreements impede global WTO negotiations (eg on the developing/developed country divide, special and differential treatment based on self-selection of less developed country status, independent and impartial third-party adjudication with appellate review); the disagreements are likely to favour regional, plurilateral, and bilateral negotiations aimed at building alliances for decentralized reforms of world trade and investment rules responding to the realities of regional power asymmetries in Asia (eg in the context of China's BRI, RCEP), the Americas (eg the hegemonic US influence on regional FTAs with Canada, Mexico, and other Latin American countries), and in EU external relations (eg with African countries). Introducing and financing some of the needed reforms of trade rules (like carbon taxes, border carbon adjustments, e-commerce, competition rules, data protection regulations) will be politically easier in FTAs, plurilateral trade agreements (PTAs), or bilateral agreements among like-minded countries than through WTO negotiations, where some WTO members (like India) eagerly defend third-world positions (eg on special and differential treatment, consensus-based WTO negotiations) in order to divert political pressures to liberalize their own protectionist market access restrictions.

5.6.3 Institutional WTO Reforms?

The reluctance of WTO members to use the expertise in the WTO Secretariat in member-driven WTO negotiations, the failure of WTO members to protect the WTO dispute settlement system as prescribed in the DSU and approved by democratic institutions, the discontinuation of regular parliamentary meetings inside the WTO, and the US blocking of the nomination of a new WTO Director-General from September 2020 to early February 2021 reveal some of the path-dependent, institutional weaknesses of WTO governance. Past GATT and WTO negotiations were dominated by bilateral market access negotiations (based on 'offer and request' bargaining) and by strategic litigation relying on bilateral enforcement of GATT/WTO dispute settlement rulings through suspension of concessions (or threats thereof). The current, plurilateral WTO negotiations (eg on services domestic regulation, investment facilitation, electronic commerce) and most regional preferential trade agreements (eg their treaty provisions on environmental, labour, competition, consumer protection, and anti-corruption commitments) prioritize general, collective obligations and corresponding rights of individuals (eg as codified in the ILO Declaration on Rights at Work, the UN Commission on International Trade Law Model Law on Electronic Commerce) rather than bilateral, reciprocal tariff concessions among governments. This shift from bilaterally negotiated concessions (eg based on bilateral requests and offers) to multilaterally agreed, general rules of conduct requires adaptations of WTO rule-making and enforcement processes.[66] It also raises other systemic and institutional questions such as: How can the WTO's deliberative functions (eg its committee structures), Trade Policy Review Mechanism, the WTO rule-making and dispute settlement systems, input from the WTO Secretariat, and cooperation with other international organizations be strengthened? How far should WTO negotiations aim at regulating non-trade issues like labour, environmental, competition, consumer protection, data protection, and cyber security standards, rather than leaving such

[66] For example, less secrecy, less focus on bilateral market access and on potential suspension of bilateral concessions, more technical and expert input and assistance from the WTO Secretariat and from specialized regulatory agencies, need for promoting plurilateral trade agreements, and for limiting the 'single Round' and consensus practices.

trade-related issues to other, more specialized organizations?[67] As the neglect for environmental pollution in trade and investment regulation has greatly contributed to climate change and the voluntary commitments under the 2015 Paris Agreement for reducing GHG emissions remain grossly inadequate, how can IEL and international environmental regulation be made mutually more coherent? Does it require closer cooperation of the WTO with UN specialized agencies (like the International Civil Aviation Organization and the International Maritime Organization), for example for the elaboration of coordinated sectoral rules on GHG emission reductions for maritime shipping and aviation and for related dispute settlement procedures?

So far, the inability to reach compromise solutions in worldwide WTO negotiations on many of the systemic WTO problems led to paralysis of the Doha Round negotiations; it moved trade negotiations increasingly away from multilateral to bilateral and regional arenas. Yet, even if regional and plurilateral trade negotiations become increasingly important, WTO law and institutions will remain essential for the worldwide coordination of trade policies and for maintaining rule of law through peaceful settlement of trade disputes. Most core principles of the GATT/WTO legal and dispute settlement system have proven to be reasonable constraints on harmful abuses of national trade policy powers assisting all governments in promoting the welfare of their citizens. Reciprocal tariff reductions, non-discriminatory treatment, transparent policy-making, prohibition of discriminatory non-tariff barriers, the rule of law, peaceful settlement of disputes, public policy exceptions reserving sovereign rights to protect non-economic PGs (like GATT Article XX), WTO rules limiting and coordinating FTAs (like GATT Article XXIV) and promoting cooperation among international organizations, special and differential treatment for least developed countries, and collective promotion of sustainable development, these and other basic WTO principles remain important even if the number of regional and PTAs increases.[68]

In order to incentivize less-developed countries to reduce their high tariffs, developed countries should offer liberalization of their protectionist farm subsidies,

[67] Some of these questions are discussed in Kolsky Lewis et al. (eds), (n 21).

[68] This conclusion is confirmed by most of the contributions to the book edited by Kolsky Lewis et al. (eds), (n 21). For instance, the chapter by BG Williams and W Zhou, 'If the WTO Were to Break Down Completely, Would We Stoop and Build It Up with Worn-out Tools?' recalls the economic and public choice theories justifying the legal ranking of trade policy instruments in GATT/WTO law according to their economic efficiency. GATT/WTO rules and dispute settlement jurisprudence have been largely consistent in serving 'the underlying function of the WTO by imposing an external constraint on domestic protectionist pressure on regulatory decision-making without restraining the capacity of governments to respond to non-trade/non-protectionist interests of other domestic constituents' (p. 106). They conclude that 'should the WTO break down, then in order to protect citizens in all countries from the economic welfare losses and possible consequent loss of political security that would flow from widespread implementation of protection, the world would need a new treaty containing rules that are very similar to the existing rules applied under the WTO'; rather than 'letting the system die and then trying to rebuild it again', WTO members should defend and improve the existing WTO rules (p. 111).

anti-dumping policies, and abuses of foreign policy powers (like justifying discriminatory import protection on grounds of national security). If consensus-based WTO reforms prove impossible, PTAs—like the EU initiative for MPIA based on Article 25 DSU—should be actively promoted among like-minded WTO members. Following the example of bilateral investment agreements and ISA, continued illegal blocking of the WTO AB system could also promote bilateral agreements on making certain WTO obligations directly applicable in domestic jurisdictions (eg following the example of the domestic review mechanism provided for in the WTO Agreement on Government Procurement), thereby depoliticizing and decentralizing WTO dispute settlements by involving independent domestic courts, judicial remedies of private economic actors, and strengthening multilevel judicial protection of transnational rule of law. For example, it has been argued that in case of disputes over domestic subsidies and discriminatory local content requirements, domestic jurisdictions may be better equipped for protecting rule of law and judicial remedies than intergovernmental WTO dispute settlement panels, provided the relevant WTO legal disciplines are applicable in domestic jurisdictions and national decisions are subject to judicial WTO remedies.[69] Recourse to more FTAs, PTAs, and bilateral agreements among WTO members would further raise the question of whether the existing, procedural, and substantive WTO rules disciplining such legal pluralism are adequate or in need of additional legal disciplines and accountability mechanisms. In certain areas like Internet commerce through digital platforms, the 'Internet of things', and 3D printing, additional WTO rules (eg on data protection and standardization of e-commerce terms) and their coordination with other international and national standardization organizations could be pursued in parallel to the particular information, communication, and technology requirements specified in regional, plurilateral, and bilateral agreements outside the WTO.[70]

5.6.4 Global Economic and Legal Dis-Integration?

The forty-six FTAs concluded by the EU with seventy-eight countries constitute the world's largest network of trade agreements. In contrast to China's BRI network of bilateral deals, the FTAs of both the EU and the United States include

[69] Cf JJ Nedumpara and A Venkataraman, 'The Rise of Import Substitution Subsidies and Local Content Requirements in a Dystopian WTO 2.0 Regime' in Kolsky Lewis et al. (eds), (n 21): 'the dispute settlement mechanisms under the existing RTAs are ill-equipped to deal with this problem' (p. 237).

[70] Cf RH Weber, A New International Trade Framework for Digital Access' in Kolsky Lewis et al. (eds), (n 21), who addresses 'the almost unsurmountable challenges caused by digital assets in the present WTO regime and . . . ideas how a new normative framework could be developed' (p. 279). Weber also identifies the major regulatory topics to be clarified through negotiations and rule-making either inside or outside the WTO. In December 2020, the Chair of the WTO negotiations on digital trade issued a first draft negotiating text reflecting the past negotiation results.

numerous provisions for promoting the consistency of trade rules with human rights and environmental rules. It seems unlikely, therefore, that increasing recourse to regional, plurilateral and bilateral trade agreements among WTO members risks causing economic and legal disintegration.[71] The EU, Japan, and the United States have already initiated negotiations on additional subsidy disciplines for industrial policies. The plurilateral WTO negotiations on additional rules for fishery subsidies, domestic regulation of services, e-commerce, investment facilitation, special and differential treatment of less-developed countries (eg for facilitating cross-border supplies of patented pharmaceuticals, other medical supplies, compulsory licensing of related intellectual property rights, rules on food security)[72] continue. They will need to be supplemented by WTO negotiations on carbon taxes, carbon border adjustments, WTO disciplines for providing vaccines to all WTO members, and WTO dispute settlement reforms. As disputes over climate change mitigation and responses to global health pandemics risk being submitted to WTO dispute settlement procedures, WTO dispute settlement reforms must enhance the legitimacy, impartiality, and independence of the WTO dispute settlement system.

Chapters 6–9 explain why increasing recourse to legal pluralism must be combined with multilevel judicial remedies so as to realize the SDG (eg in SDG 16) of promoting 'rule of law at the national and international levels and ensure equal access to justice for all' and avoid economic and legal disintegration. Chapter 6 illustrates how for twenty-five years (1995–2020), GATT/WTO jurisprudence has promoted the rule of law consistent with UN HRL and constitutional principles (eg of proportionality balancing) of judicial administration of justice. Chapter 7 examines whether the more decentralized investment law and arbitration systems offer lessons for reforming and adjusting IEL to the geopolitical rivalries and underlying value conflicts. Chapter 8 examines lessons from the increasing claims of judicial overreach—for example in bilateral ISA, regional economic law, and WTO law—for redesigning multilevel governance of PGs in favour of more decentralized, legal, and institutional checks and balances, judicial deference and judicial comity. Chapter 9 concludes that in order to maintain legal security and predictability in the global division of labour and realize the citizen-centred SDGs, the state-centred chess-board governance must be complemented by participatory, citizen-centred network governance. The increasing environmental and human rights litigation in national courts aimed at holding governments accountable for GHG emission reductions (as discussed in Chapter 9) illustrates this successful empowerment of

[71] See on this question the special issue, The Era of Disintegration—Taking Stock of the Dynamics of International Economic Governance, of the *Journal of International Economic Law* 23 (2020), 299–533.

[72] Cf FM Abbott and JH Reichman, Facilitating Access to Cross-Border Supplies of Patented Pharmaceuticals: The Case of the COVID-19 Pandemic, *Journal of International Economic Law* 23 (2020), 535–61.

citizens and NGOs using the embedded liberalism underlying IEL for legally enforcing sovereign responsibilities and corporate social responsibilities protecting the SDGs. Global economic integration agreements must also find socially and democratically more convincing responses to the tensions between transnational, functionally limited governance of global PGs (like peaceful global division of labour) and (sub)national, community-based solidarity principles (based on social trust and collective identification). The value conflicts among neo-liberal, state capitalist, and ordo-liberal conceptions of IEL reveal mutually conflicting conceptions of 'domestic justice',[73] as also reflected in the international disagreements among UN member states about civil, political, economic, social, and cultural human rights and about appropriate regulation of global Internet and environmental governance. From a European ordo-liberal perspective, American 'Wild West' neo-liberalism prioritizing negative liberties vis-à-vis state powers has become an insufficient approach, as illustrated by abuses of corporate power and social inequalities inside the United States and by arbitrary disruptions of multilateral treaty systems by US interest group politics. Authoritarian state capitalism (eg as practised in China, Russia, and many other UN member states) offers an even more dangerous 'road to serfdom' (Friedrich A Hayek). Superpower competition (eg in economic, technological, and military superiority, cybersecurity, foreign policy influence) risks spilling over into a new Cold War between (formerly) communist, authoritarian countries and US-led, democratic alliances, or even to military conflicts in response to the military threats by China (eg in the South China Sea, vis-à-vis Taiwan, China's territorial claims in the Himalaya), Russia (eg vis-à-vis Ukraine, Russia's annexation of the Crimea) and by their allies (like the military regimes in Belarus, North Korea and Myanmar). Chapters 6–9 argue that protecting third-party adjudication and transnational rule of law in world trade and investments offers democratic countries a powerful tool for containing abuses of foreign policy powers and for maintaining mutually beneficial, economic cooperation among all WTO members, including China and Russia.

[73] The justice deficits in UN law and IEL are further discussed in Chapter 9. Even among EU countries, solidarity principles often elude agreement among EU member states in view of their diverse social conditions and cultural traditions (eg the fact that more than 80 per cent of Italian households, but only less than 50 per cent of German households live in their own apartments/houses, and the savings rates of Italian households are among the highest in EU countries). Most Anglo-Saxon and non-European textbooks on IEL continue to be content with justice as economic efficiency, or justification of IEL by state-centred rather than citizen-centred theories of justice, without examining whether the sustainable development goal of transforming the world can be realized without transforming the state-centred UN and WTO legal structures; cf Suttle (n 19).

6

Protecting Rule of Law and Human Rights in the World Trading System

Humanity knows from Greek mythology and from the Bible that third-party adjudication emerged and developed in response to never-ending human tragedies (like the pursuit of Orestes by the goddesses of revenge punishing Orestes' murder of his mother, because she had killed his father, Agamemnon, who had sacrificed their daughter, Iphigenia, on his way to lead the Greeks in battle against Troy). Since the trial of Orestes in Athena's Aeropag, the trial of Socrates in the ancient constitutional democracy of Athens, or the trial of Jesus under the Roman rulers Herod and Pontius Pilate, humanity has learned that tribunals—even in constitutional republics since ancient Rome—need to be constrained by principles of justice and due process of law, as illustrated in court houses all over the world by statues of justice representing the ancient Greek goddess *Dike* and Roman goddess *Justitia* with a blindfold (representing judicial impartiality), holding a balance in one hand (symbolizing due process of law), and a sword in the other (symbolizing rule of law). Since the Second World War, human rights, judicial remedies (access to justice), and rule of law principles have become recognized in a growing number of national constitutions and international treaties, including economic law treaties and the Sustainable Development Goals (SDGs).[1] As the Permanent Court of International Justice was created in response to the First World War, so too were the International Court of Justice (ICJ), the European Court of Human Rights (ECtHR), many national constitutional courts (eg in Germany), and European courts responses to the tragedies of the Second World War. Human tragedies continue, and so do the human responses to these of establishing new national and international courts, like national and international criminal courts in response to crimes against humanity, or the World Trade Organization Appellate Body (WTO AB) in response to the previous failures of the General Agreement on Tariffs and Trade (GATT) dispute settlement system. Nationalist rulers, found in many democracies including in EU countries like Poland, challenge judicial remedies, especially if judges—or the US Congress in its impeachment proceeding against US President Trump—dare to hold rulers accountable. Chapter 3 described

[1] Cf M Kamto and Y Tyagi (eds), *The Access of Individuals to International Justice* (Hague Academy of International Law 2019). For comparative studies of individual access to economic courts, see P Wiater, *Internationale Individualkläger* (Mohr Siebeck 2020).

Transforming World Trade and Investment Law for Sustainable Development. Ernst-Ulrich Petersmann, Oxford University Press. © Ernst-Ulrich Petersmann 2022. DOI: 10.1093/oso/9780192858023.003.0007

how the US trade wars against China, and US threats of trade sanctions against other WTO members, ignored WTO rules and dispute settlement procedures. Similarly, China's military expansion in the South China Sea ignores the arbitral award rendered under the UN Convention on the Law of the Sea (UNCLOS), and Russia ignores the arbitral award rendered by the Permanent Court of Arbitration in Russia's investment dispute with the expropriated shareholders of the former Yukos oil company.[2] How should citizens and their democratic institutions respond to the illegal *de facto* incapacitation of the WTO's AB and to intergovernmental power politics (like the US blocking of the AB) disregarding the will of parliaments when they approved the WTO Agreement and, in many countries, incorporated it into their domestic legal systems? What can citizens do if their national constitutional culture tolerates nationalist and isolationist attitudes towards international law and institutions, as so often happened even in democracies like the United States, whose Congress refused joining the 1920 League of Nations and its Permanent Court of International Justice, the 1948 Havana Charter for an International Trade Organization and its dispute settlement system, the 1982 UNCLOS and its International Tribunal for the Law of the Sea, or the 1998 Rome Statute establishing the International Criminal Court, and whose government withdrew, in 1985, the US consent to the compulsory jurisdiction of the ICJ?

This chapter explains why WTO members should prioritize the rule of law objectives of the Sustainable Development Agenda and of the WTO's Dispute Settlement Understanding (DSU) (section 6.1). From 1995 to 2019, the WTO jurisprudence has protected human rights values (section 6.2), limited legal fragmentation by means of systemic treaty interpretation (section 6.3), and constrained arbitrary abuses of national security exceptions (section 6.4). Yet, the WTO legal and dispute settlement system may need to be adapted to the newly emerging security order (section 6.5). The less WTO members remain capable of amending WTO rules or agreeing on new WTO agreements and on authoritative interpretations of WTO law, the more important becomes the judicial function of the Dispute Settlement Body (DSB) to clarify the often vaguely drafted WTO provisions for the settlement of disputes in conformity with the DSU and the systemic treaty interpretation rules codified in the 1969 Vienna Convention on the Law of Treaties (VCLT).

6.1 Rule of Law at National and International Levels?

The UN 2030 Agenda for Sustainable Development 'recognizes the need to build peaceful, just and inclusive societies that provide equal access to justice and that

[2] The final award of 18 July 2014, *Yukos Universal Ltd v Russia*, PCA Case No AA 227, is available on the website of Investment Treaty Arbitration http://www.italaw.com/cases.

are based on respect for human rights (including the right to development), on effective rule of law and good governance at all levels', including international law.[3] As briefly discussed in Chapter 5, section 5.5, the EU's micro-economic common market constitution empowered citizens to invoke and enforce EU common market rules, competition rules, and fundamental rights in national and European courts directly. It was thanks to such constitutional rights and judicial accountability mechanisms that the European Court of Justice (CJEU) could emphasize:

> that the European Economic Community is a Community based on the rule of law, inasmuch as neither its Member States nor its institutions can avoid a review of the question whether the measures adopted by them are in conformity with the basic constitutional charter, the Treaty. In particular, in Articles 173 (now 263 TFEU) and 184 (now 277 TFEU), on the one hand, and in Article 177 (now 267 TFEU), on the other, the Treaty established a complete system of legal remedies and procedures designed to permit the Court of Justice to review the legality of measures adopted by the institutions. Natural and legal persons are thus protected against the application to them of general measures which they cannot contest directly before the Court by reason of the special conditions of admissibility laid down in the second paragraph of Article 173 of the Treaty.[4]

EU law and institutions continue to protect rule of law principles through primary treaty provisions (like Article 2 TEU on the EU's foundational values, Article 7 on rule of law enforcement procedures, Article 19 TEU on the CJEU, the EU Charter of Fundamental Rights), EU secondary law (like infringement procedures initiated by the EU Commission), and notably through the jurisprudence of national and European courts.[5] Yet, as in any other legal system, the dialectical tensions between legal rules (reason) and social practices (power, volition) render rule of law enforcement a never-ending task. The direct legal and judicial enforceability of the EU's micro-economic common market rules gave strong incentives for decentralized protection of rule of law. Such legal and judicial remedies are comparatively much weaker in the EU's macro-economic monetary constitution and in worldwide economic treaties on the international coordination of monetary, trade, and development policies like the Bretton Woods and GATT/WTO agreements. If the primary aim of rule of law is to prevent arbitrary abuses of public and private power and to protect equal individual rights and judicial remedies, international world order treaties coordinating, limiting, and protecting rights and duties of

[3] *Transforming our World* (2015), para 35. SDG 16 refers to promoting 'rule of law at the national and international levels and ensure equal access to justice for all'.

[4] CJEU, Case C-294/83, *Les Verts*, ECR 1986, 1339, para 23.

[5] On the progressive entrenchment and enforcement of rule of law principles in EU law, see L Pech, *The Rule of Law in the EU: The Evolution of the Treaty Framework and Rule of Law Toolbox*, Reconnect Working Paper 2020-7 (EU Commission Brussels).

states in international monetary, trade, and financial relations tend to aim more at international legality and accountability (eg for respecting the conferral of limited powers to international institutions) than at protecting individual rights vis-à-vis discretionary, economic decision-making processes invoking macro-economic margins of appreciation and economic expertise.[6] The WTO Agreement and most WTO dispute settlement rulings do not mention human rights law (HRL) in view of the democracy deficits of WTO law (like the lack of parliamentary WTO institutions) and the fact that many WTO member states—as discussed in Chapter 2, section 2.3—have accepted few human rights conventions in view of their diverse conceptions of human rights. Similarly, also neo-liberalism, state capitalism, ordo-liberalism, and constitutionalism are mentioned neither in WTO law nor in WTO publications in view of the WTO's pragmatic focus on trade regulation avoiding ideological debates.

Chapter 4, section 4.10 recalled that the UN has defined 'rule of law at national and international levels' as 'a principle of governance in which all persons, institutions and entities, including the State itself, are accountable to laws that are publicly promulgated, equally enforced and independently adjudicated, and which are consistent with internationally recognized human rights'.[7] Yet, neither UN law nor WTO law protect access to justice effectively in domestic and international courts. Nor have GATT/WTO practices applied the international state responsibility rules on reparation of injury. Arguably, by refraining from filling AB vacancies as they arise as required by Article 17.2 DSU—if necessary, by majority decisions pursuant to Article IX.1 WTO Agreement—WTO members have illegally disrupted the WTO dispute settlement and appellate review system as prescribed by parliaments when they approved the WTO Agreement. This chapter explains why the more WTO member states avoid AB nominations (since 2017), block adoption of panels reports (since 2020), and disregard WTO rules due to insufficient legal, democratic, and judicial accountability mechanisms, the less WTO law deserves being called a rule of law system. Sections 6.2 and 6.3 recall how past WTO jurisprudence protected, albeit only indirectly and imperfectly, human rights values

[6] On constitutional limits (eg under the German Constitutional Court's conception of national, parliamentary democracy accountable for national public revenue and expenditure) for delegating discretionary fiscal and economic policy powers to international institutions see Chapter 8, section 8.4 and K Tuori, *European Constitutionalism* (CUP 2015), at 218ff. According to the German Constitutional Court, conferral of rules-based monetary, trade, and competition policy powers on EU institutions is more justifiable in terms of democratic input and output legitimacy (like protecting equal freedoms and monetary stability for all) and objective economic criteria than conferral of discretionary fiscal and economic policy powers redistributing national revenue among EU member states.

[7] Cf Report of the Secretary-General, *Delivering Justice: programme of action to strengthen the rule-of-law at the national and international levels*, A/66/49 of 16 March 2012, para 2. On the need for distinguishing rule of law from rule by law, rule by men, and rule by reason, and on the need for a constitutionalist conception of the rule of law as defining the conditions under which law actually has the legitimate authority it claims to have, see M Kumm, 'Global Constitutionalism and The Rule of Law' in AF Lang and A Wiener (eds), *Handbook on Global Constitutionalism* (Edward Elgar 2017), 197–211.

and the consistent interpretation requirements of the customary rules of treaty interpretation, including interpretation 'in conformity with the principles of justice' and 'human rights and fundamental freedoms for all' (Preamble and Article 31 VCLT). The recent WTO jurisprudence limiting arbitrary invocations of security exceptions (eg under Article XXI GATT) illustrates the judicial administration of justice balancing competing principles of justice underlying WTO law (section 6.4). From 1995 to 2020, the more than 420 WTO panel, appellate, and arbitration reports provided more 'security and predictability to the multilateral trading system' (Article 3.2 DSU) than at any previous time. As maintaining a rules-based world trading system is of crucial importance for coherent, effective, and legitimate responses to the global health, environmental, economic, and governance crises, WTO members and their citizens have good reasons for defending the DSU and its compulsory jurisdiction for maintaining rule of law in multilevel trade governance as one of the constitutional foundations for realizing the SDGs.

6.2 Legitimacy Problems of Rule of Law: WTO Jurisprudence Protecting Human Rights Values

Most GATT/WTO trade diplomats argue that the 316 disputes under GATT 1947 and the 1979 Tokyo Round Agreements,[8] and the more than 600 formal dispute settlement proceedings under the WTO Agreement (1996–2020), protected—for the first time in history—transnational rule of law in trade relations among now 164 WTO members. The complex GATT/WTO jurisprudence approved by GATT/WTO members clarified the rights and duties under international trade law with due regard to general international law and the more than 400 FTAs concluded among GATT/WTO members (often providing for additional judicial remedies). As more than 85 per cent of the more than 500 GATT/WTO dispute settlement findings were approved and implemented by GATT/WTO members, the GATT/WTO dispute settlement system is widely perceived as the most frequently used worldwide dispute settlement system in the history of international law. Even if most GATT/WTO members did not allow direct application and judicial enforcement of GATT/WTO obligations in their domestic jurisdictions, many GATT/WTO disputes were preceded or followed by domestic court proceedings (eg challenging illegal trade remedies). The global interpretive community of trade lawyers, academics, and judges analysing and developing GATT/WTO law and jurisprudence strengthened this 'international trade law culture' promoting 'public reason' (eg in the sense of shared systems of public justification of multilevel trade rules and of their decentralized enforcement), providing for 'security

[8] Cf the list and analyses of cases in *GATT Disputes 1948–1995* (2 vols, WTO Geneva 2018).

and predictability to the multilateral trading system' (Article 3 DSU) and reducing transaction costs in the global division of labour.

This diplomatic conception reducing rule of law among states to the availability and relative effectiveness of international dispute settlement procedures is criticized by citizen-oriented conceptions of interactional law exploring whether the agreed international law rules become fused with a 'practice of legality' rooted in Fuller's eight criteria of legality and embraced by a community of practice that adheres to those criteria in day-to-day decision-making.[9] Regardless of how to define the rule of law in international relations, the legitimate authority and legitimacy of modern legal systems depend on the consent of free and equal citizens. As the WTO Agreement has been voluntarily approved by governments and/or democratic institutions in 163 WTO member states and by the EU and continues to promote their economic welfare through a rules-based, market-driven global division of labour, so too can the WTO legal and dispute settlement systems be assumed to have legal input and output legitimacy. The economic, social, and sustainable development objectives of the WTO (as defined in the WTO Preamble), the WTO legal rules, and multilevel, judicial remedies, and each WTO member's legal obligations to 'ensure the conformity of its laws, regulations and administrative procedures with its obligations under the annexed Agreements' (Article XVI.4 WTO Agreement) have created a global trading, legal, and compulsory dispute settlement system that has enabled member states to enhance economic welfare, peaceful legal, economic, and political cooperation and reduce poverty as never before in human history. In Article 3.2 DSU, WTO members recognize that the dispute settlement system 'serves to preserve the rights and obligations of Members under the covered Agreements, and to clarify the existing provisions of those agreements in accordance with customary rules of interpretation of public international law'. The codification of these customary rules in Articles 31–33 VCLT prescribes interpretation of treaties based not only on their text, context, object, and purpose. Interpretation must also take into account, *inter alia*, 'any relevant rules of international law applicable in the relations between the parties' (Article 31.3,c), including 'principles of justice' and 'human rights and fundamental freedoms for all', as recalled in the Preamble of the VCLT. Does the fact that human rights are nowhere mentioned in WTO law and hardly ever invoked and discussed in WTO bodies and referred to in WTO dispute settlement reports undermine the legitimacy of the WTO legal and dispute settlement system? If the incorporation of human rights into EU law and judicial remedies has promoted welfare-enhancing synergies in the EU's common market law as briefly discussed in Chapter 5, section

[9] Cf Chapter 4, section 4.2 and J Brunnée and SJ Toope, *Legitimacy and Legality in International Law: An Interactional Account* (CUP 2010), at 86. On Fuller's 'inner morality of law' based on eight principles of legality (ie generality, publicity, clarity, consistency, feasibility, constancy, prospectivity, congruence), see LL Fuller, *The Morality of Law* (revised edn, Yale UP 1969), 197–200. On constitutional conceptions of rule of law see nn 3–6 in this chapter.

5.5, why do WTO members object to incorporating universally recognized human rights into WTO law and legal practices?

Chapter 2, section 2.3 referred to the reality of reasonable disagreements on the interpretation of UN HRL and to the sovereign freedom which UN law recognizes for each UN member state to decide autonomously on whether the country wishes to ratify UN human rights conventions, and which ones. While all 30 EEA member states have ratified the European Convention on Human Rights, the disagreement on human rights among the 164 WTO members remain significant. Arguably, as WTO law does not provide for individual access to WTO dispute settlement bodies and WTO complainants and defendants hardly ever invoke human rights in WTO dispute settlement proceedings, the WTO judicial practice of focusing on the objective public goods (PGs) values underlying human rights (like public health protection underlying the human right to health), rather than on individual human rights, is justifiable on procedural grounds. It should also enable judges to protect the relevant human rights values objectively in WTO dispute settlement proceedings no less effectively than if the judges would have referred to individual human rights in interpreting and balancing WTO rights, obligations, and exceptions. This seems to be confirmed by empirical analyses of GATT/WTO jurisprudence. Even though human rights are not mentioned in WTO law, the WTO objectives and general exceptions protect human rights values like public morals, public order, human, animal, or plant life, or health, protection of national treasures of artistic, historic, or archaeological value, conservation of exhaustible natural resources, protection of the environment, essential security interests, raising standards of living, and sustainable development. WTO jurisprudence has interpreted these WTO provisions broadly. For instance:

- The 2018 WTO panel and 2020 appellate reports on complaints by tobacco-exporting countries against Australia's legislation on plain packaging of tobacco products confirmed that these health regulations restricting intellectual property rights and sales of tobacco products were consistent with WTO law (eg on technical barriers to trade and intellectual property rights). The reports refrained from referring to human rights, which had neither been invoked by the complainants nor by the defendant. But the interpretation of WTO rules in conformity with the 2001 WTO Declaration on the Agreement on Trade-Related Aspects of Intellectual Property Rights (TRIPS) and Public Health and the 2003 World Health Organization (WHO) Framework Convention on Tobacco Control (FCTC) avoided conflicts with health rights, thereby illustrating the importance of systemic treaty interpretation (Article 31.3 VCLT) for maintaining the consistency of WTO rights and obligations with other international treaty commitments.[10]

[10] Cf EU Petersmann, 'How to Reconcile Human Rights, Trade Law, Intellectual Property, Investment and Health Law? WTO Dispute Settlement Panel Upholds Australia's Plain Packaging Regulations of

- The 2014 WTO panel and appellate reports on EU import restrictions on seals products acknowledged, *inter alia*, that the EU exceptions for products from indigenous people in Greenland were justifiable under the public morals exception in GATT Article XX(a) provided they did not discriminate against seal products imported from Canada and Norway.[11]
- The 2011 panel and 2012 appellate reports on US restrictions on tuna based on the Dolphin Protection Consumer Information Act confirmed that US 'dolphin safe' labelling measures would be consistent with WTO law provided they were applied in non-discriminatory ways.[12]
- The 2007 WTO panel and appellate reports on Brazil's import restrictions on re-treaded tyres implied that the restrictions could be justified as being necessary for health protection reasons if applied in non-discriminatory ways.[13]
- The 2004 panel and 2005 appellate reports on US restrictions of cross-border gambling and betting services implied that such restrictions can be justified as being necessary for protecting public morals (Article XIV(a) of the General Agreement on Trade in Services (GATS)) if applied in non-discriminatory ways.[14]
- The 2003 panel and 2004 appellate reports on EC tariff preferences for combatting drug production and trafficking in less-developed countries implied that such preferences can be consistent with WTO law if applied in non-discriminatory ways.[15]
- The 2001 appellate report on EC import restrictions on asbestos confirmed the justifiability of these health protection measures; as health risks can affect the competitive relationship of asbestos and substitute products, non-discriminatory health protection measures may neither violate GATT Article III nor need justification under GATT law.[16]
- The 1998 and 2001 appellate reports on US import restrictions on shrimps confirmed that non-discriminatory animal protection conditioning imports of shrimp on the use of certain fishing nets protecting turtles is justifiable under GATT Article XX(g).[17]

Tobacco Products' in *The Global Community Yearbook of International Law and Jurisprudence* (2018), 69–102. The AB reports confirming the panel findings were published on 9 June 2020: WT/DS435/AB/R and WT/DS441/AB/R.

[11] Cf WT/DS400,401/R/AB adopted on 18 June 2014.
[12] Cf WT/DS/381/R/AB adopted 13 June 2012.
[13] Cf WT/DS/332/R/AB adopted on 12 December 2007.
[14] Cf WT/DS/285/R/AB adopted on 20 April 2005.
[15] Cf WT/DS246/R/AB adopted on 20 April 2004.
[16] Cf WT/DS135/R/AB adopted on 5 April 2001.
[17] Cf WT/DS58/R/AB adopted on 6 November 1998 and 21 November 2001 (Article 21.5 DSU).

All these WTO dispute settlement findings affected the regulation of business activities with potentially harmful or discriminatory, economic, health, or environmental effects. The findings influenced also global application of WTO rules beyond the specific disputes. They confirm the sovereign rights under WTO law to adopt *non-discriminatory* regulations protecting non-economic PGs like public morals (including also human rights), public health, and the environment. There is no evidence, thus far, that any of the more than 600 GATT/WTO dispute settlement findings since 1949 has violated human rights.[18]

6.3 Limiting Legal Fragmentation through Systemic WTO Interpretation: The Example of the WHO Framework Convention for Tobacco Control

The COVID-19 health pandemic is a reminder of the close interrelationships between economic and health systems. During the twentieth century, tobacco consumption killed more than 100 million people, more deaths than in both World Wars and the Holocaust combined. Yet, it was only in 2003 that the FCTC—the first multilateral treaty negotiated under Article 19 of the WHO Constitution—was signed and accepted by now 180 countries. The coexistence of fifteen separate UN specialized agencies (like the WHO) with functionally separate mandates and legal systems responds to the fact that, in a world composed of more than 200 states, the sovereign equality of states (Article 2 UN Charter) makes legal and institutional fragmentation inevitable: different states and governments have different priorities as to which bilateral and multilateral treaties each of the 193 UN member states is willing to conclude, subject to which judicial remedies, and how to implement treaty obligations inside diverse national legal and political systems. WTO jurisprudence tends to confirm that the customary rules of treaty interpretation—and judicial mandates of administering justice—offer national and international dispute settlement bodies sufficient legal flexibility for interpreting fragmented treaty rights and obligations of WTO members in mutually coherent ways.

The WTO complaints initiated in 2012 by Ukraine, Honduras, and the Dominican Republic, and in 2014 by Cuba and Indonesia, challenged the consistency with WTO law of Australia's tobacco plain packaging (TPP) measures; yet, as mentioned mainly in the third-party interventions by thirty-nine WTO members (without counting the twenty-eight member states represented by the EU) in the panel proceedings—as well as in more than forty *amicus curiae* submissions, the joint communications to the Panel by the WHO and FCTC Secretariats providing

[18] Cf EU Petersmann, 'Human Rights, Constitutional Justice and International Economic Adjudication: Legal Methodology Problems' in M Scheinin (ed), *Human Rights Norms in 'Other' International Courts* (CUP 2019), 312–52.

information on the FCTC, and in the additional information provided by the World Intellectual Property Organization (WIPO) Secretariat on provisions of WIPO conventions incorporated into the TRIPS Agreement—the complaints and defences also involved HRL, intellectual property law, investment law, health law, and Australia's constitutional law and adjudication. As tobacco use is classified as a global epidemic responsible for the deaths of nearly 6 million people annually, including 600,000 non-smokers exposed to second-hand smoke, the WTO disputes affected people and health regulations all over the world. After separate complaints by tobacco industries in the national courts of Australia[19] and in investor–state arbitration (under an investment treaty between Hong Kong and Australia) had already been rejected,[20] two of the four separate, yet largely identical WTO panel findings were adopted in August 2018.[21] The two other WTO panel reports were appealed and rejected in two WTO AB reports adopted in June 2020.[22] The four Panel reports and two AB reports dismissed all claims of violations of WTO rules; as neither the complainants nor defendant had referred to human rights (eg to health protection), the judicial balancing of economic rights (eg market access rights and intellectual property rights protected by WTO law) and public health protection focused on *governmental rights to protect public health* rather than on corresponding *human rights*. Not only the dozens of separately negotiated agreements included into the WTO Agreement and WTO treaty practices (like the 2001 WTO Declaration on the TRIPS Agreement and Public Health) were construed by the WTO dispute settlement bodies as a mutually coherent legal system. Multilateral treaties on tobacco control negotiated in the WHO (notably the FCTC of 2003), WIPO conventions, and related treaty practices were also duly taken into account in the legal findings on the consistency of Australia's tobacco plain-packaging regulations (TPPR) with the WTO Agreements on Technical Barriers to Trade (TBT), TRIPS, and GATT 1994.

The disputes concerned restrictions imposed by Australia on trademarks, geographical indications (GIs), and other plain packaging requirements applicable to all tobacco products sold, offered for sale, or otherwise supplied in Australia. The

[19] Cf *JT International SA v Commonwealth; British American Tobacco Australasia Ltd v Commonwealth*, High Court of Australia 2012, 43 (5 October 2012). For an overview of tobacco litigation in national, European, and investment courts, see EU Petersmann, *Multilevel Constitutionalism for Multilevel Governance of Public Goods* (Hart 2017), 241ff, 256ff.

[20] The tribunal's award of December 2015 was published on the website of the Permanent Court of Arbitration in May 2016.

[21] WT/DS435/R, WT/DS441/R, WT/DS458/R, WT/DS467/R of 28 June 2018 on Australia—Certain Measures Concerning Trademarks, Geographical Indications and other Plain Packaging Requirements Applicable to Tobacco Products and Packaging. The initial complaint by Ukraine (DS434) was subsequently suspended under Article 12.12 of the DSU. All facts (eg regarding Australia's TPP measures and the claims by the parties to this WTO dispute) and legal instruments mentioned in the following are quoted from and documented in more detail in these panel reports. For more detailed legal analyses, see Petersmann (n 10).

[22] The AB reports confirming the panel findings were published on 9 June 2020 (WT/DS435/AB/R and WT/DS441/AB/R) and adopted on 29 June 2020.

Panel identified the measures at issue in these disputes (the TPP measures) as comprising the following:

- the TPP Act 2011;
- the TPPR 2011, as amended by the Tobacco Plain Packaging Amendment Regulation 2012 (TPP Regulations); and
- the Trade Marks Amendment Act 2011 (TMA Act).

The TPP Act is an Act to discourage the use of tobacco products. It regulates the retail packaging and appearance of tobacco products in order to (i) improve public health and (ii) give effect to certain obligations in the WHO FCTC. The products at issue in these disputes are tobacco products, defined in the TPP Act to mean processed tobacco, or any product that contains tobacco and is manufactured for smoking, sucking, chewing, or snuffing, and is not included in the Australian Register of Therapeutic Goods maintained under the Therapeutic Goods Act 1989. This definition encompasses not only cigarettes but also non-cigarette products, such as cigars and cigarillos. As of 1 December 2012, all tobacco products sold, offered for sale, or otherwise supplied in Australia were required to comply with the TPP measures.

The Panel found that the complainants had not demonstrated that the TPP measures are inconsistent with Article 2.2 of the TBT Agreement, Articles 6*quinquies* and 10*bis* of the Paris Convention (1967) (read in conjunction with Article 2.1 of the TRIPS Agreement), Articles 15.4, 16.1, 16.3, 20, 22.2(b), and 24.3 of the TRIPS Agreement, and Article IX:4 of the GATT 1994. Honduras and the Dominican Republic appealed the Panel Reports. They challenged aspects of the Panel's findings under Article 2.2 of the TBT Agreement and Articles 16.1 and 20 of the TRIPS Agreement only.

6.3.1 Claims Relating to the Panel's Findings under Article 2.2 of the TBT Agreement

The AB recalled that for purposes of establishing that a measure is inconsistent with Article 2.2 of the TBT Agreement, a complainant must demonstrate that a technical regulation is more trade-restrictive than necessary to fulfil a legitimate objective, taking account of the risks non-fulfilment would create. The assessment of necessity, in the context of Article 2.2, involves a relational analysis of the following factors: (i) the trade restrictiveness of the technical regulation; (ii) the degree of contribution that it makes to the achievement of a legitimate objective; and (iii) the risks non-fulfilment would create. For the AB, the phrase in the second sentence of Article 2.2 that technical regulations shall not be more trade-restrictive than necessary implies that some trade restrictiveness is allowed. Establishing whether a technical regulation is more trade-restrictive than necessary may involve a comparison between (i) the trade restrictiveness and the degree of contribution of the measure at issue to the legitimate objective; and (ii) the trade restrictiveness and the degree of contribution of possible alternative measures that are reasonably available to the legitimate objective, taking account of the risks non-fulfilment would create.

In its assessment of whether the complainants had demonstrated that the TPP measures are inconsistent with Article 2.2, the Panel had examined, *inter alia*: (i) the contribution of the TPP measures to Australia's objective; (ii) the trade restrictiveness of the TPP measures; and (iii) whether the alternative measures proposed by the complainants are less trade-restrictive than the TPP measures while making an equivalent contribution to Australia's objective. The AB addressed the appellants' claims of error regarding each of these three aspects of the Panel's analysis. The AB considered that Honduras' claims implicated the Panel's appreciation of the facts and evidence, rather than its application of the legal standard under Article 2.2 to the facts of this case. Accordingly, the AB found that Honduras had not substantiated its claims that the Panel erred in its application of Article 2.2 to the facts of this case. As Honduras' arguments overlapped entirely with those made in support of its claims under Article 11 DSU, the AB addressed all of Honduras' challenges to the Panel's contribution analysis under the rubric of its claims under Article 11 of the DSU.

The appellants requested the AB to reverse the Panel's conclusion that the TPP measures were apt to, and did, make a meaningful contribution to Australia's objective of reducing the use of, and exposure to, tobacco products. The appellant's request was based, primarily, on their claims that the Panel failed in its duty under Article 11 DSU to make an objective assessment of the matter before it, with the appellant's focus being on the Panel's assessment of the facts of the case. Australia asked the AB to reject all the appellant's claims under Article 11 of the DSU, characterizing them as an unprecedented assault on a Panel's performance of its fact-finding function. In Australia's view, given both the scale and nature of the appellants' claims under Article 11 of the DSU, these claims were an invitation to the AB to determine whether the Panel's factual findings were *correct*, rather than whether the Panel was *objective* in making its assessment of the facts of the case. The AB emphasized that it would not entertain attempts by the appellant's to resubmit their factual arguments under the guise of challenging the objectivity of the Panel's assessment of the facts of the case. The AB rejected most of the claims by the appellants and upheld the Panel's conclusion that the complainants had not demonstrated that the TPP measures are more trade-restrictive than necessary to fulfil a legitimate objective, within the meaning of Article 2.2 of the TBT Agreement.

6.3.2 Claims Relating to the Panel's Findings under Article 16.1 of the TRIPS Agreement

The Panel understood the complainants to argue that, by prohibiting the *use* of certain tobacco-related trademarks on tobacco packaging and tobacco products, the TPP measures erode their distinctiveness, thereby constraining trademark owners' ability to exercise their rights under Article 16.1. For the Panel, this argument hinged on whether a reduction in the distinctiveness of a registered trademark affects the rights that members must provide to the trademark owner under Article 16.1. The Panel found that Article 16.1 provides only for a registered trademark owner's right to prevent certain activities by unauthorized third parties under the conditions set out in Article 16.1; if the activities of an unauthorized third party meet the conditions set out in the first sentence of Article 16.1, then the trademark owner must have the right under a member's domestic law to prevent such activities. It follows that in order to show that the TPP measures are inconsistent with Article 16.1, the complainants would have to demonstrate that, under Australia's domestic law, the trademark owner does not have the right to prevent third-party activities that meet the conditions set out in that provision. In the Panel's view, the text of Article 16.1 does not formulate any other right of the trademark owner, nor does it mention the *use* of the registered trademark by its owner. Thus, the Panel agreed with the parties that Article 16.1 does *not* establish a trademark owner's *right to use* its registered trademark.

Honduras requested the AB to reverse the Panel's finding that Honduras did not demonstrate that the TPP measures are inconsistent with Article 16.1 of the TRIPS Agreement, on the grounds that: (i) the Panel's interpretation of the rights conferred under Article 16.1 was in error; (ii) the Panel erred in its application of Article 16.1 to the TPP measures; and (iii) the Panel failed to comply with its obligation under Article 11 of the DSU to make an objective assessment of the matter. The AB acknowledged the unique nature of the TRIPS Agreement, which addresses *private intellectual property rights* held by natural or legal persons and derives a significant proportion of its content from pre-existing international intellectual property agreements or conventions that were negotiated outside the GATT/WTO framework. Exclusive intellectual property rights act to restrict commercial activity and require an active intervention of government to enforce these restrictions. The AB recalled that, as previous panels in *EC—Trademarks and Geographical Indications (Australia)* and *EC—Trademarks and Geographical Indications (US)* had stated, the TRIPS Agreement does not generally provide for the grant of positive rights to exploit or use certain subject matter but rather provides for the grant of negative rights to prevent certain acts. Article 1.1 imposes an obligation on members to give effect to the provisions of the TRIPS Agreement, as specified for trademarks in Articles 15–21 of the TRIPS Agreement.

Honduras claimed, *inter alia*, that the Panel erred in its interpretation of Article 16.1 by disregarding that (i) Article 16.1 of the TRIPS Agreement (read together with Articles 15, 17, 19, and 20 of the TRIPS Agreement) conferred upon the owner of a registered trademark the *right to use* its trademark; (ii) the distinctiveness of a trademark and the likelihood of confusion in Article 16.1 are closely related concepts that impose a requirement on members to protect the distinctiveness of a trademark through use; and (iii) pursuant to Article 16.1, members must guarantee a minimum level of protection relating to the distinctiveness and use of trademarks, which then guarantees particular outcomes. The AB observed that Article 16.1 grants a trademark owner the exclusive right to preclude unauthorized third parties from using, in the course of trade, identical, or similar signs for goods or services that are identical or similar to those with respect to which the trademark is registered, where such unauthorized use would result in a likelihood of confusion. While the AB agreed with Honduras that the risk of a likelihood of confusion relates to the distinguishing function of a trademark, the AB cautioned against extrapolating too broadly from this relationship. In this regard, the AB indicated that it had not come across any language in the TRIPS Agreement that endorsed Honduras' position that the *purpose* of the exclusive right articulated in Article 16.1 is to allow a trademark owner to protect the *distinctiveness* of the trademark through the trademark owner's continued *use* of that trademark. Likewise, none of the provisions of the Paris Convention (1967), which are incorporated by reference into the TRIPS Agreement, grant a trademark owner a positive right to use its trademark, or a right to protect the distinctiveness of that trademark through use. The owner of a registered trademark can exercise its exclusive right as against an unauthorized third party but not against the WTO member in whose territory the trademark is protected. Neither the TRIPS Agreement nor the provisions of the Paris Convention (1967) that are incorporated by reference into the TRIPS Agreement confer upon a trademark owner a positive right to use its trademark or a right to protect the distinctiveness of that trademark through use. In order to establish that a WTO member has acted inconsistently with Article 16.1, the complaining member must demonstrate that, under the responding member's domestic legal regime, the owner of a registered trademark cannot exercise its exclusive right to prevent the infringement of its trademark by unauthorized third parties. Based on this understanding of Article 16.1, the AB found that the Panel did not err in its interpretation of Article 16.1. As the condition on which Honduras' appeal was predicated (ie the reversal of the Panel's interpretation) had not been satisfied, the AB upheld the Panel's conclusion that the complainants had not demonstrated that the TPP measures are inconsistent with Article 16.1 of the TRIPS Agreement.

6.3.3 Claims Relating to the Panel's Findings under Article 20 of the TRIPS Agreement

With respect to the complainants claims under Article 20 of the TRIPS Agreement, the Panel concluded that the trademark requirements of the TPP measures amount to special requirements that encumber the use of a trademark in the course of trade. The Panel found, however, that the complainants failed to demonstrate that they do so 'unjustifiably'. On appeal, Honduras claimed that the Panel erred in its interpretation of the term 'unjustifiably' in Article 20 of the TRIPS Agreement or, alternatively, that it erred in applying the legal standard that it had developed to the facts of the present disputes.

The AB noted that the fact that Article 20 presupposes that the use of a trademark may be encumbered justifiably, indicates that there is no positive right of use of a trademark by its owner, nor is there an obligation on members to protect such a positive right. The term 'unjustifiably' reflects the degree of regulatory autonomy that members enjoy in imposing encumbrances on the use of trademarks through special requirements. The reference to the notion of justifiability suggests that the degree of connection between the encumbrance on the use of a trademark imposed and the objective pursued is lower than it would have been had the notion of necessity been used in this provision. The term 'unjustifiably' connotes an action for which there is no fair reason and which cannot be reasonably explained. Thus, a member that imposes encumbrances on the use of trademarks through special requirements must be able to provide a reasonable explanation of how an objective pursued by introducing special requirements warranted the resulting encumbrances. The AB agreed with the Panel that a determination of whether the use of a trademark in the course of trade is being unjustifiably encumbered could involve a consideration of (i) the nature and extent of encumbrances resulting from special requirements, taking into account the legitimate interest of the trademark owner in using its trademark in the course of trade; (ii) the reasons for the imposition of special requirements; and (iii) a demonstration of how the reasons for the imposition of special requirements support the resulting encumbrances. The AB also considered that the Panel did not err by not including an examination of alternative measures as a requisite consideration for determining whether the use of a trademark had been unjustifiably encumbered by special requirements. The AB rejected Honduras' argument that the Panel erred in relying on the Doha Declaration on the TRIPS Agreement and Public Health in its interpretation of Article 20. The AB agreed with the Panel that paragraph 5(a) of the Doha Declaration reflects the applicable rules of interpretation, which require a treaty interpreter to take account of the context and object and purpose of the treaty being interpreted. Accordingly, regardless of the legal status of the Doha Declaration, the AB saw no error in the Panel's reliance on this general principle of treaty interprctation. Reliance on the Doha Declaration had not been of decisive importance since the Panel had reached its conclusions about the contextual relevance of Articles 7 and 8 of the TRIPS Agreement to the interpretation of Article 20 before it turned to the Doha Declaration. With respect to Honduras' argument that the Panel erred by not focusing on the use of an individual trademark in terms of its distinguishing function, the AB recalled that the complainants had not sought to demonstrate before the Panel that, as a result of the trademark-related requirements of the TPP measures, consumers have been unable to distinguish the commercial source of tobacco products. The AB noted that, given the degree of regulatory autonomy provided to members under Article 20 through the use of the term 'unjustifiably', an analysis of alternative measures is not required in each and every case; it does not provide decisive guidance in determining whether the encumbrances in question are imposed unjustifiably. Having upheld the Panel's findings under Article 2.2 of the TBT Agreement and Articles 16.1 and 20 of the TRIPS Agreement, it followed that the AB agreed with the Panel that Honduras and the Dominican Republic had not succeeded in establishing that Australia's TPP measures are inconsistent with the provisions of the covered agreements at issue.

6.4 Judicial Constraints on Emergency Powers and Security Exceptions

The perennial struggles for limiting abuses of public and private power through law have led to progressive specification—in national and international legal systems since ancient times (eg the ancient Constitution of Athens and of the Roman Republic)—of ever more rule of law principles limiting legislative, administrative, and judicial powers. Examples include:

- legality (rule of law, not man);
- public monopoly of legitimate law-enforcement powers;
- supremacy of public law (also the governing institutions are bound by the law);
- separation of powers with checks and balances among independent constitutional, legislative, administrative, and judicial government branches;
- legitimation of governance powers and law through participation and consent of the governed community.

The emancipation of natural law (reflecting human reason independent from the divine laws of the church), the emergence of legal positivism (recognizing law as a product of human will rather than being discovered and inseparably linked to morality) and of social contract theories (recognizing we the people as sovereign and as delegating only limited powers to representative governments) prepared the ground for the 'Glorious Revolution' of 1688/89 in England and for the adoption of the English Bill of Rights in 1689. The democratic revolutions in the United States (eg the US Constitution of 1787 introducing a federal republic with horizontal separation of legislative, executive, and judicial powers), the US Bill of Rights of 1789 (yet without voting rights for women, slaves, and native Americans), the 1789 democratic revolution in France (eg replacing the three estates by a National Assembly adopting the 1789 Declaration of the Rights of Man and of the Citizen and the republican Constitutions of 1793 and 1795) further consolidated and specified rule of law principles. During the nineteenth and twentieth centuries, additional rule of law principles were progressively established through struggles for justice and, since 1945, universally recognized in national constitutions of UN member states as well as in ever more international agreements, UN resolutions, and rule-of-law promotion programmes.[23] The invocation (eg by the US Trump administration) of national security exceptions for imposing discriminatory trade restrictions, and the use of emergency powers of governments in the 2020/21 COVID-19 health pandemic for restricting individual freedoms and protecting public health systems (eg by executive emergency decrees, lockdowns, quarantines, travel bans, subsidization, purchase, and distribution of vaccines), have raised new challenges to the rule of law.

6.4.1 Impartial Trade Adjudication as a Rule of Law Constraint

The post-1945 decolonization, human rights revolutions, and IEL revolutions (as briefly described in Chapter 2) led to the establishment of more than forty international courts rendering thousands of international judgments reviewing governmental restraints of individual rights, rule of law, human rights, and constitutional rights.[24] The interactions between national, regional, and worldwide courts increasingly raised questions of justification and delimitation of international and national jurisdictions, notably in case of national invocations of general exceptions (like GATT Article XX on national rights to protect non-economic PGs) and national security exceptions (like GATT Article XXI), and of cooperation and judicial comity between national and international courts (eg in the context of preliminary rulings of the CJEU and advisory opinions by the European Free Trade Area (EFTA) Court at the request of national courts). The judicial clarifications of rule of law requirements were influenced by constitutional law principles such as transparency, non-discrimination, necessity, and proportionality requirements for justifying restrictions of individual freedoms and of national sovereign rights (eg

[23] For details, see M Zürn, A Nollkaemper, and R Peerenboom, *Rule of Law Dynamics in an Era of International and Transnational Governance* (CUP 2012). See also nn 5 and 7, this chapter.

[24] Cf C Romano, KJ Alter, and Y Shany (eds), *Handbook of International Adjudication* (OUP 2012).

to protect national security). As international law recognizes that similar to legal self-limitation through primacy of constitutional law over democratic legislation, a party may not invoke the provisions of its internal law as justification for its failure to perform a treaty (Article 27 VCLT), international judicial review, similar to constitutional court review, became increasingly powerful, notably whenever the jurisdiction of international courts also included substantive human rights, non-discrimination requirements, and principles of justice (like corrective justice underlying violation complaints pursuant to GATT Article XXIII.1,a, commutative justice underlying non-violation complaints pursuant to GATT Article XXIII.1,b, and equity principles underlying situation complaints pursuant to GATT Article XXIII.1,c). Extending and applying the rule of law to international organizations raised additional constitutional problems like limited delegation of powers and limited jurisdictions of international courts,[25] as illustrated by the insistence of national constitutional courts in EU member states on the constitutionally limited scope of jurisdiction of the CJEU and by increasing claims of judicial overreach (as discussed in Chapter 8). As neo-liberalism, totalitarian state capitalism, and ordo-liberal constitutionalism are rooted in diverse constitutional values, their respective willingness to accept international adjudication differs. For example, the WTO AB crisis was triggered by US politicization and rejection of impartial WTO AB jurisprudence driven by neo-liberal, US interest group politics (eg domestic industries benefitting from illegal US trade remedy practices) and by hegemonic US insistence on the self-judging nature of sovereign rights under GATT Article XXI to protect national security. The US invocation of the security exception in GATT Article XXI (eg for imposing import restrictions on steel and aluminium) illustrated how the Trump administration circumvented WTO rules (eg GATT Articles I, II, and XIX) and dispute settlement procedures whenever it suited American political interests and US interest group politics. China's rejection of the arbitration award of 12 July 2016 under the UN Convention on the Law of the Sea (UNCLOS Annex VII) was driven by China's maritime expansion disregarding its legal and judicial obligations under the UNCLOS[26] and using military force for enforcing the Chinese claims to control more than 80 per cent of the South China Sea. The EU initiative for saving WTO appellate review through agreed appellate arbitration pursuant to Article 25 DSU reflects the foreign policy mandate of the EU to consolidate and support democracy, the rule of law, human rights, and the principles of international law also in the EU's external relations (cf Articles 3, 21 TEU).

So far, the invocation by Russia, the US Trump administration, and some US allies (like Saudi Arabia) of WTO security exceptions for justifying discriminatory

[25] Cf CA Feinäugle (ed), *The Rule of Law and its Application to the United Nations* (Nomos 2016).

[26] See the Permanent Court of Arbitration Case No 2013-19 in the matter of the South China Sea Arbitration (*The Republic of the Philippines v The Peoples Republic of China*). The award is published on the PCA website at http://www.pcacases.com/web/view/7.

trade restrictions—and for denying WTO jurisdiction to review related decisions—remain contested by the EU and most other WTO members. In the WTO dispute initiated by Ukraine in 2016 against Russia's discriminatory restrictions on traffic in transit, Ukraine claimed that these transit restrictions were inconsistent with Russia's obligations under GATT Article V (freedom of transit), Article X (publication and administration of trade regulations), and with related commitments in Russia's Accession Protocol. Russia asserted that the measures were necessary for the protection of its essential security interests and had been taken in response to the emergency in international relations that occurred in 2014 (ie Russia's annexation of Crimea). Russia invoked the national security exceptions in GATT Article XXI(b)(iii) and claimed that the WTO panel lacked jurisdiction to further address this dispute. The WTO panel report, adopted on 26 April 2019, found, *inter alia*, that:

- WTO panels have jurisdiction to review some of the aspects of a WTO member's invocation of Article XXI(b)(iii);
- Russia had met the objective requirements for invoking this Article XXI(b)(iii) in relation to the transit restrictions at issue; and
- Russia's restrictions were covered by Article XXI(b)(iii).[27]

Since 2017, there has been an increasing number of WTO panel proceedings in which complainants challenged discriminatory trade restrictions that were justified by the respondent WTO members (like Saudi Arabia, United Arab Emirates, Bahrain, the United States) by invoking national security exceptions in WTO law. For instance, the US justification of its 2018 import tariffs on aluminium and steel on grounds of national security prompted China, India, the EU, Canada, Mexico, Norway, Russia, Switzerland, and Turkey to request the establishment of WTO dispute settlement panels against the United States.[28] The Panel report on *Saudi Arabia—Measures Concerning the Protection of Intellectual Property Rights* of June 2020[29] concerned discriminatory trade sanctions against Qatar and one of its companies (called beIN) operating in Saudi Arabia because of Qatar's alleged support of terrorist activities. The Panel established that the requirements of Article 73(b)(iii) of the TRIPS Agreement for justifying Saudi Arabia's violations of Articles 42

[27] WT/DS512/R, *Russia—Measures Concerning Traffic in Transit* (WTO Panel) (5 April 2019).

[28] See WTO documents DS 544, 547, 548, 550, 551, 552, 554, 556, and 564, respectively. Some of these WTO members adopted trade restrictions against the US as countermeasures under Article 8 of the Safeguards Agreement (arguing that the US measures are in reality disguised safeguards). The US challenged these countermeasures as unjustified (eg requesting WTO dispute settlement proceedings against Canada, China, the EU, Mexico, and Turkey; cf WTO documents DS 557, 558, 559, 560, and 561 respectively).

[29] WT/DS567/R, *Saudi Arabia—Measures Concerning the Protection of Intellectual Property Rights* (16 June 2020); adoption of this panel report was prevented by Saudi Arabia's 'appeal into the void'. In the following quotations from this Panel report, the footnotes are omitted.

and 41 of the TRIPS Agreement on national security grounds were met. Yet, the additional Panel finding of Saudi Arabia's violation of Article 63 TRIPS Agreement had not been justified by Saudi Arabia under the security exception of Article 73(b)(iii). In examining the security exception in Article 73 TRIPS Agreement, the Panel noted (in paragraph 7.230) that:

> Article XXI(b)(iii) of the GATT 1994, which is identical to Article 73(b)(iii) of the TRIPS Agreement, was recently addressed by the panel in *Russia—Traffic in Transit.* It held that a panel must determine for itself whether the invoking Member's actions were 'taken in time of war or other emergency in international relations' in subparagraph (iii) of Article XXI(b) of the GATT 1994. It further found that a panel's review of whether the invoking Member's' actions are ones 'which it considers necessary for the protection of its essential security interests' under the chapeau of Article XXI(b) of the GATT 1994 requires an assessment of whether the invoking Member has articulated the 'essential security interests' that it considers the measures at issue are necessary to protect, along with a further assessment of whether the measures are so remote from, or unrelated to, the 'emergency in international relations' as to make it implausible that the invoking Member implemented the measures for the protection of its 'essential security interests' arising out of the emergency. According to the panel in *Russia—Traffic in Transit,* the obligation of a Member to interpret and apply Article XXI(b)(iii) of the GATT 1994 in 'good faith' requires 'that the measures at issue meet a minimum requirement of plausibility in relation to the proffered essential security interests, i.e. that they are not implausible as measures protective of these interests'.
>
> 7.231. In this dispute, both parties interpreted Article 73(b)(iii) of the TRIPS Agreement by reference to, and consistently with, the interpretation of Article XXI(b)(iii) of the GATT 1994 developed by the panel in *Russia—Traffic in Transit.* However, the parties' arguments reveal divergent views on three fundamental issues pertaining to the applicability of the security exception in Article 73(b)(iii) to the facts and measures at issue: (a) whether there is an 'emergency in international relations' in the sense of subparagraph (iii) of Article 73(b); (b) whether Saudi Arabia has articulated its 'essential security interests' with sufficient clarity and precision; and (c) whether—and, if so, how—the measures that Saudi Arabia characterizes as the 'action which it considers necessary for the protection of its essential security interests' under the chapeau of Article 73(b) relate to any of the specific measures challenged by Qatar in this dispute.

The Panel further noted that the parties in this dispute and multiple third parties each express agreement with the general interpretation and analytical framework enunciated by the panel in *Russia—Traffic in Transit.* These parties and third parties therefore considered that both can be transposed to Article 73(b)(iii) of the

TRIPS Agreement.[30] Following detailed examinations of these contested issues, the Panel concluded:

> With respect to Saudi Arabia's invocation of the security exception in Article 73(b)(iii) of the TRIPS Agreement:
>
> i. the requirements for invoking Article 73(b)(iii) are met in relation to the inconsistency with Article 42 and Article 41.1 of the TRIPS Agreement arising from the measures that, directly or indirectly, have had the result of preventing beIN from obtaining Saudi legal counsel to enforce its IP rights through civil enforcement procedures before Saudi courts and tribunals; and
> ii. the requirements for invoking Article 73(b)(iii) are not met in relation to the inconsistency with Article 61 of the TRIPS Agreement arising from Saudi Arabia's non-application of criminal procedures and penalties to beoutQ.
>
> 8.2. Under Article 3.8 of the DSU, in cases where there is an infringement of the obligations assumed under a covered agreement, the action is considered *prima facie* to constitute a case of nullification or impairment. The Panel concludes that, to the extent that the measures at issue are inconsistent with the TRIPS Agreement, they have nullified or impaired benefits accruing to Qatar under that Agreement.
>
> 8.3. Pursuant to Article 19.1 of the DSU, the Panel recommends that Saudi Arabia bring its measures into conformity with its obligations under the TRIPS Agreement.

It remains to be seen whether the legal reasoning in the two panel reports reviewing the good faith invocation of WTO security exceptions—and confirming the partial justiciability of such unilateral invocations of security exceptions—will be followed in future WTO jurisprudence on other invocations of security exceptions. It is likely that the currently pending WTO panel proceedings on US invocations of the security exception in GATT Article XXI for justifying other trade sanctions (eg on steel and aluminium) will follow the convincing reasoning of the above-mentioned panel reports and confirm the inconsistency of these US invocations of Article XXI GATT with WTO rules.[31] At the DSB meeting on 22 February 2021, the US invoked Article XXI GATT in response to Hong Kong's complaint against US requirements that goods produced in Hong Kong must be marked to indicate that their origin is China.[32] The US objected to the establishment of a panel on the following grounds:

[30] Panel report (n 29), para 7.243.

[31] In this sense also former AB chairman J Bacchus, 'WTO signals national security no longer trump card in trade disputes', *Newsweek* 7 July 2020.

[32] US—Origin Marking Requirement (WTO document DS597/5 of 15 January 2021).

- The clear and unequivocal U.S. position, for over 70 years, is that issues of national security are not matters appropriate for adjudication in the WTO dispute settlement system. We therefore do not understand the purpose of this request for panel establishment, seeking WTO findings that the United States has breached certain WTO provisions. The WTO cannot, consistent with Article XXI of the General Agreement on Tariffs and Trade 1994, consider those claims or make the requested findings.
- No WTO Member can be surprised by this view. For decades, the United States has consistently held the position that actions taken pursuant to Article XXI are not subject to review in GATT or WTO dispute settlement. Each sovereign has the power to decide, for itself, what actions are essential to its security, as is reflected in the text of GATT 1994 Article XXI.
- Infringing on a Member's right to determine, for itself, what is in its own essential security interests would run exactly contrary to the efforts to revitalize and reform the WTO that are necessary to ensure that it lives up to its potential.[33]

China's WTO complaint of 6 December 2018 leading to the WTO Panel report of 15 September 2020 on *United States—Tariff Measures on Certain Goods from China*[34] illustrated how systemic incoherencies among state capitalist and liberal economic systems may provoke also other systemic WTO disputes. The US invoked the findings in the USTR's Section 301 report on China's unfair trade practices as demonstrating violations of the public morals and standards of right and wrong enshrined in US legislation (like norms against theft and misappropriation of intellectual property and unfair competition) as justification of the additional tariff sanctions imposed by the US government. Both China and the WTO Panel rejected the US request not to examine China's request for findings under GATT Articles I and II with respect to the US tariff measures and, instead, to issue a report with a brief description of the pertinent facts of the dispute and reporting that a solution had been reached by the parties, as prescribed by Article 12.7 of the DSU. The Panel report confirmed that the US tariff increases were inconsistent with the US obligations under GATT Articles I and II. As regards the US invocation of the public morals exception in GATT Article XX(a) as justification of discriminatory US tariff sanctions, the Panel concluded that the standards of right and wrong invoked by the United States (including norms against theft and misappropriation of intellectual property, unfair competition) could be covered by the term 'public morals' within the meaning of Article XX(a) of the GATT 1994. In its assessment of whether the United States had demonstrated the necessity of the import tariffs at

[33] US Statements at the DSB meeting on 22 February 2021, USTR website. The panel was established as requested by Hong Kong.

[34] The Panel report is published in WT/DS543/R.

issue, the Panel examined the existence of a *genuine relationship of ends and means* between the public morals objective as invoked by the United States and the measures at issue. After lengthy examinations of the nexus between the measures the United States had chosen (ie additional duties on a wide range of products) and the US public morals concerns, the Panel concluded that the United States had not provided an explanation that demonstrates how the imposition of additional duties on the selected imported products contributes to the achievement of the public morals objective as invoked by the United States. It follows that the United States has not adequately explained how the measures the United States has chosen are necessary to protect such public morals.[35] As the United States had not met its burden of demonstrating that the measures were justified under Article XX(a) of the GATT 1994, the Panel upheld its previous findings that the US measures at issue were inconsistent with Articles I:1, II:1(a), and II:1(b) of the GATT 1994. The US appealed the Panel report, once again, into the void of a dysfunctional WTO AB. The panel report has not been adopted, thus far.

6.4.2 WTO Adjudication as Constitutional Justice?

The three recent WTO disputes just discussed illustrate how independent third-party adjudication complying with the DSU mandate of clarifying the often imprecise WTO rules in accordance with customary rules of interpretation of public international law (Article 3.2 DSU) can protect the WTO's normative legal order by balancing the WTO market access obligations of WTO members with their sovereign rights to invoke WTO exceptions for protecting non-economic values like national security and public morality. The alternative claims of Russia, Saudi Arabia, and the United States to limit judicial review (eg by supporting authoritarian claims of the self-judging nature of unilateral invocations of WTO security or public morals exceptions) were convincingly rejected in all three panel reports. As recalled in Chapter 2, section 2.3 and Chapter 5, section 5.2, theories of justice (eg by John Rawls) explain why the basic legal structure of legal systems—including international law—requires justification in terms of agreed principles of justice from the different perspectives of constitutional contracts among citizens, democratic legislation, and administrative and judicial application and enforcement of the constitutional and legislative rules to individual situations. The diverse procedural, constitutional, distributive, corrective, commutative principles of justice and equity justifying the basic structures of legal system have progressively been clarified in national and international legal systems over centuries. As the politics of international legal practices tends to be dominated by utilitarian self-interests

[35] WT/DS543/R, para 7.238.

of the actors concerned (eg complainants and defendants in WTO disputes), impartial third-party adjudication has been accepted by all WTO members and their democratic institutions as a necessary constitutional self-constraint for protecting independent public reason in both national and international trade law systems. The post-1945 creation of more than forty new international courts and tribunals reflects this constitutional limitation of power politics in international legal practices and the emergence of a common law of international adjudication.[36]

By settling disputes, protecting the rule of law, and impartially clarifying the often disputed meaning of WTO rules for the benefit of the global trading community, WTO dispute settlement bodies have clarified what the law is (*juris dictio*) and have provided security and predictability to the multilateral trading system as prescribed in Article 3 DSU. This enhancement of the rule of law in international relations also enhanced the rule of law for the benefit of citizens inside states. Yet, the international judicialization processes focus on certain areas only (like HRL, criminal law, economic law, administrative law); they remain more developed in the Americas and Europe than, for instance, in the Asia Pacific and Arab world. The 2012 UN General Assembly Declaration on the rule of law[37] emphasizes the link between national and international judiciaries and their judicial protection of rule of law in national and international legal systems; the independence, impartiality, and integrity of the judiciary as essential prerequisite for upholding the rule of law; and the need for non-discriminatory administration of justice in conformity with human rights and equal access to justice for all against arbitrary or unlawful use of power. UN member states reaffirmed that human rights, the rule of law, and democracy are interlinked and indivisible core values and principles of the United Nations.[38] Just as rule of law cannot exist in international relations without international adjudication and jurisprudence promoting a common law of adjudication,[39] so too did it not exist under the GATT 1947 legal system (eg due

[36] Cf Romano, Alter, and Shany (eds) (n 24); N Grosman, H Grant Cohen, A Follesdal, and G Ulfstein (eds), *Legitimacy and International Courts* (CUP 2018). For comparative studies of eleven international and domestic trade courts—ie the WTO adjudicating bodies; the CJEU; the EFTA Court; the US Court of International Trade; the Federal Court of Canada; the Mercosur courts; the Andean Court of Justice; the Economic Court of the Commonwealth of Independent States; the Common Market for Eastern and Southern Africa Court of Justice; the West African Economic and Monetary Union Court of Justice; and the ASEAN Trade Dispute Settlement Mechanism—see R Howse, H Ruiz-Fabri, G Ulfstein, and MQ Zang (eds), *The Legitimacy of International Trade Courts and Tribunals* (CUP 2018). Each of these case studies refers to the emergence of rules regarding (i) selection and composition of the adjudicators; (ii) procedural rules; (iii) fact finding; (iv) interpretative approaches; (v) forum shopping; (vi) implementation and interaction with national courts; and (vii) tribunal-specific legitimacy concerns resulting, eg, from the embeddedness of each court into a particular legal and political regime. Common judicial practices reinforce this emergence of a common law of international adjudication.

[37] UNGA Resolution Doc A/RES/67/1.

[38] UNGA Resolution Doc A/RES/67/1, para 5.

[39] Cf de Baere and Wouters (eds) (2015).

to the politicization of GATT dispute settlement practices, for instance by arbitrary blockage of the adoption of some GATT panel reports).[40]

The WTO dispute settlement system, by contrast, evolved into the most frequently used (quasi)judicial procedure for the settlement of disputes among states (including also sub-state actors like Hong Kong, Macau, and Taiwan, and supranational actors like the EU) ushering in a comprehensive jurisprudence based on more than 420 WTO panel, appellate, and arbitration reports (1995–2020).[41] The independence of the AB jurisprudence has been demonstrated, *inter alia,* by the judicial clarification of due process of law principles (like admissibility of *amicus curiae* submissions, of public observation of AB hearings, presumption of persuasive precedential effects of AB jurisprudence) that have remained contested by some WTO members. The main problem of the WTO AB jurisprudence has been its relative success compared with the failures of the political WTO bodies to conclude their Doha Round negotiations since 2001 and their DSU reform negotiations since 1998. Yet, these political failures of the rule-making branch of WTO negotiators offer no legal justification for violating WTO law and blocking independent, impartial WTO dispute settlement procedures. As the remaining three AB members decided in late 2019 to complete only the three pending appeals in which the hearings had already been held before the end of the AB terms of Ujal S Bhatia and Tom R Graham on 12 December 2019, only these three proceedings led to the adoption of AB reports in 2020 leaving the other ten pending AB proceedings unresolved.[42] Due to the regular appeals into the void since the incapacitation of the AB in December 2019, there were more than thirty WTO panel—and more than fifteen WTO appellate—proceedings pending in April 2021 without clear prospects whether and when WTO member would be willing to comply with their existing DSU obligations again. Even if the DSB should reach agreement on reforming the AB procedures and filling the seven AB vacancies, it could take years until the existing backlog of pending WTO panel and appellate proceedings could be worked up and enable the adoption of past and new WTO dispute settlement findings.

[40] For a comparison of the GATT and WTO dispute settlement systems, see EU Petersmann, *The GATT/WTO Dispute Settlement System. International Law, International Organizations and Dispute Settlement* (Kluwer 1997). On more demanding definitions of rule of law by 'interactional conceptions' of international law see n 9 in this chapter, and related text.

[41] Cf P van den Bossche, 'The Appellate Body of the WTO' in de Baere and Wouters (eds), (n 39), 176–202.

[42] For summaries of the three adopted appellate reports and of the additional pending AB proceedings see the latest (currently also the last) Appellate Body Annual Report (2019–2020) at https://www.wto.org/english/tratop_e/dispu_e/ab_anrep_2019_e.pdf. According to Article 15 of the Working Procedures for Appellate Review, the three AB members could have completed the disposition of all pending appeals beyond the end of their term in office.

6.5 Adapting the WTO Legal and Dispute Settlement System to the New Security Order?

This chapter suggests that it remains in the reasonable self-interest of all WTO members to (i) return to the rule of law in their WTO practices and (ii) negotiate a new compromise on adjusting WTO rules to the regulatory challenges of state capitalism, climate change, global health pandemics, and other regulatory challenges of the twenty-first century such as the newly emerging security order. Academic claims that law is incapable of providing convincing justifications to the solution of normative problems[43] are unreasonable: legal decision-making procedures and institutions are preconditions for social peace; reasonable citizens and governments tend to comply with (inter)national court judgments, as illustrated by the continued compliance by most WTO members with the institutionalized public reason of WTO dispute settlement rulings adopted by the DSB. The DSU requires the DSB to reclaim its legitimate authority and collective legal duty to protect the balance (reason) as well as the sword (power) of justice (as represented by *Justitia*, the blindfolded Roman goddess of law and justice armed with scales and a sword) so as to continue the success story of the WTO dispute settlement system from 1995 to December 2019. Since 2020, the regular appeals of most WTO panel reports into the void of a dysfunctional AB continues to prevent legally binding dispute settlements; the voluntary appellate arbitration procedures based on Article 25 DSU had not yet produced any appellate report by November 2021. Without a functioning WTO dispute settlement system, rules-based responses to the global governance challenges risk becoming ever more contested.

6.5.1 Return to the Rule of Law in WTO Legal Practices?

Normative legal orders—like the WTO legal and dispute settlement system—cannot remain effective if the legal practices (such as law-making, administrative, and judicial decisions) and legal institutions (like the DSB) no longer support the principles of justice underlying the normative legal system. As discussed earlier, the non-compliance by the United States and by the DSB with Article 17 DSU—and with the separation and limitation of legislative, executive, and judicial powers in the WTO Agreement (cf Articles III, IX)—is disrupting the WTO legal and dispute settlement system. Most of the USTR's criticism of the AB jurisprudence remains unconvincing (as explained in Chapter 3) and has not been supported by most other WTO members. Yet, due to domestic interest group politics and the mid-term US elections in 2022, the US Biden administration lacks domestic

[43] Cf M Koskenniemi, *From Apology to Utopia. The Structure of International Legal Argument* (CUP 2005), at 69, and my criticism in Chapter 2, section 2.1 and Chapter 4, section 4.2.

support for returning to the WTO AB system (eg based on the mediation proposals by Ambassador Walker plus some face-saving DSU clarifications aimed at preventing judicial overreach). Resolving the AB's appointments crisis is further complicated by the US insistence on the unreasonable ninety days time-limit for AB proceedings in Article 17.5 DSU and on US interpretations (eg of DSU rules), which are inconsistent with the DSU requirements of impartial, judicial administration of justice (as specified in the working procedures for WTO panels and the AB) in conformity with the customary rules of treaty interpretation (as prescribed in Article 3 DSU). How should the WTO membership respond to the continued US blocking of AB nominations in violation of Article 17.2 DSU and the prevention of the adoption of panel reports by appeals into the void?

According to Article 17 DSU, the 'Appellate Body … shall be composed of seven persons, three of whom shall serve on any one case' (paragraph 1). 'Vacancies shall be filled as they arise' (paragraph 2). What is the relationship between these legal requirements and Article 2.4 DSU ('Where the rules and procedures of this Understanding provide for the DSB to take a decision, it shall do so by consensus')?[44] Many DSB members expressed the view that Article 17 DSU entails a collective legal obligation of all WTO members to maintain the AB as legally prescribed in Article 17 DSU, and that the US blocking of the filling of AB vacancies since 2017 on grounds not related to the personal qualifications of the AB candidate violates the US legal duties under Article 17 DSU. The US minority view is that the positive consensus rule in Article 2.4 DSU (as distinguished from the negative/reverse consensus rules in Articles 16.4 and 17.14 DSU) permits the US blockage of AB nominations based on the US objections to the jurisprudence of the AB (as discussed in Chapter 3, sections 3.3 and 3.4). Arguably,[45] the legal requirements of good faith, of systemic treaty interpretation, and the unqualified legal duty of filling AB vacancies as they arise as part of the judicial functions of WTO dispute settlement bodies require taking into account, *inter alia*:

- the explicit separation (eg in Articles III, X of the WTO Agreement) of the rule-making, administrative, and dispute settlement functions of the WTO: while *law-making procedures* must be inclusive and representative, *administrative* and *judicial decision-making powers* tend to be allocated to different institutions applying different decision-making procedures. For example, the DSU allocates the elaboration of dispute settlement findings to panels, the AB, and arbitration, and protects the respective independence and impartiality of these dispute settlement bodies through, *inter alia*, working procedures (eg as

[44] Footnote 1 to Article 2.4 DSU clarifies: 'The DSB shall be deemed to have decided by consensus on a matter submitted for its consideration, if no Member, present at the meeting of the DSB when the decision is taken, formally objects to the proposed decision.'

[45] For more detailed arguments, see EU Petersmann, How Should WTO Members React to their WTO Governance Crises? *World Trade Review* 18 (2019), 503–25.

codified in Appendix 3 to the DSU) and rules of conduct; the DSU provides for administrative and (quasi)judicial functions of the DSB for completing and adopting panel and AB findings as prescribed in the DSU—amending the DSU is regulated separately in Article X.8 WTO Agreement by providing for the jurisdiction of the WTO Ministerial Conference rather than the DSB.

- Article IX.1 WTO Agreement explicitly provides for decision-making by voting: 'Except as otherwise provided, where a decision cannot be arrived at by consensus, the matter at issue shall be decided by voting. At meetings of the Ministerial Conference and the General Council, each Member of the WTO shall have one vote'.
- This voting rule was confirmed in the WTO General Council Decision adopted 10 December 2002 on Procedures for the Appointment of Directors-General, which provided in paragraph 20: 'Recourse to a vote for the appointment of a Director-General shall be understood to be an exceptional departure from the customary practice of decision-making by consensus, and shall not establish any precedent for such recourse in respect of any future decisions in the WTO.'[46] As WTO law does not authorize exceptions from filling AB vacancies as they arise (Article 17.2 DSU), Article IX.1 WTO Agreement provides for administrative majority decisions by the WTO Ministerial Conference and the WTO General Council for overcoming illegal blockage of AB nominations in the DSB. Similarly, Article 8.7 DSU allocates administrative decision-making powers to the Director-General to nominate members of WTO panels even against the will of the parties to the dispute.[47] The wording of Article 8.7 DSU ('shall') makes clear that the Director-General has a legal obligation to complete the composition of the panel without administrative discretion to decline such a request. Likewise, Articles 2.4 and 17 DSU make clear the legal obligations of the DSB ('shall') to appoint—by consensus—seven AB members and fill vacancies as they arise. The text of Article IX.1 of the WTO Agreement[48] confirms that the WTO Ministerial

46 *Procedures for the Appointment of Directors-General*, WT/L/509 (20 January 2003).

47 'If there is no agreement on the panelists within 20 days after the date of the establishment of a panel, at the request of either party, the Director-General, in consultation with the Chairman of the DSB and the Chairman of the relevant Council or Committee, shall determine the composition of the panel by appointing the panelists whom the Director-General considers most appropriate in accordance with any relevant special or additional rules or procedures of the covered agreement which are at issue in the dispute, after consulting with the parties to the dispute. The Chairman of the DSB shall inform the Members of the composition of the panel thus formed no later than 10 days after the date the Chairman receives such a request.'

48 'The WTO shall continue the practice of decision-making by consensus followed under GATT 1947. Except as otherwise provided, where a decision cannot be arrived at by consensus, the matter at issue shall be decided by voting.' 'Decisions of the Ministerial Conference and the General Council shall be taken by a majority of the votes cast, unless otherwise provided in this Agreement or in the Multilateral Trade Agreements.' Arguably, the DSU provisions for consensus-based decision-making by the DSB (eg pursuant to Articles 2.4, 16.4, 17.14 DSU) do not prevent the Ministerial Conference or General Council from meeting collective WTO legal obligations by voting if a decision cannot be arrived at by consensus in the DSB due to 'bad faith blocking' of consensus in the DSB.

> Conference and General Council are *legally required* ('shall') to overcome illegal blocking in the DSB of the filling of AB vacancies by majority decisions in order to meet the collective WTO legal duties to maintain the AB as prescribed in Article 17 DSU (eg being 'composed of seven persons', with 'Appellate Body membership (being) broadly representative of membership in the WTO'). The practice of the WTO General Council—for example the convening of a General Council meeting in order to discuss the contested AB findings on admission of *amicus curiae* briefs after proposals for a consensus-based DSB decision on this legal interpretation had been vetoed in the DSB—confirms this legal interpretation of the residual decision-making powers of the WTO Ministerial Conference and the General Council as the hierarchically superior WTO institutions responsible for protecting the WTO judicial functions as prescribed in the DSU.[49]

The DSB's pragmatic toleration of the US Trump administration's abuse of veto powers has rendered the *judicial WTO institutions* dysfunctional and entailed *de facto* amendments of WTO rules that run counter to the democratic mandate given by parliaments to implement and modernize but *not* to destroy WTO rules and institutions. Just as President Trump has abused executive powers for undermining democracy inside the United States (as illustrated by criminal condemnations of several collaborators of Trump in the White House who were subsequently granted presidential pardons suspending enforcement of their criminal sentences), the Trump administration's assault on the WTO AB, and the failures of other WTO members to refute the false USTR claims regarding AB jurisprudence, have undermined the WTO dispute settlement system. If the effectiveness of the DSB and of its administration of the WTO dispute settlement system is defined by 'the level to which this body attains the goals set for it by the WTO and its Member States ... those that fund, monitor and use this adjudicative system',[50] the essential WTO and DSU objectives—like providing security and predictability to the multilateral trading system, maintaining and restoring the balance of benefits between WTO members by prompt resolution of disputes, sustaining the operation of the WTO and realizing its objectives, legitimizing WTO law and WTO practices and promoting rule of law—have obviously been impaired since 2019. At

[49] The footnote to Article IX.1 WTO ('Decisions by the General Council when convened as the Dispute Settlement Body shall be taken only in accordance with the provisions of paragraph 4 of Article 2 of the Dispute Settlement Understanding') is no legal obstacle to majority decisions by the WTO Ministerial Conference or by the General Council deliberately *not* convening as DSB in order to meet the collective duties of WTO members to comply with Article 17 DSU. Such convening of the WTO General Council in order to overcome disagreements in the DSB has been practised already in the past, for instance when WTO Members wanted to censure the AB for its handling of *amicus curiae* briefs; cf General Council, *Minutes of Meeting—Held in the Centre William Rappard on 22 November 2000*, WT/GC/M/60 (23 January 2001).

[50] S Shlomo Agon, *International Adjudication on Trial—The Effectiveness of the WTO Dispute Settlement System* (OUP 2019), at 9.

the request of WTO members, New Zealand's Ambassador David Walker engaged in consultations and mediation resulting in a WTO General Council draft decision proposing AB reforms in exchange for an agreement by the United States to initiate the WTO procedures for the filling of the vacant AB positions.[51] As adoption of such a WTO General Council Decision continued being blocked by the United States, the 12th WTO Ministerial Conference in November 2021 could have considered whether to adopt a majority decision on the filling of AB vacancies pursuant to Article IX.2 WTO Agreement (possibly combined with a waiver allowing non-participation by outvoted WTO members in future appellate procedures). In view of the past WTO consensus practices and the fear of provoking unpredictable US responses to any WTO majority voting on the filling of AB vacancies, the 12th WTO Ministerial Conference is, however, more likely to proceed pragmatically by continuing the multi-party interim appeal arrangements under Article 25 DSU and by further postponing any WTO decisions on restoring the WTO appellate review system. This failure—not only by the United States but also by WTO institutions—to uphold a rules-based WTO legal and dispute settlement system adversely affects also other areas of WTO negotiations (eg on new trade liberalization commitments, prohibiting fisheries subsidies contributing to illegal overfishing, granting waivers from certain provisions of the TRIPS Agreement for the prevention, containment, and treatment of COVID-19).

6.5.2 Need for Adapting WTO Rules to the New Security Order?

Chapter 3 described why, in view of the US assault on the WTO legal and dispute settlement system, WTO members avoided a legalistic insistence on majoritarian filling of AB vacancies aimed at maintaining the AB as prescribed by democratic institutions when they approved the WTO and DSU agreements. The EU initiative for multi-party appellate arbitration based on Article 25 DSU offered a pragmatic response protecting the reasonable self-interests of WTO members in WTO appellate review without provoking US President Trump to intensify his assault on the WTO (eg by ordering a complete US withdrawal from the WTO Agreement). Up to November 2021, the United States continued to block the regular requests in DSB meetings by 121 WTO members to appoint the vacant AB positions—without any indication by the USTR on how the Biden administration intends to resolve

[51] Reports of Ambassador Walker regarding the informal process on matters related to the functioning of the Appellate Body conducted under the auspice of the General Council are contained in the following WTO documents: WT/JOB/215, WT/JOB/217, WT/JOB/220, WT/JOB/222, and WT/JOB/225. As a result of the informal process, a draft General Council decision regarding the functioning of the Appellate Body was prepared and introduced for adoption in the General Council meeting on 9–10 December 2019. However, WTO members were not able to reach a consensus to adopt the draft decision (WT/GC/M/181).

the WTO AB crisis, for instance based on Ambassador Walker's informal mediation proposals as discussed in WTO General Council meetings, or by responding to the EU proposal of 18 February 2021 to negotiate more comprehensive DSU reforms.[52]

If the preceding analysis should prove correct that the geopolitical crises, illegal trade sanctions, their justification by unilateral 'self-judging interpretations of WTO security exceptions' (as discussed above), and the neo-liberal interest group politics inside the United States will render a return to the WTO dispute settlement system (as prescribed in the DSU) politically impossible, how will the newly emerging geo-economic security order change the future world trading system?[53] Will the disruption of the post-1989 paradigm of 'world peace through world trade'—with rare invocations of national security exceptions and with legal and judicial 'good faith review' (as discussed above)—also adversely affect the needed, international cooperation in the global environmental, health, migration, and other governance crises? How will third states respond to the US strategy of economic decoupling from totalitarian states like China, and to China's strategy of digital decoupling from democratic societies and of sanctioning of external criticism (eg by trade sanctions against Australia and by individualized, political sanctions against members of the European Parliament)? Will new regional strategic alliances (like AUKUS, the new security pact announced by Australia, the United Kingdom, and the United States on 15 September 2021 for the Indo-Pacific region) continue to distort trade relations (like the Australian-French procurement contract for nuclear-powered submarines)?

The global health crisis has been characterized by the UN Secretary-General as a 'pandemic of human rights abuses', both those caused directly by COVID-19 itself and frequently compounded by restrictive measures imposed by states purportedly to combat it.[54] Yet, the proposals by India and South Africa for a WTO waiver from certain provisions of the TRIPS Agreement for the prevention, containment, and treatment of COVID-19[55] has not been supported by a number of European and other WTO members on the ground that cooperation between governments, pharmaceutical industries, and international organizations had proven to be more

[52] See 'An open, sustainable and assertive trade policy', EU Commission, 18 February 2021 (available on the EU website https://ec.europa.eu/commission/press).

[53] Cf A Roberts, H Choer Moraes, and V Ferguson, Toward a Geoeconomic Order, *Journal of International Economic Law* 22 (2019), 655.

[54] Cf Antonio Guterres, The World Faces a Pandemic of Human Rights Abuses in the Wake of COVID-19, The Guardian, 22 February 2021 (available at: https://www.theguardian.com/global-development/2021/feb/22/world-faces-pandemic-human-rights-abuses-covid-19-antonio-guterres.10Statem).

[55] Cf WTO doc IP/C/W/669 (2 October 2020) and IP/C/W/677 (18 May 2021). See also the Expert Legal Opinion by the International Commission of Jurists of November 2021 on 'Human Rights Obligations of States to not impede the Proposed Covid-19 TRIPS Waiver' (https://docs.google.com/forms/d/19SfhnfRtFcRhP59kq5XBdsMOSrKg2mx7cSpSMYstmp8/edit?ts=617886db, https://www.dropbox.com/s/cvdybd04uqwvdf7/Legal%20Opinion.pdf?dl=0).

suitable for promoting inventions, production, and worldwide supply of COVID-19 vaccines and related medical products than the proposed TRIPS waivers, which could disrupt the existing public–private partnerships in inventing, producing, and supplying COVID-19 vaccines worldwide.[56] Arguably, the contradictions between the claims by less-developed countries for broad suspensions of intellectual property rights protected under the TRIPS Agreement and the insistence by European countries that the proposed TRIPS waiver is neither suitable nor necessary and proportionate for speeding up vaccine production and distribution reflect the increasing ideological divergences among WTO members.

6.5.3 Leadership by Democratic Alliances of WTO Members?

European ordo-liberalism and American neo-liberalism face common regulatory challenges (like authoritarian state capitalism, climate change, global health pandemics, threats to cybersecurity, regulatory gaps for digital trade) and share common foundations (like democratic constitutionalism, use of institutional economics and constitutional economics for responding to market and governance failures). Hence, democracies should join forces in responding to the regulatory challenges of the changing global economy and international order by joint leadership for multilateral, rules-based reforms.[57] Arguably, the Geneva ordo-liberalism underlying many WTO legal and dispute settlement rules offers coherent constitutional and competition principles also for modernizing WTO rules on non-discriminatory conditions of trade competition, special and differential treatment of less-developed economies, and transnational rule of law—which were the three main targets of US criticism of inadequate WTO rules and practices. If the WTO consensus practices should prevent agreement on global WTO reforms, more decentralized approaches (eg based on plurilateral trade agreements or enlargement of existing mega-regional FTAs, such as through EU and US accession to a revised Comprehensive and Progressive Trans-Pacific Partnership (CPTPP)) could progressively strengthen or supplement WTO competition, environmental, labour,

[56] The Max-Planck Institute for Innovation and Competition—in its *Opinion 05/07/2021* on 'Covid-19 and Intellectual Property: 10 Arguments Against a Waiver of Intellectual Property Rights'—offered detailed expert arguments why a suspension of intellectual property rights would neither foster vaccine production nor lead to a more equitable distribution of vaccines. These alternative, more effective policy instruments for promoting production and distribution of COVID-19 vaccines in less-developed countries were not even examined in the communications and human rights report mentioned in n 55.

[57] Notably of WTO rules for SOEs and market-based policies; notification and limitation of subsidies; new rules for e-commerce; special and differential treatment of less-developed countries; taxation and limitation of greenhouse gas emissions; collective responses to global health pandemics; transparent WTO deliberations with more input from the WTO secretariat (eg by means of annotated agendas and factual background papers); facilitation of plurilateral agreements; impartial WTO dispute settlement and appellate review procedures.

and dispute settlement rules necessary for transforming the global economy into a green economy mitigating climate change through sustainable development.

The WTO agreements on trade in goods, services, intellectual property rights, civil aircraft, and government procurement include already numerous rules for protecting non-discriminatory conditions of competition and preventing anti-competitive abuses of public and private powers, like Article 8 TRIPS Agreement on 'abuses of intellectual property rights by right holders or the resort to practices which unreasonably restrain trade or adversely affect the international transfer of technology'.[58] The WTO Working Group on the Interaction of Trade and Competition Policy (1997–2003) systematically explored the competition policy dimensions of WTO rules and the impact of anti-competitive practices of enterprises on international trade; its work promoted the general acceptance among WTO members of mutual synergies between WTO rules and competition law principles (eg on non-discrimination, transparency, procedural fairness, prohibitions of price-fixing cartels, and discriminatory market-sharing agreements).[59] The Group suspended its work on proposals for a possible multilateral framework on competition policy following the WTO Ministerial Conference decisions at Cancun in 2003. Yet, it could be reconvened whenever WTO members should reach agreement on negotiating more precise competition disciplines in the WTO, for instance in view of the fact that more than 130 WTO members (including all five BRICS economies: Brazil, Russia, India, China, and South Africa) now have national competition laws. The inadequacy of WTO rules for restraining anti-competitive abuses of state capitalism (such as forced technology transfer), other trade distortions (eg in new sectors like electronic commerce and digital markets), and SOEs is increasingly recognized as one of the biggest regulatory challenges of WTO members. Recent analyses of competition policies emphasize that—also inside the US—antitrust policies are less and less effectively enforced vis-à-vis powerful market actors (like the FAANG: Facebook, Apple, Amazon, Netflix, and Google) in many economic and technology sectors.[60] Hence, all WTO members, including China, might find it in their national self-interests to de-escalate unilateral trade sanctions against alleged unfair competition. Rather than overloading the WTO dispute settlement procedures with competition-related disputes, the WTO Working Group on the Interaction of Trade and Competition Policy could

[58] On the clarification of the TRIPS rules on unfair competition in the recent WTO panel reports on *Australia—Plain-Packaging of Tobacco Products* (28 June 2018) WT/DS435/R, WT/DS441/R, WT/DS458/R, WT/DS467/R, see Petersmann (n 10), 69, 94ff.

[59] See RD Anderson, WE Kovacic, AC Müller, A Salgueiro, and N Sprorysheva, Competition Policy and the Global Economy: Current Developments and Issues for Reflection, *The George Washington Law Review* 88 (2020) 1421–76.

[60] See T Wu, *The Curse of Bigness: Antitrust in the New Gilded Age* (Colombia Global Reports 2018); J Tepper and D Hearn, *The Myth of Capitalism: Monopolies and the Death of Competition* (Wiley 2018). The Executive Order on promoting competition in the US economy, signed by President Biden on 9 July 2021, may present a generational shift in US competition policy; cf 'Joe Biden styles himself as a 21st century "trust buster"', *Financial Times* 13 July 2021.

be tasked to elaborate member-driven guidelines for additional WTO competition disciplines in particular policy areas (like anti-competitive state-trading, intellectual property practices, and green energy markets).

Ordo-liberalism would suggest that embedding trade competition into social market economies—following the examples of President Franklin D Roosevelt's New Deal of the 1930s, the social market economy progressively established in Germany since the 1960s, the EU law commitments to a competitive social market economy (Article 3 TEU) with guarantees of social rights (eg for education, professional training, access to labour markets, fair working conditions, social protection, and health), and the SDGs accepted by UN member states—could offer coherent, domestic policy responses to the regulatory challenges of economic globalization and changes in technologies (like automation, robotics, and artificial intelligence) without resorting to the general WTO exception rules, which risk being abused. The adoption by the US Congress of President Biden's $1.9 trillion coronavirus relief legislation on 10 March 2021 could enable such a policy reorientation in favour of non-discriminatory, domestic economic reforms. In the WTO, special and differential treatment (S&D) of less-developed WTO member countries should be defined more precisely in terms of local capacity building (as in the WTO Trade Facilitation Agreement), in conformity with the universally agreed 2030 Agenda for Sustainable Development. Developed, less developed and least developed WTO members often disagree on the contents and scope of S&D to be included in different kinds of WTO agreements (eg providing for longer implementation periods, flexibilities, lesser obligations, capacity building, and technical assistance for implementation). The more the disconnect between UN/WTO law and citizens undermines social and democratic support from citizens, the more important become ordo-liberal approaches to applying trade and economic rules not only as rights of governments but also of citizens and other, non-governmental actors in order to promote legal, democratic, and judicial accountability of governance agents vis-à-vis citizens as their democratic principals. The less citizens with, today, universally recognized human rights can perceive WTO rules and dispute settlement procedures as just,[61] the less they are likely to support international rules politically and comply with them voluntarily. Even if the British proposal to transform the G7 into a 'D10' (by adding Australia and Asian democracies like India and South Korea) should be realized, these ten democracies require much broader support by other WTO members for leading democratic and constitutional reforms of the WTO legal and dispute settlement systems. Moreover, democratic alliances defending regional order in transatlantic relations are bound to differ from

[61] On defining justice in terms of 'justification' by agreed procedural, constitutional, distributive, corrective, and commutative principles of justice and equity, as they underlie many GATT/WTO provisions like GATT Article XXIII.1 on 'violation complaints', 'non-violation complaints', and 'situation complaints', cf Petersmann (n 19), 38f, 177ff, 334f.

democratic alliances defending regional order in the Indo-Pacific, or in Africa and in the Americas. And even democracies (like India and South Africa) might block consensus on WTO legal reforms and related plurilateral trade agreements (eg if other democratic WTO members should decide to incorporate plurilaterally agreed standards into their respective WTO schedules of concessions in order to apply them on a non-discriminatory basis towards all WTO members).[62]

[62] In their communication of 19 February 2021 on 'The Legal Status of "Joint Statement Initiatives" and their Negotiated Outcomes' (WTO doc. WT/GC/W/819), India and South Africa emphasized the need for consensus on integrating into WTO law 'PTAs' (eg on electronic commerce, investment facilitation for development, small and medium-sized enterprises, domestic regulation in services) negotiated among only some of the WTO members as a means of overcoming deadlock among all WTO members; their insistence on the WTO's single undertaking approach and consensus requirements for amending the WTO agreements is widely criticized as an attempt at increasing their respective leverage for their negotiation proposals (eg on agricultural subsidies) eluding agreement among WTO members.

7

Rule of Law and Human Rights in Investment Arbitration—Need for Judicial Reforms

Investments are a crucial part not only of the world trading system but even more so of realizing most Sustainable Development Goals (SDGs) like 'greening' and decarbonizing the global economy, promoting public health by providing vaccines to all, and protecting data privacy and cybersecurity in Internet governance. The UN 2030 Agenda acknowledges the important role of foreign investment for creating and financing sustainable development projects like infrastructure projects, medical facilities, water and sewerage systems, power plants, or through the sustainable exploitation and use of a state's natural resources.[1] Similarly, Articles 9–11 of the Paris Agreement provide for financial assistance, technology transfer, and capacity building, assisting less-developed countries to invest in renewable energies and 'green' (environmentally sound) technologies and helping them to transit from brown to green economies. The necessary phasing out of coal-fired power plants and promotion of green energies (eg by feed-in tariffs) will affect existing investments and inevitably give rise to regulatory challenges. For example, which measures will distort competition, amount to indirect expropriation, and require compensation? What role can bilateral investment treaties (BITs) play as incentives for investments in green economies or as impediments to effective regulation of decarbonizing brown economies?

Even though most BITs do not explicitly refer to sustainable development, the more recently concluded BITs tend to include provisions referring to sustainable development issues (eg by reserving sovereign rights to regulate sustainable development goals). From the liberal perspective of utilitarianism, the domination of the world economy during the eighteenth and nineteenth centuries by colonial policies and colonial preferences for overseas trade with European colonial powers and their multinational corporations reflected a money-driven extension of feudal and liberal interest group politics inside the major European trading countries. Colonial excesses like slave trade, colonial trading and shipping monopolies, gunboat diplomacy, opium wars, and related legal privileges and immunities (eg for

[1] UN 2030 Agenda, paras 28, 41, and 67.

Transforming World Trade and Investment Law for Sustainable Development. Ernst-Ulrich Petersmann, Oxford University Press. © Ernst-Ulrich Petersmann 2022. DOI: 10.1093/oso/9780192858023.003.0008

commercial arbitration centres abroad) had been preceded by feudal and authoritarian power politics inside Europe and around the Mediterranean Sea. Until the International Court of Justice (ICJ) judgment in the *ELSI* dispute,[2] most international investment disputes were decided either by recourse to domestic courts or by diplomatic protection of the foreign investor by the home state which, occasionally, submitted the dispute to international courts like the ICJ or its predecessor, the Permanent Court of International Justice. Yet, as illustrated by the *ELSI* judgment delivered by the ICJ more than twenty-five years after the dispute arose between the US investor and the local authorities in Sicily, most foreign investors perceive prior exhaustion of local remedies in national courts—followed by politicized, lengthy, and costly procedures of diplomatic protection and disputes among states in international courts—as insufficient legal and judicial safeguards of investor rights (especially in less developed countries). In addition, other investment disputes in the ICJ—like the 2007, 2010, and 2012 judgments in the *Diallo* dispute—illustrated the limited jurisdiction (eg due to narrow interpretations of the customary law rules on effective nationality and diplomatic protection of company shareholders), long duration (ie more than twenty years), and inadequate remedies of the ICJ for deciding complex investment and human rights disputes after prior exhaustion of local remedies.[3]

From the post-1945 ordo-liberal perspective of European democracies protecting equal economic liberties, private property rights, monetary stability, and rule of law as legal preconditions for non-discriminatory conditions of mutually beneficial trade and competition, the export of investment protection standards and institutions (like arbitration) through rights-based bilateral and multilateral agreements was a logical response to decolonization, foreign nationalizations, the international disagreements on the minimum standards for the protection of foreign property, and the widespread discontent with the related ICJ jurisprudence.[4] Section 7.1 recalls how the first BITs were concluded by Germany and Switzerland since 1959 and laid the foundations for today's global network of more than 3,200 bilateral and multilateral agreements on investment protection standards and investor–state arbitration (ISA) procedures. Yet, civil societies criticize investor biases in ISA practices and contest whether the more than 1,100 publicly known ISA awards extant today truly reflect rule of law at national and international levels as defined by the United Nations (ie as 'a principle of governance in which all persons, institutions and entities, including the State itself, are accountable to

[2] *United States v Italy, ELSI* case, ICJ Reports 1989, 15.

[3] Cf A Vermeer-Künzli, Diallo: Between Diplomatic Protection and Human Rights, *Journal of International Dispute Settlement* 4 (2013) 487.

[4] Cf EU Petersmann, 'German and European Ordo-Liberalism and Constitutionalism in the Post-War Development of International Economic Law' in P Hilpold (ed), *The European International Law Tradition* (Springer 2020), 305–32; N Tzouvala, 'The Ordo-Liberal Origins of Modern International Investment Law: Constructing Competition on a Global Scale', *European Yearbook of International Economic Law* (Springer 2018), 37–54.

laws that are publicly promulgated, equally enforced and independently adjudicated, and which are consistent with internationally recognized human rights').[5] Section 7.2 offers empirical evidence on why complainants, host states, third parties, and arbitrators increasingly invoke human rights as applicable law or relevant systemic context for the settlement of investment disputes. In most cases, however, the impact of such human rights arguments on the outcome of ISA awards remained marginal. Section 7.3 concludes this brief analysis of the post-1945 evolution of international investment law and adjudication by referring to the ongoing proposals and negotiations for reforming the multilateral arbitration procedures elaborated by the International Center for the Settlement of Investment Disputes (ICSID), the UN Commission on International Trade Law (UNCITRAL), and in the international trade and investment agreements of the EU. Numerous less-developed countries review their investment legislation and BITs (eg their protection standards) in order to reconcile investment promotion with the SDGs.[6] The conflicting attitudes among ordo-liberal and neo-liberal countries vis-à-vis appellate review in the World Trade Organization (WTO) are visible also in the ongoing negotiations on whether investment arbitration should provide for appellate review by a standing public law appellate body (AB). Neither the China–EU draft investment agreement signed on 30 December 2020 nor the Regional Comprehensive Economic Partnership Agreement (RCEP) agreement of November 2020 provide for multilateral investment adjudication as proposed by the EU. It seems unlikely that the ISA reform negotiations can serve as a model for reforming the ordo-liberal WTO dispute settlement system.

7.1 Bilateral Investor–State Arbitration: Neo-Liberalism vs Ordo-Liberalism

Germany's conclusion, in 1959, of its first BIT with Pakistan was followed by more than 135 additional BITs protecting foreign direct investments through reciprocal

[5] Cf ML Marceddu and P Ortolani, What Is Wrong with Investment Arbitration? Evidence from a Set of Behavioural Experiments *European Journal of International Law* 31 (2020), 405–28. The protection standards of BITs and of the Energy Charter Treaty (ECT) tend to protect foreign investor rights more comprehensively than the protection of property rights in constitutional law, where governmental restrictions of property rights and their only limited (eg appropriate) financial compensation may be justifiable on grounds of general interests as lawful, general limitation of private rights without being qualified as expropriation requiring prompt, full and effective compensation. Such a balancing between the private property interests of foreign investors and the general interest of the host state in regulating the social dimensions of property rights (eg as in the case of Germany's decision—following the Fukushima nuclear accident in Japan—to phase out nuclear energy) was regularly not provided for in the protection standards of BITs until recently (eg depending on the drafting of new BIT provisions acknowledging the host state's rights to regulate).

[6] See, eg, GM Zagel, India's International Investment Agreements and Sustainable Development: Friends or Foes? *Indian Journal of International Economic Law* XII (2020), 1–39.

guarantees of non-discrimination, full protection and security, fair and equitable treatment, access to judicial remedies and other legal protection standards aimed at transforming international investment law (IIL) from a Westphalian into a more cosmopolitan system, as it evolved since the 1960s in essentially 5 phases:

- Following the first BIT between Germany and Pakistan in 1959, the number of BITs has dynamically increased to now more than 3,200 agreements. Yet, the first-generation BITs did not provide for direct access of the foreign investor to independent international arbitration.
- The 1965 World Bank Convention establishing the ICSID, which entered into force in 1966 (following twenty ratifications), offered a multilateral legal framework for institutionalized, transnational arbitration of investment disputes based on consent between the states and investors involved. The first ICSID disputes were based on investor–state contracts[7] or on national legislation that provided for direct access of foreign investors to international arbitration.[8]
- Treaty-based investor–state arbitration was provided for only in the second-generation BITs concluded since 1969. In view of its many advantages for private investors (eg in terms of direct access to independent international arbitration usually without prior exhaustion of local remedies, direct control of the procedures without dependence on diplomatic protection, availability of institutionalized ICSID procedures), most modern BITs provide for treaty-based investor–state arbitration.[9]
- In contrast to the less than 400 BITs concluded prior to 1989, the number of new BITs increased dramatically since the 1990s and exceeds now 3,200 BITs and corresponding treaty provisions in free trade agreements (like USMCA chapter 14) and other sectorial agreements (like the ECT, which entered into force in 1998). The number of BITs and related ISA among LDCs also continues to increase.
- Since the 1990s, the number of treaty-based ICSID disputes, or investor–state disputes based on UNCITRAL or other commercial arbitration procedures, and the emergence of case law referring to ISA awards and related ICSID annulment decisions or national court decisions as relevant precedents, increased dramatically. The general ICSID and BIT provisions on arbitration procedures (eg transparency of the arbitral procedure, burden and standard of proof, multiplicity of procedures, annulment, and execution) and on substantive standards (eg protection of good faith, reasonable expectations, non-discriminatory treatment, proportionality, due process in expropriations, fair

[7] The first ICSID dispute based on an investor–state contract was *Holliday Inns v Morocco*, ICSID Case No ARB/72/1.

[8] The first ICSID dispute based on national legislation was *SPP v Egypt*, ICSID Case No ARB/84/3.

[9] The first ICSID dispute based on a BIT clause was *AAPL v Sri Lanka*, ICSID Report IV, at 250.

and equitable treatment, full protection and security and of public interests of the host state, prohibitions of denial of justice and unjust enrichment, compensation also in case of indirect expropriations) leave open many specific legal questions (eg concerning also their relationships to WTO law, EU law, and commercial arbitration). Judicial clarification of incomplete investment treaty rules and principles (eg on the necessity of governmental emergency measures) has progressively developed and clarified IIL. Yet, there is also widespread criticism of incoherencies among, and institutional biases in ISA practices, for instance due to inadequate transparency and inclusiveness of arbitration procedures, conflicts of interests of commercial arbitrators (eg when acting also as advisors to TNCs (transnational corporations)), and their sometimes inadequate regard to public national and international law and jurisprudence. This need for protecting the regulatory duties of states and the public law nature of ISA prompt ever more states to revise their BITs and related arbitration procedures. The ordo-liberal traditions of European economic regulation have prompted the EU to promote multilateral investment court procedures (eg in the free trade agreements (FTAs) of the EU with Canada, Singapore, and Vietnam) strengthening the public law dimensions of investment arbitration.

7.2 Legitimacy Challenges and Human Rights in Investor–State Arbitration

How should investment arbitrators and judges respond to the criticism that the legal privileging of foreign investors in IIL and ISA risks undermining the human rights of citizens? Justice (eg in the sense of justifying law by the hypothetical consent of all affected citizens), the customary law rules on treaty interpretation, and the universal recognition of human rights require construing IIL in conformity with the human rights obligations of states rather than only in terms of economic utility and autonomy (eg of investors, arbitrators, and states). Prioritizing foreign investments risks undermining constitutional justice and human rights law. In ISA, complainants, respondents, third parties (eg *amici curiae*), and arbitrators increasingly invoke human rights as procedural due process rights, part of the applicable law or relevant context for systemic interpretation. Yet, just as the adoption of the proposed UN Agreement on Business and Human Rights remains contested, so remain judicial references to human rights—as applicable law or systemic interpretation—in the settlement of investment disputes controversial. Arguably, *judicial references* to human rights law (HRL) can increase the source- and process-based normative legitimacy and result-oriented, internal and external social legitimacy of economic adjudication. Yet, judicial administration of justice is no substitute for *legislative reforms* of IIL, which are necessary—as discussed in sub-section 7.3—for protecting constitutional and human rights integrity, deliberative and constitutional democracy and public reason in multilevel governance of public goods (PGs) (like sustainable development). HRL requires *legislative* and *judicial* reforms aimed at limiting neo-liberal interest group politics and authoritarian state capitalism in IIL and ISA.

7.2.1 Legitimacy Challenges of Investment Arbitration

The EU negotiations of FTAs with Canada and the United States providing for transatlantic investment protection and ISA revealed what EU trade commissioner Malmström called huge scepticism in civil societies over whether legal and judicial privileges for foreign investors remain justifiable in relations among constitutional democracies with well-functioning domestic judicial systems.[10] Even from an investor perspective, the legal findings in the more than 1,100 publicly known ISA awards tend to be fact-specific and replete with inconsistent interpretations of protection standards (like the scope of the most-favoured nation clause, the extent of security exceptions, the nature of umbrella clauses), thereby undermining legal security.[11] From a human rights perspective, the claims advanced also by Canadian constitutional lawyers like David Schneiderman—that the 'constitution-like features' of BITs aimed 'to bring constitutional order to international economic law' and resembled 'the ordoliberal version of the rule of law'[12]—remained methodologically and normatively unconvincing.[13] Constitutional guarantees of equal private autonomy rights—also in the field of commercial arbitration subject to the

[10] Cf EU Petersmann, 'Democratic Legitimacy of the CETA and TTIP Agreements?' in T Rensmann (ed), *Mega-Regional Trade Agreements and the Future of International Trade and Investment Law* (Springer 2017), 37–59. The criticism by human rights advocates of ISA in relations among developed and less-developed countries—eg that ISA among capital-exporting developed countries and less-developed, capital-importing countries was not only designed to protect basic requirements of justice like non-discrimination, fair treatment, prohibition of expropriation without compensation, and due process of law; BITs were often concluded with despotic and corrupt governments that disregarded human rights and enriched themselves through collaboration with foreign investors (eg in the oil and minerals sector)—is hardly relevant in relations among the transatlantic democracies.

[11] An extreme example were the *CME* and *Lauder* cases against the Czech Republic, where related entities brought cases arising out of the same facts against the Czech Republic under the Netherlands–Czech Republic BIT and the comparable BIT between the United States and the Czech Republic. The two tribunals reached different conclusions as to the law and its application to the facts; cf *CME v The Czech Republic*, Award of 13 September 2001 (https://www.italaw.com/sites/default/files/case-documents/ita0180.pdf) and *R.S. Lauder v The Czech Republic*, Award of 3 September 2001, (https://www.italaw.com/sites/default/files/case-documents/ita0451.pdf).

[12] Cf D Schneiderman, 'Global Constitutionalism and International Economic Law: The Case of International Investment Law' in *European Yearbook of International Economic Law 2016* (Springer 2017), 23–44.

[13] Cf EU Petersmann, 'From Fragmentation to Constitutionalisation of International Economic Law? Comments on Schneiderman's Constitutionalism' in *European Yearbook of International Economic Law 2016* (Springer 2017), 45–65. On the interpretation of investment protection standards by arbitration tribunals, see A Reinisch and S Schreuer, *International Protection of Investments. The Substantive Standards* (CUP 2020).

proviso that national courts (eg if requested to enforce private commercial arbitration awards) must review the legal consistency of the awards with the public policy and constitutional law in the country where the complainant seeks recognition and enforcement of the award—must be construed and applied in conformity also with procedural human rights of access to justice and substantive (eg *jus cogens*) human rights guarantees, not only for foreign investors but also for other citizens affected by the investments (like workers in the host country).[14] As BITs fail to effectively limit market failures as well as governance failures and constitutional failures in host states and usually avoid references to the human rights obligations of both home and host states of investors, they do not meet the constitutive and regulative principles advocated by ordo-liberal economic constitutionalism aimed at protecting a social market economy based on equal constitutional rights, institutional checks and balances and legislative restraints of market failures through competition, environmental and social laws and remedies.

The social legitimacy of courts (eg understood as socially accepted authority) depends not only on the internal rules constituting the legal regimes in which the courts operate. It is also influenced by the principles of justice underlying legal and judicial systems, and by judicial jurisprudence promoting social acceptance in the constituencies concerned. For example, due to the lack of judicial independence inside China's communist party state, the source legitimacy, procedural legitimacy, and result-based legitimacy of Chinese courts are widely perceived as inadequate, even if national courts inside China offer low-cost judgments compared with more expensive arbitration or international dispute settlement procedures. Comparative studies of international trade and investment courts point to both converging developments (eg in judicial interpretations of national treatment and most-favoured-nation treatment obligations in trade and investment agreements, proportionality balancing) and diverging structures (eg regarding *prospective remedies* in WTO dispute settlement procedures, *retroactive reparation of injury* in investment arbitration, cooperation between national courts and investment arbitral tribunals, lack of similar cooperation among national and WTO trade tribunals).[15] Evaluating the legitimacy and comparative advantages of national, regional, and worldwide trade and investment courts and of their increasing interactions raises also political, sociological, and moral legitimacy questions going beyond 'positive law',[16] for instance whether the legitimacy of international courts is ultimately a matter of justifiability towards individuals (eg in terms of protecting citizens against arbitrary domination, protecting equal freedoms as individual rights) rather than only vis-à-vis government agents representing states (eg in terms of

14 Cf A Jaksic, *Arbitration and Human Rights* (Lang 2002).

15 Cf J Kurtz, *The WTO and International Investment Law. Converging Systems* (CUP 2016).

16 Cf G Ulfstein, M Zhang, R Howse, and H Ruiz-Fabri (eds), *The Legitimacy of International Trade Courts and Tribunals* (CUP 2017).

helping them solve collective action problems).[17] The behaviour of international judges is influenced not only by law but also by political constraints and uncertainty depending on their independence, accountability, and the multilevel allocation and separation of powers (eg in Chinese arbitration centres and courts, which are perceived as failing adequate legitimacy standards like judicial independence from political interference, impartiality, due process of law, legal expertise in international law).

7.2.2 Human Rights Law Can Increase Input- and Output-Legitimacy of ISA

Foreign investments (eg in exploitation of natural resources) affect the interests and rights not only of investors but also of workers, consumers, competitors, and many other people in host states. Yet, most BITs focus one-sidedly on the legal and judicial protection of foreign investors without offering similar legal and judicial protection to other natural or legal persons, which may be adversely affected by foreign investments or by ISA awarding foreign investors financial compensation (often amounting to millions and, recently, billions of dollars). In no other area of international law have natural and legal persons received such comprehensive, procedural, and substantive legal privileges as in IIL and ISA. Even if domestic courts found the property rights claimed by foreign investors to be unconstitutional and invalid,[18] or adversely affected domestic citizens sought legal protection by regional human rights bodies,[19] violations of domestic constitutional law

[17] Cf EU Petersmann, 'International Dispute Settlement and the Position of Individuals under EU and International Law' in M Cremona, A Thies, and R Wessels (eds), *The European Union and International Dispute Settlement* (Hart 2017), 213–34.

[18] For example, in *Awdi v Romania* (ICSID Case No ARB/10/13, award of 2 March 2015), the arbitration Tribunal noted that the property rights claimed by the investor had been found unconstitutional and invalid by Romania's Constitutional Court; this had breached the legitimate expectations of the investor (as protected by Romania's fair and equitable treatment obligations under the BIT) and required compensation of the damages and related expenses of the investor.

[19] For example, in the *Endorois* case, the African Commission on Human and Peoples' Rights confirmed that the eviction—without consultation or compensation—of hundreds of families belonging to the indigenous Endorois people from their ancestral lands to create game reserves for tourism, and to grant concessions for forestry and mining, violated the Community's rights to protection of religion, culture, property, and freedom to dispose of its natural resources and wealth; *Centre for Minority Rights Development (Kenya) on behalf of Endorois Welfare Council v Kenya*, Merits and Provisional Measures, Decision African Commission HPR No 276/03 (25 November 2009). In the *Kilwa* case, the same African Commission found that the government and military of the Democratic Republic of Congo, with support from an Australian-Canadian mining company operating a copper and silver company near Kilwa, had engaged in extrajudicial executions, torture, arbitrary arrests, and forced displacement violating numerous rights under the African Charter on Human and Peoples' Rights; *Institute for Human Rights and Development in Africa and Others v Democratic Republic of Congo*, Communication 393/10 (2017). In *Sawhayamaxa Indigenous Community v Paraguay*, the Inter-American Court of Human Rights rejected the argument that the governmental taking of the community's ancestral lands and related violations of the Inter-American Convention on Human Rights could be justified by the governmental sale

or HRL may not prevent ISA awards protecting foreign investor rights as defined in BITs. In response to the long-standing civil society criticism that the prioritization of procedural and substantive investor rights in IIL and ISA may unduly disregard the rights of other persons (eg labour rights of local workers, citizens affected by environmental pollution), the complainants, respondents, arbitrators, and third parties participating in ISA are increasingly invoking human rights in ISA—as procedural due process rights, part of the applicable law, or relevant context for systemic interpretation—in order to prevent, or remedy, abuses of human rights (eg of indigenous people) by foreign investors and host states. Examples also include cases of local governments engaging or colluding in violations of human rights, particularly if domestic laws and courts in host and home states failed to offer effective remedies. This sub-section briefly discusses the limited possibilities for investment arbitrators and judges to enhance judicial administration of justice in investment disputes (sub-section 7.2.2.1) and the past efforts at rendering HRL more effective in ISA (sub-section 7.2.2.2).

7.2.2.1 Increasing invocation of human rights by investors, host states, third parties, and arbitrators in ISA

HRL, property law, and investment law have evolved separately based on different structures and value principles.[20] Is it wise that most BITs and ISA awards do not refer to human rights in view of the often diverging legal traditions of, and views on HRL in the home and host states of the foreign investor, in national and international jurisdictions and among commercial arbitrators?[21] Is there any need for invoking HRL in ISA in view of the fact that investment treaties and ISA procedures tend to specify the applicable protection standards and due process guarantees in greater detail than the often vague human rights guarantees of private property and access to justice? Does the increasing invocation of human rights in ISA confirm a change in international HRL[22] and in the commercial law culture

of the land to a foreign investor and by the protection of this foreign property through a BIT; cf judgment on merits, reparations, and costs of 29 March 2006, Inter-Am. Ct.HR (ser. C), No 146.

[20] For instance, HRL perceives governmental restrictions as exceptions that need to be justified (eg in terms of legality, public interests, proportionality) subject to limited standards of review (eg due to margins of appreciation). BITs protect foreign investments through international obligations (rather than exceptions from fundamental rights) and tend to prescribe full, prompt, and effective compensation as a condition of the legality of expropriation of investor rights.

[21] Most UN human rights conventions—like many national Constitutions (eg of Canada)—do not provide for protection of private property rights.

[22] Note the *obiter dicta* by the tribunal in *Urbaser v Argentina*: 'international law accepts corporate social responsibility as a standard of crucial importance for companies operating in the field of international commerce. This standard includes commitments to comply with human rights in the framework of those entities' operations conducted in countries other than the country of their seat or incorporation. In light of this more recent development, it can no longer be admitted that companies operating internationally are immune from becoming subjects of international law.' *Urbaser S.A. and Consorcio de Aguas Bilbao Bizkaia, Bilbao Biskaia Ur Partzuergoa v Argentine Republic*, ICSID Case No ARB/07/26, Award, 8 December 2016, paras 1194–1195. ('*Urbaser v Argentina*'). See also UN Human

of many arbitrators avoiding references to HRL? How should investment adjudicators define and protect procedural and substantive rule of law in transnational ISA as a restraint on abuses of public and private power (eg in cases of bribery and corruption) and reconcile private and public interests? The answers to these questions often remain controversial, just as the UN negotiations on implementing the UN Guiding Principles on Business and Human Rights remain contested. Does judicial avoidance of such controversies enhance the judicial task of ISA to settle investment disputes?

Path-dependent investment law approaches are challenged by civil society claims that the universal recognition of human rights also protects access to justice, judicial remedies, and rights to justification requiring that governmental restrictions of individual rights remain consistent with human rights and procedural and substantive principles of justice.[23] Human rights are increasingly recognized as part of the applicable law in ISA procedures (eg as defined in Article 42 of the ISCID Convention) and as relevant rules of international law for systemic interpretation of IIL pursuant to Article 31.3(c) of the Vienna Convention on the Law of Treaties (VCLT) (eg in conformity with regional and UN human rights conventions accepted by host and home states of investors). Hence, 'justice as justification'[24] prompts participants in ISA to increasingly challenge investment regulations from the point of view of human and constitutional rights of adversely affected investors, workers, consumers, and other citizens (eg suffering from adverse impacts of foreign investments), for instance by:

- construing BIT jurisdiction, applicable law, and human rights clauses in conformity with the human rights obligations of states;
- defining protected investments in conformity with local and international law;
- interpreting the customary rules of treaty interpretation, BIT references to public interests, investment law protection standards (like full protection and security, fair and equitable treatment, non-discrimination), rules on awarding damages and quantification of compensation in conformity with human rights;

Rights Council, Eighth Session 7 April 2008, 'Protect, Respect and Remedy: A Framework for Business and Human Rights. Report of the Special Representative of the Secretary-General on the issue of human rights and transnational corporations and other business enterprises, John Ruggie', UN Doc A/HRC/8/5, para 54: 'whereas governments define the scope of legal compliance, the broader scope of the responsibility to respect (human rights) is defined by social expectations—as part of what is sometimes called a company's social licence to operate'. Such soft law obligations may evolve into hard international law (as defined in Article 38 of the Statute of the International Court of Justice) by incorporation into the formal sources of national or international law.

[23] Cf n 5.

[24] Cf R Forst, *The Right to Justification. Elements of a Constructivist Theory of Justice* (Columbia UP 2012).

- expanding judicial reason-giving, third-party participation, and legal accountability of public and corporate actors involved; and
- supplementing commercial law-approaches to ISA (eg emphasizing private autonomy of investors and arbitrators) and public international law-approaches (eg emphasizing sovereignty and responsibility of home and host states) by constitutional law-methodologies acknowledging constitutional duties of states and adjudicators to reconcile protection of foreign investments with broader state and judicial duties to protect public interests, human and constitutional rights.[25]

In the limited number of investment disputes before the ICJ initiated at the request of home states exercising diplomatic protection for foreign investments by their nationals, human rights were invoked only exceptionally.[26] In investment disputes initiated directly by investors in national and European courts like the European Court of Human Rights (ECtHR) and the European Court of Justice (CJEU), private property and investor rights tend to be protected with due respect for democratic regulation aimed at reconciling economic and non-economic rights and public interests.[27] In ISA, empirical studies confirm that, *inter alia*, human rights of access to water, health protection, access to courts, due process of law, and the rights of indigenous peoples are increasingly invoked before ISA tribunals, notably if jurisdiction and remedies gaps are perceived to exist in domestic legal systems of host countries and in non-binding UN recommendations on business and human rights adopted by ever more international organizations and transnational corporations. The role of human rights in ISA—and the kind of human rights invoked—vary depending on the actor who (i) introduces them into the dispute and who (ii) asserts human rights and their violation. These may be investors, home and host states, *amici curiae*, and the arbitrators themselves. Investors have introduced human rights either as independent claims (eg violations of human rights of investors) or in support of the alleged violation of a BIT (eg to substantiate certain interpretations of treaty terms such as expropriation). Host states have occasionally invoked human rights as respondents to justify governmental limitations of

[25] Cf EU Petersmann, 'Introduction and Summary: "Administration of Justice" in International Investment Law and Adjudication' in PM Dupuy, F Francioni, and EU Petersmann (eds), *Human Rights in International Investment Law and Arbitration* (OUP 2009), 3–39. It remains contested whether protection of foreign investments should be limited by proportionality balancing rather than by the more limited necessity exception of international state responsibility law; how to weigh foreign investments and adversely affected public interests; and how to define the indivisible core of interdependent civil, political, economic, social, and cultural human rights with due respect for constitutional pluralism and sovereign rights to refuse ratifying UN human rights conventions. Arbitral discretion is especially wide regarding quantification of compensation (eg by taking into account an investor's contributory fault so as to avoid inequitable outcomes).

[26] Cf Vermeer-Künzli (n 3).

[27] Cf V Kosta and B de Witte, 'Human Rights Norms in the Court of Justice of the European Union' in M Scheinin (ed), *Human Rights Norms in 'Other' International Courts* (CUP 2019), 263ff.

investor rights in terms of protecting human rights of third persons. The success of such defences hinges upon whether the regulatory objective (eg health protection) and proportionality balancing play a role in determining the breach of investor rights, or whether only the severity and impact on the investor are the decisive criteria. The respondent state may also introduce counterclaims alleging human rights abuses by the investor or related violations of corporate social responsibilities. Finally, arbitrators have occasionally referred to human rights *ex officio* in their reasoning (eg for justifying admission of third party submissions including human rights arguments).[28]

7.2.2.1.1 Human rights as investor claims

In past investment disputes, investors invoked human rights either in support of claims based on breaches of the applicable IIL (eg based on systemic interpretation pursuant to Article 31:3(c) VCLT) or independently (eg claiming that the host state had—in addition to breaching an investment agreement—also violated its human rights obligations, and that these human rights violations were covered by the broad jurisdiction and applicable law clauses underlying the Investor–State Dispute Settlement (ISDS) case). For example, in *Biloune v Ghana*, a Syrian investor based his claim on violations of human rights (arbitrary detention and deportation) besides contractual breaches of an agreement between him and Ghana. In this case, the tribunal declared that it lacked jurisdiction to rule on human rights issues as an independent cause of action. This conclusion was based on the jurisdictional clause in the agreement, according to which arbitration only covers disputes arising in respect of the enterprise. The actions alleged to be human rights violations were nevertheless taken into consideration when deciding on expropriation. The relation was deemed sufficient for factoring it in when determining the severity of the intrusion, which precisely for that reason was found to be tantamount to expropriation.[29]

The investment arbitrations following Russia's criminal proceedings against its successful oil company Yukos and its management for tax evasion,[30] and the parallel human rights complaints before the ECtHR, reveal diverging conceptions of property and diverging judicial methodologies in HRL and IIL. The tribunals in *Quasar de Valors SICAV SA et al v Russian Federation* and *Veteran Petroleum Ltd*

[28] For a much more detailed discussion of recent ISA awards referring to human rights see: EU Petersmann, 'Can Invocation of Human Rights Enhance Justice and Social Legitimacy in Investment Adjudication?' *Indian Journal of International Economic Law* XII (2020), 58–105. Sub-section 7.2.2.1.1 discusses only a few selected cases as examples of some of the regulatory and judicial challenges.

[29] *Biloune and Marine Drive Complex Ltd v Ghana Investments Centre and the Govt. of Ghana*, Award Jurisdiction and Liability, 27 October 1989, 95 ILR 184, at 30.

[30] *Hulley Enterprises Ltd (Cyprus) v Russian Federation*, PCA Case No 2005-03/AA226, Final Award (18 July 2014); *Yukos Universal Ltd (Isle of Man) v Russian Federation*, PCA Case No 2005-04/AA227, Final Award, § 765 (18 July 2014); *Quasar de Valors SICAV SA et al v Russian Federation*, SCC Case No 24/2007, Award, § 25 (20 July 2012); *Veteran Petroleum Ltd. (Cyprus) v Russian Federation*, PCA Case No 2005-05/AA228, Final Award, § 765 (18 July 2014).

(Cyprus) v Russian Federation denied any binding force of the ECtHR's jurisprudence on the tribunals, yet declared to take them into consideration when needed. In *Quasar de Valors SICAV SA et al v Russian Federation,* the tribunal stressed the differences of the required assessment; unlawfulness or *bona fide* regulations did not play a role for determining the existence of an expropriation under IIL, which was primarily aimed at inducing foreign investment. Even though the assessments of the ECtHR did not have any legal force for the given proceedings, the tribunal discussed the arguments brought forward before the ECtHR. In *Veteran Petroleum Ltd. (Cyprus) v Russian Federation,* Russia invoked *res judicata* as a ground for lack of jurisdiction by pointing to the ECtHR proceeding. The tribunal responded that it was not a human rights court; it would assess the alleged human rights violations of the individuals linked to Yukos as part of the factual matrix of the claimants' complaints that the Russian Federation violated its obligations under the ECT.[31] No legal force was ascribed to ECtHR judgments for the arbitration proceedings; the human rights violations played only a role in the assessment of violations of the ECT. While human rights courts protect *human rights* against undue governmental restraints, ISA tends to interpret BITs as *international obligations* protecting *foreign investments* regardless of whether investors invoke HRL. ISA may prioritize procedural autonomy of participants in ISA (eg to insist on confidential, bilateral arbitration without publication of awards).

7.2.2.1.2 Human rights as a defence of the host state

In past ISA cases, host states invoked human rights at the jurisdiction, merits or quantum phases of the arbitral proceedings in order to persuade tribunals that (i) they lacked jurisdiction (eg because the investment had been made in violation of applicable domestic HRL); (ii) no investment protection standards had been violated (eg because the investor had no legitimate expectations that his investment project and related government regulations could disregard HRL); (iii) damages ought to be calculated in a certain manner (eg in case of complicity in human rights violations, or of non-discriminatory, non-compensable regulations protecting the human rights obligations of the host state in a severe financial crisis); and/or (iv) the tribunal should accept jurisdiction for counterclaims by the state for damages due to human rights violations caused by the foreign investor in the conduct of its investment project.[32] The latter situation arose in *Urbaser v Argentina,* where a tribunal interpreted Article 46 ICSID and the BIT as allowing for host state

[31] *Veteran v Russian* (n 30) §§ 76, 765.

[32] Cf F Baetens, 'Invoking Human Rights: A Useful Line of Attack or a Defence Tool for States in Investor–State-Dispute Settlement?' in Scheinin (n 27), Chapter 8. Even though focusing on environmental law rather than HRL, in *Burlington Resources Inc v Republic of Ecuador* (ICSID Case No ARB/08/5), the Decision on Counterclaims of 7 February 2017 made history by ordering the investor to pay more than $39 million to Ecuador as compensation for the costs of restoring environmental damage caused by the complainant (a mining company).

counterclaims and engaged in a discussion of such a claim based on human rights (like the right to water) and corresponding corporate obligations accepted by the investor.[33] Most often, human rights only play a minor role as justification for state measures undertaken to comply with HRL.

For instance, the duty of the state to ensure just and favourable conditions of work may compel states to enact legislation that is to the detriment of the investors' profit. Host states often invoke their regulatory discretion without specifying their concrete human rights obligations in investment disputes. Tribunals have recurrently stressed that the objective behind a state measure does not play a role for their assessment of potential BIT breaches.[34] Even in cases in which a regulation's objective was discussed, the examination tends to focus on general terms—such as public/social welfare or public policy—without engaging with concrete human rights obligations of the host state. One exception concerns the right to water cases, which illustrate the diverse possibilities of approaching human rights justifications. The right to water is part of the International Covenant on Economic, Social and Cultural Rights (ICESCR);[35] it is also recognized in other human rights treaties, and was confirmed in a 2010 UN General Assembly resolution as well as in a 2012 UN Human Rights Council resolution as being part of HRL.[36] The water-related investment disputes mostly arose following the privatization of water supply and sewage systems and subsequent termination of concessions (or tariff freezing) by the state authorities in order to secure adequate access to water at affordable prices, notably in response to Argentina's emergency measures mitigating the social impact of its economic and financial crisis starting in 1999.

In *Azurix*, the tribunal failed 'to understand the incompatibility' with human rights as the facts had not been sufficiently established.[37] In seeking guidance in the case law of the ECtHR for interpreting the scope of property rights and the role that public purpose ought to play for determining expropriation, the Tribunal concluded that the public purpose of a measure plays a less significant role when the affected individual is a non-national. In *Siemens*, the human rights relevance was rejected because Argentina failed to develop the argument that state measures to protect the human rights of domestic citizens may justify expropriation of foreign investors without full compensation.[38] In *Suez/Vivendi*, Argentina—as well as five

[33] *Urbaser v Argentina* (n 22), §§ 1144, 1188–92, 1200. As most BITs do not mention counterclaims, ISA has tended to reject such claims on grounds of lack of jurisdiction, inadmissibility (eg due to lack of a close 'connection' with the main claim), or lack of legal obligations of the investor concerned.

[34] See, eg, *Compañia del Desarrollo de Santa Elena SA v Republic of Costa Rica*, ICSID Case No ARB/96/1, Final Award, a § 72 (17 February 2000).

[35] According to General Comment 15 the right to water is part of the right to an adequate standard of living (Article 11), to adequate housing and adequate food (Article 11), and of the highest attainable standard of health (Article 12); Committee on Economic, Social and Cultural Rights (CESCR), *General Comment 15, The right to water*, § 3, UN Doc. E/C.12/2002/11 (20 January 2003).

[36] Cf P Thielbörger, *The Right(s) to Water. The Multilevel Governance of a Unique Human Right* (Springer 2014).

[37] *Azurix Corp v Argentina Republic*, ICSID Case No ARB/01/12, Award, § 261 (14 July 2006).

[38] *Siemens v Argentina*, ICSID Case No ARB/02/8, Award, §§ 79, 121 (6 February 2007).

non-governmental organizations as *amici*—stressed the importance of the right to water that Argentina aimed to protect by freezing water tariffs. The tribunal acknowledged that safeguarding sufficient water supply was 'vital for the health and well-being of 10 million people'.[39] Nevertheless, it concluded that adopting measures in breach of investors' rights were not the only means available. The tribunal stated that human rights obligations as well as BIT obligations must be respected equally, which it found to be possible in the given case. In *SAUR International v Argentina*, Argentina explicitly argued that its most basic human rights obligation—with constitutional hierarchy in the Argentinian legal system—made it indispensable for Argentina to intervene in the investors' business; such human rights protection could not constitute an expropriation. The tribunal responded by emphasizing 'that human rights in general, and the right to water in particular, are one of the various sources that the tribunal should take into account to resolve the dispute'; however, Argentina had the possibility to comply with its human rights obligations while compensating the investor.[40]

In other Argentinian crisis cases, the defence claims were based on the necessity clause in the US–Argentina BIT (which was interpreted in the light of customary international law[41] or of Article XX GATT)[42] or on the 'exceptional circumstances', which should have influenced the 'legitimate expectations' of the investors.[43] The precise criteria for preclusion of liability differed depending on the legal interpretation of the necessity exception, for example as being based on the customary law rules on state responsibility (eg excluding recognition of necessity of emergency measures if the state could have prevented the emergency situation) or on more flexible treaty exceptions providing for proportionality balancing between the competing rights and legal values concerned. As explained in the *Continental Casualty* award, interpreting BIT exceptions similar to the WTO jurisprudence regarding GATT Article XX enables arbitrators to balance the competing rights and obligations more flexibly.

In *Philip Morris v Uruguay*, the dispute concerned restrictions on the packaging of cigarettes. The claimants argued that Uruguay's restrictions amounted to an expropriation of their intellectual property rights.[44] The tribunal recalled that public health protection is widely accepted as an expression of the state's police powers

[39] *Suez et al v Argentine Re*, ICSID Case No ARB/03/19, Decision on Liability (30 July 2010), §§ 252, 256, 260

[40] *SAUR International SA v Republic of Argentine*, ICSID Case No ARB/04/4, Decision on Jurisdiction and Liability, §§ 328, 330–1 (6 June 2012).

[41] For example: *CMS Gas Transmission Co v Argentine Republic*, ICSID Case No ARB/01/8, Award, §§ 315–17 (12 May 2005)

[42] *Continental Casualty Co. v Argentine Republic*, ICSID Case No ARB/03/9, Award, §§ 192–5 (5 September 2008)

[43] *Total SA v Argentine Republic*, ICSID Case No ARB/04/01, Decision on Liability, 308–14 (27 December 2010).

[44] *Philip Morris Brands Sàrl, Philip Morris Products SA and Abal Hermanos SA v Oriental Republic of Uruguay*, Award (2016) ICSID Case No ARB/10/7.

in accordance with international customary law. By applying the ECtHR's doctrine of margin of appreciation, the tribunal held that any state measure that is reasonable, not arbitrary, non-discriminatory, adopted in good faith, and not wholly disproportionate, does not constitute a breach of expropriation.[45] Specific weight was given to the fact that public health is protected by Uruguay's Constitution and in numerous international treaties (like investment treaties, the Framework Convention on Tobacco Control). Uruguay's tobacco packaging restrictions were found to be non-discriminatory and proportionate limitations of intellectual property rights that did not amount to illegal expropriation.

7.2.2.1.3 Human rights introduced by third party interveners

As host states tend to justify their regulatory action by reference to public policy concerns, the participation of third parties is an important avenue for bringing in concrete human rights interests that otherwise risk being ignored. Third party interventions by civil society groups as *amici curiae* are increasing. Such interveners often act as advocates for affected populations or communities in response to the reluctance of governments to introduce their own human rights duties into the investment dispute. The human rights argumentation may play a role for the acceptance of an *amicus* submission when ISA tribunals acknowledge that public interests are at stake. *Amici* submissions may promote the examination of human rights issues as part of the investment dispute.

Amicus curiae participation started with *Methanex v US* in 2001.[46] The applicable North American Free Trade Agreement (NAFTA) and UNCITRAL procedural rules did not include provisions on third-party intervention. The tribunal nevertheless declared that it had the power to accept third-party submissions in view of the public interests involved.[47] *Suez/Vivendi* was the first ISA where an arbitration tribunal working under ICSID procedures decided to accept participation of civil society organizations as *amicus curiae* even though the complaining companies had objected to it. It stated that the given case 'involved matters of public interest of such a nature that have traditionally led courts and other tribunals to receive *amicus* submissions from suitable non-parties'; 'the investment dispute centres around the water distribution and sewage systems of a large metropolitan area'.[48] In the decision on the merits, the tribunal explicitly responded to the human rights argumentation by Argentina and the *amici*; it made clear that it saw no incompatibility between the right to water and the BIT obligations and

[45] *Philip Morris v Uruguay*, Award (n 44) § 305. The application of the ECtHR's margin of appreciation doctrine was sharply criticized in the *Concurring and Dissenting Opinion of Co-Arbitrator Gary Born* (2016) ICSID Case No ARB/10/7, §§ 87, 138.

[46] *Methanex Corpn v United States of America*, UNCITRAL, Decision of the Tribunal on Petitions from Third Persons to intervene as *amici curiae* (15 January 2001).

[47] *Methanex Corpn v United States of America*, § 49.

[48] *Suez et al v Argentine Republic*, ICSID Case No ARB/03/19, Order in Response to a Petition for Transparency and Participation as Amicus Curiae (19 May 2005), §§ 19, 20.

examined Argentina's plea of the defence of necessity in terms of Article 25 of the Draft Articles on State Responsibility (codifying the customary rules on state responsibility) without giving any relevance to the human rights at stake.[49]

In *UPS v Canada* (2007), the tribunal made no reference to human rights in the acceptance of the *amicus* submission; it followed the argumentation of the *amici* by rejecting the parts of the claim that were based on labour rights, yet without explicit reference to the *amici* nor to their arguments.[50] In *Suez v Argentina*, the tribunal accepted the *amicus* submission on the ground that the operation of water and sanitary systems affects human rights.

This connection also led the *Biwater Gauff v Tanzania* tribunal to accept *amicus* participation; however, in its final award, there is no reference to the human rights raised in the submission. This case law suggests that the rationale behind accepting third-party intervention is not primarily to ensure legal remedies for affected individuals or communities; third-party intervention is rather meant to assist the tribunal in evaluating public interests and enhancing the transparency and legitimacy of the investment arbitration concerned. For example, in accepting an *amicus* submission, the *Philip Morris v Uruguay* tribunal referred to the fact that 'granting the request would support the transparency of the proceeding and its acceptability by users at large'.[51] As stated by the tribunal in *Suez*, the

> purpose of *amicus* submissions is to help the Tribunal arrive at a correct decision by providing it with arguments, and expertise and perspectives that the parties may not have provided. The Tribunal will therefore only accept *amicus* submissions from persons who establish to the Tribunal's satisfaction that they have the expertise, experience, and independence to be of assistance in this case.[52]

7.2.2.1.4 Human rights introduced by adjudicators ex officio

Arbitrators have also referred to human rights *ex officio*, that is without having a dispute party referring to the specific argument. This was mainly the case in the context of determining procedural rights (eg promoting transparency of ISA in disputes involving public interests transcending the two parties), admitting *amicus curiae* submissions, and clarifying the scope of property rights, the existence of an expropriation, and the amount of compensation. For instance, in *Azurix*, the tribunal sought guidance in the ECHR and corresponding case law.[53] The tribunal in *Tecmed v Mexico* referred to the case law of the ECtHR and the Inter-American

[49] See n 39, § 262.

[50] *United Parcel Service of America Inc. v Govt. of Canada*, UNCITRAL, Award on the Merits, §§ 185–7 (May 24, 2007).

[51] *Philip Morris v Uruguay* (n 44), § 30.

[52] *Suez/Vivendi v Argentina* Order, ICSID Case No ARB/03/17, Order in Response to a Petition for Participation as Amicus Curiae, § 24 (17 March 2006).

[53] See n 37.

Convention on Human Rights for determining the existence of an expropriation and for stressing the legitimacy of distinguishing between nationals and non-nationals in this context.[54] In *Saipem v Bangladesh*,[55] ECtHR case law was cited to confirm the assertion that also immaterial rights can be property rights protected by IIL, and also that judicial acts may amount to illegal interference with property rights. ISA tribunals have also resorted to HRL and jurisprudence to support the use of proportionality balancing of investor rights with public interests as defined by human rights.[56] For example, in *Mondev v US*, when assessing the claim that the granting of a special governmental immunity for domestic tort law was in breach of NAFTA law, the tribunal turned to ECtHR case law by stating that it could provide guidance by analogy.[57] In *Phoenix*, the tribunal acknowledged that 'nobody would suggest that ICSID protection should be granted to investments made in violation of the most fundamental rules of protection of human rights, like investments in pursuance of torture or genocide or in support of slavery or trafficking of human organs'.[58] In addition, in cases in which human rights arguments were dismissed as not excluding liability, ISA tribunals referred back to human rights considerations when assessing compensation for damages. In the case of *Bear Creek v Peru*, for example, the arbitrator Philippe Sands issued a dissenting opinion that an International Labour Organization Convention on the protection of the rights of indigenous peoples was part of the applicable law and the investor's contribution to events which led to the indirect expropriation of its investment (ie social protests against its allegedly adverse environmental impact and disregard for indigenous rights) justified reduction of damages by 50 per cent.[59] Yet, the occasional references by arbitrators to human rights for interpretative guidance—in particular to human rights jurisprudence on property rights—do not follow a transparent, legal methodology transcending the commercial law culture of many arbitrators.

[54] *Tecmed SA v The United Mexican States*, ICSID Case No ARB (AF)/00/2, Award, §§ 116, 122 (29 May 2003).

[55] *Saipem S.p.A. v The People's Republic of Bangladesh*, ICSID Case No ARB/05/07, Decision on Jurisdiction and Recommendation on Provisional Measures, §§ 130, 132 (21 March 2007)

[56] See n 37, § 122, with reference to ECtHR case law. Necessity and proportionality balancing are recognized as general principles in Article 5:4 TEU (no action shall 'exceed what is necessary to achieve the objectives of the Treaties').

[57] *Mondev International Ltd v United States of America*, ICSID Case No ARB(AF)/99/2 (NAFTA), Award, § 144 (11 October 2002).

[58] *Phoenix Action, Ltd v Czech Republic*, ICSID Case No ARB/06/5, Award, § 78 (15 April 2009).

[59] *Bear Creek Mining Corpn. v Republic of Peru*, ICSID Case No ARB/14/21, Award of 30 November 2017, Partial Dissenting Opinion of Professor Philippe Sands QC, para 39. Using contributory fault for reducing damages is based on the customary international law principle codified in Art 39 of the International Law Commission's Articles on State Responsibility for Internationally Wrongful Acts, which primarily deals with the determination of damages. Contributory fault must not be conflated with issues of illegality or corruption that concern the admissibility of a claim or a tribunal's jurisdiction, as opposed to its merits or quantum.

7.2.2.2 Marginal impact of human rights law in investor–state arbitration

Why is it that even if ISA awards explicitly refer to human rights invoked by investors, host states, third parties or *ex officio* by the arbitrators themselves, the judicial *ratio decidendi* of the awards is rarely based on such invocations of human rights? Chapter 2, section 2.2 recalled how the moral theories (eg on personal freedoms, capabilities, justice, basic needs, agency, human dignity) and political theories underlying HRL and democratic constitutionalism remain contested among UN member states. While neo-liberal capital-exporting countries (like the United Kingdom and the United States) still refer to libertarian justifications of property rights,[60] many less-developed, capital-importing countries prioritize egalitarian justifications of the social functions of property reconciling individual and democratic autonomy in ways protecting the basic needs and human rights of *all* affected persons. Invocation of human rights (eg of access to water, food, medicines, health protection, and judicial remedies) may not change the judicial balancing of economic rights (like market access rights, property and investor rights) with non-economic human rights if judges protect the human rights values by prioritizing governmental *duties to protect PGs* (like public health) rather than corresponding *human rights*. Empirical evidence confirms that investment arbitrators remain reluctant to respond to their 'legitimacy crisis',[61] for instance by acknowledging HRL as applicable law or relevant interpretative context in ISA (eg for promoting transparency and *amicus curiae* submissions for taking into account public interests transcending the litigating parties). The commercial law background of many investment arbitrators, their commercial arbitration culture (eg prioritizing party autonomy, confidentiality, and *inter partes* dispute settlement), rational ignorance (eg vis-à-vis the complexities of multilevel HRL and adjudication), and prioritization of ordinary virtues over the burdens of judgment demanded by cosmopolitan HRL[62] offer additional reasons for path-dependent focus on state-centred IIL as narrowly defined in BITs and ISA procedures, rather than to propose integrated approaches to IEL and HRL in order to justify ISA more comprehensively vis-à-vis all citizens affected by ISA. The denial of human and constitutional rights in China's communist party state,[63] and the EU's insistence on protecting human

[60] Examples include J Locke's labour theory justifying private property rights as moral entitlements to the fruits of one's labour provided the valuable good was acquired or produced without violating the rights and basic needs of others, or R Nozick's theory of historical entitlements ('justice in holdings') if the acquisition, transfer, and distribution of private property rights were lawful according to the rules in effect at the time.

[61] Cf M Langford and D Behn, Managing Backlash: The Evolving Investment Treaty Arbitrator, *European Journal of International Law* 29 (2018), 551–80.

[62] Cf M Ignatieff, *The Ordinary Virtues: Moral Order in a Divided World* (Harvard UP 2017). Cf also EU Petersmann,' Constitutional Theories of International Economic Adjudication and Investor–State Arbitration' in Dupuy, Francioni, and Petersmann (eds), (n 25), 137–94

[63] Cf EU Petersmann, International Economic Law without Human and Constitutional Rights? Legal Methodology Questions for my Chinese Critics, *Journal of International Economic Law* 21 (2018), 213–31.

rights also in trade and investment agreements with third countries, may explain why China has remained so reluctant over many years to conclude a China–EU investment protection agreement as proposed by the EU (eg with public law investment adjudication rather than only commercial arbitration).

7.3 From Investor–State Arbitration to Public Interest Adjudication?

In IIL and arbitration, transnational investments and related disputes tend to be governed by (i) the national laws of both the host country and the investor's home country; (ii) contracts between the investor and the host country or among investors and their associates; and (iii) applicable international treaties, customary law rules, and general principles of law.[64] The ordo-liberal idea underlying Germany's BITs since 1959—that foreign direct investments in less-developed countries should be promoted in exchange for the same constitutional protection standards (like non-discriminatory treatment, fair and equitable treatment, full protection and security, compensation in case of expropriation) applicable to investments in the home country—was hardly consistent with the neo-liberal, business-driven idea of depoliticizing and decentralizing investment disputes by means of investor–state arbitration based on commercial arbitration principles (like appointment of arbitrators and financing of arbitration costs by the parties to the dispute), as codified in the ICSID Convention. The constitutional and administrative law features of investor–state disputes (eg requiring the balancing of public interests, private property rights, and treatment of aliens) tend to be much more important than the contractual and commercial dimensions of concession contracts of the foreign investor with the host country. BITs are public international law treaties, and their principles, dispute settlement procedures, object, and purpose are dominated by public law rights and obligations, even if foreign direct investors are granted rights to directly invoke BIT provisions and ISA procedures vis-à-vis the host country as an alternative to politicized diplomatic protection by the home country. An EU submission of December 2017 to the UNCITRAL review process on 'Possible Reforms of Investor–State Dispute Settlement (ISDS)' focused on the following six public law features of ISDS:

1. A constitutional/administrative law component: the obligations set down in the investment treaties are intended to protect investors from certain (limited) state conduct. Hence applying the obligations implies striking a

[64] Cf JW Salacuse, *The Three Laws of International Investment. National, Contractual and International Frameworks for Foreign Capital* (OUP 2013).

balance between the right to exercise sovereign authority and the duty to protect individuals, typical of constitutional/administrative law determinations;
2. A unidirectional system: the investor initiates the case against the state because the investor accepts the standing offer to arbitrate provided in the treaties;
3. A vertical relationship: disputes predominantly concern foreign investors bringing cases against host states that arise from the vertical, regulatory relationship between those actors due to the fact that the investor enters into the host State territory and its economic and legal order;
4. A repeat function: the treaties in question potentially will give rise to multiple disputes over a potentially extended period of time. This is to be distinguished from legal instruments establishing one-off contractual arrangements;
5. A determinacy component: the substantive obligations are indeterminate in the sense that they set down general, high-level standards intended to apply in multiple different fact patterns, much like constitutional law provisions; and,
6. A predictability/consistency function: given the general formulation of investment protection standards and conscious of the repeat function, stakeholders (governments, investors, civil society) look at precedents in order to understand how obligations in the treaties are being or should be interpreted. This occurs both within the same treaty and across treaties, given the relatively high degree of homogeneity of the treaties. This means the adjudicative role is key in elaborating and further refining the precise meaning of the substantive obligations.[65]

7.3.1 Changing Applicable Laws

The more the applicable national and international legal systems include guarantees of human rights, private property rights, and related judicial remedies, the more frequently complainants, defendants, judges, or third-party participants in investment disputes invoke human rights too. The historical influence of commercial arbitration on the design and development of ISA is increasingly limited by acknowledgment of ISA's public law dimensions as illustrated by increasing transparency and inclusiveness of ISA procedures, comprehensive judicial balancing

[65] Submission from the European Union, 12 December 2017, A/CN.9/WG.III/WP.14 available at https://undocs.org/en/A/CN.9/WG.III/WP.145. The call for stronger public law adjudication aims at strengthening the personal and financial independence, impartiality, transparency, permanency, predictability, and possibilities of appealing investment adjudication compared with ISA, whose current financing, high costs, and *ad hoc* procedures are widely perceived as creating potential conflicts of interests (eg in case of 'double hatting' of *ad hoc* arbitrators working simultaneously as legal counsels for TNCs) and as insufficiently protecting the rule of law (eg in the sense of consistency and predictability of ISA jurisprudence, legal security).

of investor rights with public interests, recognition of social corporate responsibilities, publication of ISA arbitration awards, and the ongoing EU, ICSID, and UNCITRAL initiatives for strengthening the public law dimensions in ISA procedures. As discussed in Chapter 5, the EU's micro-economic common market constitution (eg based on EU competition law, common market freedoms, social law, constitutional rights, and multilevel judicial remedies of EU citizens) and the EU Charter of Fundamental Rights (EUCFR) confirm the constitutional significance of HRL for protecting individual access to justice and judicial protection of economic and non-economic rights in transnational economic cooperation. Similar to the increasing democratic challenges of one-sided legal protection of foreign investor rights in IIL, also the EU's macro-economic monetary constitution and protection of foreign creditor rights in over-indebted EU member states (like Greece) are increasingly challenged by citizens and courts of justice inside the EU, for instance if citizens are adversely affected by the 'financial conditionality' and austerity measures imposed by creditor states.[66]

This constitutional dimension of ISA was illustrated by the *Achmea* judgment of the CJEU,[67] which—according to the EU Commission—implies 'that all investor–State arbitration clauses in intra-EU BITs are inapplicable and that any arbitration tribunal established on the basis of such clauses lacks jurisdiction due to the absence of a valid arbitration agreement'.[68] In democracies, the ongoing negotiations on reforming ICSID, UNCITRAL, and other ISA procedures—and on strengthening corporate social responsibilities—are driven by social and democratic claims that justice and HRL, even if they may not prescribe specific economic policies, entail duties for governments, courts of justice, and corporate actors that require constitutionalizing the path-dependent investor privileges in BITs and ISA so that citizens are legally and judicially protected more comprehensively in non-discriminatory ways. Protecting constitutional and human rights, including also the right of 'everyone . . . to a social and international order in which the rights and freedoms set forth in this Declaration can be fully realized' (Article 28 UDHR), is particularly urgent at times when cosmopolitan conceptions underlying HRL are challenged by authoritarian state capitalism and neo-liberal interest group politics (eg neglecting human and labour rights of local workers in global supply chains) and nationalist restrictions on religious and cultural minorities (eg indigenous peoples affected by foreign direct investments in natural resources and by related environmental pollution).

The reluctance of investment arbitrators to engage in human rights discourse often reflects their limited judicial mandates and the diversity of the applicable

[66] Cf the case studies in Parts II and III of HCH Hofmann, L Pantazatou, and G Zaccaroni (eds), *The Metamorphosis of the European Economic Constitution* (Edward Elgar 2019).

[67] Case C-284/16 *The Slovak Republic v Achmea BV* [2018] ECLI:EU:C:2018:158.

[68] Cf *Protection of Intra-EU Investment, Communication from the Commission to the European Parliament and the Council*, COM (2018) 547 (19 July 2018), at 26.

national and transnational legal rules rather than judicial disregard for legitimate public interests. But reliance on investors and host states to present the relevant human rights issues to investment arbitrators may not be sufficient, for instance if corrupt governments collude with foreign investors in circumventing human rights obligations or have political self-interests in avoiding judicial accountability. As investor rights need to be reconciled with all other human and constitutional rights of citizens, the civil society opposition against ISA privileges and related collusion among foreign investors and host state rulers is constitutionally justified. Remedying the current situation that, apart from references to procedural rights and property rights, references in ISA to civil, political, economic, social, and cultural human rights and collective third-generation rights (like self-determination of indigenous people adversely affected by foreign investments exploiting natural resources) remain rare and of marginal legal importance, would require legislative and treaty clarifications (like insertion of human rights clauses and competition rules into BITs) and judicial reforms (as promoted by the EU and pursued also in ICSID and UNITRAL negotiations on reforming ISA procedures).[69] The increasing interactions of HRL, IIL, and ISA reduce problems of structural biases (eg resulting from legal fragmentation and forum shopping driven by vested interests) and enhance the legitimacy of law and adjudication (eg in terms of access to justice, due process rights, legitimacy of rule-making, justification of adjudication vis-à-vis citizens in terms of their human rights). The path-dependent prioritization of protection of foreign investments in IIL and ISA procedures prompts ever more countries to review and change their national investment laws, BITs, and multilateral regulation of ISA procedures. National investment laws and ISA procedures should regulate more specifically the needed reconciliation of privileged procedural and substantive rights of foreign investors with other public and private rights (eg of workers, consumers, indigenous peoples) in order to avoid that public rights to regulate, corporate responsibilities (eg to respect HRL and protect the environment), and the impact of HRL on the outcome of ISA based on existing BITs and ISA procedures remain insufficiently protected.

The case studies in both Chapters 6 and 7 confirm that economic law and adjudication can complement HRL by offering legal and judicial remedies and protecting PGs beyond the still limited scope of HRL and limited jurisdiction of human rights courts. Inside constitutional democracies, regulation of trade and investment law, property rights of investors, and judicial administration of justice

[69] On global (eg financial) markets as complex systems where constitutional and competition rules protecting undistorted competition and legal liability of economic actors are often superior to discretionary, government regulation in limiting the knowledge problems, incentive problems, and reputation problems of private market actors, see V Vanberg, 'Consumer Welfare, Total Welfare and Economic Freedom—On the Normative Foundations of Competition Policy' in J Drexl, W Kerber, and R Podszun (eds), *Competition Policy and the Economic Approach. Foundations and Limitations* (Edward Elgar 2011), 44–71.

in trade and investment disputes have become restrained by constitutional law guarantees of human and constitutional rights. Reconciling the diverse principles of justice underlying the commercial and private law dimensions of IIL (eg in UNCITRAL arbitration and its enforcement through national courts), its transnational law dimensions (eg in concession contracts of foreign investors and host states), and the public international law dimensions of IIL and related ISA remains a challenging task, for which the United Nations Conference on Trade and Development (UNCTAD) and its World Investment Network have recommended numerous reforms.[70] The continuing challenges—by civil societies and governments—of the post-war embedded neo-liberalism underlying international trade and investment law, the increasing geopolitical rivalries, and the hegemonic weaponization of trade, investment and internet restrictions (eg by China, Russia, and the United States) suggest that the impact of HRL on ISA will remain contested and limited. Paradoxically, while the EU initiated (ordo-liberal) multilateral reform negotiations for strengthening the public law dimensions of ISA following the (ordo-liberal) model of the WTO panel and appellate review systems, the US Trump administration allowed (neo-liberal) US interest-group politics to destroy the WTO dispute settlement system as legally prescribed in the WTO/DSU agreements. In its negotiations on transforming NAFTA into the new USMCA free trade agreement, the US Trump administration also limited the availability of ISA in its relations with Canada.[71] The RCEP between China, the ten ASEAN countries, Australia, Japan, South Korea, and New Zealand does not provide at all for ISA. Inside the EU, the CJEU confirmed the legal view of the EU Commission that, in relations among EU member countries, ISA has become legally inconsistent with the more comprehensive, multilevel legal and judicial guarantees of EU law (as discussed in Chapter 8). Procedural and substantive reforms of IIL and ISA are legally required also in the external relations of the EU in order to protect the SDGs more effectively.

7.3.2 Impact of EU Law and Adjudication

EU law protects fundamental rights as constitutional restraints on the exercise of all public authority by EU institutions, including external policy powers of the EU.[72] Hence, ISA arbitration in intra-community relations challenging EU

[70] See, eg, UNCTAD, *World Investment Report 2019* (Geneva 2020).

[71] Chapter 14 USMCA on investment protection and investor–state dispute settlement has significantly reduced ISA in relations between Canada and the United States to legacy investments and pending claims.

[72] In Case C-263/14, *Parliament v Council*, ECLI:EU:C:2016, 435, the CJEU confirmed (para 47) that ensuring compliance of external EU agreements with human rights is required by Articles 21:2 and 3 TEU.

member states has been found to be inconsistent with EU constitutional law and its guarantees of multilevel judicial protection of fundamental rights.[73] Respect for human rights is a condition of the lawfulness of Community acts also in the external relations of the EU.[74] The jurisprudence of European courts confirms that HRL may both *legitimize* the protection of foreign investors and *justify limitations* on procedural and substantive investor rights as protected in IIL, for instance if—in foreign debt crises—compensation claims of foreign creditors and investors may have to be reconciled (balanced) with state duties to protect existential needs of domestic citizens as recognized in HRL.

In Opinion 1/2017 rendered by the CJEU on 30 April 2019, the ISA procedures in the EU's 2016 Comprehensive Economic and Trade Agreement (CETA) with Canada were found to be consistent with EU law in view of the legal limitations of the potential reach of ISA by CETA guarantees of, *inter alia*, the legal autonomy of EU law, the EU judicial system, the democratic regulatory freedom to protect non-economic PGs, and of fundamental rights (eg of access to judicial remedies, equal treatment) as protected in the EUCFR.[75] ISA in the external relations of the EU must remain consistent with EU constitutional law and HRL. The EU–Vietnam Investment Protection Agreement of 2019 limits the potential reach of ISA rulings, *inter alia*, by explicit references—in its Preamble—to 'the principles articulated in *The Universal Declaration of Human Rights*, adopted by the General Assembly of the United Nations on 10 December 1948', so as to compensate for the inadequate HRL inside communist Vietnam. The EU objective of progressively replacing bilateral *ad hoc* ISA by a permanent public law tribunal with full-time adjudicators and an appeal process may further strengthen judicial protection of human and constitutional rights. Also outside the EU, an increasing number of trade and investment agreements of developed and less-developed countries, and some of their BITs (eg based on the 2012 Model BIT of the Southern African Development Community, Article 12.1(v) of India's 2015 Model BIT, the 2018 Model BIT of the Netherlands) and the Draft Pan-African Investment Code,[76] include provisions referring to human rights and investor obligations. In the UNCITRAL reform negotiations, the EU submitted a concept paper on how a multilateral investment court could operate:[77]

[73] Cf n 67.

[74] Opinion 2/94 CJEU, ECLI:EU:C:1759, para 34. On the *Kadi* jurisprudence annulling smart sanctions of the EU (like seizure of foreign property) on grounds of human rights violations even if these sanctions were ordered by the UN Security Council against alleged terrorists, see M Avbelj et al. (eds), *Kadi on Trial: A Multifaceted Analysis of the Kadi Trial* (Intersentia 2014).

[75] Opinion 1/2017 CJEU of 30 April 2019, ECLI:EU:C:2019:341.

[76] Cf *The Legal Nature of the Draft Pan-African Investment Code and its Relationship with International Investment Agreements*, South Center Investment Policy Brief 9 (July 2017).

[77] See A/CN.9/WG.III/WP.159/Add.1 of 24 January 2019 (https://undocs.org/en/A/CN.9/WG.III/WP.159/Add.1); cf M Bungenberg and A Reinisch, *From Bilateral Arbitral Tribunals and Investment Courts to a Multilateral Investment Court* (2nd edn, Springer 2020); M Bungenberg and A Reinisch, *Draft Statute of the Multilateral Investment Court* (Nomos 2021).

- a permanent court would function at two levels, with a first instance which would be the main locus for resolving a dispute and an appeal function;
- adjudicators would be appointed on a full-time basis without any other activities outside of their appointment (other than with the permission of the President of the court—for example academic activities);
- independence would be ensured through long, non-renewable terms of appointment;
- expertise would be required in public international law, with additional experience in judicial or dispute settlement functions being desirable;
- adjudicators would be appointed by a qualified majority of contracting parties after being subject to a screening mechanism to check their suitability;
- requirements would be built into the system to ensure that gender and regional diversity is respected in the appointment of adjudicators;
- there would be an opt-in mechanism to permit coverage of the large number of existing treaties without having to amend individual treaties;
- enforcement of decisions would take place via a system providing for enforcement in the convention establishing the permanent court and, as far as possible, via existing systems.

7.3.3 Human Right Jurisprudence in Economic Courts?

Complementing human rights jurisprudence of specialized human rights courts by human rights references in other international courts and economic regulation—as suggested in Chapters 6 and 7—can be seen as a necessary, albeit controversial transition phase in multilevel governance of transnational PGs aimed at institutionalizing public reason and social support for reconciling IEL with HRL and constitutional law.[78] HRL outside Europe has neglected the human rights dimensions of economic law. Both HRL and IEL can benefit from mutual dialogue and criticism among economic and human rights courts clarifying the human rights dimensions of IEL. This may contribute to reforming 'state-centred investment paradigms' (eg in the context of China's Silk Road investment projects) and 'neo-liberal investment paradigms' (eg underlying many US BITs and their ISA rules), and to making them more compatible with 'ordo-liberal investment paradigms' underlying EU law and the UN Guiding Principles on Business and Human Rights.[79] In the increasing number of investor claims under the ECT over the governmental phasing out of coal and nuclear energy plants as part of clean energy policies, human rights arguments are likely to play an increasing role for justifying

[78] Cf Scheinin (n 27).

[79] UN Guiding Principles on Business and Human Rights, adopted by UN Resolution A/HRC/RES/17/4 (2011).

environmental protection measures. Yet, the marginal impact of HRL on past WTO and ISA jurisprudence also reflects the need for *legislative reforms* of international trade and investment laws—and also of the ECT, which is increasingly criticized as an impediment to decarbonization of economies—in order to reconcile protection of trade and investor interests with other domestic citizen interests more effectively. The continuing review and revision of national investment laws and ISA procedures (eg in multilateral ICSID and UNCIRAL negotiations) reflects increasing social and democratic discontent with utilitarian, embedded neo-liberalism underlying post-war IEL, for example in order to better reconcile legal protection of *foreign* investments with governmental rights to regulate and duties to protect public interests and related human rights.

Why is it that after more than fifty years of bilateralism and incoherent ISA jurisprudence in IIL, ISA reformers aim at strengthening multilateralism, institutionalized public law adjudication and appellate review, whereas the WTO appellate court system sees a transformation towards bilateral arbitration and legal and judicial disintegration? The multiple problems of bilateralism, regulatory capture, and incoherent ISA jurisprudence in the decentralized evolution of IIL since the ICSID Convention of 1966 was driven by insufficient leadership and neo-liberal privileging of investor interests in multilateral investment agreements and investment adjudication. Similarly, the US Trump administration's assault on the WTO dispute settlement system reflects the regulatory capture of US trade policies by protectionist interest group politics. Unfortunately, the US Biden administration seems to lack domestic political support for returning to the systemic advantages of the multilateral WTO dispute settlement system and its institutionalized, judicial protection of rule of law, and for insisting on similar public law reforms in investment law and arbitration. Similarly, also authoritarian governments show little interest in strengthening multilateral judicial protection of transnational rule of law and stronger, multilevel cooperation among national and international courts, as discussed in Chapter 8. The risks of trade and investment adaptation to the SDGs being impeded by trade and investment litigation (eg by coal, gas, and oil industries requesting financial compensation) requires procedural and substantive adjustments of economic, investment, and environmental legislation as it has been advocated since the UN Stockholm conference on trade and environment in 1972 and as it is increasingly enacted in new national and European climate change laws as discussed in Chapters 8 and 9.

8

Judicial Overreach? Constitutional Justice Requires Multilevel Judicial Comity

What are the legal relationships between multilevel judicial protection of transnational rule of law at national, regional, and worldwide levels of governance? Why are there an increasing number of disputes over alleged judicial overreach in national courts (eg in EU member states like Germany and Poland), European courts, worldwide courts (like the WTO Appellate Body (AB)), and in investor–state arbitration (ISA)? Can such disputes be avoided through judicial comity among national and international jurisdictions, or do they require procedural and substantive reforms of adjudication (eg as envisaged in EU free trade agreements (FTAs) with Canada and Singapore and in the UN Commission on International Trade Law (UNCITRAL) negotiations on reforms of ISA)? This chapter discusses constitutional principles (like proportionality balancing, judicial deference towards subsidiarity and margins of interpretation in domestic jurisdictions with more expertise and more democratic support and accountability) that should govern judicial administration of justice and judicial comity in multilevel protection of rule of law in national and international jurisdictions and related claims of judicial overreach (eg by China regarding the UN Convention on the Law of the Sea (UNCLOS) arbitration finding China's territorial expansion in the South China Sea to be in violation of international law).

As discussed in Chapters 4 and 6, the UN and the Sustainable Development Goal (SDG) 16 emphasize that in a globally integrating world in which many PGs demanded by citizens can be provided only through multilevel governance of public goods (PGs), the rule of law requires protecting legal and judicial remedies in both national and international legal systems.[1] Access to justice and judicial administration of justice in national and international courts reflect agreed principles of constitutional justice that have evolved in European legal systems since ancient times. Human rights law (HRL) and democratic constitutional law (eg Article 47 of the EU Charter of Fundamental Rights (EUCFR)) postulate that law and governance must recognize citizens as free and equal legal subjects entitled to judicial protection of procedural and substantive principles of justice. Social agreements constituting independent, impartial courts of justice represent more

[1] Cf Chapter 4, section 4.10 and Chapter 6, section 6.1.

Transforming World Trade and Investment Law for Sustainable Development. Ernst-Ulrich Petersmann, Oxford University Press. © Ernst-Ulrich Petersmann 2022. DOI: 10.1093/oso/9780192858023.003.0009

ancient forms of constitutional justice than democratic constitutionalism (eg in ancient Athens) and republican constitutionalism (eg in ancient Rome). Chapter 5 explained why multilevel judicial cooperation in protecting transnational rule of law and constitutional rights remains an indispensable complement of democratic and republican constitutionalism in Europe. This chapter discusses the disconnect between citizens and UN/WTO governance (section 8.1) and recent claims of judicial overreach in ISA (section 8.2), WTO appellate review (section 8.3), and in the European Court of Justice (CJEU), and related constitutional principles for limiting judicial overreach (section 8.4).

Complaints over judicial overreach reflect the broader backlash against the creation of more than forty international courts since the Second World War, notwithstanding the increasing recognition also of private access to international courts (like regional human rights and economic courts, investment tribunals, the Seabed Chamber of the International Tribunal for the Law of the Sea). This backlash is illustrated by the *de facto* abolishment of the Tribunal of the Southern African Development Community; the widespread criticism of the International Criminal Court (eg by African countries); withdrawals form the Inter-American Court of Human Rights (eg by Trinidad and Tobago, Venezuela) and from the African Court of Human Rights (by Rwanda); and by the backlash against ISA discussed in Chapter 7.[2] The backlash reveals diverse motives, such as denial of international jurisdiction (eg in case of China's rejection of the 2016 UNCLOS arbitral award in favour of the complaint by the Philippines against China's extraterritorial expansion in the South China Sea) or criticism of previous jurisprudence (eg US criticism of the AB jurisprudence on trade remedies as the main US justification of its blocking of appointments of WTO AB members). Resistance to international adjudication in international environmental agreements is often due to the particular nature of environmental protection obligations, to insufficient resources in less-developed countries, and to the need for external capacity building assistance aimed at conflict prevention through protection of the environment. For example, the UN Framework Convention on Climate Change and the Paris Climate Agreement do not include provisions for third-party adjudication. Yet, climate justice and trade and investment disputes over harmful effects of climate change measures (eg WTO disputes over green subsidies, ISA challenging government restrictions on fossil and nuclear power generation) and human rights disputes (eg over the rights of climate refugees) are bound to assume increasing importance in the implementation of the SDGs. This risks aggravating the politics of legal practices (as discussed in Chapter 2, section 2.1, Chapter 3, section 3.1, and Chapter 4, sections 4.1 and

[2] Cf MR Madsen, P Cebulak, and M Wiebusch, Backlash against International Courts. Explaining the Forms and Patterns of Resistance to International Courts, *International Journal of Law in Context* 14 (2018), 197–220; P Clark, *Distant Justice: The Impact of the International Criminal Court on African Politics* (CUP 2018).

4.2), for instance if protection of human rights to a healthy environment depends on contested climate facts and scientific evidence, or legal and judicial balancing (eg among the seventeen SDGs, their respective human rights values, diverse legal safeguards) hinges on a turn to ethics and to climate science.[3] As in the COVID-19 health emergencies, climate emergencies too risk being abused by governments for restricting individual rights (eg of climate refugees, victims of natural catastrophes) through executive emergency measures without adequate parliamentary control and judicial remedies against transnational harm (eg caused by foreign pollution). The efforts by the Palau islands to secure an advisory legal opinion from the International Court of Justice (ICJ) on assigning responsibility for causing climate change reveal inadequacies of international law rules (eg on collective state responsibilities), judicial remedies and precautionary measures in the increasing justice versus order dilemmas of UN law.[4] Insufficient legislative, administrative, and judicial protection of UN human rights law (HRL) and of other international legal obligations inside states facilitates violations of human rights with transnational effects (eg by Belarus' military actions forcing the international Ryanair flight 4978 to land in Minsk on 23 May 2021 in order to arrest two members of the Belarusian political opposition on board the plane) that often provoke secondary international conflicts which could have been avoided by more effective domestic implementing legislation of international legal obligations.

8.1 Need for Reducing the 'Disconnect' between UN/WTO Governance and Citizens

National and international legal systems vary enormously in their respective design of legal and judicial remedies, notably regarding cooperation among national and international jurisdictions and reparation of injury (which was excluded from the WTO dispute settlement system). Chapter 2 recalled that UN and WTO law failed to establish a truly global community law protecting citizens and peoples as democratic principals of governments and states with limited, delegated powers and duties to protect PGs for the benefit of humankind. Even though WTO law protects judicial remedies at the international level among WTO members and inside domestic jurisdictions for the benefit of citizens and non-governmental actors—and each WTO member is legally required to 'ensure the conformity of its laws, regulations and administrative procedures with its obligation as provided in the annexed Agreements' (Article XVI.4 WTO Agreement)—most domestic legal systems (eg in China, the EU, and the United States) do not empower citizens

[3] Cf Chapter 2, section 2.1 and Chapter 4, section 4.2.

[4] Cf S Beck and E Burleson, Inside the System, Outside the Box: Palau's Pursuit of Climate Justice and Security at the United Nations, *Transnational Environmental Law* 3 (2014), 17–29.

to invoke and enforce WTO rules directly in domestic courts. As a result of this disconnect between international and domestic trade governance, most inconsistencies between WTO rules and domestic laws can be challenged only by WTO members *ex post* in WTO dispute settlement proceedings rather than by adversely affected citizens in domestic courts of justice. In international investment law, ISA awards can be requested by non-governmental actors and tend to be enforceable in domestic jurisdictions. Yet, contrary to judicial comity procedures such as preliminary rulings of the CJEU and advisory opinions of the European Free Trade Area (EFTA) Court at the request by national courts in the judicial interpretation and enforcement of European common market law, equivalent judicial comity procedures exist neither in WTO law nor in international investment law and adjudication. The lack of direct applicability of WTO rules in domestic jurisdictions weakens the effectiveness and democratic legitimacy of multilevel trade law and governance inside and outside the EU and the European Economic Area (EEA). 'Localizing' the legal and judicial remedies for decentralized enforcement of the SDGs requires reducing the disconnect between *international* law and governance and *domestic* citizens and civil society institutions (like business and trade unions) so as to enable joint struggles for realizing the SDGs as illustrated by the constitutional, human rights and environmental litigation in Europe discussed in Chapter 9.

In many national and international legal systems, judicial remedies of individuals and of (non)governmental actors were recognized only after long 'struggles for justice',[5] or continue being resisted by political rulers (eg in communist countries). Courts of justice have good reasons for promoting cooperation among national and international courts in order to promote the rule of law at national and international levels and hold rulers and interest groups accountable if they disregard rule of law and judicial remedies. Just as the assault by the US Trump administration on the WTO dispute settlement system reflected self-interests of US government officials (like President Trump and his US Trade Representative (USTR)) and of their neo-liberal business supporters (as discussed in Chapter 3), many other governments also neglect their WTO legal obligation (eg under Article XVI.4 WTO Agreement) to ensure the conformity of their laws, regulations, and administrative procedures with (their) obligation as provided in the WTO Agreements.

The establishment of more than twenty permanent international courts of justice following the Second World War, in addition to hundreds of *ad hoc* arbitration tribunals and the General Agreement on Tariffs and Trade (GATT)/WTO dispute settlement panels, confirmed that struggles for protecting and improving access to justice, transnational rule of law, and better protection of equal rights of states, human rights, and constitutional rights can be successful. The jurisdictions

[5] This was famously described by the German law professor Rudolf Jhering in his lecture on *The Struggle for Law (Der Kampf ums Recht)* of 11 March 1872.

of international courts remain, however, limited and often contested.[6] In European integration law, the CJEU has confirmed the legal claim of the EU Commission that the EU's 'common market constitution' has rendered ISA in relations among EU member states unconstitutional (section 8.2). In contrast to this transformation of ISA into multilevel public law adjudication inside the EU, the WTO dispute settlement system is currently facing an opposite substitution of voluntary appeal arbitration pursuant to Article 25 Dispute Settlement Understanding (DSU) for the compulsory yet dysfunctional AB adjudication system provided for in Article 17 DSU (as discussed in section 8.3). Claims of executive overreach and of judicial overreach were made also in the ruling of the German Constitutional Court of 5 May 2020, as discussed in section 8.4, that the European Central Bank (ECB) exceeded its limited monetary policy competences—and the CJEU violated its limited powers of judicial review—by not examining whether certain ECB decisions were consistent with the proportionality requirements in Article 5 TEU. Similar political and judicial claims of judicial overreach risk being raised whenever systemic conflicts between neo-liberal, state capitalist, and ordo-liberal conceptions of IEL are submitted to international jurisdictions, as illustrated by the contested WTO AB jurisprudence on 'zeroing methodologies' in anti-dumping calculations, and on when state-owned enterprises (SOEs) are public bodies in the sense of the WTO Agreement on Subsidies. Even though China has a comparatively good record of implementing adverse WTO dispute settlement rulings against China (as discussed in Chapter 3), some disputes over the interpretation of WTO legal disciplines (eg regarding discriminatory market distortions by state capitalist WTO members, their often non-transparent subsidies, SOEs, and government procurement practices) may involve political questions that elude settlement through WTO litigation and jurisprudence alone. This chapter focuses on judicial methodology, judicial review standards, and alleged judicial overreach and their close relationships with applicable constitutional law standards for judicial administration of justice.

8.2 From Investor–State Arbitration to Multilevel Investment Adjudication in the EU

Constitutional democracies protect equal private autonomy rights and judicial remedies in the field of commercial and investment arbitration subject to the

[6] On legitimacy of international courts, see N Grosman, H Grant Cohen, A Follesdal, and G Ulfstein (eds), *Legitimacy and International Courts* (CUP 2018). *Legitimacy of origin* of international courts may be distinguished from the *personal legitimacy* of judges; operational *legitimacy of judicial exercise*; *output legitimacy* of judgments and jurisprudence; the perception of their *sociological legitimacy* by compliance constituencies; and social reactions by governments, diplomatic communities, or civil society (eg perceived judicial biases of investment arbitrators, judicial overreach by the WTO AB).

proviso that national courts (eg if requested to enforce private commercial arbitration awards) must review the legal consistency of the awards with the public policy and constitutional law in the country where the complainant seeks recognition and enforcement of the award. The more than 135 bilateral investment treaties (BITs) concluded by Germany since 1959 were perceived as an export of ordoliberal justice principles protecting foreign direct investments—in relations with less-developed countries—through reciprocal guarantees of non-discrimination, full protection and security, fair and equitable treatment, access to judicial remedies, and other legal protection standards. The 1966 ICSID Convention provided a multilateral, procedural framework for investor–state arbitration (ISA) and for judicial enforcement of arbitration awards in the 163 (2020) International Center for the Settlement of Investment Disputes (ICSID) member states. As discussed in Chapter 7, the more than 775 ICSID ISA proceedings (2019) and the altogether more than 1,100 known ISA cases have given rise to increasing criticism, for instance on the ground that BITs, ISA, and commercial arbitrators privilege foreign investor rights without adequate regard to the regulatory duties of host states to protect human and constitutional rights of all citizens, and without adequately reconciling investment regulation with all other economic and non-economic public interest regulation.[7]

The 2018 *Achmea* judgment of the CJEU[8]—according to which ISA in relations among EU member states is inconsistent with the EU constitutional law guarantees of the autonomy of EU law, the exclusive jurisdiction of the CJEU for interpreting EU law, and with multilevel judicial protection of individual rights and judicial remedies by the CJEU in cooperation with national courts—illustrates how Europe's multilevel constitutionalism imposes constitutional restraints on path-dependent conceptions of commercial autonomy and state sovereignty embedded into national constitutionalism 1.0. The CJEU continues to recognize private party autonomy to submit private and commercial law disputes to private arbitration. Yet, according to the *Achmea* judgment, both private legal autonomy and the national sovereignty of EU member states have become limited by the autonomy of EU constitutional law to the effect that the more than 200 intra-EU BITs among EU member states can no longer justify ISA in view of the EU Treaty provisions reserving multilevel judicial protection of EU law, individual rights, and non-discriminatory treatment to national courts and European courts.[9] In January 2019, EU member states adopted three Declarations committing themselves to:

[7] Cf S Puig, Debiasing International Economic Law, *European Journal of International Law* 30 (2019), 1339–57.

[8] Case C-284/16 *The Slovak Republic v Achmea BV* [2018] ECLI:EU:C:2018:158.

[9] Cf CJEU (n 8), referring especially to Article 18 of the Treaty on the Functioning of the European Union (TFEU) (prohibition of discrimination), Article 19 of the Treaty on European Union (TEU) (judicial protection of rule of law in the EU), Article 3 267 TFEU (preliminary rulings reference procedure), and Article 344 TFEU (exclusive jurisdiction of the CJEU for interpreting EU law), to 'the preservation of "the particular nature" of EU law' and of the 'EU principle of mutual trust'. The judgment did not review the compatibility of the substantive clauses of intra-EU BITs with EU law.

- the termination of their intra-EU BITs before the end of 2019;
- request all courts to set aside arbitration awards based on intra-EU BITs; and
- inform ISA tribunals in all pending cases about the legal consequences of the *Achmea* judgment.[10]

According to the EU Commission, the legal reasoning of the *Achmea* judgment—which concerned an intra-EU BIT providing for ISA governed by UNCITRAL arbitration procedures, with EU law being part of the applicable law—applies also to ISA governed by the Energy Charter Treaty (ECT) and by ICSID procedures. It requires a modernization of the ECT and ICSID procedures for ISA similar to the EU initiatives for a new investment court system in EU trade and investment agreements with third countries (as discussed in Chapter 7, section 7.3). Another agreement on the termination of BITs among twenty-three EU member states of 6 May 2020 confirmed the incompatibility with EU law of ISA among EU member states, including 'sunset' clauses in these BITs; all related investment disputes must now be decided by domestic courts in these EU member states with preliminary rulings by the CJEU, if required.[11] Yet, many legal questions regarding the relationships between intra-EU arbitration awards based on the ECT or ICSID procedures and enforcement actions by national courts inside EU member states remain controversial.[12] Opinion 1/2017, in which the CJEU interpreted the ISA provisions in the EU–Canada Comprehensive Economic and Trade Agreement as being consistent with EU law,[13] could suggest that the CJEU may support the view of the EU Commission that also ECT and ICSID arbitration procedures need to be modernized in order to make them compatible with EU constitutional law principles. Based on the Lisbon Treaty's conferral of exclusive EU competence for the common commercial policy, including foreign direct investment, the EU Commission continues to pursue international negotiations aimed at transforming ISA into multilateral investment court systems, for instance by modernizing the UNCITRAL, ECT, and ICSID arbitration procedures and ISA provisions in EU trade and investment agreements with third states. It remains uncertain how

[10] For a detailed analysis of these Declarations and of the legal consequences of the *Achmea* judgment on ISA proceedings and on intra-EU BITs, see M Fanou, *The EU as an Actor Shaping the Future of ISDS: Unveiling the Interplay between the Clash of Two Autonomies and the Reform of Investor–State Arbitration* (EUI doctoral thesis publicly defended on 14 February 2020).

[11] Cf M Fermeglia and A Mistura, Killing all Birds with One Stone: Is this the End of Intra-EU BITs? in *European Journal of International Law Talk* Blog of 26 May 2020. It remains contested whether this applies also to disputes based on the ECT and involving foreign investors of EU member states and their investments inside the EU.

[12] In the *Micula et al. v Romania* ICSID Case No ARB/05/20, the final award of 11 December 2013 ordered Romania to pay compensation for the revocation of state aid that had been found by the EU Commission to violate EU state aid prohibitions. The investors successfully challenged in the EU General Court the European Commission's decision to block the enforcement of the award (Cases T-624/15, T-694/15, and T-704/15 *Micula and Others v Commission*, ECLI:EU:T:2019:423 of 18 June 2019); the appeal by the Commission is pending before the CJEU.

[13] Case C-1/17, EU:C:2019:341 (30 April 2019).

the ongoing reform negotiations (eg in UNCITRAL and ICSID institutions) will respond to the widespread criticism of traditional ISA—like the lack of an appeal mechanism, insufficient transparency, and incoherence of ISA jurisprudence, inadequate independence, and impartiality of arbitrators, pro-investor biases threatening the regulatory powers of host states, limiting access to justice, burdening taxpayers, and undermining the legitimacy of ISA—by improving the UNCITRAL, ICSID, and other ISA procedures and protection standards. If economic efficiency is determined not only by utility maximization (eg in the sense of Kaldor–Hicks efficiencies) but also by compliance with democratically agreed rules protecting informed preferences of citizens, the progressive replacement of FDI privileges by more inclusive investment rules and investment court procedures protecting all affected citizen interests inside the EU offers social, democratic, and legal efficiency gains strengthening rule of law.[14]

8.3 From WTO Appellate Body Adjudication Back to Arbitration?

Constitutionalism 2.0 refers to multilateral treaty constitutions establishing organizations for multilevel governance of PGs, like the constitutions (*sic*) establishing the International Labour Organization (ILO), the World Health Organization (WHO), the Food and Agriculture Organization (FAO), the UN Educational, Scientific and Cultural Organization (UNESCO), and regional human rights conventions establishing regional human rights courts for the benefit of citizens.[15] Each of these UN specialized agencies is embedded into the broader UN system (establishing global security, human rights, and development systems). The UN treaty constitutions justify their mandates to protect aggregate PGs by labour rights (ILO), health rights (WHO), rights to food (FAO), and rights to education and participation in the benefits of science and cultural development (UNESCO). As described in Chapter 6, section 6.1, the multilevel GATT/WTO dispute settlement system was the most frequently used, worldwide dispute settlement system in the history of international law (with, since 1948, more than 85 per cent of the more than 500 GATT/WTO panel, appellate, and arbitration findings approved and implemented by GATT/WTO members). Chapter 3, section 3.3 explained why President Trump's assault on the WTO AB was illegal and offered no evidence that the AB jurisprudence had violated the customary rules of treaty interpretation.

[14] Cf Chapter 4, section 4.10.

[15] On the historical development from 'constitutionalism 1.0' to 'constitutionalism 4.0' see EU Petersmann, *Multilevel Constitutionalism for Multilevel Governance of Public Goods* (Hart 2017), 321ff.

8.3.1 Appellate Arbitration as a Pragmatic Response to US Power Politics

The US blockage of the AB system confronted WTO members with four strategic choices so as to avoid that also the adoption of WTO panel reports could be blocked by appealing into the void and, without a functioning AB review, the negative consensus principle for (quasi)automatic adoption of panel reports by the DSB would no longer be applicable (cf Article 16.4 DSU):

- *First*, some WTO members pragmatically avoided the risk of appeals into the void leading to potential blocking of adoption of panel reports by concluding bilateral agreements to accept panel findings as final without appeals.
- *Second*, a progressively increasing group of (in 2020 more than 120) WTO members regularly requested in DSB meetings the initiation of the DSB procedures for filling the AB 'vacancies … as they arise' (Article 17.2 DSU); some of these WTO members also referred to the legal authority and obligation of the WTO Ministerial Conference and WTO General Council under Article IX.1 WTO Agreement to overcome illegal abuse of veto powers in the DSB by majority-voting so as to comply with the collective legal obligation of filling AB vacancies as they arise and maintain the AB as approved by all WTO members and by their domestic parliaments.[16]
- *Third*, WTO members requested New Zealand's Ambassador David Walker to engage in consultations and mediation resulting in a WTO General Council draft decision proposing AB reforms in exchange for an agreement by the United States to initiate the WTO procedures for the filling of the vacant AB positions. Yet, adoption of this draft General Council decision regarding the functioning of the Appellate Body continued to be blocked by the US delegation.[17]
- *Fourth*, after the AB was reduced to one single member on 10 December 2019, the EU's initiative for MPIA arbitration based on Article 25 DSU[18] was accepted

[16] As this interpretation of Article IX.1 WTO Agreement remains contested in view of the consensus rule prescribed for DSB decisions in Article 2.4 DSU, it was also proposed to clarify this authority and obligation of the WTO Ministerial Conference, and of the exercise of its functions by the WTO General Council 'in the intervals between meetings of the Ministerial Conference' (Article IV.2 WTO Agreement), through a majoritarian authoritative interpretation of Article IX.1 WTO Agreement pursuant to Article IX.2 WTO Agreement. So far, the WTO consensus practice has avoided recourse to majority decisions pursuant to Article IX:1 WTO Agreement. The exceptional character of the illegal US abuse of *de facto* veto power under the DSU for reasons unrelated to the personal qualifications of AB candidates would, however, politically and legally justify protection of the rule of law in WTO decision-making by using the majority voting provided for in Article IX.1; cf EU Petersmann, How Should WTO Members React to their WTO Governance Crises? *World Trade Review* 18 (2019), 503–25.

[17] See Chapter 6, section 6.5, note 50 and related text.

[18] The text of the MPIA was notified to the WTO in WTO document JOB/DSB/1/Add.12 of 30 April 2020 and was accepted by the EU and 22 (October 2020) other WTO members. On the history of this EU initiative, see E Baroncini, 'The EU Approach to Overcome the WTO Dispute Settlement Vacuum: Article 25 DSU Interim Appeal Arbitration as a Bridge between Renovation and Innovation'

and used—as a temporary substitute for the dysfunctional AB—by some WTO members since 2020. In a recent WTO dispute on EU anti-dumping measures involving imports from Russia, the EU appealed certain issues in the panel report into the void subject to the following declaration:

> In commencing this appeal, in accordance with Article 16(4) of the DSU and Rule 20(1) of the Working Procedures for Appellate Review, the European Union is aware that, as a matter of fact, temporarily, there are currently an insufficient number of Appellate Body Members to constitute a division due to the obstruction of appointments by the United States. In these circumstances, the European Union stands ready, as it will always stand ready, to move, together with the Russian Federation, to final resolution of the dispute in appeal proceedings pursuant to Article 25 of the DSU, on a reciprocal basis, based on the Multiparty Interim Arrangement (MPIA) and an arbitration agreement as set forth in the standard agreed default procedures contained in Annex 1 of the MPIA.[19]

Since early 2020, almost all WTO panel reports submitted to the DSB have been appealed into the void, leaving the disputes unsettled. As the WTO AB legal secretariat was dissolved in 2020 in response to US threats of blocking the WTO annual budget and the Trump administration blocked the EU request for making WTO Secretariat legal staff available for assistance in appellate arbitration pursuant to Article 25 DSU, this lack of institutionalized legal assistance and financial support from the WTO Secretariat confronted the ten WTO *ad hoc* appellate arbitrators with problems similar to those in ISA arbitration. For instance, while AB members represented the whole WTO membership defending systemic public interests, interim appeal arbitrators have a more limited mandate and may focus more on bilateral dispute settlement rather than on systemic WTO interpretations protecting the general interests of all WTO members. As the EU Commission gave in to the US pressures to renegotiate the AB rules and procedures as one part of more comprehensive WTO reforms (eg also aimed at settling some of the long-standing EU–US trade disputes), both the DSU review negotiations since 1998 (based on the December 1993 Ministerial Decision) and Ambassador Walker's WTO mediation for a WTO Ministerial Decision enabling the filling of WTO AB vacancies seem to have been abandoned in 2021.

in M Kolsky Lewis, H Nakagawa, RJ Neuwirth, CB Picker, and PT Stoll (eds), *A Post-WTO International Legal Order. Utopian, Dystopian and other Scenarios* (Springer 2020), 115–32.

[19] WT/DS494/7, at p 11.

8.3.2 WTO Members Should Comply with Their Duties to Fill AB Vacancies

If China or Russia should follow the short-sighted US strategy of using the WTO AB as a bargaining chip in WTO reform negotiations, the WTO trading, legal and compulsory WTO dispute settlement system could quickly become replaced by geopolitical and climate change power politics. Hence, all four strategic responses to the illegal US blockage of the AB should be pursued in parallel in accordance with the subsidiarity principle, that is bilaterally and plurilaterally agreed dispute settlement solutions should be used as pragmatic substitutes as long as the appellate procedures in Article 17 DSU remain illegally blocked. The reasons why, during the Uruguay Round negotiations in 1993, the US insisted on Article 17 DSU continue to remain valid. Most WTO panels are composed of diplomats without judicial training and detailed knowledge of GATT/WTO jurisprudence. Hence, the availability of institutionalized review of panel findings by AB members with legal expertise and independent legal support remains of crucial importance for the confidence of governments and their citizens that the quasi-automatic adoption of WTO panel and AB findings by the DSB will take into account the legitimate interests of all WTO members in a coherent WTO jurisprudence clarifying the often vague and disputed meaning of WTO rules. The US Trump administration was well known for its disdain of third-party adjudication and for its preference to impose US views through power politics. Yet, other WTO members have no reason to give in, once again, to short-sighted US interest group politics. Even without the United States, continuation of the compulsory AB system among 'willing countries' could provide more 'security and predictability to the multilateral trading system' (Article 3.2 DSU) than allowing the United States to destroy the AB system illegally. The current proposals for including a self-standing dispute settlement procedure into a future WTO Agreement on limitation of fishery subsidies suggest a return to the methodology of the 1979 Tokyo Round Agreements: WTO members seem unwilling to negotiate new WTO rules without functioning dispute settlement and enforcement procedures.

The illegal US destruction of the WTO AB in December 2019 was unilaterally imposed on the WTO membership by long-standing US trade lobbyists whose successful capture of key positions in the US trade policy bureaucracy (like USTR Robert Lighthizer and WTO Ambassador Dennis Shea) enabled them to prioritize US business interests (eg in rejecting the AB jurisprudence limiting US trade remedies). US trade policies returned to earlier, aggressive unilateralism by imposing bilateral protectionism (eg as during the 1980s regarding imports of steel and automobiles) and proposing legalization of protectionist US practices through new WTO rules (as it had been done in the 1979 GATT and 1994 WTO agreements on trade remedies and trade-related intellectual property rights). Likewise, the US criticism of the AB jurisprudence reflected the interests and demands of

US business lobbies (eg for more flexible trade remedy rules) and disregarded the customary rules of treaty interpretation and the (quasi)judicial AB mandate for impartial, independent, and prompt third-party adjudication.[20]

It remains to be seen whether a more comprehensive WTO compromise on how to improve the WTO legal and dispute settlement system, adjust WTO rules to the global regulatory challenges (eg of health pandemics and climate change), and strengthen the rule of law in international trade can be negotiated in 2021. As long as all five BRICS countries (Brazil, Russia, India, China, and South Africa) continue supporting the WTO dispute settlement system and the continuation of WTO appellate review, the EU should support leadership for maintaining, or further improving the WTO AB system. Majority voting on the filling of AB vacancies based on Article IX.1 WTO Agreement (possibly with a simultaneous, authoritative interpretation of Article IX.1)—together with offering pragmatic opt outs from Article 17 DSU for outvoted WTO members—might offer better fall-back alternatives than allowing one single WTO member to illegally destroy the WTO legal and dispute settlement systems.

8.4 Judicial Comity and Judicial Overreach in the EU's Constitutionalism 3.0: Lessons for Multilevel Judicial Protection of the SDGs

From the beginnings of European integration in the 1950s up to the Maastricht Treaty of 1992, the progressive transformation of European economic integration into a multilevel constitutional order was driven by the jurisprudence of the CJEU (eg on legal primacy, direct effect, direct applicability of EU law, judicial

[20] See Chapter 3, sections 3.3 and 3.4 on why the 2020 USTR Report—notwithstanding its valid criticism of some WTO rules and dispute settlement practices (eg that the AB no longer consulted with the parties when deciding to disregard the Article 17.5 deadline)—revealed systemic biases and incorrect claims. Even the AB's disregard for the ninety-day deadline for AB proceedings (Article 17.5 DSU) may have been justifiable on grounds of judicial administration of justice in view of the objective impossibility of meeting this unreasonable deadline (imposed by US negotiators in 1993) in view of the illegal US obstruction of the normal functioning of AB procedures (eg due to illegal blocking of the filling of AB vacancies, withholding of adequate administrative and financial resources at times of large numbers of simultaneously pending AB proceedings). The 2018 Chair of the AB, in his presentation of the annual AB Report for 2018, noted in this respect, *inter alia*: 'In recent months, several delegations have lamented the delays incurred by appellate proceedings beyond the 90 days set out in the DSU. Sadly, these critiques are accurate: the average duration of appeals completed in 2018 was 395 days. These slippages—which worry us as much as they worry Members—were often due to the AB's inability to staff cases with the reduced number of Appellate Body members and supporting lawyers, as well as the complex nature of the issues raised. However, focusing exclusively on delays in appellate proceedings risks obscuring the broader issue of duration of WTO disputes. In fact, appellate review is but a fraction of the total length of time of proceedings, which has been steadily increasing in recent years. Suffice it to say that the panel reports the AB reviewed in 2018 took, on average, 859 days to complete against the stipulated 6 months as of panel composition, or, at most, 9 months as of panel establishment' (quoted from WTO Appellate Body Annual Report for 2019–2020, WT/AB/30, at p. 161).

protection of human and constitutional rights, implied EU powers) and its acceptance and implementation by national courts and parliaments inside EU member states. Successive treaty reforms (eg introducing direct elections of the European parliament and its co-decision powers) and independent EU institutions (like the EU Commission as guardian of non-discriminatory conditions of competition) maintained a 'political equilibrium' respecting 'exit, voice and loyalty'.[21] From the 1992 Maastricht Treaty (eg consolidating the EU's single market, introducing the Economic and Monetary Union) until the 2009 Lisbon TEU, EU member states progressively 'constitutionalized' EU law (eg by the EUCFR) and improved the EU's micro-economic common market constitution, macro-economic monetary constitution, and multilevel foreign policy constitution,[22] thereby maintaining democratic support based on input legitimacy, output legitimacy, and respect for multilevel constitutional pluralism. The global financial crisis of 2008, Britain's referendum on EU membership of 2016, the US assault on the world trading system since 2017, the EU parliament's declaration of a global climate emergency of 2019, and the COVID-19 health pandemic of 2020/21 illustrated successive regulatory challenges testing the limits of EU law and policies, and of their implementation inside EU member states (eg in southern EU member states disregarding EU fiscal and debt disciplines, Hungary and Poland disregarding EU constitutional rights). In contrast to political and economic claims that global economic integration is incompatible with national sovereignty and democratic decision-making,[23] the EU's multilevel economic constitutionalism and multilevel constitutional, parliamentary, participatory, and deliberative democracy principles (cf Articles 9–12 TEU) can be reconciled through multilevel, judicial protection of transnational rule of law and fundamental rights, as illustrated by the following case studies.

8.4.1 *Ultra Vires* Acts in EU Governance?

The constitutional complaints, initiated in 2015 in Germany's Federal Constitutional Court (FCC) on behalf of more than 1,700 citizens, contended, *inter alia*, that the European Central Bank (ECB) decisions introducing the Public Sector Asset Purchase Programme (PSPP) and the Corporate Sector Purchase

[21] Cf J Weiler, The Transformation of Europe, *Yale Law Journal* 100 (1991), 2403–83; MP Maduro and M Wind (eds), *The Transformation of Europe Twenty-Five Years After* (CUP 2017).

[22] Cf Chapter 5, section 5.5 and EU Petersmann, The EU's Cosmopolitan Foreign Policy Constitution and its Disregard in Transatlantic Free Trade Agreements, *European Foreign Affairs Review* 21 (2016), 449–69.

[23] Cf D Rodrik, *The Globalization Paradox. Democracy and the Future of the World Economy* (WW Norton & Company 2011) and the convincing refutation of his 'incompatibility proposition' (ie that we cannot have national sovereignty, democratic politics, and global economic integration at once (cf at 200–1)—in the critical book review by RM Lastra in *International Journal of Constitutional Law* 11 (2013), 809–12. The EU's multilevel democratic constitutionalism offers the clearest refutation of Rodrik's state-centred views.

Programme (CSPP) constituted *ultra vires* acts violating the EU prohibition of monetary financing (Article 123.1 TFEU) and the principle of conferral of limited EU powers (Article 5.1 TEU in conjunction with Articles 119, 127 ff TFEU). The complainants asserted violations of their constitutional rights to democratic self-determination and of the constitutional identity enshrined in Germany's Basic Law to the extent that the ECB programmes infringed the budgetary powers of the German *Bundestag*. They challenged the omission on the part of the Bundestag, the Federal Government, and the Federal Central Bank to take steps against the PSPP; their constitutional complaints sought a judicial declaration from the FCC that the Federal Government and the Bundestag had violated their constitutional responsibilities with regard to European integration. In 2017, the second senate of the FCC suspended the proceedings and referred a number of related questions to the CJEU for a preliminary ruling pursuant to Article 267.1 TFEU. By the judgment of 11 December 2018,[24] the CJEU responded that its consideration of the questions from the FCC had disclosed no such factor as to affect the validity of the ECB decisions concerned. The FCC judgment of 5 May 2020[25] declared the constitutional complaints 'well-founded to the extent that they challenge the omission on the part of the Federal Government and the Bundestag to take suitable steps to ensure that the ECB, by means of purchasing securities under the PSPP, does not exceed its monetary policy competence and encroach upon the economic policy competence of the Member States' (paragraph 97). This finding was based, *inter alia*, on the following conclusions:

- 'The democratic legitimation by the people of public authority exercised in Germany belongs to the essential contents of the principle of the sovereignty of the people and thus forms part of the Basic Law's constitutional identity protected in Art. 79(3) GG; it is therefore beyond the reach of European integration in accordance with Art. 23(1) third sentence in conjunction with Art. 79(3) GG' (paragraph 101).
- 'The Basic Law … prohibits conferring upon the European Union the competence to decide on its own competences (Kompetenz-Kompetenz) … dynamic treaty provisions must be subject to suitable safeguards that enable the German constitutional organs to effectively exercise their responsibility with regard to European integration' (paragraph 102).

[24] CJEU, *Weiss and others*, C-493/17, EU:C:2018:1000.

[25] Bundesverfassungsgericht 2 BvR 859/15, 1651/15, 2006/15, and 980/16; an English translation of the judgment is available on the website of the FCC: https://www.bundesverfassungsgericht.de. The judgment does not rule on the Pandemic Emergency Purchase Programme (PEPP) that the ECB announced on 18 March 2020 to address the effects of the COVID-19 pandemic. Nonetheless, it calls into question also the legality of this programme and makes further constitutional complaints against the PEPP more likely.

- 'It is for the German Bundestag, as the organ directly accountable to the people, to take all essential decisions on revenue and expenditure; this prerogative forms part of the core of Art. 20(1) and (2) GG, which is beyond the reach of constitutional amendment . . . a transfer of sovereign powers violates the principle of democracy at least in cases where the type and level of public spending are, to a significant extent, determined at the supranational level, depriving the Bundestag of its decision-making prerogative' (paragraph 104).
- 'Where measures taken by institutions, bodies, offices and agencies of the European Union exceed the limits of the European integration agenda (*Integrationsprogramm*) in a manifest and structurally significant manner, it is incumbent upon the Federal Government and the Bundestag to actively address the question how the order of competences can be restored and to make a positive determination as to which course of action to pursue' (paragraph 109).
- 'While the Federal Constitutional Court must review substantiated *ultra vires* challenges regarding acts of institutions, bodies, offices and agencies of the European Union, the Treaties confer upon the CJEU the mandate to interpret and apply the Treaties and to ensure uniformity and coherence of EU law (cf Art. 19(1) subpara. 2 TEU, Art. 267 TFEU); it is imperative that the respective judicial mandates be exercised in a coordinated manner . . . the Member States remain the "Masters of the Treaties" and the EU has not evolved into a federal state' (paragraph 111).
- 'The *ultra vires* review must be exercised with restraint, giving effect to the Constitution's openness to European integration . . . The methodological standards recognized by the CJEU for the judicial development of the law are based on the (constitutional) legal traditions common to the Member States (cf also Art. 6(3) TEU, Art. 340(2) TFEU), which are notably reflected in the case-law of the Member States' constitutional and apex courts and of the European Court of Human Rights . . . the mandate conferred in Article 19(1) second sentence TEU is exceeded where the traditional European methods of interpretation or, more broadly, the general legal principles that are common to the laws of the Member States are manifestly disregarded' (paragraph 112).
- 'If the CJEU crosses the limit set out above, its actions are no longer covered by the mandate conferred in Article 19(1) second sentence TEU in conjunction with the domestic Act of Approval; at least in relation to Germany, its decision then lacks the minimum of democratic legitimation necessary under Art. 23(1) second sentence in conjunction with Article 20(1) and (2) and 79(3) GG' (paragraph 113).
- 'Where such acts of institutions, bodies, offices and agencies of the European Union give rise to effects that bear on Germany's constitutional identity enshrined in Art. 1 and 20 GG, they exceed the limits of open statehood set by the Basic Law . . . This concerns the protection of the human dignity core

enshrined in fundamental rights under Art. 1 GG ... as well as the basic tenets that inform the principles of democracy, the rule of law, the social state and the federal state within the meaning of Art. 20 GG. With a view to the principle of democracy enshrined in Art. 20(1) and (2) GG, it must *inter alia* be ensured that the German Bundestag retain for itself functions and powers of substantial significance ... and that it remains capable of exercising its overall budgetary responsibility' (paragraph 115).

- 'Based on these standards, the Federal Government and the German Bundestag violated the rights of the complainants ... by failing to take suitable steps challenging that the ECB, in Decision (EU) 2015/774 as amended ... neither assessed nor substantiated that the measures provided for in these decisions satisfy the principle of proportionality. In light of this, Decision (EU) 2015/774 and amending Decisions ... constitute a qualified, i.e. manifest and structurally significant, exceeding of the competences assigned to the ECB in Art. 119, Art. 127 *et seq.* TFEU and Art. 17 *et seq.* ESCB Statute. The differing view of the CJEU set out in its judgment of 11 December 2018 does not merit a different conclusion, given that on this point, the judgment is simply not comprehensible so that, to this extent, the judgment was rendered *ultra vires*... Nevertheless, it cannot be definitively determined whether the ECB decisions at issue satisfy the principle of proportionality'[26]

Arguably, German constitutional law, the Lisbon Treaty, and their multilevel judicial interpretation and application illustrate systemic constitutional problems of multilevel governance of aggregate PGs (like transnational economic markets, rule of law, democratic governance, the SDGs) that are of importance also in multilevel governance of global PGs (eg in the WTO) and related judicial challenges (eg in AB and ISA jurisprudence). For instance, the focus of the FCC on the constitutional principles of conferral (limited delegation of power), proportionality review, subsidiarity, democracy, and respect for national constitutional identities may offer lessons also for challenges of judicial overreach in the AB and in ISA.

[26] These very incomplete excerpts from the long FCC judgment are sufficient for the limited purposes of this chapter. For a more complete summary and criticism of the reasoning of the FCC see, eg, I Feichtner, The German Constitutional Court's PSPP Judgment: Impediment and Impetus for the Democratization of Europe, *German Law Journal* 21 (2020), 1090–103. As regards the diverse, recent challenges of the primacy of EU law by national courts in EU member states (like France, Germany, Hungary, and Poland), it is important to distinguish national challenges of the EU rule of law principles (eg by Poland's government disregarding the independence of judicial powers) from national courts protecting the diverse constitutional identities of EU member states (like Germany's FCC protecting democratic constitutionalism as prescribed in the German Basic Law).

8.4.2 The Principle of Limited Delegation of Powers

All international organizations for multilevel governance of transnational PGs operate on the basis of limited delegation of powers by member states. Democratic constitutions delegate limited governance powers to representative, majoritarian institutions (like parliaments and elected governments) and non-majoritarian institutions (like central banks and courts of justice) subject to requirements of rule of law and judicial remedies; as emphasized by the FCC in the judgment on *ultra vires* acts of EU institutions cited earlier; they do not confer on international organizations competence-competence to enlarge their limited powers for imposing new obligations without consent of member states on behalf of their peoples. Moreover, discourse theories justifying democratic discourse (eg by relying on transparent, inclusive, general, and reciprocal reasoning) differ from those for judicial deliberations and judicial comity (eg focusing on judicial dispute settlement functions different from legislative and administrative decision-making).[27]

The WTO's DSU acknowledges: 'Recommendations and rulings of the DSB cannot add to or diminish the rights and obligations provided in the covered agreements' (Article 3.2). This provision, introduced during the Uruguay Round negotiations at the request of the US delegation, was construed in conformity with the recognition by member states that the DSU 'serves to preserve the rights and obligations of Members under the covered agreements, and to clarify the existing provisions of those agreements in accordance with customary rules of interpretation of public international law' (Article 3.2 DSU). WTO, ISA, and EU judicial bodies apply customary rules of treaty interpretation common to the member states. As the constitutional context of EU law differs from the international legal context of WTO law, 'systemic treaty interpretation' (Article 31.3,c VCLT) clarifying treaty provisions on the basis of general principles of law common to the member states may differ among international organizations depending on their respective legal contexts. According to the AB, WTO legal interpretations clarifying WTO provisions in conformity with the customary rules of treaty interpretation cannot simultaneously violate the DSU prohibitions of 'add[ing] to or diminish[ing] the rights and obligations provided in the covered agreements' (Articles 3.2 and 19.2 DSU).[28] Yet, as emphasized in the *Achmea* judgment, the EU constitutional principles (eg on fundamental rights) and judicial remedies prevail over the applicable law in ISA

[27] Cf A Follesdal and G Ulfstein (eds), *The Judicialization of International Law. A Mixed Blessing* (OUP 2018); R Forst, *Normativity and Power: Analyzing Social Orders of Justification* (OUP 2017); EU Petersmann, 'Constitutional Theories of International Economic Adjudication and Investor-State Arbitration' in PM Dupuy, F Francioni, and EU Petersmann (eds), *Human Rights in International Investment Law and Arbitration* (OUP 2009), 137–96; J Habermas, *Between Facts and Norms. Contributions to a Discourse Theory of Law and Democracy* (MIT Press 1998), at 194ff.

[28] Cf AB Report, WT/DS110/AB/R, *Chile-Alcoholic Beverages* (2000), para 79. For an explanation of the interpretative approaches of the AB, see P Van den Bossche and W Zdouc, *The Law and Policy of the World Trade Organization. Text, Cases and Materials* (4th edn, CUP 2017), 190ff.

involving EU member states; they create directly applicable rights. As emphasized by the FCC, the EU member states and their national constitutional identities are protected by EU law against unjustified (eg disproportionate) interference by EU institutions. Article 5.1 TEU, for instance, clarifies the principle of conferral by specifying '[t]he use of Union competences is governed by the principles of subsidiarity and proportionality'. In its judicial examination of whether the contested ECB decisions and the related CJEU judgment are consistent with the proportionality principle as defined in the common constitutional traditions of EU member states as applied by their highest courts, the German FCC criticized both the ECB decisions and the related judgment of the CJEU for failing to examine whether the ECB's use of monetary policy instruments disproportionately affected the national economic and fiscal policy competences of EU member states; according to the FCC, they 'manifestly fail[ed] to give consideration to the importance and scope of the principle of proportionality (Art. 5(1) second sentence and Art. 5(4) TEU), which also applies to the division of competences'.[29]

8.4.3 Democratic Constitutional Pluralism and Subsidiarity

Western democracies proceed from human rights, the rule of law, and democracy as three core principles of democratic constitutionalism. Yet, their national constitutions, democratic legislation, administration, and jurisprudence differ, depending on their diverse histories and democratic preferences. For instance, the German Basic Law's protection of judicially enforceable, constitutional rights to democratic self-determination, including the parliamentary prerogative of taking all essential decisions on revenue and expenditure as an indispensable element of constitutional democracy in Germany, differs from constitutional traditions in other EU member states. This diversity of democratically defined national identities must be respected by the law of international organizations, as explicitly prescribed in Article 4 TEU and as explained in the German FCC judgment of 5 May 2020:

[29] Note 25, para 119. According to the FCC, the CJEU had examined only the suitability and necessity of the PSPP for realizing the monetary policy objective without judicial proportionality *stricto sensu* review balancing the monetary policy effects with the PSPP's adverse effects on the economic policy competences of EU member states. Such transparent proportionality balancing by the ECB and by the CJEU would enhance rule of law and also democratic accountability of EU monetary policies (eg by helping parliaments and governments to exercise what the FCC calls their 'integration responsibility'). On 18 May 2021, the FCC rejected applications to revisit its judgment of May 2020; it found, *inter alia*: 'The applications are also unfounded given that the federal government and the Bundestag substantially addressed and appraised the monetary policy decisions taken by the ECB governing council following the judgment of May 5 2020, including the proportionality assessment conducted and substantiated by the ECB' (quoted from *Financial Times* 19 May 2021).

> The democratic legitimation by the people of public authority exercised in Germany belongs to the essential contents of the principle of the sovereignty of the people and thus forms part of the Basic Law's constitutional identity protected in Art. 79(3) GG; it is therefore beyond the reach of European integration in accordance with Article 23(1) third sentence in conjunction with Art. 79(3) GG.[30]

Constitutional democracy as a constitutional constraint on multilevel governance of PGs—as defined in German constitutional law and protected by Articles 4 and 5 TEU—differs from merely majoritarian, political conceptions of democratic governance. Yet, the EU Treaty definitions of respect for national identities (Article 4.2 TEU) and of the principles of conferral and subsidiarity in Articles 5.2 and 5.3 TEU are context-dependent; they may differ from those in other treaty systems, for instance the legal principles applied by the European Court of Human Rights (ECtHR) for interpreting the ECHR (like purpose-oriented interpretation, dynamic interpretation, subsidiarity, margin of appreciation, significance of national and international law).

In its 2020 Report on the WTO AB, the USTR complained of 'persistent overreaching' by the AB in its interpretation of WTO rules:'this overreaching also violates the basic principles of the United States Government. There is no legitimacy under our democratic, constitutional system for the nation to submit to a rule imposed by three individuals sitting in Geneva, with neither agreement by the United States nor approval by the United States Congress.'[31] Yet, the very long USTR Report identifies no AB interpretation that could not be justifiable based on the (quasi)judicial DSU mandate 'to clarify the existing provisions of those agreements in accordance with customary rules of interpretation of public international law' for the 'prompt settlement' of disputes (Article 3 DSU). Nor does the Report identify a US constitutional law provisions prohibiting US consent to international third-party adjudication. As both the US government and the US Congress approved the WTO Agreements and the DSU provisions (including Article 17 on the establishment of the AB), and the US government consented to the appointment of each AB member, the USTR claims are factually wrong, as are so many other populist claims of the US Trump administration. Such political claims by majoritarian government institutions cannot justify non-compliance with democratically approved treaty obligations, such as the US blocking of AB nominations aimed at

[30] BVerfG (n 25), para 101. The FCC's interpretation of the budgetary and fiscal responsibilities of the German Bundestag as a core element of democratic self-determination, constitutional identity, and integration responsibility in Germany will be relevant for deciding the pending constitutional complaint challenging the German legislation approving the EU Council Decision 2020/2053 of 14 December 2020 based on Article 311.3 TFEU for the financing of the EU Recovery and Resilience Facility and Next Generation EU investment program through EU credits/bonds of up to €750 billion.

[31] See the 'Introduction' in *Report on the Appellate Body of the WTO*, Washington, DC, February 2020, (https://ustr.gov/about-us/policy-offices/press-office/press-releases/2020/february/ustr-issues-report-wto-appellate-body).

rendering the AB dysfunctional in violation of Article 17.2 DSU. The democratic approval of the WTO Agreement by parliaments confers limited, democratic legitimacy also on the AB as long as it operates within its legal constraints and respects the subsidiarity principle, for instance by choosing judicial interpretations that respect legitimate constitutional pluralism in the interpretation of the general and security exceptions in WTO law (eg on sovereign rights to protect public morals, public order, and essential security interests). There is no evidence, so far, that the related WTO jurisprudence (as discussed in Chapter 6) has exceeded what the German FCC called the traditional European methods of interpretation or, more broadly, the general legal principles that are common to the laws of WTO Member States.

8.4.4 Multilevel Judicial Comity in Protecting Rule of Law

All UN member states have introduced judicial remedies in multilevel courts of justice in view of the fact that judicial procedures and judgments risk being affected by human mistakes which, on request, should be subject to legal review by courts of higher instance. Chapters 5–7 described the emergence of multilevel judicial remedies and rule of law at national, regional, and international levels of governance in international trade, investment, and economic integration law. As recalled in Chapter 5, access of individuals, juridical persons (eg companies), governments, and European institutions (like the EU Commission, the EFTA Surveillance Authority) to European courts (like the CJEU, the EFTA Court, the ECtHR)—and the preliminary ruling procedures and advisory opinion procedures for multilevel cooperation among national and European courts—offered more comprehensive judicial remedies for protecting human, constitutional, and other rights than are provided for in other international legal systems. In all national and international legal systems, judicial dialogues among lower and upper courts of justice have been crucial for cultivating public reason and for resolving allegations of judicial overreach, as discussed earlier with regard to ISA inside the EU, the AB jurisprudence in the WTO, and the contested limits of reciprocal review of CJEU judgments and national constitutional courts inside the EU.[32] By giving reasons, protecting the rule of law through impartial third-party adjudication and cooperating by means of judicial comity,[33] courts of justice contribute to the clarification of public reason and of constitutional justice as a restraint on judicial overreach, thereby enhancing the collective capability and democratic legitimacy of multilevel governance and

[32] See also F Fontanelli, G Martinico, and P Carozza (eds), *Shaping Rule of Law Through Dialogue* (Intersentia 2009), and my Introduction to this book on '"Constitutional Justice" Requires Judicial Cooperation and "Comity" in the Protection of "Rule of Law"', at 1–19.

[33] Cf JH Fahner, *Judicial Deference in International Adjudication. A Comparative Analysis* (Hart 2020).

of its democratic support by citizens. Power-oriented sovereignty claims that governments can always reject judicial deductions from general treaty rules and legal principles by invoking their lack of specific consent to such deductive clarifications of legal rules[34] were shown to be inconsistent with the modern international law rules on treaty interpretation. As illustrated by the GATT/WTO and ISA jurisprudence discussed in Chapter 6, the consistent and systemic treaty interpretation requirements of the customary rules of interpretation also require judicial comity taking into account relevant jurisprudence of other jurisdictions (eg WTO dispute settlement bodies accepting factual advice from the World Intellectual Property Organization (WIPO) Secretariat on past interpretations of WIPO conventions, or from the Framework Convention on Tobacco Control (FCTC) Secretariat on past interpretations of FCTC provisions).

As international organizations do not have competence-competence, disagreements over *ultra vires* acts of international institutions (like the CJEU, ISA, or the WTO AB) must be resolved either through multilevel judicial cooperation or agreed compromises among governments with due respect for legitimate constitutional pluralism and for constitutional law principles common to the member states concerned. 'Manifest' and 'structurally significant' *ultra vires* acts, as criticized in the German FCC judgment of 5 May 2020, have remained very rare and contested in the evolution of international law and jurisprudence. The FCC rightly emphasizes that, as member states remain the 'masters of the treaties', and the EU has not evolved into a federal state, such conflicts 'must be resolved in a co-operative manner, in keeping with the spirit of European integration, and mitigated through mutual respect and understanding'.[35] As the German government accepted the subsequent 'proportionality justifications' by the ECB, academic proposals for introducing additional EU law remedies for reviewing alleged '*ultra vires* acts' were not pursued so far.[36] Yet, as the EU Commission started infringement proceedings challenging the disregard for CJEU judgments by the FCC as well as by other national constitutional courts (eg in Poland), additional legal compromise and judicial comity procedures for agreed demarcations of the scope of national and international jurisdictions may be needed also inside the EU.

Due to the lack of evidence that the WTO AB engaged in arbitrary *ultra vires* acts violating the customary rules of treaty interpretation, WTO members and WTO institutions remain legally required to protect the AB as defined in Article 17

[34] Cf M Koskenniemi, *From Apology to Utopia. The Structure of International Legal Argument* (CUP 2005), at 69; M Koskenniemi, *The Politics of International Law* (Hart 2011). Among his fourteen articles republished in the latter book, only one seems to acknowledge—at 238ff—that constitutional approaches to interpretation and development of treaty systems can protect human rights and community interests more effectively.

[35] Note 25, para 111.

[36] Cf J Weiler and D Sarmiento, The EU Judiciary after Weiss—Proposing a new Mixed Chamber of the Court of Justice: A Reply to our Critics, *European Journal of International Law Talk* Blog of 8 July 2020.

DSU and to clarify the legal constraints limiting the AB jurisprudence. In contrast to the finding of the German FCC that insufficient proportionality balancing in delimiting EU monetary policy powers from national economic and fiscal policy powers infringed the democratic rights of citizens and the parliamentary responsibilities under German constitutional law, the scope of the proportionality principle in WTO AB jurisprudence remains limited to reviewing and protecting rights and obligations of WTO members. In view of the broad interpretation of national competences under the general exceptions of GATT/WTO law (as discussed in Chapter 6), there is no evidence that the AB jurisprudence has disproportionately limited national competences (eg to restrict trade on grounds of public morals). The compromise proposal by the WTO Facilitator Ambassador Walker for resolving the WTO AB crisis,[37] the EU initiative for a plurilateral agreement on using appellate arbitration based on Article 25 DSU as an interim solution pending the illegal US blocking of AB nominations,[38] the EU initiatives for transforming ISA into a multicourt system inside the EU as well as in the context of external EU trade and investment agreements offer reasonable, political responses to the ongoing challenges of WTO and ISA jurisprudence.

Due to the interdependencies between trade, investment, environmental, economic integration, and human rights agreements, their mutual coherence—and efficient solutions of the global economic, health, environmental, and political governance crises—require multilevel, legal and judicial protection of transnational rule of law. The mere fact that US trade politicians and trade lobbyists do not wish to comply with legal constraints (like the customary rules of treaty interpretation) and with the separation of legislative, executive, and judicial powers in WTO law (eg in Articles III, IX WTO Agreement, the DSU) is no reason for other WTO members to accept the illegal incapacitation of the WTO AB contrary to what democratic institutions prescribed in Article 17 DSU. As long as the legislative procedure for amending the DSU has not been followed, the DSU does not authorize illegal blocking of the filling of AB vacancies as an arbitrary means for *de facto* amendments of the DSU contradicting the approval of the WTO Agreement by democratic institutions; for the reasons explained in Chapter 6, section 6.4, the WTO Ministerial Conference and the General Council remain legally required to fill the vacant AB positions as prescribed in Article 17 DSU, if necessary by majority decisions as prescribed in Article IX.1 WTO Agreement—possibly backed up by related authoritative interpretations confirming the powers of the WTO Ministerial Conference and the General Council to such protection of respect for Article 17 DSU.

[37] Cf WTO doc. JOB/GC/222 of 15 October 2019.

[38] Cf WTO doc. JOB/DSB/1/Add.12 of 30 April 2020 (on behalf of the EU and nineteen other WTO members participating in this interim appellate arbitration system).

8.4.5 Lessons for Judicial Balancing of the SDGs? The Example of the 2019 German Climate Protection Act

This chapter argued that the global economic, health, environmental, and political crises cannot be resolved in coherent and legitimate ways without multilevel legal and judicial remedies protecting transnational rule of law. As discussed in the concluding Chapter 9, the international community's incapacity to effectively regulate global environmental problems (like climate change, biodiversity losses, pollution of the oceans) confirms the need for interpreting the WTO objective of sustainable development in conformity with the UN's 2030 Agenda for Sustainable Development in order to make it clear for citizens, democratic institutions, and governments that the seventeen SDGs protecting citizens and their human rights (eg to health and environmental protection) cannot be realized without multilateral treaties and institutions coordinating national, regional, and worldwide governance, including WTO law and WTO third-party adjudication protecting lawful use of trade policy instruments (like border adjustments of national carbon taxes aimed at reducing GHG emissions, non-discriminatory access to vaccines and medical equipment) in common responses to the regulatory challenges of the global health, environmental, economic, and rule of law crises. Regulatory competition among WTO members with mutually inconsistent neoliberal, state capitalist, ordo-liberal constitutional, or third-world conceptions of economic regulation entails not only that judicial remedies and judicial balancing of the human rights values underlying the seventeen SDGs are likely to differ at national levels of governance. The global interdependence of the increasing health and climate emergencies also requires stronger regional and worldwide judicial remedies, notably a strong WTO dispute settlement system preventing trade wars, promoting independent judicial rule clarifications and peaceful dispute settlements, and assisting UN and WTO members in realizing their universally agreed SDGs. The politics of climate change litigation must be limited by taking into account scientific knowledge and independently established facts in evidence-based judicial balancing and clarification of SDGs and indeterminate principles (eg for protection of climate justice and climate refugees from island states risking being submerged by rising sea levels).

The advantages of institutional checks and balances were illustrated by the Order of the German Constitutional Court of 24 March 2021 protecting the constitutional complaints by German climate activists against Germany's Federal Climate Change Act of 2019.[39] The Federal Climate Change Act makes it obligatory

[39] The Constitutional Court decision can be found on the website of the German Constitutional Court (BVerfG, decision of the First Senate of March 24, 2021—1 BvR 2656/18, Rn. 1-270, http://www.bverfg.de/e/rs20210324_1bvr265618.html); for a brief discussion, see note 44 and the related text in Chapter 4. The official press release summarizing this Order in English is available on the same website of Germany's FCC.

to reduce greenhouse gas (GHG) emissions by at least 55 per cent by 2030 relative to 1990 levels; it sets out the reduction pathways applicable during this period by means of sectoral annual emission amounts. The complainants claimed that the legislation failed to introduce a legal framework sufficient for swiftly reducing GHG, especially carbon dioxide (CO_2). The Court found that the legislative emission reduction targets respond to the constitutional duty (Article 20a Basic Law) to protect the claimants from harm against climate change at present. Yet, the challenged provisions were found to violate the freedoms of young complainants by irreversibly offloading major emission reduction burdens onto periods after 2030. The Court defined the constitutional climate goal arising from Article 20a Basic Law, which protects the natural foundations of life like the environment, in accordance with the Paris target as being to limit the increase in the global average temperature to well below 2 °C and preferably to 1.5 °C above pre-industrial levels. For this target to be reached, the reductions still necessary after 2030 will have to be achieved with ever greater speed and urgency. These future obligations to reduce emissions have an impact on practically every type of constitutional freedoms because virtually all aspects of human life still involve the emission of GHG and are thus potentially threatened by drastic restrictions after 2030. Therefore, the legislator should have taken precautionary steps to mitigate these major burdens in order to safeguard the freedoms guaranteed by fundamental rights. The statutory provisions on adjusting the reduction pathway for GHG emissions from 2031 onwards are not sufficient to ensure that the necessary transition to climate neutrality is achieved by the deadline. The legislator must enact provisions by 31 December 2022 that specify in greater detail how the reduction targets for greenhouse gas emissions are to be adjusted for periods after 2030. The Court held that the provisions of the Federal Climate Change Act governing national climate targets and the annual emission amounts allowed until 2030 are incompatible with fundamental rights insofar as they lack sufficient specifications for further emission reductions from 2031 onwards. In all other respects, the constitutional complaints were rejected. By protecting constitutional complaints against insufficient climate mitigation measures from individual natural persons in Germany and abroad (some of the complainants lived in Bangladesh and Nepal), the Court opened access to justice for future complaints challenging the adequacy of German climate mitigation measures.

Four legally innovative features of this judgment are that (i) climate change mitigation measures are recognized as a constitutional requirement, and (ii) carbon reductions are legally interpreted as limitations of constitutional freedoms; (iii) legal carbon reduction commitments have to be distributed in proportionate ways; and (iv) individual constitutional complaints are admitted and successfully protected not only for the benefit of individual complaints by German citizens, but also—albeit in more limited ways—by foreign citizens adversely affected by climate change.[40] Legislation placing too much of the GHG reduction burdens on future generations requires democratic justification; it may necessitate emergency measures in the coming years that risk burdening younger complainants disproportionately. The judgment illustrates the importance of multilevel constitutional theories of justice (as discussed above in Chapter 2, section 2.3.1) interpreting national constitutions and multilateral treaties for protecting global PGs in mutually consistent ways. Germany's constitutional commitments to protecting human and constitutional rights (eg in Articles 1–19 Basic Law) as well as the natural foundations of life (Article 20a Basic Law) were construed in conformity with European and UN treaty obligations accepted by the German parliament for protecting the fundamental rights of present and future generations; they require distributing the adjustment burdens to climate change in proportionate ways to be determined by the democratic legislator. As regards future emission reductions for the time after 2030, the court found a 'heightened risk of serious losses of freedom because there would then be a shorter timeframe for the technological and social developments required to enable today's still heavily CO_2-oriented lifestyle to make the transition to climate-neutral behavior in a way that respects freedom'. According to the court, a climate target that allows for the depletion of the remaining carbon budget constitutes an advance interference-like effect (*eingriffsähnliche Vorwirkung*) on individual freedoms: if the remaining carbon budget is used too quickly, there must be important restrictions of individual freedoms protected by the Basic Law at a later stage. Such a risk of serious individual rights restrictions has constitutional law implications at present. Every amount of CO_2 that is allowed today narrows the remaining options for reducing emissions in compliance with Article 20a Basic Law as specified in Article 2 of the 2015 Paris Agreement and the German commitment to climate neutrality by 2050 (§ 1 Climate Protection Act). To avoid such interference-like effects on practically every type of individual freedoms, the court ordered the legislator to enact (until 31 December 2022) provisions on emission reductions from 2031 onwards, which are for now lacking in the Act: 'In order to be constitutional, the advance interference-like effect of current emission provisions—an effect that arises not only de facto, but also de jure—must be compatible with the objective obligation to take climate action as enshrined in Art 20a (Basic Law).' The Constitutional Court's protection of justiciable rights aimed at protecting future generations and intergenerational equity as a constitutional law requirement are of importance far beyond Germany; in the words of the Court, 'one generation must not be allowed to consume large portions of the CO_2 budget while bearing a relatively minor share of the reduction effort if this would involve

[40] In this respect, individual access to the German Constitutional Court is less restrictive than individual access to the CJEU, which rejected similar actions for annulment by EU citizens for 'lack of individual concern' in a Judgment of the Court (Sixth Chamber) of 25 March 2021 (*Armando Carvalho and Others v European Parliament and Council of the European Union*, Case C-565/19 P, ECLI:EU:C:2021:252).

leaving subsequent generations with a drastic reduction burden and expose their lives to comprehensive losses of freedom'.[41] By relying on multilateral treaty obligations for overcoming the counter-majoritarian difficulty in judicial review of democratic legislation on protection of SDGs,[42] the Constitutional Court not only clarified the complex interrelationships between national and international law, legislatures, governmental institutions (like the Intergovernmental Panel on Climate Change), and courts of justice in multilevel governance of PGs like climate change mitigation and the SDGs. It also recognized constitutional duties to protect the human rights of people outside Germany, which—in this case—Germany had fulfilled by ratifying and implementing the 2015 Paris Agreement. Interpreting national Constitutions in conformity with multilateral treaty obligations accepted by national parliaments reflects the multilevel constitutional restraints of multilevel governance of PGs, without excluding judicial insistence (as in the *Weiss* judgment of the Constitutional Court discussed above) that multilevel constitutional requirements (eg of proportionality balancing) must be respected by EU institutions with limited, delegated powers subject to constitutional and judicial restraints.

The more current political discourse neglects scientific facts and the limited time for keeping temperature increases below the UN goal of 'well below 2 degrees Celsius above pre-industrial levels', courts of justice have good reasons for insisting that democratic lawmakers take into account the explicit acknowledgment in the 2030 Agenda for Sustainable Development that the seventeen SDGs are 'integrated and indivisible and balance the three dimensions of sustainable development: the economic, social and environmental' (Preamble). As the seventeen SDGs are mutually supportive—and climate change poses a foreseeable threat to civilization, living conditions, and the earth's systems—climate justice (eg in terms of burden-sharing among generations) supports the arguments from constitutional justice that justifying law and governance vis-à-vis citizens and their human rights requires stronger, multilevel judicial remedies, proportionality balancing, and judicial comity in multilevel UN and WTO governance protecting the SDGs and related constitutional and human rights.[43] The four years of climate change denial

[41] For more detailed analyses of the Constitutional Court order, see AJ Saiger, The Constitution Speaks in the Future Tense: On the Constitutional Complaints against the Federal Climate Protection Act, in *Verfassungsblog* of 29 April 2021 (https://verfassungsblog.de/the-constitution-speaks-in-the-future-tense/, DOI:10.17176/20210429-221250-0).

[42] In an order of 15 December 2015 (see Press Release No. 9/2916, available on the website of the German Constitutional Court), the German Constitutional Court acknowledged that treaty overrides by later national legislation may be permissible under the German Constitution ('The principle of democracy requires that, within the boundaries set by the Basic Law, later legislatures be able to revoke legal acts of previous legislatures. Neither the rule of law nor the principle of the Constitution's openness to international law (*Grundsatz der Völkerrechtsfreundlichkeit des Grundgesetzes*) yield a different result. Although the latter principle is also of constitutional rank, it does not entail an absolute constitutional duty to obey all rules of international law.').

[43] On the challenges of reconciling civil, political, economic, social, cultural, and environmental constitutional and human rights, see JH Knox and R Pejan (eds), *The Human Right to a Healthy Environment* (CUP 2018).

practised by the US Trump administration—similar to the Trump administration's systemic disinformation in justifying its arbitrary assault on the WTO legal and appellate review system (as discussed in Chapter 3)—confirm what was emphasized in Chapter 2, section 2.1 and Chapter 4, section 4.2: Authoritarian refusal to escape from one's 'self-incurred immaturity' (Immanuel Kant)—and to use inclusive reasonableness and evidence-based science for participating in open 'conjectures and refutations' (Karl Popper) for problem-solving—reveals not only bad faith and lack of truthfulness; it also disregards the human right to justification of governmental restrictions of human and constitutional rights.[44] The more climate change, global health pandemics, and related economic crises proceed, the more measures protecting the SDGs risk interfering with human and constitutional rights (like intellectual property rights of pharmaceutical and green technology companies). The related adjustment burdens must be distributed in proportionate, justifiable ways among citizens and future generations. Moreover, as emphasized in the Constitutional Court judgment, the national democratic legislator and government executives, European law and institutions, and UN law and institutions with limited, delegated powers must cooperate in multilevel governance of global PGs with due respect for their different, yet complementary legal and political functions. This multilevel legislative, executive and judicial cooperation for constituting, limiting, regulating, and justifying multilevel governance of global PGs requires new twenty-first century constitutionalism in order to save humanity from global governance failures like climate change, unnecessary poverty, and global health pandemics, as discussed in the concluding Chapter 9.

[44] On the human right to justification see R Forst, *The Right to Justification. Elements of a Constructivist Theory of Justice* (Columbia UP 2012). On the decay of deliberative democracy under US President Trump, see J Kavanagh and M Rich, *Truth Decay. An Initial Exploration of the Diminishing Role of Facts and Analysis in American Public Life* (Rand Corporation 2018); M Wolf, 'The struggle for the survival of US democracy', *Financial Times* 11 May 2021.

9
Conclusions: Multilevel Governance of Sustainable Development Requires Multilevel Twenty-First Century Constitutionalism

If 'justice is the first virtue of social institutions'[1] and the existential impact of global climate change, health pandemics, and other governance failures on peoples, citizens, and interpersonal relations beyond states render the path-dependent treatment of citizens as mere objects of United Nations (UN) and World Trade Organization (WTO) governance unjust, how can citizens meet their moral and political responsibilities and duties to support and further just institutions and abolish unjust institutions? This book has argued that the universally agreed Sustainable Development Goals (SDGs), their objective of realizing just societies (social justice), and their moral foundations (like respect for individual and democratic autonomy) offer citizens reasonable justifications and standards for criticizing power politics of UN member states. The objective of transforming the world in order to realize the SDGs requires transforming UN and WTO *legal practices* in order to better protect transnational rule of law and judicial remedies against abuses of foreign and domestic policy powers. Amending the UN Charter and the WTO Agreement may neither be politically feasible nor legally necessary. For example, just as the UN Security Council has addressed global health problems through Security Council resolutions (known as 'securitization of global health'),[2] so are global environmental problems and other SDGs likely to increasingly become the subject of Security Council actions or—in case of inaction by the Security Council—of humanitarian interventions by democratic alliances. The judicial function of peaceful settlement of disputes through impartial clarifications of the disputed content of legal rights and obligations helps to maintain the consistency of national and international legal systems with new regulatory challenges, as illustrated in Chapters 6–8 by the examples of judicial protection of human rights

[1] J Rawls, *A Theory of Justice* (Revised edn, Harvard UP 1999), at 3.

[2] Cf P Villarreal, The Security Council and Covid-19: Towards a Medicalization of International Peace and Security, *ESIL Reflections* 9(6) (2021).

Transforming World Trade and Investment Law for Sustainable Development. Ernst-Ulrich Petersmann, Oxford University Press. © Ernst-Ulrich Petersmann 2022. DOI: 10.1093/oso/9780192858023.003.0010

values in the interpretation of trade and investment agreements even in the absence of explicit references to human rights in the relevant treaty provisions.

As the power politics inside the UN Security Council is inconsistent with democratic governance and respect for human rights, reasonable citizens (eg subject to military dictatorship and human rights abuses in some African and Eurasian UN member states) cannot regard themselves as democratic co-authors of the lack of support of human rights by UN institutions against governance failures inside so many UN member states.[3] As explained in Chapters 2–5, authoritarian power politics in UN and WTO member states remains the biggest impediment to realizing citizen-oriented SDGs (section 9.1). Rendering WTO law consistent with climate change mitigation and with other environmental SDGs—like Sustainable Development Goal 6 (availability and sustainable management of water and sanitation for all), Goal 7 (access to affordable, reliable, sustainable, and modern energy for all), Goal 14 (conserve and sustainably use the oceans, seas, and marine resources for sustainable development), and Goal 15 (protect, restore, and promote sustainable use of terrestrial ecosystems, sustainably manage forests, combat desertification, halt and reverse land degradation, and halt biodiversity loss)—requires making the WTO's embedded liberalism consistent with modern international environmental law (section 9.2). Recent environmental and human rights litigation in Europe illustrates the potential synergies between human rights law (HRL), economic and environmental law and adjudication (section 9.3). Yet, Europe's cosmopolitan constitutionalism empowering citizens to challenge governmental disregard for the SDGs in national and European courts is resisted in multilevel governance outside Europe (section 9.4). The SDG of a 'Global Partnership for Sustainable Development ... with the participation of all countries, all stakeholders and all people', including 'multi-stakeholder partnerships that mobilize and share knowledge, expertise, technology and financial resources, to support the achievement of the Sustainable Development Goals in all countries, in particular developing countries',[4] can be realized through more inclusive, legal practices of UN/WTO institutions and member states, for instance by strengthening of private–public partnerships (like COVAX), network governance (eg among independent competition, health, and environmental agencies similar to the institutionalized cooperation among central banks), multilevel

[3] Cf D Hovell, *On Trust: The UN Security Council as Fiduciary*, LSE Legal Studies Working Paper 05/2021. According to Habermas, for any law to be legitimate, its addressees must be able to regard themselves as their co-authors; agency-oriented justice (eg focusing on state consent to international law, citizen consent to democratic legislation) cannot be secured by unjust means (like inadequate respect for human rights in UN Security Council practices and in many authoritarian UN member states), J Habermas, *Between Facts and Norms. Contributions to a Discourse Theory of Law and Democracy* (MIT Press 1998), at 408. As recognized in the SDGs, the legitimacy of UN and WTO law (notably of their basic structures) depends on promoting human rights, social welfare, and other forms of input- and output-oriented justice for all (like access to judicial remedies as discussed in Chapters 6–8).

[4] *Transforming our World* (2015), para 17.16.

judicial remedies (including also WTO appellate review and multilateral investment courts), individual rights, and transnational rule of law (sections 9.5 and 9.6). The more civil societies and non-governmental organizations are directly involved in health and environmental protection treaties (like the global pandemic treaty proposed by the EU) and insist on defining the common interests of states in terms of protecting human and constitutional rights of their citizens (rather than self-interests of governments), the better they can monitor and resist abuses of public and private power. Alleged conflicts among state interests can be depoliticized by focusing on the shared interests of their citizens as expressed in the SDGs and in third-party adjudication of disputes through judicial administration of justice.

9.1 Need for Strengthening Rule of Law and Democratic Participation in UN/WTO Practices

This book proceeded from the value premise of HRL that states, governments, politics, economics, and international economic law (IEL) are mere *instruments* for realizing the human rights and related SDGs of citizens. The history of politics and of states confirms that power-based governance and legal systems (eg by feudal kings, emperors, military rulers, tribal chiefs)—and their justification by mandates from heaven (as claimed by Chinese, Jewish, Christian, and Muslim rulers)—prevailed for millennia before 'enlightenment', anti-colonial struggles, and democratic revolutions enabled the emergence of republican and democratic governance forms in ever more states. UN law and institutions were shaped by the power realities of the Second World War; regulatory capture (eg of the UN Security Council by the five veto powers, the Bretton Woods institutions by the United States providing the US dollar as global reserve currency) and blockage of many UN decision-making processes by authoritarian rulers (eg rejecting ratification of UN human rights conventions, impeding domestic protection of democracy and human rights, opposing humanitarian interventions) continue prioritizing state-centred principles of power politics, which impede effective protection of human rights and of related SDGs. As the SDGs acknowledge the need for protecting the human rights of all and for inclusive, democratic governance, Chapters 5–8 explained why limitation of intergovernmental power politics and of regulatory competition by multilevel protection of transnational rule of law must remain a priority for UN and WTO governance in pursuit of the SDGs. UN and WTO *practices* must respect the UN and WTO *agreements* ratified by parliaments and democratic institutions for the benefit of their citizens. The *jus cogens* core of HRL excludes conceptions of international law among states prioritizing unlimited policy powers of authoritarian rulers.

The EU's human rights constitution, common market, monetary and foreign policy constitutions are functionally limited by the scope of EU law (as described in Chapter 5, section 5.5). UN and WTO law allows much higher degrees of regulatory competition among member states, including systemic competition among neo-liberal, state capitalist, ordo-liberal, and third-world conceptions of multilevel trade regulation as long as countries comply with their specific WTO legal obligations. WTO law provides for interface rules (eg in Articles III, X, XV–XXV GATT) limiting rules-based regulatory competition (eg through non-discrimination and transparency requirements) and providing for compulsory, peaceful settlement of disputes over related regulatory conflicts (eg over the calculation of anti-dumping duties and countervailing duties on goods exported by SOEs). The WTO transparency and consultation requirements, trade policy review mechanisms, and obligations for cooperation with UN and other international organizations promote public reason and legal and political accountability of governments vis-à-vis civil societies. If WTO rules (eg for plurilateral agreements, special and differential treatment, waivers) and WTO practices (eg for consensus-based negotiations and single undertakings) prove insufficient for reaching agreements on new global rules (eg on electronic commerce, more precise competition rules for state-owned enterprises (SOEs), aircraft, fisheries, and environmental subsidies, calculation of carbon taxes and border carbon adjustments aimed at reducing greenhouse has (GHG) emissions), WTO members can resort to free trade agreements (FTAs), plurilateral trade agreements (PTAs), or multilateral agreements outside the WTO (eg on climate change mitigation) without formal amendments of WTO law. The WTO legal and dispute settlement constraints did not prevent the illegal trade wars initiated by US President Trump and China (as discussed in Chapter 3). In view of the geopolitical rivalries and political abuses of trade policy powers, strengthening the WTO legal and dispute settlement remedies—and continuing the efforts at reforming IEL and related third-party adjudication—are important for rule of law in international trade, investment, environmental, and health cooperation aimed at limiting global governance crises and protecting the SDGs. The case analyses in Chapters 6 and 7 suggest that in both trade and investment disputes, WTO dispute settlement bodies and investor–state arbitration (ISA) are taking the customary law requirements of treaty interpretation increasingly seriously.

The input and output legitimacy of member-driven WTO governance disconnected from human and constitutional rights of citizens—and from effective parliamentary and democratic control—remains weak, as illustrated by the collective toleration by WTO members of the illegal blocking of the WTO appellate review system contrary to Article 17 Dispute Settlement Understanding (DSU). The main sources of input and output legitimacy of WTO law derive from its parliamentary approval, protection of rule of law through the WTO dispute settlement system, systemic treaty interpretation in conformity with UN law, and the empowerment of member states—and indirectly also of non-governmental actors—to enhance their respective freedoms and economic welfare through mutually beneficial trade and its efficient regulation. The environmental and global health crises confirmed that citizens perceive national and European community law systems as more important guarantors of public goods (PGs) (like public health and sustainable development) than worldwide organizations. Yet, functionally limited cooperation in the context of the UN and UN specialized agencies (eg protecting public health, sustainable development, monetary stability, providing financial and development assistance, regulating international air, maritime, postal transports, and other communication systems) remains important for protecting transnational PGs. The Trump administration's disregard for UN and WTO rules confirmed that power-oriented UN/WTO governance practices—if not effectively constrained by democratic constitutionalism and controlled by national parliaments—risk undermining global institutions (like the WTO, the World Health Organization (WHO), the UN Convention on the Law of the Sea (UNCLOS), the UN Framework Convention on Climate Change (UNFCCC), and the Paris Agreement on climate change mitigation, as illustrated in Chapter 3). The geopolitical rivalries impede the emergence of global community law for responding more effectively to the global health, economic, environmental, migration, and political crises. Yet, the UN and WTO remain indispensable frameworks for global supply of vaccines, global poverty reduction, and climate change mitigation. Responsible citizenship requires continuing democratic struggles for more justice and accountability for the ubiquity of public and private abuses of power.

Chapters 4 and 5 explained how the value conflicts underlying neo-liberal, state capitalist, and ordo-liberal conceptions of economic and political orders require more decentralized forms of cooperation among like-minded countries based on regional, plurilateral, and bilateral agreements for bottom-up supply of the SDGs and of other—diversely defined—aggregate PGs (like cyber security and data privacy). Chapters 6–8 demonstrated how the overall coherence of such multilevel governance of aggregate PGs depends on legal and judicial protection of transnational rule of law. The hundreds of separate trade, investment, and human rights agreements interact and create incentives for free-riding and harmful externalities (like carbon leakage), which challenge the overall coherence of fragmented treaty systems and require stronger, multilevel judicial remedies aimed at protecting transnational rule of law.

As recognized by all UN member states in their 2030 UN Sustainable Development Agenda, the global division of labour remains the most important *instrument* for promoting sustainable development in a world with unlimited demand for scarce economic and environmental resources. Maintaining and reforming the WTO legal and multilevel dispute settlement system is in the reasonable self-interest of all UN and WTO members in order to realize their universally agreed SDGs efficiently and peacefully. Worldwide trade and investment regulation remain characterized by conflicting neo-liberal, state capitalist, and ordo-liberal conceptions. International regulation of companies and of their private foreign investments—and related dispute settlement procedures—are based more on bilateral and regional agreements without worldwide investment agreements similar to WTO law. The cultural and value differences underlying diverse neoliberal, state capitalist, and ordo-liberal economic regulation are confirmed by the fact that regional human rights conventions and human right courts—as they protect human and constitutional rights of citizens and of NGOs (including companies) in the thirty European Economic Area (EEA) member countries—have so far not been accepted by North American democracies and Asian countries. In Russia and many other authoritarian countries, human rights lack effective legal protection. The EU initiatives for judicial reforms in international trade and investment law were described—in Chapters 3, 6, 7, and 8—as being aimed at defending multilevel, judicial protection of transnational rule of law among willing countries by providing interim solutions for protecting PGs. Similar plurilateral reforms are needed for responding to the global environmental, health, and other governance crises, for example by agreements on coordinating carbon border taxes necessary for climate change mitigation, regulating e-commerce, data privacy, and Internet governance, protecting universal access to medicines and providing medical equipment for responding to health pandemics. The global epistemic community of UN and WTO lawyers and practitioners remains divided on whether UN and WTO legal systems should be developed as international law among sovereign member states (prioritizing state sovereignty) or as multilevel governance of PGs for the benefit of peoples and citizens as the ultimate democratic principals of governments with limited, delegated powers (ie prioritizing individual and democratic autonomy).

9.2 Greening Embedded Liberalism: Need for Rendering WTO Law Consistent with Climate Change Mitigation

Trade liberalization before the First World War reflected disembedded liberalism based on *laissez faire* attitudes in most countries vis-à-vis the social adjustment problems created by colonialism, the first industrial revolution (based on machines driven by steam power), and by the first globalization during the second half of the nineteenth century. The post-war second industrial revolution (based on mass assembly line production driven by electricity) was embedded into domestic economic regulation, competition, and social policies in most industrialized countries, notwithstanding the social disembedding resulting from the global financial crises and economic disintegration during the 1930s.[5] The embedded liberalism underlying the General Agreement on Tariffs and Trade (GATT) 1947 not only *acknowledged* sovereign rights to regulate market failures, related governance

[5] As criticized by K Polanyi, *The Great Transformation: The Political and Economic Origins of our Time* (2nd edn, Beacon Press 1944/2001).

failures, and constitutional problems. It also *enabled* and *promoted* welfare states through reciprocal trade liberalization enhancing mutually beneficial division of labour and economic and legal cooperation in producing private and public goods. As explained in Chapter 4, the economic theory of optimal intervention justified GATT's legal ranking of alternative policy instruments in terms of their economic efficiency and enabled mutually welfare-enhancing, legal harmonization reducing transaction costs and political conflicts—without limiting national sovereignty over non-discriminatory, domestic regulation of the economy and polity.[6]

WTO law responded to the third industrial revolution of computers and telecommunications by additional, multilateral harmonization of product and production standards, competition and trade remedy rules, liberalization and regulation of services trade, protection of intellectual property rights, and of transnational rule of law through compulsory jurisdiction for settlement of trade disputes through domestic judicial remedies and WTO dispute settlement procedures. WTO law changed the embedded liberalism underlying GATT 1947 in ways reflecting both neo-liberal Anglo-Saxon interest-group politics (eg resulting in the WTO Anti-dumping and the Trade-Related Aspects of Intellectual Property Rights (TRIPS) Agreements)[7] and ordo-liberal insistence on rule compliance (through the compulsory jurisdiction of the WTO dispute settlement system and the (quasi)automatic adoption of more than 420 WTO panel, appellate, and arbitration reports), non-discriminatory conditions of competition (eg as reflected by the non-discrimination and necessity requirements in the WTO Agreements on technical barriers to trade and (phyto)sanitary standards, the phasing out of the Agreement on Textiles and Clothing) and sustainable development commitments. Compared with the provisional application, lack of parliamentary ratification, and 'grandfather' exceptions of the intergovernmental GATT 1947, the WTO Agreement strengthened the constitutional dimensions of WTO law, as illustrated by parliamentary approvals of the WTO Agreement, its incorporation into the domestic legal systems of many WTO members, the separation of legislative, administrative, and judicial powers of WTO institutions (cf Article III WTO Agreement), provisions for majority voting (cf Article IX), and for domestic implementation of WTO rules (Article XVI.4), and the compulsory WTO dispute settlement system.

[6] Cf Chapter 4, sections 4.3–4.5.

[7] The inconsistencies of anti-dumping laws and practices with non-discriminatory competition rules are widely recognized; they prevented WTO negotiators from agreeing on a Preamble text explaining the economic rationale of the WTO Anti-dumping Agreement. Many competition lawyers express concerns (eg in H Ullrich, RM Hilty, M Lamping, and J Drexl (eds), *TRIPS Plus 20. From Trade Rules to Market Principles* (Springer 2016)) that some anti-dumping and TRIPS rules—whose drafting was dominated by domestic industry lobbyists—offer too much protection stifling competition and innovation (eg as exemplified by recent complaints of thirty-five major technology companies that 'patent trolls' are being abused for rent-seeking licensing practices blocking development and use of new technologies; cf 'Apple, Microsoft and BMW urge EU to stop patent trolls', *Financial Times* 16 January 2020, available at https://www.ft.com/content/26230960-37a7-11ea-a6d3-9a26f8c3cba4).

The progressive adjustment of the embedded liberalism underlying GATT/WTO law—for example to the emergence of social welfare states,[8] decolonization,[9] and to European economic integration[10]—needs to be continued in order to render WTO law consistent with the regulatory challenges of globalization, climate change, and other SDGs. WTO law does not explicitly refer to climate change. Decisions on GHG emission reductions have to be coordinated in the specialized UN bodies (like the UNFCCC, the International Maritime Organization, the International Civil Aviation Organization), regional, and national institutions outside the WTO. Yet, trade and climate rules inevitably interact and must remain consistent and mutually supportive. The 2015 Paris Agreement on climate change entered into force in November 2016; it was ratified by 190 Parties (2021); 182 countries plus the EU notified their nationally determined contributions (NDCs) by 2019. These voluntary contributions to reduce GHGs differ enormously and remain insufficient. President Trump's withdrawal of the United States, as the largest economy and second-largest emitter of GHGs, from the Agreement entailed that, during the UN climate conference in Madrid in December 2019 focusing on carbon market systems, other major emitters of GHGs (like China, India, Australia) avoided committing to ambitious limitations of GHGs. In January 2021, US President Biden recommitted the United States to join the Paris Agreement and to transform the country into a carbon-neutral economy by 2050. Yet, the lack of effective legal disciplines for NDCs, for the WTO-consistent application of climate measures or—in case of inconsistencies with WTO law—for WTO exemptions (eg waivers granted by the WTO Ministerial Conference), WTO surveillance measures (eg by the WTO Trade Policy Review Mechanism), and for mutually consistent dispute settlement procedures (eg in the context of the UNFCCC and the WTO) risk provoking legal collisions between WTO rules and climate mitigation policies—unless WTO members can agree on a peace clause for climate actions, or on how to determine the likeness of competing products based on the amount of carbons used in producing them, and on standards for calculating border carbon adjustments (eg border tax adjustments) on the basis of carbon use, carbon emissions, agreed carbon prices, and an agreed framework for emissions trading. For example, WTO members could define the conditions under which specified climate measures taken in conformity with the UNFCCC are covered by WTO exceptions (eg Articles XX GATT, XIV of the General Agreement on Trade in Services (GATS)) or by WTO waivers. Protecting a level playing field between

[8] For example, by providing for GATT-consistency of social policies under Articles III, XVI, XIX, XX GATT.

[9] For example, by providing in GATT Article XXVI:5,c for easy transition from 'dependent' to 'independent' GATT membership, Part IV GATT on Trade and Development, 'special and differential treatment' provided for in many WTO provisions.

[10] For example, by recognizing sovereign rights to form customs unions and admitting EU membership in the WTO.

clean and fossil energies, promoting the sustainable production of goods and services and use of low-carbon products, and coordinating diverse emissions trading systems, environmental standards, tax, subsidy, government procurement and border adjustment rules (cf Article II.2,a, III.2 GATT) will require close cooperation between UN, WTO, and regional institutions in their respective design and administration of climate change mitigation measures in order to avoid unilateral trade sanctions and trade wars.[11] The more UN and WTO negotiations on multilateral climate mitigation rules (like carbon taxes, financial and technological assistance for LDCs) and plurilateral agreements (eg on coordination and mutual recognition of emissions trading systems) lag behind, the more inevitable become unilateral initiatives and multilateral disputes settlement procedures for protecting and clarifying the legal consistency of unilateral measures with the existing multilateral trade and environmental treaties. For example, the increasing number of emissions trading systems (eg in the EU, California, China) cannot remain effective in the long run without a border carbon tax ensuring that imports and domestic producers are treated the same (eg by equalizing the difference between carbon prices in the importing and exporting countries concerned).

The EU Commission is committed to supplementing the EU emissions trading system (ETS) by carbon taxes and carbon border adjustment mechanisms (CBAMs) for imports from third countries in order to avoid trade distortions and carbon leakage (by relocating emissions-intensive production to countries with less or no taxes on carbon use). Such CBAMs aim at (i) increasing carbon prices so as to (ii) reduce carbon emissions; (iii) preventing carbon leakage; (iv) inducing polluting industries (notably steel, aluminium, iron, cement, fertilizers, electricity, aviation, shipping, road transport) and free-riding countries to participate in climate mitigation (eg by waiving the CBAM among members of the same carbon club); and (v) maintaining non-discriminatory conditions of competition (trade neutrality).[12] Objectively calculating the carbon footprint of imported goods and

[11] For an overview of linking trade to environmental standards, see O de Schutter, *Trade in the Service of Sustainable Development. Linking Trade to Labour Rights and Environmental Standards* (Hart 2017). For a comparison of diverse emissions trading systems, see J Munro, *Emission Trading Schemes under International Economic Law* (OUP 2018). The EU legislative proposals of 14 July 2021 envisage creation of a second emissions trading system for road transport and buildings leading to (temporary) coexistence of two separate carbon pricing systems inside the EU, which are likely to converge in the long run.

[12] A CBAM, which the EU plans to introduce as of 2026 (with procedural requirements of reporting emissions embedded in imported goods starting already in 2023), would aim at ensuring that the carbon emissions of imports are charged the same cost as their EU equivalents in order to prevent carbon leakage by 'internalizing' the cost of carbon emissions of EU producers and of the EU's trading partners. One way of introducing a CBAM could be to incorporate foreign producers into the EU's ETS. This would require them to buy the permits that European producers must use to be able to compete with them in the EU market. In order to make carbon taxes compatible with WTO rules on non-discriminatory treatment and avoid protectionist abuses and competitive distortions, an *import CBAM* would tax emissions-intensive imports at a rate equivalent to that for an average domestic producer (with possibility of tax rebates if the foreign producer can demonstrate lower carbon usage, for instance due to use of renewable energy); an *export CBAM* could reimburse domestic carbon taxes paid to the extent they exceed carbon taxes in the country of destination. For finished goods rather than raw materials, assessing the costs of inputs and emissions by product and by producer will require complex emissions

services can be difficult, for instance if carbon dioxide (CO_2) is not included in the final product and the product includes components from many countries. In order to avoid green protectionism (eg from the free allowances granted to some EU producers under the ETS), discrimination against LDCs and related WTO disputes, CBAMs should be based on multilaterally agreed—rather than unilateral—rules, preferably to be negotiated in the context of the Paris Agreement or in the WTO.[13] The EU's CBAM draft rules of July 2021 provide for transition phases up to 2025 and progressive extension of the scope of the CBAMs (eg starting with steel, aluminium, and iron products). The EU's decarbonization policies also provide for a Social Climate Fund and income redistribution in conformity with the EU's social market economy; it remains to be clarified how less-developed countries will benefit from preferential treatment under the Generalized System of Preferences, as well as from financial and technological assistance (eg pursuant to Article 9 Paris Agreement and Article 66 TRIPS Agreement) so as to promote support for CBAMs. Challenges of the legal technicalities of CBAMs (eg by Australia, Brazil, China, and the United States) remain likely, especially if the US Biden administration cannot convince the US Congress to introduce CBAMs as it was already proposed in 2010 under the Obama administration. The consistency of any CBAM with GATT non-discrimination requirements (eg Articles I and III GATT), tariff bindings (Article II GATT), environmental exceptions (eg in Articles XX GATT and XIV GATS), and subsidy disciplines (eg in view of continuing free allocations of emission allowances for some EU industries) depends on its specific design features and administration.[14] As WTO rules were not drafted to address climate change problems, WTO supervision of CBAMs and the availability of WTO dispute settlement procedures are crucial for maintaining transnational rule of law among WTO members introducing CBAMs. EU leadership for introducing CBAMs must be coordinated with China and the United States and reconcile WTO rules with climate mitigation policies under the Paris Agreement.[15] In order

certifications inside and outside the EU; even if carbon taxes and CBAMs were introduced progressively in coordination with the major trading partners, they are bound to give rise to trade disputes. For the complex details of potential CBAMs and of making them WTO consistent (notably GATT Articles I–III and XX, the WTO Subsidy Agreement) see: D Kleimann and J Pauwelyn, *Trade Related Aspects of a Carbon Border Adjustment Mechanism. A Legal Assessment* (European Parliament Document PE 603.502, April 2020); T Kuusi *et al.*, *Carbon Border Adjustment Mechanisms and their Economic Impact on Finland and the EU* (Finland's Prime Minister Office, Publication of the Government's Analysis Activities 2020-48).

[13] On the need for elaborating the rules on CBAMs among like-minded countries (including the United States and China) so as to reduce foreign policy conflicts, see M Leonard, J Pisani-Ferry, J Shapiro, S Tagliapietra, and G Wolff, *The Geopolitics of the European Green Deal*, Policy Contribution 04/2021 (Bruegel 2021).

[14] Cf n 12 and MA Mehling, H van Asselt, K Das, S Droege, and C Verkuijl, Designing Border Carbon Adjustments for Enhanced Climate Action, *American Journal of International Law* 113 (2019), 433–81.

[15] For example, by means of WTO waivers, WTO peace clauses, agreed interpretations of WTO exceptions, WTO agreements limiting fossil fuel subsidies and regulating carbon emission trading.

to be credible, such EU leadership requires also EU compliance with other agreed environmental policy objectives (like preventing over-fishing and plastics pollution in the oceans, phasing out of fossil fuel subsidies). Additional UN and WTO agreements (eg on limiting fishery subsidies and fossil fuel subsidies, reducing pollution caused by use of plastics) are necessary for avoiding further disruption of multilevel governance of interdependent PGs.

The needed adaptations of WTO rules are facilitated by the systemic interpretation requirement of customary international law (as codified in Article 31.3(c) VCLT). It calls for clarification of the WTO's sustainable development objectives in conformity with the seventeen SDGs accepted by UN member states and the Paris Agreement. The 2030 Agenda for Sustainable Development aims at implementing its seventeen SDGs (like overcoming poverty, hunger, and global warming, protecting health, education, gender equality, access to water, sanitation, and clean energy, urbanization, the environment, human rights, and social justice) by localizing the SDGs so as to engage local institutions, actors, and civil society support. As the SDGs aim at reconciling climate mitigation measures with other sustainable development objectives (like poverty reduction, sustainable agriculture, sustainable use of marine resources, terrestrial ecosystems) and with trade rules, they may offer relevant context for interpreting WTO rules, for balancing competing policy measures, for evaluating NDCs under the Paris Agreement, and for other WTO governance reforms as discussed in the following.

9.3 Citizen-driven Climate Change Litigation in Europe

The European Convention on Human Rights (ECHR) does not explicitly protect rights to a clean and quiet environment and to preservation of the environment. But the European Court of Human Rights (ECtHR) has interpreted environmental protection into Articles 2 (right to life) and 8 (right to privacy, family life, and a home); it has discussed state duties to protect citizens from real and imminent environmental risks and natural disasters also in the context of the right to property (Article 1 Protocol 1). Applicants in climate cases communicated by the ECtHR have further invoked Article 3 (prohibition against inhuman and degrading treatment), Article 6 (access to court), Article 13 (right of remedy), and Article 14 (prohibition against discrimination). Notwithstanding the few possibilities under the UNFCCC and related, transnational climate regulation for holding governments legally and judicially accountable for insufficient climate change mitigation measures, national and European courts interpret HRL and environmental legislation in conformity with other international law obligations of the states concerned.[16] By

[16] Cf M Meguro, Litigating Climate Change through International Law: Obligations Strategy and Rights Strategy, *Leiden Journal of International Law* 33 (2020), 933–51; I Alogna, C Bakker, and JP Gauci (eds), *Climate Change Litigation. Global Perspectives* (Brill Nijhoff 2021).

mid-2021, the ECtHR had not yet decided on the increasing number of complaints (eg from Portugal, Norway, and Switzerland) invoking Convention rights and corresponding state duties to mitigate climate harm. Yet, an increasing number of national courts confirmed legal state duties under Articles 2 and 8 ECHR to reduce GHG emissions.[17] The European climate law, adopted by the European Parliament and European Council in June 2021,[18] makes the EU's goals of cutting GHG emissions 55 per cent by 2030 (compared with 1990 levels) and reaching climate neutrality by 2050 legally binding and establishes a governance framework for climate mainstreaming and progress control; it envisages extending the EU's ETS (eg to automobiles and housing), tightening EU reduction requirements for car emissions, and providing for carbon taxes on polluting imports. As illustrated by the successful constitutional complaints against Germany's Federal Climate Protection Act (discussed in Chapter 8 section 8.4.5), the agreed specifications of some of the SDGs (eg in terms of human rights) and of GHG reduction commitments in democratic legislation are being used by citizens and NGOs for judicial remedies aimed at enforcing governmental commitments to GHG reductions. The European Climate Law, the 'Fit for 55' package of thirteen EU legislative proposals published on 14 July 2021 aimed at aligning EU policies with the 55 per cent reduction goal by 2030, the direct applicability of precise and unconditional rules in these EU regulations in domestic courts, and the constitutional right to effective remedies (Article 47 EUCFR) offer citizens legal and judicial remedies to hold EU institutions and EU member states accountable for implementing the agreed climate mitigation objectives.

9.3.1 Climate Litigation against Governments

The ruling of the Dutch Supreme Court on 20 December 2019 in *State of the Netherlands v Urgenda*[19] (a Dutch non-governmental organization (NGO) suing the state on behalf of around 900 citizens)—confirming the 2018 Court of Appeals judgment that Articles 2 (right to life) and 8 ECHR (right to private and family life) entail legal duties of the Dutch government to reduce GHG emissions by at least 25

[17] Cf J Sandvig, P Dawson, and M Tjelmeland, Can the ECHR Encompass the Transnational and Intertemporal Dimensions of Climate Harm? *European Journal of International Law Talk* Blog of 23 June 2021. For detailed summaries of national court cases, see also *Climate Change and Human Rights in the European Context* (European Network of National Human Rights Institutions 2021).

[18] Regulation (EU) 2021/1119 of the European Parliament and of the Council establishing the Framework for Achieving Climate Neutrality and Amending Regulations (EC) No 401/2009 and (EU) 2018/1999 ('European Climate Law'), adopted 30 June 2021.

[19] De Staat der Nederlanden (Ministerie van Economische Zaken en Klimaat) tegen Stichting Urgenda, Hoge Raad der Nederlanden, Civiele Kamer, Nummer 19/00135, 20 December 2019.

per cent (compared to 1990 levels) by the end of 2020—sets important precedents for climate litigation,[20] notably by the following legal findings:

- HRL (eg the ECHR) and related constitutional and environmental law guarantees (like the 1998 Aarhus Convention on access to justice in environmental matters) may be invoked by citizens in order to enforce positive obligations to take appropriate measures mitigating climate change.
- Even if the respondent state is only a minor contributor to climate change, a court can determine the legal responsibilities to reduce emissions of an individual state that shares responsibility with other actors for climate change (partial causation justifies partial responsibility; the failure of other states to meet their responsibilities does not justify non-performance).
- As the disputing parties agreed that climate change presents serious risks, the court did not need to decide on these facts; it relied on the precautionary principle and the internationally agreed need for reducing emissions by at least 25 per cent by 2020, leaving it to the political government branches to determine how to implement this legal obligation.

The Dutch government's commitment to comply with the judgment sets a welcome political precedent for rules-based legal, judicial, and political protection of PGs like climate change mitigation. In November 2020, the *Conseil d'État*—France's highest administrative court—delivered another climate-related ruling in *Commune de Grande Synthe I* by acknowledging France's obligation to reduce GHG emissions.[21] The *Conseil d'État* accepted that the municipality of *Grande Synthe* had *locus standi* resulting from its direct and certain exposure to climate change (notably sea level rise); its request relating to GHG emissions reductions had been based on international, European, and French legal obligations for emissions reduction, notably the EU's second Energy climate package of 2018 and its implementation in French law, which made the objective of GHG emissions reductions enforceable against the government.

On 30 November 2020, the ECtHR communicated its first climate change case brought by six Portuguese children and young people, with the crowd-funded support of the *Global Legal Action Network*, against all twenty-seven EU countries plus Norway, Russia, Switzerland, Turkey, the United Kingdom, and Ukraine.[22] It alleges that the contribution by each of these states to global GHG emissions means that they share responsibility for the existing and impending harms caused

[20] Cf A Nollkaemper and L Burgers, A New Classic in Climate Change Litigation: The Dutch Supreme Court Decision in the Urgenda Case, *European Journal of International Law Talk* Blog of 6 January 2020. References to climate change lawsuits can be found at http://climatecasechart.com/.

[21] Cf N de Arriba-Sellier, verfassungsblog.de/another-urgenda-in-the-making of 25 November 2020.

[22] Request No 39371/20 of 7 September 2020 *Duarte Agostinho and Others v Portugal and 32 other States.*

by global warming and climate change. Furthermore, the applicants make an argument based on extraterritorial jurisdiction for significant transboundary environmental harm. They call on the Court to determine whether the respondent States are doing their fair share towards mitigation efforts. In their application, the applicants invoked states' positive obligations under Articles 2 and 8 ECHR (life and respect for private and family life, respectively), read in the context of the 2015 Paris Agreement. They also made a discrimination claim based on Article 14 ECHR (arguing that their generation will particularly suffer the effects of climate change). When the Court communicated the case, it asked the parties to comment not only on the alleged violations of Articles 2, 8, and 14 ECHR but it also invoked Article 3 ECHR (prohibition of inhuman and degrading treatment) as well as the right to property in Article 1 of Protocol No 1 to the Convention.[23] It remains to be seen whether the increasing number of human rights complaints in national and European courts challenging insufficient GHG reductions will offer citizens effective legal and judicial remedies regarding the harmful effects of climate change. The absence of similar complaints in American, Chinese, and Russian courts illustrates, once again, the value differences between neo-liberal, authoritarian, and European ordo-liberal legal systems. Arguably, the embedded liberalism and sustainable development objectives of WTO law imply that non-discriminatory climate change litigation, border taxes, CBAMs, and other climate change mitigation measures in conformity with UN law must be presumed to be consistent with WTO law as long as WTO dispute settlement bodies do not find otherwise.

9.3.2 Climate Litigation against Companies

Climate change litigation is increasingly targeting fossil fuel companies and investment funds based on claims that most industrial GHG emissions are caused and financed by private companies, which—as in the case of tobacco litigation—should be held legally accountable for the environmental and social harm produced by their actions. The more EU climate legislation refers to the UNFCCC, the Paris Agreement, and to the EU's obligations to reduce GHG emissions, the more national and European courts are likely to be seized for protecting environmental rights and related human rights to protection against harmful climate change.

The CJEU, the EFTA Court, and the ECtHR emphasize the need for mutual cooperation in their judicial reconciliation (balancing) of human rights, constitutional rights, and common market freedoms, notwithstanding methodological

[23] For details, see C Heri, The ECtHR's Pending Climate Change Case: What Has Ill-Treatment Got to Do with It? *European Journal of International Law Talk* Blog of 22 December 2020.

differences in their judicial reasoning.[24] On 28 November 2019, the European parliament declared a global climate emergency and requested the EU Commission to cut emissions by 55 per cent to ensure a carbon-neutral circular economy with net-zero GHG emissions in the EU by 2050. On 11 December 2019, the EU Commission presented its New Green Deal, followed by additional proposals—in spring 2020—for a European Green Deal Investment Proposal, a Just Transition Plan, and a European Climate Law to ensure a climate-neutral EU by 2050. The ruling of the District Court of The Hague on 26 May 2021 in *Milieudefensie v Royal Dutch Shell* (RDS) is the first judgment of its kind in which a multinational corporation is held responsible for its contribution to climate change on the basis of national and international law.[25]

The case was brought as a public interest class action by a Dutch NGO; it does not focus on compensation for past damages but on corporate obligations to reduce emissions and invest more in cleaner fuels to protect the common interest of current and future generations in preventing dangerous climate change. Similar litigation against energy companies focusing on corporate responsibilities for climate change is pending in many countries. Even though the judgment is based on corporate duties of care under Dutch tort law, the Court's references to international law and to the shared responsibilities of RDS and other actors may influence the reasoning in future judgments by other courts. The Court found that the total CO_2 emissions of the Shell group exceeded the emissions of many states, including the Netherlands. The group's global CO_2 emissions contributed to global warming and climate change in the Netherlands, and entailed significant risks for residents of that country.[26] The court agreed with the complainants that Shell had an obligation to reduce CO_2 emissions of the Shell group's entire energy portfolio, holding that:

- RDS is obliged to reduce the CO_2 emissions of the Shell group's activities by net 45 per cent by the end of 2030 relative to 2019 through the Shell group's corporate policy;

[24] Cf HP Graver, The Demise of Viking and Laval: The Holship Ruling of the ECtHR and the Protection of Fundamental Rights in Europe, *Verfassungsblog* of 16 June 2021, https://verfassungsblog.de/holship/, DOI:10.17176/20210616-193402-0.

[25] Cf A Nollkaemper, Shell's Responsibility for Climate Change. An International Law Perspective on a Groundbreaking Judgment, *Verfassungsblog* of 28 May 2021, https://verfassungsblog.de/shells-responsibility-for-climate-change/. The judgment has been appealed by Shell. On the promotion of the implementation of Article 2 Paris Agreement by constitutional, human rights, and climate change litigation, see F Ekardt, Shell's Climate Obligation: Climate, Civil Courts, Human Rights, and Balance of Powers, *VerfBlog* of 9 June 2021, https://verfassungsblog.de/shells-climate-obligation/, DOI:10.17176/20210610-004138-0

[26] The Court refers, *inter alia*, to health risks and deaths due to climate change-induced hot spells, as well as health problems and an increased mortality risk due to increasing infectious diseases, deterioration of air quality, increase of ultraviolet (UV) exposure, an increase of water-related and foodborne diseases, as well as water-related health risks.

- the policy, policy intentions, and ambitions of RDS for the Shell group imply an imminent violation of this obligation;
- the Court, therefore, allowed the claimed order for compliance with this legal obligation.

The judgment was based on the duty of care under Dutch tort law as the complainants could not directly invoke—with respect to RDS—human rights (notably to life and the right to respect for private and family life under the ECHR and the International Covenant on Civil and Political Rights (ICCPR), as they apply in relationships between states and citizens). But the Court took into account the human rights value and the Paris Agreement in its interpretation of the unwritten standard of care.[27] The Court also referred to the UN Guiding Principles on Business and Human Rights (UNGP), which it found to constitute an authoritative and internationally endorsed soft law instrument setting out the responsibilities of states and businesses in relation to human rights; even though the UNGP 'do not create any new right, nor establish legally binding obligations', they 'are suitable as a guideline in the interpretation of the unwritten standard of care'.[28] According to the Court, 'the responsibility to respect human rights encompasses the company's entire value chain' including the end-users of the products produced and traded by the Shell group at the end of RDS' value chain.[29] As to the scope of RDS' reduction obligation, the Court found the goals of the Paris Agreement to represent the best available climate science, supported by widespread international consensus and scientific evidence; this supported the conclusion that the appropriate reduction target is a net 45 per cent reduction of CO_2 emissions in 2030, relative to 2010 levels. It is these reduction pathways that 'offer the best possible chances to prevent the most serious consequences of dangerous climate change'; the Court emphasized that this does not formulate a legally binding standard for RDS, but that this broad consensus was relevant in its interpretation of the unwritten standard of care.[30] To buttress the conclusion that the Paris goals were legally relevant for RDS, the Court found it relevant that under the Paris Agreement, the signatories ensured support of non-state stakeholders. The Court concluded that the human rights standards, the UNGP, and the Paris agreement all support the conclusion that RDS should be ordered to reduce the CO_2 emissions of the Shell group's activities by net 45 per cent at the end of 2030 relative to 2019 through the group's corporate policy. Similar to the *Urgenda* case, the District Court clarified the shared

[27] In this respect, the Court followed the *Urgenda* judgment (see nn 19–21 this chapter and related texts) where the Dutch Supreme Court found that Articles 2 and 8 ECHR offer protection against the consequences of dangerous climate change caused by CO_2 emissions-induced global warming, also referring to the practice of the UN Human Rights Committee and the UN Special Rapporteur on Human Rights.

[28] Para 4.4.11 of the judgment (ECLI: NL: RBDHA:2021:5339) as cited by Nollkaemper (n 25).

[29] Para 4.4.18 of the judgment (n 28).

[30] Para 4.4.29.

responsibility for climate change mitigation: given the broad international consensus that each company must independently work towards achieving net zero emissions by 2050, RDS must be expected to do its part; the fact that RDS is not the only party responsible for tackling dangerous climate change in the Netherlands did not absolve RDS of its individual partial responsibility to contribute to the fight against dangerous climate change according to its ability.

The complainants celebrated the ruling as a landmark victory setting a global precedent for the legal obligations of corporate polluters to reduce their carbon emissions by accelerating their decarbonization plans.[31] The *Shell* case not only confirms the judicial trend in various European countries to strengthen judicial remedies for enforcing GHG emission reductions that have been recognized as necessary in international treaties, national legislation and other governmental commitments. The judicial clarification of corporate responsibilities also limits compensation claims of fossil fuel companies in ISA proceedings (eg based on investor claims that GHG emission reduction obligations amount to unforeseen interferences into their property and investor rights); it thereby contributes to the limitation of the procedural and substantive investor biases in ISA as discussed in Chapter 7.[32]

9.4 Cosmopolitan Constitutionalism as Democratic Defence against Power Politics beyond Europe?

Rights to the protection of the environment are recognized in the laws of more than 150 states, regional treaties, and by the UN Human Rights Council (HRC).[33] Environmental and human rights have been invoked by litigants all over the world in hundreds of judicial proceedings on protection of environmental interests over the past years.[34] Democratic and judicial control (eg of emergency restrictions of fundamental rights) and science-based governance helped to limit governance failures in 'executive emergency measures'; they increased calls for 'environmental constitutionalism' limiting the human destruction of eco-systems ('anthropocene') and disregard for 'planetary boundaries'.[35]

The increasing recognition of judicial remedies in HRL, constitutional, environmental, social, and IEL empowers civil societies to hold governments

[31] Cf A Raval, Dutch Court orders Shell to accelerate emission cuts, *Financial Times* 26 May 2021.

[32] Cf. C Eckes, *The Courts Strike Back: The Shell Case in Light of Separation of Powers*, *Verfassungsblog* of 15 June 2021, https://verfassungsblog.de/the-courts-strike-back/, DOI:10.17176/20210615-193332-0.

[33] See Resolution 48/13 adopted by the HRC on 8 October 2021, recognizing that having a clean, healthy, and sustainable environment is a human right.

[34] Cf P de Vilchez Moragues/A Savaresi, The Right to a Healthy Environment and Climate Litigation: A Mutually Supportive Relation?, April 18, 2021, http://dx.doi.org/10.2139/ssrn.3829114.

[35] Cf L Kotzé, A Global Environmental Constitution for the Anthropocene? *Transnational Environmental Law* 8 (2019), 11–33.

accountable—at least inside constitutional democracies—not only through political but also judicial means for violations of government duties to protect the SDGs and related PGs. Both HRL and IEL confirm that states may have legal duties not only vis-à-vis individuals inside their respective territory, but also extraterritorial duties vis-à-vis individuals and companies under their jurisdiction (eg investments and human rights violations by their nationals abroad) or suffering from the extraterritorial effects of state actions (like environmental pollution, human rights violations across national boundaries). As discussed in Chapter 2, section 2.2, global administrative law conceptions of IEL argue that UN specialized agencies and the WTO can be likened to regulatory agencies necessary for collective protection of PGs demanded by citizens; constitutional conceptions of international law emphasize that in order to remain democratically legitimate and prevent abuses of their limited, delegated powers, international organizations, like national regulatory agencies, must remain embedded into national systems of constitutional checks and balances so that citizens and their democratic institutions can control and hold accountable multilevel governance of PGs. From social contract and democratic citizen perspectives, all governance institutions are ultimately owned by citizens rather than by governments as agents with limited, delegated powers and corresponding duties to protect their citizens.[36] Courts of justice and democratic governments in Europe may be willing to support such cosmopolitan claims by citizens. Yet, authoritarian rulers and their supporters continue to be loath to accept such legal restraints on government powers. Likewise, many citizens give priority to their local and national identities and interests (eg in vaccine nationalism) and neglect or deny cosmopolitan responsibilities. Cosmopolitanism acknowledges that in a globalized world sharing an endangered planet with limited resources, the tribal traditions of humanity must be replaced by human rights and democratic responsibility for sustainable development beyond national frontiers.

In the judgment of 29 January 2021 on three separate lawsuits brought by four Nigerian farmers concerning large-scale oil spillage in three villages in the Niger Delta, the Hague Court of Appeals held, for the first time, a parent company (ie Royal Dutch Shell headquartered in The Hague) liable for breach of duty of care regarding abuses (ie oil spills rendering the claimants' farmlands and fishponds unusable) committed abroad by its foreign subsidiary company (ie Shell Petroleum Development Company in Nigeria).[37] This judgment, and its recognition of corporate duties of care towards victims of multinational corporate activities in foreign jurisdictions is likely to improve the ability of persons affected by the operation of subsidiary companies in developing countries to seek and obtain remedy

[36] Cf EU Petersmann, WTO Adjudication@me.too: Are Global Public Goods like the World Trade Organization Owned by Governments or by Peoples and Citizens? *Journal of East Asia and International Law* 13 (2020), 21–52.

[37] *Milieudefensie v Shell*, Gerechtshof Den Haag, 29 January 2021, document ECLI:NL:GHDHA:2021:132.

from the parent company in home states (eg if the subsidiary company has insufficient assets or no longer exists, or the judicial system in the host state fails to protect the victims).

Similarly, the French law on duty of vigilance of 27 March 2017 allows victims to hold French-based parent companies liable for abuses committed by their subsidiary companies if the damage is due to breach of the duty of vigilance. In common law jurisdictions, such as the United Kingdom and Canada, victims seeking to hold parent companies liable continue circumventing the barrier of limited liability by bringing their claims based on breach of the duty of care.[38] Similar to the successful tobacco litigation holding tobacco companies legally accountable for the health damages caused by smoking and prompting governments to drive attempts to limit tobacco consumption (as discussed in Chapter 6, section 6.3), tort-based and human rights-based climate litigation against fossil fuel companies and the energy industry aimed at enforcing carbon reduction commitments is expected to increase in the coming years.

Changing environmentally harmful conduct (like oil spills, carbon emissions, use of plastics, illegal over-fishing) requires changing conduct of citizens and companies all over the world. This cannot be realized without stronger legal and judicial protection of human and environmental rights and decentralized accountability mechanisms that can be invoked and enforced by civil societies. UN and WTO paradigms of member-driven governance have proven to be not enough for changing power politics and social conduct governing daily lives of citizens, politicians, and diplomats. Climate change mitigation and adaptation require following the multilevel governance approaches of the UN SDGs and of the Paris Agreement empowering also non-state and non-governmental actors, civil society institutions, and citizens to participate in multilevel governance, for instance by using domestic parliamentary and judicial institutions for holding governments accountable for non-compliance with UN SDGs and human rights. Ordo-liberal democracies acknowledge that human rights, democracy, and respect for human dignity require recognizing citizens as legal subjects of constitutional contracts, as democratic principals of government agents with limited, delegated powers, and as being entitled to inalienable human rights and judicial remedies, as recognized in HRL and democratic constitutions. European and UN HRL can be construed as cosmopolitan legal systems not only of states but also of citizens and peoples

[38] Cf W Tiruneh, Holding the Parent Company Liable for Human Rights Abuses Committed Abroad: The Case of the Four Nigerian Farmers and Milieudefensie v. Shell, *European Journal of International Law Talk* Blog of 19 February 2021. On the recent limitation by the US Supreme Court of jurisdiction under the US Alien Tort Statute for private claims alleging legal liability of US corporations for violations of human rights outside the United States, see D Desierto and D Song, SCOTUS Further Narrows Parent Corporate Liability under the Alien Tort Statute: Ambiguities and Evidentiary Thresholds in the June 2021 Judgment in Nestle USA Inc. v Doe et al., *European Journal of International Law Talk* Blog of 25 June 2021.

entitled to human rights for holding all governance powers accountable by democratic, legal, and judicial remedies.[39]

Yet, even if such normative conceptions of international law are reasonable and citizen-driven remedies can be effective (eg in European constitutional, HRL, and IEL), international legal *practices* remain dominated by power-oriented politics of international law (as discussed in Chapter 2, section 2.2), including opposition by many powerful rulers—also in democratic states like Hungary, Poland, and the United States under President Trump—against effective democratic and judicial accountability. Authoritarian and neo-liberal governments resist constitutionalization of international law empowering citizens to invoke international legal obligations in domestic legal systems. The realities of geopolitical rivalries and underlying value conflicts (described in Chapter 3) render it unlikely that, for example, China's communist party and US governments will ever follow the example of Europe's multilevel constitutionalism by limiting their respective powers through international and constitutional constraints and institutions empowering citizens to enforce civil, political, economic, and social human rights guarantees through international courts. Due to the bounded rationality of human beings (as discussed in Chapter 5), and due to the political opposition against making international legal rules and court decisions directly applicable and enforceable for the benefit of citizens inside national legal systems, the realities of power politics inside and among so many UN and WTO member states are likely to continue. This is confirmed by the only very few instances where courageous legal advisers of worldwide organizations (like C Wilfrid Jenks at the International Labour Organization, Ibrahim Shihata at the World Bank) argued for cosmopolitan human rights approaches.[40] As long as citizens allow their rulers to separate international law from domestic law so as to exempt foreign and trade policy powers (eg for taxing and restricting domestic citizens, redistributing their income) from effective democratic and judicial constraints, legal empowerment of cosmopolitan citizens depends on struggles for justice. It risks remaining a utopia beyond Europe's borders. Even if citizens legitimately invoke HRL and EU law as cosmopolitan legal orders, the state-centred UN/WTO *practices* undermine normative ideals of cosmopolitan constitutionalism. The UN Guiding Principles on Business and Human Rights, as adopted by the UN Human Rights Council in

[39] Cf EU Petersmann, 'Cosmopolitan Constitutionalism: Linking Local Engagement with International Economic Law and Human Rights' in L Biukovic and P Pitman (eds), *Local Engagement with International Economic Law and Human Rights* (Edward Elgar 2017), 26–54. See also S Charnovitz, 'The WTO and Cosmopolitics' in EU Petersmann (ed), *Reforming the World Trading System: Legitimacy, Efficiency and Democratic Governance* (OUP 2005), 437–46.

[40] Cf D van den Meerssche, Performing the Rule of Law in International Organizations: Ibrahim Shihata and the World Bank's Turn to Governance Reform, *Leiden Journal of International Law* 32 (2019), 47–69; GF Sinclair, Wilfred Jenks, and the Future of International Organizations Law, *European Journal of International Law* 31 (2020), 525–42; CW Jenks, *The Common Law of Mankind* (Praeger 1958).

2011, have induced thousands of companies to accept corporate social responsibility for integrating social, environmental, ethical, consumer and human rights concerns into their business strategies and operations. They are also reflected in recent (eg German) legislation and EU draft directives on corporate supply chain responsibilities for respecting human rights and could evolve (eg with the help of judicial case law) into customary law duties of corporations to respect human rights and address adverse corporate impact on human rights. Yet, as discussed in Chapter 7, their impact on ISA awards and on enforceable legal corporate duties remains limited, so far. How should citizens respond to this power-oriented reality of the politics of international law recognizing state power and corporate power as sources of law even if public and private power disregard human and democratic rights?

9.5 Participatory Public–Private Partnerships in Multilevel Network Governance of Sustainable Development

Just as democratic and republican constitutionalism resulted from struggles of citizens for supply of national PGs (like rule of law, democratic peace), so were the post-war developments of international labour law, HRL, IEL, international criminal and environmental law often initiated by democratic institutions, labour unions, economic associations (like chambers of commerce), and non-governmental human rights and environmental organizations. For instance, the UN Guiding Principles on Business and Human Rights were endorsed by the UN Human Rights Council in 2011 even though their legal methodology ('protect, respect and remedy') and content were elaborated by non-governmental advocacy groups (under the intellectual leadership of Professor John Ruggie) in consultation with business representatives supporting social contracts that may never have been reached through purely intergovernmental UN negotiations. The 2030 Sustainable Development Agenda and its 'call for changing our world' through a 'global partnership' with the 'participation of all countries, all stakeholders and all people' acknowledges the importance of bottom-up private sector participation and civil society initiatives (eg for voluntary sustainability standards) for realizing the SDGs.[41] This need for 'transforming our world' responds to the changing structures and functions of international law as an instrument of multilevel governance of PGs in a globally integrated world.

[41] See the case studies in C Beverelli, J Kurtz, and D Raess (eds), *International Trade, Investment and the Sustainable Development Goals* (CUP 2020), 175–315.

9.5.1 Changing Structures of International Law

Similar to the transformation of the Westphalian international law of coexistence among states into an international law of cooperation based on networks of hundreds of intergovernmental and thousands of non-governmental organizations for the collective supply of transnational PGs, globalization continues to transform the structures of the international legal system by empowering citizens and NGOs to participate in the governance of *transnational PGs* like protection of public health (eg by inventing, producing, and distributing vaccines and other medical goods and services), the environment (eg by reducing environmental pollution, protecting animals and plants), and protection of human rights (eg by challenging governmental violations of human rights in national and international courts). This empowerment of transnational civil societies reinforces globalization and legal accountability, the emergence of global law (like UN HRL, rights to participate in global Internet and transport communications), and the incentives for citizen-driven, participatory forms of governance (eg of the Internet, air and shipping transportation); they challenge state-centred 'chess-board' conceptions of international law among sovereign states (eg as practised in the UN Security Council) by global network governance linking citizens, governments, and NGOs in most international economic, social, environmental, and human rights organizations (eg participation of NGOs in the ILO, in international standardization organizations, in the public *fora* of the WTO, the International Air Transport Association, the International Telecommunications Union, UN human rights and environmental bodies).[42] The WorldWideWeb confirms the increasing frequency and intensity of civil society networks influencing intergovernmental cooperation and regulation.

The systemic importance of public–private partnerships is confirmed also by the fact that citizen-driven network governance can threaten multilevel governance of PGs (eg by security threats from terrorist networks, criminal drug cartels, or cybercriminals). The legal empowerment of network governance—like labour rights empowering workers and trade unions; electronic communication systems enabling working from home during lockdowns imposed during health pandemics; electronic platform companies selling electronic services by using international commercial and investment law; sub-national and supra-national customs territories as WTO members; cities in climate change prevention agreements; individual victims in international criminal law, and the legal empowerment of every

[42] Cf AM Slaughter, *The Chess-Board and the Web. Strategies of Connection in a Networked World* (Yale UP 2017), elaborating strategies for designing, improving, and managing social networks for resolving collective action problems at local, national and transnational levels of governance; J von Bernstorff, New Responses to the Legitimacy Crisis of International Institutions: The Role of 'Civil Society' and the Rise of the Principle of Participation of 'The Most Affected' in International Institutional Law, *European Journal of International Law* 32 (2021), 125–58.

human being through HRL—changes the law-creating processes and incentive structures of international law. For instance, a UN Press Release of 21 September 2020 noted that the

> number of commitments to reach net zero emissions from local governments and businesses has roughly doubled in less than a year, as many prioritize climate action in their recovery from Covid-19. Cities and regions with a carbon footprint greater than the emissions of the US, and companies with a combined revenue of over $11.4 trillion (equivalent to more than half of the US GDP), are now pursuing net zero emissions by the end of the century, according to a major report published by the *Data-Driven EnviroLab* and the *NewClimate Institute* today. The majority of these actors are aiming for a zero-carbon economy by 2050, as part of the UN Race to Zero campaign, the largest alliance of local governments, businesses, investors and others aiming for zero emissions in the 2040s. This now encompasses 22 regions, 452 cities, 1,101 businesses, 549 universities and 45 of the biggest investors.[43]

9.5.2 Changing Functions of International Law

Chapter 2, section 2.1 described legal systems as being characterized by dialectic tensions between *normative legal orders* (based on public reason) and *legal practices* driven by rational self-interests and/or politics of individual and social legal actors. Chapters 4 and 5 emphasized that the domestic policy functions of multilevel governance and regulation of PGs (like rules-based, mutually beneficial trade, environmental, health, and human rights systems) are increasingly recognized not only in constitutional democracies but also in many non-democratic countries (like China using WTO law to drive domestic economic and legal reforms). Regulatory competition and geopolitical rivalries are bound to increase the regulatory challenges of global health, environmental, economic, and humanitarian crises and, as explained in Chapters 6–8, the systemic importance of maintaining multilevel legal and judicial remedies in international trade, investment, and environmental policies for protecting rule of law and mutual coherence in the legally and institutionally fragmented, yet interdependent, multilevel governance systems for the SDGs and related overlapping global PGs (like mutually beneficial trade, investment, environmental, and legal systems). Transforming our world for implementing the SDGs requires reviewing all three major functions of national and international legal systems:

[43] UN Climate Press Release of 21 September 2020, https://unfccc.int/news/commitments-to-net-zero-double-in-less-than-a-year.

- The *instrumental function of law* for normative ordering of social cooperation must respond to the definition of the SDGs in terms of human rights and welfare of domestic citizens, that is acknowledging the domestic policy and constitutional functions of many international law rules protecting PGs for the benefit of domestic citizens. The universal recognition of inalienable human rights confirms that the needed limitations on mutually harmful politics (like pollution, human rights violations) must be constructed from the bottom up, for instance by strengthening democratic accountability vis-à-vis citizens, parliamentary and judicial accountability, and institutional checks and balances by science-based, regulatory agencies (like independent central banks, competition, environmental, and public health institutions). *International* legal accountability and dispute settlement mechanisms are only second lines of constitutional entrenchment for protecting PGs like the rule of law beyond state borders for the benefit of domestic citizens.
- The *systemic function of law* for justifying the reasonable coherence of legal primary rules of conduct and secondary rules of recognition, change, and adjudication must acknowledge that modern positive law includes inalienable human rights and principles of justice deriving their legitimacy from the bottom-up consent of citizens. Just as national courts in Europe and European courts base their jurisprudence on constitutionally agreed principles common to EU member states, the 'general principles of law recognized by civilized nations' (Article 38.1,c ICJ Statute), as well as 'judicial decisions and the teachings of the most highly qualified publicists of the various nations, as subsidiary means for the determination of rules of law' (Article 38.1,d ICJ Statute) must be more actively used for interpreting treaties and customary rules in conformity with agreed SDGs (like food security, public health and education, gender equality, decent work for all).
- The *cultural function of transforming law as it is written* into living law must seek more effective ways of promoting legal socialization and institutionalization of public reason so as to induce legal actors to comply voluntarily with agreed legal rules and principles in domestic jurisdictions. Empowering citizens and domestic court of justice to challenge abuses of power (such as inadequate implementation of GHG emission reductions and other SDGs) can promote compliance and accountability cultures protecting transnational rule of law and other PGs.

9.5.3 Democratic Network Governance as a Restraint on Power Politics

This book emphasized that, as illustrated by statues of justice in courthouses all over the world and at the entrance of the WTO building at Lake Geneva, law and governance require justification in terms of agreed principles of justice as recognized in national and international legal systems. According to David Hume, moderate scarcity of resources (ie all humans can have enough resources, but not everything they desire) and limited altruism (humans tend to focus on their own goals before acknowledging the claims of others) constitute the circumstances of justice necessitating theories of justice (justifications) on how the competing distributive claims of individuals and groups should be reconciled. Other philosophers proceed from respect for human dignity, human rights, constitutional contract theories, and democratic discourse as foundations of justice and justification of legal systems.[44] The inevitable conflicts about distributive justice raise procedural and constitutional justice problems for elaborating social and constitutional contracts on (i) how reasonable societies should define just rules and institutions; (ii) institutionalize their agreed principles of procedural, constitutional, distributive, corrective, commutative justice and equity; and (iii) design democratic legislation, administration, and judicial protection of equal individual rights enabling citizens to satisfy their legitimate demand for private and public goods.[45] Chapters 2 and 3 concluded that UN and WTO law are not enough for protecting global PGs (like human rights and other SDGs) and for responding to legitimate civil society demands for justice. Even if UN HRL can be construed as a constitutional foundation for an international law of states, peoples, and citizens, UN and WTO law have failed to constitutionalize the power-oriented *practices* of UN and WTO member states. Chapters 4 and 5 explained why, even if the return to hegemonic power politics should make it impossible to transform UN/WTO law into inclusive global community law empowering citizens and democratic institutions, HRL and democratic constitutionalism require protecting human rights, democracy, rule of law, international courts, and democratic accountability mechanisms not only among democracies but also in external relations vis-à-vis third countries, as prescribed in the EU's domestic and foreign policy constitutions (cf Chapter 5,

[44] On justice as justification based on respect for human rights and other, agreed principles of justice reconciling equal liberties with democratic governance and social justice see: EU Petersmann, *Multilevel Constitutionalism for Multilevel Governance of Public Goods* (Hart 2017), 89ff. For a discussion of distributive justice from a state-centred IEL perspective see: O Suttle, *Distributive Justice and World Trade Law. A Political Theory of International Trade Regulation* (CUP 2018). Suttle emphasizes 'state coercion as a key factor triggering distributive duties domestically' (at 9), which are different from distributive duties resulting from coercive relations among states (at 10). Suttle understands coercion as 'imposition of nonvoluntary institutions' (at 11). He perceives external trade measures as 'just if and only if they pursue global equality of individual opportunity, through improving the position of less-advantaged individuals, subject to a reasonable principle of self-determination' (at 25). He applies his 'equality of individual opportunity' principle in practice 'by considering per capita income of groups, as a proxy for the opportunity sets enjoyed by individuals within those groups' (at 26).

[45] On such constitutional and human rights approaches to international law see Petersmann (n 44). Both neo-liberal Anglo-Saxon nationalism and power-oriented state capitalism tend to neglect constitutional justice problems of international legal systems and the priority of justice over efficiency also in IEL, which remains dominated by state-centred legal positivism and economic theories neglecting human rights.

section 5.5) and in FTAs concluded by the EU with third countries. Yet, most UN/WTO member states and their civil societies have failed to constitutionalize foreign policies and to follow the EU example of justifying IEL in terms of human and constitutional rights and multilevel democratic constitutionalism. These constitutional failures and the reality of intergovernmental power politics render successful implementation of the SDGs highly uncertain.

Economic lawyers should acknowledge also outside the EU that—as explained in Chapter 4 and confirmed by the universally accepted SDGs—neither economic efficiency (eg in terms of Kaldor–Hicks efficiency) nor state-centred theories of justice offer sufficient justifications for legally designing IEL and multilevel governance of transnational PGs for the benefit of citizens: both economic markets and states are mere *instruments* for enabling citizens to develop their personalities (eg by pursuing non-market values like human rights and PGs).[46] In democracies, conclusion and implementation of multilateral treaties depend no longer only on intergovernmental negotiations and on their *ex post* parliamentary approval; civil society participation in preparing, negotiating, and implementing agreements is often no less important for the democratic legitimacy, approval, and effectiveness of international agreements. A more internationalist United States under democratic President Biden may prove a passing phase before another nationalist, Republican US President may again withdraw the US from multilateral agreements. Hence, Anne-Marie Slaughter has explained why involving civil society groups and NGOs in multilateral treaties like the Paris Agreement can promote 'network governance' with broader and deeper 'democratic engagement' that will be more 'impervious to the efforts of any future president to withdraw from the world'.[47] As one example, she mentions a Biden/Bloomberg Climate Coalition, which would bring together the US government; the more than 7,000 members of the Global Covenant of Mayors for Climate and Energy, an alliance helped by Bloomberg Philanthropies; as many of the companies in the US Roundtable as possible; and civic groups working on climate change. Similar political coalitions could be formed for global health policies, where the Gates Foundation has already pioneered the creation of the Global Alliance for Vaccines and Immunisation, which brings together governments, international organizations, pharmaceutical companies, and civic organizations. Environmental experts in the United States also argue that US carbon taxes and carbon emission trading systems could provide a degree of permanency to climate policy in the changeable political landscape of the United States, where the merry-go-round of Democratic and Republican legislatures means that regulation can be changed every few years: fiscal policy could

[46] Cf EU Petersmann, *International Economic Law in the 21st Century* (Hart 2012), arguing for constitutional and human rights approaches to IEL.

[47] AM Slaughter, 'There is a way to keep America globally engaged', *Financial Times* 19 November 2020.

become more durable, longer term, and less subject to legal and administrative challenges and risks. Public–private partnerships and participatory approaches involving business, citizens, and social resources in transnational problem-solving have proven important for the conclusion and operation of many other multilateral agreements in the field of human rights, environmental protection, international criminal justice, and other PGs that may affect ordinary lives more than geopolitical power politics. As states can no longer protect the SDGs and most PGs without international law and multilateral institutions, they should recognize and protect rights and duties of their citizens to participate in multilevel governance of PGs, including everyone's right 'to a social and international order in which the rights and freedoms set forth in this Declaration can be fully realized' (Article 28 UDHR). For example, a global health pandemic treaty on preventing disease outbreaks (eg by reducing the risk of pathogens jumping from animals to humans), limiting local, national, and international disease spread (as regulated in the WHO International Health Regulations), and on assisting countries in disease control (eg through scientific advice, provision of medical equipment and vaccines) should involve not only governments and multilevel health authorities; it must promote and protect also more decentralized information and cooperation networks (like financial and technical support from NGOs).

9.6 Will Constitutional Reforms of UN/WTO Governance Be Politically Feasible?

Chapter 1 referred to the social and political premisses of Henry Kissinger's analysis of world order. Kissinger's final chapter, 'World Order in our Time?', acknowledges that both the legitimacy and the balance of power of the twenty-first-century international order are increasingly challenged due to, *inter alia*, the emerging multipolarity of power and the injustices of globalization (like repeated financial crises). One of his policy conclusions—'(t)he contemporary quest for world order will require a coherent strategy to establish a concept of order *within* the various regions, and to relate these regional orders to one another'[48]—is reflected in the GATT/WTO provisions on embedded liberalism, non-discriminatory competition, free trade areas, customs unions, and plurilateral agreements, which are increasingly used for diverse regional trade agreements among like-minded countries. The embedded liberalism underlying both UN law and WTO law serves the purpose of coordinating diverse national and regional orders and related regulatory competition (eg among neo-liberal, state capitalist, European ordo-liberal, and third-world approaches to economic regulation). Kissinger's recommendation for retaining

[48] H Kissinger, *World Order. Reflections on the Character of Nations and the Course of History* (Penguin 2014), at 371.

the United States as the 'indispensable geopolitical force for the vindication of humane values'[49] has been taken up in this book by supporting proposals for alliances of democratic WTO members, who should defend the consistency of multilevel trade, health, and environmental governance with human rights and rule of law. Yet, other conclusions of this analysis of *transforming world trade and investment law for sustainable development* go beyond those of Kissinger's state-centred methodologies, for instance by calling for constitutional reforms rather than only for 'deconstructive criticism' (like that of M Konkenniemi) and 'evolutionary constitutionalism' (eg as advocated by P Allott).[50] As explained in Chapter 5, as long as the definition of state interests is left to the discretion of rulers instead of defining them in terms of equal rights and remedies of citizens vis-à-vis constitutionally accountable governance institutions, foreign policy powers always risk being abused for protecting particular interests of the rulers rather than general interests and equal rights of their citizens.

9.6.1 Protecting the WTO Legal and Dispute Settlement System for Non-Discriminatory Regulatory Competition

Chapters 2–6 explained why the WTO legal and dispute settlement system must be protected as a framework for non-discriminatory, regulatory competition among WTO members with often diverse conceptions of economic and political regulation. Even if the systemic conflicts between the neo-liberal Washington consensus, China's totalitarian state capitalism, and Europe's ordo-liberal Brussels consensus render WTO negotiations more difficult, WTO law and the WTO dispute settlement system remain of constitutional importance for a rules-based world trading system. In contrast to the WTO ideology of member-driven governance based on 'chess-board' conceptions of international law among sovereign states, the 2030 UN Agenda for Sustainable Development seeks 'to realize the human rights of all' through more inclusive legal systems protecting 'all countries, all stakeholders and all people' so as to build a 'world of universal respect for human rights and human dignity, the rule of law, justice, equality and non-discrimination'.[51] Interpreting the WTO sustainable development objectives in conformity with the UN Sustainable Development Agenda requires interpreting WTO rules with due respect for the diverse constitutional and human rights traditions of WTO members. The global economic, health, and environmental crises illustrate the systemic importance of

[49] Kissinger (n 48), at 373.

[50] For my criticism of Koskenniemi's 'interpretation games' and Allot's refusal to support 'constitutional constructivism' see: EU Petersmann, 'Constitutional Constructivism' for a Common Law of Humanity? Multilevel Constitutionalism as a 'Gentle Civilizer of Nations', *MPIL Research Paper Series* No. 2017-24.

[51] Transforming our World (2015), Preamble and para 8.

maintaining the legal coherence of UN law (eg WHO law, the UNFCCC, the Paris Agreement) with the WTO legal and dispute settlement system and of reducing the disconnect in private and public, national and international network governance of PGs, as successfully realized in the WTO panel and AB reports on tobacco control measures in conformity with the WHO FCTC (as discussed in Chapter 6, section 6.3). Just as trade and investment litigation have successfully promoted transnational rule of law in international trade and investment cooperation (as illustrated in Chapters 6–8), the recent human rights and climate change litigation (as discussed in Chapter 8, section 8.4 and this chapter) has promoted more legal accountability of governments for their commitments to reduce GHG emission. Interpreting world trade and investment laws and adjudication in conformity with HRL is important for preventing WTO rules, ISA, and notably the ECT from becoming major obstacles to climate change mitigation and implementation of the SDGs. If the needed reforms cannot be agreed among governments (eg due to the WTO consensus practices), third-party adjudication of disputes based on systemic treaty interpretations offers second-best modalities for promoting systemic coherence between fragmented treaty systems and for adjusting their interpretations to new regulatory challenges.

The insufficient information by the Chinese government on the COVID-19 outbreak in Wuhan in 2019—despite the reporting and early warning mechanisms that had been established in response to the 2003 SARS crisis in China—was revealed by civil society criticizing the politicized censorship of public opinion and inadequacies of the national and international public health emergency information systems with respect to new and emerging infectious diseases.[52] The unilateral, uncoordinated trade restrictions imposed by WTO members in response to the COVID-19 global health pandemic confirmed the need for stronger WHO transparency and cooperation requirements (eg on early notification of outbreaks of health pandemics and their origins) and for additional WHO and WTO rules protecting access to information, medicines, and medical equipment so as to limit the impact of global health emergencies threatening welfare and human rights throughout the world. In the EU, the regulatory challenges of COVID-19 have led to comprehensive EU initiatives—complementing the national EU member state competences for health policies—for EU financial aid and EU guarantees of access to medical supplies and vaccines aimed at securing better health and economic policy responses to the COVID-19 pandemic and to the resulting economic and financial challenges. In the UN, the UN Security Council—for instance in Resolution 2532 adopted on 1 July 2020—underscored the potential danger posed by the COVID-19 health pandemic to the maintenance of international peace and security; it called upon parties to armed conflicts to engage in a humanitarian

[52] Cf C Ding, Fatal Lack of Information Transparency in Public Health Emergency: Lessons from the COVID-19 Outbreak in China, *Hong Kong Law Journal* 50 (2020, forthcoming), 781–808.

ceasefire for at least ninety days.[53] The WTO participated in G20 and WHO initiatives promoting more coherent trade, financial, and health policy responses to the COVID-19 health pandemic. The pandemic revealed the need for making the health regulations of the WHO more effective through better coordination among UN Specialized Agencies (eg the WHO and the Chicago Convention establishing the International Civil Aviation Organization, notably its Article 14 regulating prevention of the spread of diseases through air travel) and UN human rights bodies.[54] Keeping markets open, in compliance with WTO law, for the post-COVID-19 recovery will be important for creating jobs and economic growth and for providing global access to vaccines and medical supplies necessary for coping with health pandemics.[55]

9.6.2 The SDGs and the Geneva Consensus Require Leadership by Democratic Alliances

US President Biden has described the great-power competition among democracies and autocracies as the defining challenge of the twenty-first century. Democracies acknowledge that, as emphasized in Chapters 4 and 5, the bounded rationality of private and public actors, and the existence of market failures, governance failures and constitutional failures in multilevel governance of PGs, require legal protection of human and constitutional rights, democratic governance, and rule of law. Even though formerly communist countries have embraced economic liberalism, autocracies continue to insist on political monopoly powers and reject political competition, democratic disagreements, and constitutional limitations of their political powers and privileges—notwithstanding the historical evidence that monarchies and oligarchies, and their abuses of power, have been challenged and ultimately reversed throughout history by democratic struggles for justice. The universal recognition of human rights and rule of law in UN law and in the SDGs reflects not only such humanist lessons from political history (as described in Chapter 5); it also suggests that the twenty-first-century competition among democracies and autocracies remains rooted in power struggles by autocrats lacking moral and political legitimacy in their suppression of human rights. The SDGs require a new twenty-first century constitutionalism protecting human rights and rule of law in multilevel governance of PGs.

[53] Cf n 2.

[54] Cf A von Bogdandy and PA Villarreal, *International Law on Pandemic Response: A First Stocktaking in Light of the Coronavirus*, MPIL Research Paper Series No 2020-07.

[55] See the various speeches (on the WTO website) given by former WTO Deputy Director-General A Wolff throughout 2020 on how WTO law can assist governments in better responding to the COVID-19 health pandemic.

The failures of the WTO's Doha Round negotiations reflect disagreements among neo-liberal, state capitalist, ordo-liberal, and third-world conceptions of multilevel trade regulation (eg regarding abuses of trade remedies, subsidies, intellectual property rights, anti-competitive distortions of digital trade, tax evasion, private data protection). Some of these disagreements (eg on Internet governance) may be overcome only at more decentralized levels of trade regulation among like-minded countries. In some areas (like designing rules for CBAMs), WTO negotiations could become more depoliticized by relying on scientific input from independent think tanks, UN specialized agencies, and annotated background papers by the WTO Secretariat. In other areas—like global financial, health, and environmental crises—the G20 countries, or the now thirty-eight Organisation for Economic Co-operation and Development (OECD) countries as an alliance of democracies—could initiate new institutional frameworks for coordinating global emergency responses (like the Financial Stability Board established by the G20 in 2009). Even if the G20 responses to the global health and environmental challenges have, so far, been disappointing, the G20 and the OECD countries remain the best chance for reforming the UN and WTO governance failures (eg for providing vaccines to all and decarbonizing the global economy). As explained in Chapter 2, the regulatory competition among WTO members practising different varieties of capitalist economic orders should be accepted as long as they comply with their existing WTO legal obligations. The illegal trade wars and trade distortions described in Chapter 3 reflect governance failures and constitutional failures inside WTO member states; they need to be reduced by returning to WTO negotiations, the rules-based WTO dispute settlement procedures, and WTO third-party adjudication, which will be indispensable for maintaining transnational rule of law in responding to the global governance crises. Chapters 4 and 5 explained and supported the EU efforts at promoting multilevel, democratic, and republican constitutionalism also in the external relations law of the EU, for instance by insisting on human rights clauses and environmental protection commitments in EU trade and investment agreements with third countries, promoting multi-party interim appellate arbitration as a substitute for the dysfunctional AB in the WTO, and pushing for public law reforms of ISA. The psychological insight that constitutionalism enables more reasonable self-government by means of agreed self-commitments to just rules and institutions of a higher legal rank, remains important also for authoritarian states like China, whose national Constitution of 1982 cannot be invoked and enforced by citizens in national courts. China's commitment to labour law reforms in the EU–China Investment Agreement of December 2020 illustrates why constructive engagement may help also authoritarian governments in reforming obvious market failures and governance failures.[56] The proposed

[56] The panel of experts report of 21 January 2021 under the EU–Korea FTA, and the US–Guatemala panel report of 2017 under the US–Central America FTA, concerning labour practices (in Korea and Guatemala, respectively) interpreted the respective FTA provisions referring to the ILO's fundamental

democratic alliances of WTO members should encourage civil society struggles—as they are increasingly taking place in Russia and other authoritarian countries (notably in Eurasia, Africa, Asia, and Latin America)—for democratic reforms and compliance with the human rights obligations of UN member states in order to avoid that authoritarian governments and kleptocratic élites undermine protection of the SDGs, for instance by provoking military conflicts, health pandemics, environmental pollution, corruption, and violation of human rights. More importantly, as illustrated by the contribution of the EU and EEA to promoting democratic peace in Europe, democratic alliances should focus on reducing existing weaknesses inside democracies like insufficient enforcement of competition, environmental, and digital privacy rules, decarbonization and digitalization of economies, limitation of tax evasion and cybercrimes, joint promotion of strategic technologies (like semiconductors where 75 per cent of current production is concentrated in China and East Asia) and of public health and social security. Demonstrating the legitimacy and effectiveness of democratic governance systems is the best response to disruptive policies from China (like Chinese steel dumping) and other authoritarian governance systems suppressing human and democratic rights.[57]

9.6.3 Multilevel Adjudication as Guardian of Rule of Law and of Systemic Treaty Interpretation

Chapters 5–8 argued that multilevel judicial remedies—for example in regional economic and human rights law, for the settlement of the more than 600 invocations of WTO dispute settlement procedures (1995–2020), and for the more than 1,100 ISA procedures—remain of systemic importance for maintaining rule of law in international trade, investment, and environmental cooperation. Systemic treaty interpretations (eg of state duties to protect public health, the environment and public order) through impartial third-party adjudication promoted respect for human rights values even if, due to the politics of legal practices and strategic interpretation by self-interested actors, human rights were hardly ever invoked in WTO dispute settlement proceedings and remained of marginal importance for the settlement of most ISA disputes. Multilevel judicial cooperation in trade and investment adjudication enhances respect for due process of law, rule of law, proportionality balancing, and subsidiarity principles; it limits abuses of trade policy powers (eg in case of trade remedies and invocations of national security

labour rights conventions in different ways; cf D LeClercq, Guest Post in the International Economic Law and Policy Blog of 9 February 2021. On linking trade to labour rights, see de Schutter (n 11).

[57] Cf M Lassus, *The Revival of Democracy in America and the Better Angels of Your Nature* (Odile Jacob 2021).

exceptions) and can strengthen parliamentary, judicial, and constitutional restraints protecting citizens against rent-seeking lobbies and rogue rulers.[58]

The global environmental, health, and economic crises confirmed the systemic importance of WTO law for efficient responses to the global climate, health pandemic, economic and geopolitical crises. WTO law offers sufficient instruments for preventing or settling systemic regime conflicts among WTO members, for instance by agreeing on additional clarifications of WTO rules (eg on subsidies and CBAMs) and complying with WTO dispute settlement procedures for the peaceful settlement of trade disputes. Neither human rights nor international environmental law and health law need to be incorporated into WTO law; systemic treaty interpretation, politically agreed clarifications for the interpretation and application of existing WTO rules (eg for calculation of border carbon adjustments), multilateral treaty negotiations outside the WTO in the competent institutions (like the UNFCCC, the WHO), and close cooperation of the WTO with other international organizations aimed at maintaining the Geneva consensus may suffice for preventing systemic conflicts in realizing the SDGs for the benefit of citizens.

9.6.4 Promoting SDGs through Private–Public Partnerships and Multilevel Constitutionalism

Lack of legal and judicial accountability of authoritarian governments, their support by kleptocratic oligarchs, the often selfish politics of international legal practices, and the insufficient institutionalization of public reason for stronger protection of human rights and rule of law were described as major impediments to realizing the SDGs. Climate change mitigation requires following the multilevel governance approaches of the UN SDGs and of the Paris Agreement by empowering non-state and non-governmental actors, civil society institutions, and citizens to participate in multilevel trade, environmental, and health governance, for instance by private development of green energy technologies and vaccines, by using domestic parliamentary and judicial institutions for holding governments accountable for compliance with UN SDGs and human rights, and by promoting cosmopolitan and interactional conceptions of international law enabling citizens to invoke and enforce precise and unconditional treaty rules in domestic jurisdictions. This chapter used the examples of recent litigation in European courts (eg on human rights, climate mitigation and corporate responsibilities) and of civil

[58] For detailed proposals, see AM Wolff, *Stressed in an Age of Populism: Recommendations for Changes in US Trade Law and Policy* (IIEL Issue Brief 04/2017, 2017); EU Petersmann, The 2018 Trade Wars as a Threat to the World Trading System and to Constitutional Democracies, *Trade, Law and Development* X (2018), 179–225.

society involvement in multilevel health and environmental governance to explain why empowerment of citizens and their direct participation in protecting SDGs can reduce collective action problems.[59] European integration law shows how stronger legal and judicial remedies for citizens in multilevel governance of PGs are politically easier to realize through reciprocal, plurilateral agreements among like-minded countries. Yet, the global Brussels effects of EU data and chemicals regulations and of the *Schrems I and II* judgments of the CJEU (confirming the illegality of EU–US data transfer arrangements) were also mentioned as examples of how civil society initiatives, judicial and democratic leadership can promote reforms (eg of Internet governance) far beyond Europe. The proposed extension of the EU's ETS, carbon taxes, and CBAMs to international movements of goods, services, persons, and capital was discussed as another example for responding to the collective action problems of climate change mitigation, for instance by making internal carbon reduction regulations compatible with external legal obligations under the WTO (which would require, *inter alia*, a phasing out of free allowance subsidies under the ETS for some EU industries). With direct access to more than a third of the world's population as their users, global tech companies (like Facebook and Twitter) could play a central role in private–public governance of PGs. Yet, as demonstrated by the Twitter politics of Donald Trump and the manipulation of public opinion through social networks (as illustrated by misinformation and misappropriation of private data by Cambridge Analytica distorting the UK's 2016 referendum on EU membership), corporate Internet governance remains in urgent need of additional public law regulation, especially outside the scope of the EU's General Data Protection Regulation 2016/679 of 14 April 2016 (effective as of May 2018).

Multilevel constitutional reforms and more decentralized, multilevel governance of PGs are called for also by the subsidiarity- and margin of appreciation-principles of HRL, especially in a multipolar world suffering from geopolitical rivalries, trade wars, and non-homogeneous societies. Power politics can ultimately be overcome only by democratic bottom-up reforms of national and international legal systems, as demonstrated by the successful constitutionalization of European common market law and HRL. The needed constitutional reforms depend on stronger domestic struggles for justice by citizens and people invoking their human rights against abuses of public and private power. Democratic institutions must insist that modern UN/WTO law has become constitutionally

[59] For example, through reduction and decentralized control of environmental pollution; invention, production and distribution of vaccines against infectious diseases; private–public partnerships in the joint administration of common pool resources (cf the research of economic Nobel Prize winner E Ostrom on more efficient private–public governance of common pool resources allowing resource appropriators and local institutions to participate in the governance of global commons like the atmosphere: E Ostrom, *Governing the Commons: The Evolution of Institutions for Collective Action* (CUP 1990); E Ostrom, *Understanding Institutional Diversity* (Princeton UP 2005).

constrained by inalienable human and democratic rights and other *jus cogens* rules. Just as neo-liberal shareholder conceptions of corporate governance are increasingly being replaced by responsible stakeholder conceptions of inclusive corporate governance (ie recognizing also employees, consumers, suppliers, local communities, and the environment as corporate stakeholders whose interests will affect the value and success of corporate activities), so do the SDGs and recent climate litigation acknowledge that multilevel trade and environmental governance must empower and serve all affected citizens and stakeholders.

The new nationalism (eg in the United States, the United Kingdom, 'ethnic nationalism' in China, India, and Russia) suggests that regional, economic constitutionalism may remain limited to plurilateral agreements among European democracies. Yet, as discussed in Chapters 5–8, the harmful externalities of nationalism render transnational third-party adjudication, judicial comity among national and international courts, and judicial respect for constitutional principles of justice ever more urgent for maintaining rule of law, containing abuses of power and preventing systemic regime conflicts undermining the SDGs. UN law (eg the 1992 UNFCCC and the 1994 UNCLOS) and WTO law have failed to prevent climate change, ocean pollution, biodiversity losses, disregard for UNCLOS and WTO adjudication, and widespread disregard for human rights. Without stronger civil society and democratic struggles for constitutional restraints on the ubiquity of abuses of public and private power, many SDGs risk remaining a utopia.

Select Bibliography

Boucher D and Kelly P (eds), *The Social Contract from Hobbes to Rawls* (Routledge 1994)

Brunnée J and Toope SJ, *Legitimacy and Legality in International Law: An Interactional Account* (CUP 2010)

Cohen A, *Supreme Inequality: The Supreme Court's Fifty-Year Battle for a More Unjust America* (Penguin Press 2019)

Cooter RD, *The Strategic Constitution* (Princeton UP 2000)

de Baere G and Wouters H (eds), *The Contribution of International and Supranational Courts to the Rule of Law* (Edward Elgar 2015)

de Schutter O, *Trade in the Service of Sustainable Development. Linking Trade to Labour Rights and Environmental Standards* (Hart 2017)

Fallon RH, *Law and Legitimacy in the Supreme Court* (Harvard UP 2018)

Forst R, *The Right to Justification. Elements of a Constructivist Theory of Justice* (Columbia UP 2012)

Furubotn E and Richter R, *Institutions and Economic Theory. The Contribution of the New Institutional Economics* (2nd edn, University of Michigan Press, 2005)

Gosepath S and Lohmann G (eds), *Philosophie der Menschenrechte* (Suhrkamp 1998)

Grosman N, Grant Cohen H, Follesdal A, and Ulfstein G (eds), *Legitimacy and International Courts* (CUP 2018)

Habermas J, *Between Facts and Norms. Contributions to a Discourse Theory of Law and Democracy* (MIT Press 1998)

Hien J and Joerges C (eds), *Ordoliberalism, Law and the Rule of Economics* (Hart 2020)

Hilf M and Petersmann EU (eds), *National Constitutions and International Economic Law* (Kluwer 1993)

Hilf M, Jacobs FG, and Petersmann EU (eds), *The European Community and GATT* (Kluwer 1986)

Hofmann HCH, Pantazatou K, and Zaccaroni G (eds), *The Transformation of the European Economic Constitution* (Edward Elgar 2019)

Joerges C and Petersmann EU (eds), *Constitutionalism, Multilevel Trade Governance and International Economic Law* (Hart 2011)

Kaupa C, *The Pluralist Character of the European Economic Constitution* (Hart 2016)

Kissinger H, *World Order. Reflections on the Character of Nations and the Course of History* (Penguin 2014)

Kjaer PF (ed), *The Law of Political Economy: Transformation in the Function of Law* (CUP 2020).

Kolsky Lewis M, Nakagawa H, Neuwirth RJ, Picker CB, and Stoll PT (eds), *A Post-WTO International Legal Order. Utopian, Dystopian and other Scenarios* (Springer 2020)

Koskenniemi M, *From Apology to Utopia. The Structure of International Legal Argument* (CUP 2005)

Koskenniemi M, Constitutionalism as Mindset: Reflections on Kantian Themes About International Law and Globalization, *Theoretical Inquiries in Law* 8 (2006), 9–36

Koskenniemi M, *The Politics of International Law* (Hart 2011)

Kotzé LJ, *Global Environmental Constitutionalism in the Anthropocene* (Hart 2016)

Lamy P, *The Geneva Consensus. Making Trade Work for All* (CUP 2013)
Maduro MP and Wind M (eds), *The Transformation of Europe: Twenty-Five Years After* (CUP 2017)
Mahbubani K, *Has the West Lost It? A Provocation* (Penguin 2018)
Ménard C and Shirley MM (eds), *Introduction to a Research Agenda for New Institutional Economics* (Edward Elgar 2018)
Morsink J, *Inherent Human Rights. Philosophical Roots of the Universal Declaration* (University of Pennsylvania Press 2009)
Moyn S, *Not Enough. Human Rights in an Unequal World* (Harvard UP 2018)
Petersmann EU, 'International Economic Theory and International Economic Law—On the Tasks of a Legal Theory of International Economic Order' in RSJ Macdonald and DM Johnston (eds), *The Structure and Process of International Law* (Nijhoff 1983) 227–61
Petersmann EU, *Constitutional Functions and Constitutional Problems of International Economic Law. International and Domestic Foreign Trade Law and Foreign Trade Policy in the United States, the European Community and Switzerland* (Fribourg UP/Westview Boulder Press 1991, reprinted by Routledge 2019)
Petersmann EU, Time for a United Nations 'Global Compact' for Integrating Human Rights into the Law of Worldwide Organizations: Lessons from European Integration, *European Journal of International Law* 13 (2002) 621–50
Petersmann EU (ed), *Reforming the World Trading System: Legitimacy, Efficiency and Democratic Governance* (OUP 2005)
Petersmann EU, *International Economic Law in the 21st Century* (Hart 2012)
Petersmann EU, The EU's Cosmopolitan Foreign Policy Constitution and its Disregard in Transatlantic Free Trade Agreements, *European Foreign Affairs Review* 21 (2016), 449–69
Petersmann EU, *Multilevel Constitutionalism for Multilevel Governance of Public Goods* (Hart 2017)
Petersmann EU, The 2018 Trade Wars as a Threat to the World Trading System and to Constitutional Democracies, *Trade, Law and Development* X (2018), 179–225
Petersmann EU, How Should WTO Members React to Their WTO Governance Crises? *World Trade Review* 18 (2019), 503–25
Petersmann EU, Economic Disintegration? Political, Economic and Legal Drivers and the Need for 'Greening Embedded Liberalism', *Journal of International Economic Law* 22 (2020), 347–70
Petersmann EU, Can Invocation of Human Rights Enhance Justice and Social Legitimacy in Investment Adjudication? Indian Journal of International Economic Law XII (2020), 58–105
Petersmann EU, WTO Adjudication@me.too: Are Global Public Goods like the World Trade Organization Owned by Governments or by Peoples and Citizens? *Journal of East Asia and International Law* 13 (2020), 21–52
Pinker S, *Enlightenment Now. The Case for Science, Reason, Humanism and Progress* (Penguin 2018)
Polanyi K, *The Great Transformation: The Political and Economic Origins of our Time* (2nd edn, Beacon Press 1944/2001)
Rawls J, *Political Liberalism* (Harvard UP 1993)
Rawls J, *A Theory of Justice* (Revised edn, Harvard UP 1999)
Ruggie JG, International Regimes, Transactions and Change: Embedded Liberalism in the Postwar Economic Order, *International Organization* 36 (1982), 379–415
Scheinin M (ed), *Human Rights Norms in 'Other' International Courts* (CUP 2019)
Slobodian Q, *Globalists: The End of Empire and the Birth of Neoliberalism* (Harvard UP 2018)

Soave T, European Legal Culture and WTO Dispute Settlement: Thirty Years of Socio-Legal Transplants from Brussels to Geneva, *The Law and Practice of International Courts and Tribunals* 19 (2020), 107–33

Suttle O, *Distributive Justice and World Trade Law. A Political Theory of International Trade Regulation* (CUP 2018)

Stone Sweet A, A Cosmopolitan Legal Order: Constitutional Pluralism and Rights Adjudication in Europe, *Global Constitutionalism* (2012) 1, 53

Tiedemann P, *Philosophical Foundations of Human Rights* (Springer 2020)

Trachtman JP, *The Economic Structure of International Law* (Harvard UP 2008)

Tuori K, *European Constitutionalism* (CUP 2015)

United Nations, *Transforming our World: the 2030 Sustainable Development Agenda*, UN General Assembly Resolution A/RES/70/1 of 25 September 2015

VanGrasstek C, *Trade and American Leadership. The Paradoxes of Power and Wealth from Alexander Hamilton to Donald Trump* (Harvard UP 2019)

Index

For the benefit of digital users, indexed terms that span two pages (e.g., 52–53) may, on occasion, appear on only one of those pages.